DEVELOPMENT OF A LEGEND

Studies on the Traditions concerning Yoḥanan Ben Zakkai

DEVELOPMENT OF A LEGEND

Studies on the Traditions concerning Yoḥanan Ben Zakkai

Jacob Neusner

Classics in Judaic Studies
Global Publications, Binghamton University
2001

First printed by E. J. Brill, Leiden in 1970.

Cover artwork entitled "Leaping Flower" by Suzanne R. Neusner.

Library of Congress Cataloging-in-Publication Data:

Jacob Neusner, *Development of A Legend: Studies on the Traditions Concerning Yoḥanan Ben Zakkai*

1. Judaism 2. Yoḥanan Ben Zakkai 3. Religious Traditions

ISBN 1-586841-20-3

Published and Distributed by:
Classics in Judaic Studies
Global Publications, Binghamton University
State University of New York at Binghamton
LNG 99, Binghamton University
Binghamton, New York, USA 13902-6000
Phone: (607) 777-4495 or 777-6104; Fax: (607) 777-6132
Email: pmorewed@binghamton.edu
http://ssips.binghamton.edu

CLASSICS IN JUDAIC STUDIES

Publisher: Global Publications, State University of New York at Binghamton
Address: LNG 99, SUNY-Binghamton, Binghamton, New York 13902-6000

Editor-in-Chief
Jacob Neusner, *Bard College*

Editorial Committee
Alan J. Avery-Peck, *College of the Holy Cross*
Bruce D. Chilton, *Bard College*
William Scott Green, *University of Rochester*
James F. Strange, *University of South Florida*

For Morton Smith

האומר שלי שלך ושלך שלך — חסיד

TABLE OF CONTENTS

Preface XI
List of Abbreviations XVIII

INTRODUCTION 1
i. The Problem 1
ii. The Broken Process of Tradition 2
iii. Event and Tradition 3
iv. *Ipsissima Verba* 5
v. Editorial Tendencies 6
vi. Talmudic "Historiography". 8
vii. The Growth of the Normative Tradition 9

PART ONE

THE TRADITIONS IN HISTORICAL SEQUENCE

I. TANNAITIC MIDRASHIM 15
i. School of R. Ishmael 15
ii. School of R. ʿAqiva 24
iii. General Comments 32
iv. Midrash Tannaim 36

II. MISHNAH AND TOSEFTA 41
i. Mishnah 41
ii. General Comments 61
iii. Tosefta 65
iv. General Comments 78

III. TANNAITIC MATERIALS IN THE *Gemarot* OF PALESTINE AND BABYLONIA 83
i. Palestinian Talmudic Traditions Attributed to Tannaim 83
ii. Babylonian Talmudic Traditions Attributed . . . . to Tannaim *(Beraitot)* 86
iii. General Comments 110

IV. Avot De Rabbi Natan 113
i. Texts 113
ii. General Comments 131

V. Amoraic Traditions 133
i. Palestinian Talmud 133
ii. Babylonian Talmud 142
iii. General Comments 155

VI. Some later Midrashim 159
i. Genesis Rabbah 159
ii. Lamentations Rabbati 162
iii. Pesiqta deRav Kahana 167
iv. Pesiqta Rabbati 169
v. Tanḥuma 171
vi. Qohelet Rabbah 174
vii. Numbers Rabbah 176
viii. Deuteronomy Rabbah 178
ix. Song of Songs Rabbah 178
x. Midrash on Psalms 179
xi. Scholion to Megillat Ta'anit 180
xii. General Comments 182

PART TWO

SYNOPTIC STUDIES

VII. Introduction 187

VIII. Legal Sayings and Stories 192
i. "Conventional" Sayings 192
ii. Woe if I say it 193
iii. Further Subscriptions 195
iv. The Story Is Told 197
v. His Disciples Asked 199
vi. Laws reported by Disciples 201
vii. Disputes 203
viii. The Ordinances of Yavneh 206
ix. Conclusion 209

IX. Biographical Materials 213
i. One-hundred-twenty Years 213
ii. Eighty Disciples 216
iii. They Said Concerning Yoḥanan 218
iv. Death Scene 221
v. A Good Court 224
vi. Conclusion 226

X. Historical Stories 228
i. The Escape 228
ii. The Destruction 234
iii. Because You Did Not Serve 235
iv. Conclusion 238

XI. Stories about Disciples 240
i. The Five 240
ii. Eliezer's Origins 242
iii. The *Merkavah*-Sermon and Related Materials 247
iv. Conclusion 252

XII. Scriptural Exegesis 253
i. Disputes with Gentiles 253
ii. Exegesis in "Standard" Form 256
iii. Analogical Exegeses *(Kemin Ḥomer)* 257
iv. Conclusion 262

PART THREE

CONCLUSION

XIII. Formation of a Legend 265
i. The Cumulative Tradition 265
ii. Yoḥanan and the Tannaim 273
iii. Yoḥanan and the Amoraim 293
iv. Conclusion 297

Index of Biblical and Talmudic Citations 302
General Index 307

PREFACE

In my *Life of Yoḥanan ben Zakkai*[1] I attempted to give that picture of his life which can now be composed by summation of all extant sour ces, early and late. Here my task is critically to study and analyze those sources, to try to locate the origins of different parts of them, to see how the whole structure grew. My purpose is thus not to produce a connected history of the man and his time, but to offer systematic observations on the tradition about him and through it, on the development of a sample body of talmudic literature. I shall try to review the sources as they appear in talmudic and midrashic collections, to type and categorize the various kinds of sayings and stories, to see whether we can locate characteristic forms used in transmitting particular sorts of material—in all to develop a form-critical structure and system. In my *Life*, I described the content, and now turn to the formation, of the traditions.

I do not suppose we can come to a final and positive assessment of the historicity of various stories and sayings. We surely cannot declare a narrative to be historically reliable simply because it contains no improbabilities or merely because some details are accurate. We must not confuse verisimilitude with authenticity. At best we may reach a more comprehensive and critical estimate of what we know about Yoḥanan than was available earlier. At the end I shall offer some suggestions on what I regard as more reliable and what less so.

The complex relationships between one rabbinical document and another are not under study here, except in so far as similar sayings of Yoḥanan occur in two or more compilations of sources. The study of such relationships, e.g. of the Mishnah to the Tosefta, of both to *beraitot* in the Babylonian *Gemara*, of the Tannaitic halakhic *midrashim* to the citations of those same *midrashim* in the Babylonian *Gemara*, and the like—that study has made substantial progress over the past century, and it is not likely that the few particulars considered here will be significant. The results of the more general study are, however, only indirectly relevant to the study of the traditions on Yoḥanan. To show how the general relationships of one document to another are

---

[1] Leiden, E. J. Brill: first edition, 1962; second edition, completely revised, 1970.

illustrated by synopses of Yoḥanan's sayings would carry us far beyond our limited objective. It indeed would make our objective nothing other than the explanation of the history and structure of the whole of rabbinical literature. "The best is the enemy of the good." Here I do not claim to have completed the larger task. On the other hand, where necessary, I have tentatively undertaken a small part of it. In all I continue to ask historical, not literary questions; but the historical questions cannot be answered without attention to literary-critical considerations.

I have had to make use of awkward constructions and to invent a few adjectives for the purposes of presenting my results. Rather than turn "Yoḥanan" into an adjective such as "Yoḥanine," or "Yoḥananean," I preferred to preserve the name as a noun and, when used as an adjective, to connect it to the modified noun with a hyphen. I have referred to the school of R. Ishmael as Ishmaelean, rather than Ishmaelite, because the latter adjective has other, fixed meanings, which do not apply here. Aqiban is fairly well accepted as an adjective from ʿAqiva. Other such invented adjectives include Yavnean, from Yavneh. I have not found it easy to find a style appropriate to literary studies, since all my former experience concerned historical narrative.

Each item is listed according to chapter, section, and subsection; thus the capitalized Roman numeral signifies the chapter; the following uncapitalized Roman numeral, the section; and the Arabic numeral, the item within the section. IV.i.3, for instance, indicates that the item is found in Chapter Four, section one, third item in the document there under study.

Where translations of scientific quality existed, I have used them with little modification. This results in a measure of inconsistency in presenting pretty much the same texts. The reader will benefit from seeing how various translators have dealt with identical materials. On the other hand, I have imposed stylistic consistency in minor details. When a single, consistent version was important for synoptic purposes, I have provided it. The synoptic studies were prepared by comparing the various Hebrew texts.

Names of translators and of editors of critical editions are invariably cited when their work is quoted. Translations not attributed to others are my own. Where variants seem to me to have been important, I have included them; otherwise they are ignored. The state of our textual traditions is so unsatisfactory that I saw no point in making much of variant readings for the purposes of any particular argument.[1] Little I say here depends upon the supposedly greater reliability of one reading over another or one text over another.

On the other hand, I have had to rely upon the conventional and accepted opinions of literary scholars as to the origin and approximate dates of various rabbinical documents. If Y. N. Epstein expressed an opinion on a document, that opinion entered my study as a matter of fact, and he provides the court of final appeal in any contested matter. I have further assumed that current scholarship has been correct in concluding that certain texts were cited at certain times and thereafter additions and changes were not made in them. I regard the consequent documents as fixed and final. Any other assumption would have rendered the task utterly impossible.[2] At the same time I should make it explicit that these two assumptions are merely provisional. Should

[1] In III.i.6, the reading Eliezer, instead of Eleazar, is significant for my argument, but I have tried to analyze the problem with both readings as possibilities.

[2] An example of the implications of this assumption is to be derived from Ben Zion Wacholder, "The Date of the Mekilta de-Rabbi Ishmael," *Hebrew Union College Annual* 39, 1968, pp. 117-144. Wacholder holds that the Mekhilta of R. Ishmael "may not be dated much later than the year 800..." (p. 142). The evidences Wacholder assembles cannot be ignored, but generally are susceptible of more than one explanation, frequently not the explanation he offers. Yet if in time Wacholder's thesis *were* to find acceptance, then his assertions that the bulk of the Mekhilta is post-Talmudic and references to Tannaitic authorites are pseudepigraphic would require the complete revision of all conclusions offered here with reference to Yoḥanan ben Zakkai in the Mekhilta. I am prepared to undertake such revisions if need be; for now, Wacholder's interesting hypothesis merely serves to underline the tentative nature of my studies.

With reference to Yoḥanan, Wacholder states (p. 127), "Also notable is the role of Rabbi... Yoḥanan ben Zakkai, founder of the academy of Yavneh in the year 70, who is listed in the Mekilta seven times, but only in haggadic texts, some of which are rephrasings from the Babylonian Talmud and postamoraic lore." In his accompanying note (pp. 127-8 n. 38), Wacholder states that Mekhilta Neziqin II, p. 253, Laut. III, p. 16 (cited below, I.i.3) depends on b. Qid. 22b, not on Tos. B.Q. 7:5, where the passage is cited anonymously. Mekhilta Neziqin XV, 299, Laut. III, p. 115 (below, I.i.5) depends on b.B.Q. 79b, rather than on Tos.; Mekhilta Baḥodesh I, p. 203f., Laut. II, p. 193f (I.i.1) seems to follow Avot deRabbi Nathan XVII, p. 33a "(a posttalmudic source)," rather than b. Ket. 66b-67a, or Sifré Deut. 305 etc., "for only Avot deRabbi Nathan, and after it the Mekhilta, attributes the story to Yoḥanan ben Zakkai; the talmudic sources and the Tosefta cite here Simeon ben Eleazar." (Sic!—See III.ii.16). Mekhilta Bahodesh XI, p. 245, Laut. II, p. 290 (I.i.2) is related to Sifra Qedoshim rather than to Tos. B.Q. 7.6, which reports this passage anonymously. The passage of Mekhilta Neziqin XII, p. 292, Laut. III, p. 99 (I.i.4) is related to Tosefta B.Q. 7:10, but the Mekhilta "strings together here B. *ibid.* 67b, resulting that Yoḥanan ben Zakkai follows Meir and precedes Akiba in a controversy. There is no reason to assume that the author of the Mekilta ever used Yohanan ben Zakkai's name fictitiously, but there is no doubt that his sources were primarily the Babylonian Talmud or posttalmudic works." So Wacholder.

In fact, every item has an equivalent in talmudic, not post-talmudic materials. As

future scholars demonstrate that the formation, dating, and editing of rabbinical literature in Talmudic times were in large part different from the accounts followed here, the whole work will have to be redone. I depend upon the results of the best literary scholars known to me, an act not of faith but of judgment.[1]

In the comments on texts, various questions are brought to bear, according to the character of the texts themselves. In the beginning, the primary questions are form-critical and historical. The chief interest is the analysis of the components of stories, possible life-situations underlying them, and the history of the pericope. Later on, questions of literary analysis become important. Finally, in the last stratum of materials, the primary concern is for the editorial or redactional context in which an earlier tradition is later on discussed.

I have made no contribution toward the study of the relationship between opinions held by Yoḥanan and those held by other Tannaim and Amoraim. This is an important question, to be sure, but the

---

to the comparison of Mekhiltan materials to equivalent items in other documents, for I.i.1, 7,—see Chapter Ten, section iii; I.i.3, 2, 5,—Chapter Twelve, Section iii; etc. Wacholder's thesis cannot be tested within so limited a framework as Yoḥanan-sayings; but it also cannot be proved within it.

More generally, Wacholder supposes that agreements between the Mekhilta and Mishnah prove the former must be later; but I do not see why. He points out that rare or unknown authorities occur in the Mekhilta—an argument for the lateness of the Mekhilta. The contrary would seem to me the case. A later forger would put his ideas in the mouths of famous authorities. Normally pseudepigraphic writing is in the name of famous and well-known figures, not the contrary. The immense problems of the reliability of the transmission of the texts and of the possibilities of later interpolations are not faced by Wacholder. Wacholder's assertions that the Mekhilta is by a single author prove nothing; uniformity of the frame of reference is not strong evidence, for a later interpolator could easily imitate the framework of the text he was doctoring. And, as is clear, Wacholder has not yet laid the form-critical foundations for his work.

[1] Still, I have not treated as components of the Yoḥanan-tradition the segments of Mishnah and Tosefta designated by Y. N. Epstein as deriving from Yoḥanan ben Zakkai. My interest is in only those pericopae definitively attributed to Yoḥanan in the period in which the tradition was taking shape. In any event, I am not yet able to understand the methodological criteria by which Epstein and others come to such judgments; as it stands, his arguments seem to me rather circular in places, facile in others. See his *Mevo'ot leSifrut haTanna'im* (Jerusalem, 1957), pp. 40-41.

In presenting the Tannaitic Midrashim before the Mishnah-Tosefta, I do not mean to imply they date before the latter collections. Scholarly opinion is that the Mishnah-Tosefta were redacted before the Tannaitic Midrashim. However, the Yoḥanan-data in the Tannaitic midrashic collections are, on the whole, quite different from, and probably earlier in final formulation, though not in redaction, than those in the Mishnah-Tosefta.

history of Talmudic law and theology is not the subject before us. To show, for example, how Yoḥanan's Scriptural exegeses may have influenced those of later masters would carry us far afield; we could not ignore other possible influences, confluences of opinion through the rigorous and autonomous exegetical process itself, and similar complex questions. Whenever I knew that an opinion attributed to Yoḥanan is elsewhere attributed in pretty much the same language to another master, I have said so, so far as I could find out. My chief interest, however, is in the configuration of the traditions about Yoḥanan, not in the relationship of those to other talmudic traditions about other masters.

The difficulty with the synoptic studies is that the numerous parallel versions exhibit differences I have no way of systematically explaining. It is not easy to evaluate these differences. I have dealt with one chief issue only, and that is, Do the parallel versions appearing in later documents seem in fact to be composed later than the ones appearing in earlier documents? I believe the synoptic studies produce a definitive reply in the affirmative. That fact allows us to proceed to a tentative estimate of the historical value of materials appearing for the first time in later documents. Since it has a along been maintained that אין מוקדם ומאוחר בתורה applies to the oral, as well as the written Torah, I believe the evidence to the contrary is important.

But, as I said, only when careful study of the relationships of the entire structures of collections has been undertaken shall we be able to explain many of the differences before us. We know too little of the literary characteristics, methods, and motives of the major documents. We therefore can hardly make proper allowances in evaluating the material contained in them. Literary source criticism must precede form criticism—as it did in New Testament studies. And it must apply not to a single problem, let alone to a single rabbi, but rather to whole tractates and collections. Hence this study stands at the very beginning of a great task, one in which many generations will likely participate. At this time, I cannot even say for certain that the appearance of identical words and sentences in several documents—e.g. Mekhilta, Tosefta, and Babylonian *beraita*—means that a single, anterior, written source lies behind the whole lot. I am never sure whether one document copies another. I think it beyond question that the Mishnah was "published" and therefore quoted later on. (But quotations of the Mishnah in the two Talmuds show interesting variants.) As to collections, we have not got much certainty as to whether, when, and how, they were published, let alone to what degree and in what way they were used by later editors.

All our information about Yoḥanan comes from rabbinical documents edited after his death, some long afterward. As we shall see, few of the traditions about him can have derived from his own lifetime, not many more from his immediate disciples. Nothing comes to us from non-rabbinical circles. This means that our interpretation is circular. From rabbinic literature of various periods I have drawn a picture of Yoḥanan; from my picture of Yoḥanan I have proceeded to interpret the literature in a form-critical framework. Still, my heuristic framework is not elaborate and has not been imposed, rather deduced. I take it as fact that Yoḥanan survived the war of 70; that he opposed it earlier; that he afterward undertook the first stages of reconstruction. These are the only "facts" that have governed my interpretation of all materials. I further assume that the rabbinical movement was not a monolith, but that various schools preserved individual viewpoints and that these affected the formation and transmission of sayings, including the ones under study here. I take it for granted that ʿAqiva and his circle did not oppose war and probably did not approve Yohanan's policies toward the war of 66-73. These are the chief notions brought to the interpretation of the texts; they do not seem to me outrageous or farfetched. But they do derive from the materials for the criticism of which they then are used, and this represents a circularity to be specified and admitted.[1]

My only defense for this primitive beginning is that, to my knowledge, no one has ever attempted what I have done here, unsatisfactory though is my method; tentative, limited, and modest though are my results.

The dedication to my teacher and friend, Morton Smith, is simply one more effort to pay a debt that can never be—and that neither party would want to see—fully discharged. My most recent obligation is for his careful, critical reading of the first three chapters in the first draft, not to mention hundreds of letters and conversations preceding and during its composition. Many of his specific contributions are so labelled; there were many more.

Professors Ernest S. Frerichs, Baruch A. Levine, Robin J. Scroggs, Brevard S. Childs, and W. Sibley Towner, Rabbi Joel Zaiman and my students, Rabbis Robert Goldenberg and David Goodblatt graciously

[1] I here am guided by Robert M. Grant, *After the New Testament* (Philadelphia, 1967), pp. xiii-xiv.

read the manuscript as well. Professor Levine kindly translated a pericope that dumbfounded me (V.i.16).

Brown University continues generously to pay all costs of my research, including typing, preparation of indices, and many incidental expenses. During the summers of 1968 and 1969 I enjoyed a Summer Research Stipend of Brown University. I am especially grateful for this support. My typist, Mrs. Marion Craven, performed patiently and valiantly.

My wife, Suzanne, and sons, Samuel Aaron and Eli Ephraim, frequented my study during this work, cheering me on and sharing my pleasure in it. I could accomplish nothing without them.

Providence, Rhode Island
28 July 1969
13 Av 5729

JACOB NEUSNER

ABBREVIATIONS

ʻArakh.	=	ʻArakhin
A.Z.	=	ʻAvodah Zarah
b.	=	Babylonian Talmud
B.B.	=	Bava' Batra'
Bekh.	=	Bekhorot
Ber.	=	Berakhot
Bez.	=	Beẓah
Bik.	=	Bikkurim
B.M.	=	Bava Meẓiʻa'
B.Q.	=	Bava' Qamma'
Chron.	=	Chronicles
Dan.	=	Daniel
Deut.	=	Deuteronomy
ʻEd.	=	ʻEduyyot
Epstein, *Mevo'ot*	=	Y. N. Epstein, *Mevo'ot leSifrut HaTanna'im*
ʻEruv.	=	ʻEruvin
Ex.	=	Exodus
Ez.	=	Ezekiel
Gen.	=	Genesis
Git.	=	Giṭṭin
Hab.	=	Habbakuk
Hag.	=	Haggai
Ḥag.	=	Ḥagigah
Ḥal.	=	Ḥallah
Hos.	=	Hosea
Ḥul.	=	Ḥullin
Jer.	=	Jeremiah
Jos.	=	Joshua
Ju.	=	Judges
Kel.	=	Kelim
Ket.	=	Ketuvot
Kil.	=	Kil'ayim
Lev.	=	Leviticus
Ma.	=	Maʻaserot
Mak.	=	Makkot
Mal.	=	Malachi
Meg.	=	Megillah
Men.	=	Menaḥot
Mid.	=	Middot
Miq.	=	Miqva'ot
M.Q.	=	Moʻed Qaṭan
M.S.	=	Maʻaser Sheni
Naz.	=	Nazir
Ned.	=	Nedarim
Neg.	=	Negaʻim
Neh.	=	Nehemiah
Nid.	=	Niddah
Num.	=	Numbers
'Oh.	=	'Ohalot ['Ahilot]
Par.	=	Parah
Pes.	=	Pesaḥim
Prov.	=	Proverbs
Ps.	=	Psalms
Qid.	=	Qiddushin
Qoh.	=	Qohelet
R.H.	=	Rosh Hashanah
Sam.	=	Samuel
Sanh.	=	Sanhedrin
Shab.	=	Shabbat
Shev.	=	Sheviʻit
Sheq.	=	Sheqalim
Song	=	Song of Songs
Sot.	=	Soṭah
Suk.	=	Sukkah
Ter.	=	Terumot
Toh.	=	Ṭoharot
Tos.	=	Tosefta
y.	=	Yerushalmi, Palestinian Talmud
Yad.	=	Yadaim
Yev.	=	Yevamot
Zev.	=	Zevaḥim

INTRODUCTION

I. The Problem

No "life of Rabban Yoḥanan ben Zakkai" has come down to us from antiquity. We have no traces whatever of biography, no chronological sketch of the story of his life and deeds. No equivalents either to Christian hagiographies or to pagan lives of great and meritorious men exist for rabbis. Biblical, not rabbinical, heroes were subjects of rabbinical biographers, and in any event they did not even write connected accounts. We have only single stories, pericopae, which are never put into a systematic framework of Yoḥanan's life. They are rather episodically set into several frameworks established by editors for entirely other purposes. We shall first review the discrete elements of the tradition, roughly in order of the dates of the collections in which they occur, to see how they were used in various places and for various purposes. We shall then pursue synoptic studies and raise the questions of source- and form-criticism which have hitherto been neglected. We shall finally consider the interests of various schools and circles in particular components of the Yoḥanan-tradition and suggest what motives may have led to such interests.

It is possible to do so to begin with because of the completed effort, for which I claim limited success at best, to offer a comprehensive, if primitive, life of Rabban Yoḥanan ben Zakkai. I now wish to take up the latter part of the challenge, phrased in terms of literary studies, offered by Morton Smith:

> ....If the Christians have done little to describe this important parallel [structure] between the Gospels and Tannaitic Literature, the Jews have done nothing. I cannot recall even a word by any Jewish scholar remarking—for example—that the problem of the relationship between Tosetta and the Mishnah is similar to the synoptic problem, and this in spite of the fact that they are so similar as to be practically inseparable, *and that any theory begun from a study of the one literature should have immediate application in the study of the other.*[1]

Still, we cannot suppose that the problems connected with recovering the life of Jesus are entirely congruent to those of the biography of

[1] *Tannaitic Parallels to the Gospels* (Philadelphia, 1951), p. 143. Italics supplied.

Yoḥanan, for nothing like the Gospels' accounts exists with reference to any rabbinic master.

One may wish to argue—though I do not—that the traditions on Jesus's life and teachings must have circulated in brief oral accounts, just as the traditions on Yoḥanan supposedly did. Even so, we can hardly imagine that the rabbinical schools invested so much energy in preserving stories about, and sayings of, Yoḥanan, as did the Christians for Jesus. In no degree did Yoḥanan play a role in the rabbinical schools remotely similar to that of Jesus in the Christian schools (if there *were* Christian schools, complete with Tannaitic memorizers, rabbinical masters, and obsequious disciples, as has been alleged).[1] To no individual in the history of Tannaitic and Amoraic Judaism was half so much attention ever devoted as was given to Jesus. Whether or not the data or the conditions for their preservation, redaction, and transmission were similar, however, the *problem* is identical, namely, to find out who *was* this man who meant much in his own time and even more to subsequent generations? What can we know about him? Most important, *how* do we know it? Since both men lived in the same century, in the same country, the beginning of the parallel is the obvious, historical one. But further, since the conditions for the preservation of historical information were, in both cases, unsatisfactory, methods and inquiries devised for research on the life of Jesus cannot be ignored when Tannaitic rabbis, particularly those who flourished before the destruction of the Temple, are under study. Any theory begun from a study of the one ought to be tested in the study of the other, as Smith said.

II. The Broken Process of Tradition

The study of both Yoḥanan and Jesus is complicated by the serious break in the processes of transmission marked by the destruction of Jerusalem in 70 A.D. The kind of evidence we have for later Tannaitic and Amoraic times is simply *not* available about rabbis who lived before 70 A.D. After 70, academies were established and the traditions cultivated in them were handed down, orally or in notes, without substantial interruption, except for the Bar Kokhba War, until they were

[1] Birger Gerhardsson, *Memory and Manuscript. Oral Tradition and Written Transmission in Rabbinic Judaism and Early Christianity* (Uppsala, 1961). His is the most extreme statement of the case.

redacted. The Bar Kokhba War caused no drastic break in the transmission of either Aqiban or Ishmaelean traditions, for some of the students of the two great rabbis escaped from Palestine, and preserved their traditions in Mesopotamia and Babylonia. (The Aqibans returned to Palestine ca. 145.) By contrast for the period before 70, we have no quite unaltered traditions, because whatever schools formerly existed were destroyed and their traditions either lost or drastically reshaped in the new academies created after 70.

The paucity of information about Hillel, Gamaliel I, Simeon b. Gamaliel I, their colleagues, not to mention Yoḥanan himself, is by no means accidental. We do not know much because not much survived the destruction, and, what we *do* know underwent thorough revision in the post-70 academies. No sayings of Yoḥanan are attributed by him to an identifiable master of the immediately preceding generation. His laws go back to the prophets and Moses, but never to Gamaliel I or even Hillel. His exegeses invariably begin the rabbinical exegetical tradition on a verse. He stands, therefore, not at the end of the former period, but at the beginning of the new one. Yet most of his life, most of his teaching, and most of his effective actions came before 70. Therefore either he himself, conscious of beginning a new period, set forth laws on his own authority without reference to his teachers, or his successors looked back to him as the beginning of their school and attributed later laws to him, or both.

Even if one grants, therefore, that some close relationship exists between event and tradition or between a saying and the person to whom it is attributed, the necessary conditions for preserving the tradition did not exist (or at least survive) for the data emerging from pre-70 academies.

III. Event and Tradition

But one can hardly grant that things happened as the sources allege. It is by no means clear how a given event was cast into literary form. No one seriously supposes that the rabbinic sources supply either eyewitness accounts of great events or stenographic records of men's speeches or lectures. By the time we hear of a speech or an event, it has already been recast. It is rarely possible to know just what, if anything, originally was said or happened. We sometimes have an obvious insertion which provides evidence that a given tradition originated very early, before the date of that insertion, and possibly quite close to the time it purports to discuss. A striking example is the comment attributed to ʿAqiva or Joseph on the alleged conversation between Yoḥanan and Vespasian. Vespasian asked, "Now ask me what I may grant you," to which Yoḥanan replied, "Give me Yavneh and its sages, the chain of Rabban Gamaliel, and a physician to heal Rabbi Ẓadok." The source continues:

> R. Joseph said, and some say, Rabbi ʿAqiva said, "*He turneth the wise backward* (Is. 44:25). For he should have asked him to leave them alone that time, but he thought that perhaps so much he would not grant, and then there would be no relief whatever."
>
> (b. Giṭ. 56b)

Still later, Lamentations Rabbati I.5.31 was corrected to conform to the criticism of ʿAqiva, or (more likely) of the fourth-century Babylonian Amora, Joseph. The inserted criticism gives us a *terminus ante quem*, a date before which the story must have been current. In this case the date is either that of ʿAqiva (c. 120) or of Joseph (c. 330), more likely the latter.

Of greater significance, the preceding story occurs in a document, the Babylonian Gemara, generally thought to come later than The Fathers according to Rabbi Nathan, chapter four, which preserves an utterly different account of Yoḥanan's excape. Obviously two accounts of the same event cannot both be right, and probably *neither* provides the kind of factual information historians need and do not have for this period. They tell us, rather, what differing schools of thought chose to recall about a controversial event. That the story in ARN is commonly supposed to be "earlier" than the one in b. Giṭ. 56b is certainly no proof of its truth.

If a detail of a story appears in a later, but not an earlier account of the event, we may account for that fact in one of three ways: Either (a) the earlier source was ignorant of it, or (b) the earlier source knew the detail but omitted or suppressed it, or (c) each was entirely separate. That is, it continued independent of the rest of the tradition because of the isolation of a tradent or school, so was neither suppressed earlier nor invented later on. Each of these hypotheses leads to consequences of its own. If a later source is ignorant of a story concerning an earlier man, then the ignorance must be explained. Is the story a late invention? Or was it handed down in secret material? If a later source contains details which prove it knew an earlier story itself, then the reason for omission or suppression must be found.

IV. Ipsissima Verba

It might be tempting to suppose that, whatever happened, the *words* ascribed to a given rabbi were actually said by him. I so assumed in my first studies of Yoḥanan. It was only later on that I found evidence to suggest otherwise. Certain sayings of Rav and Samuel, cast into precisely the form one would expect, were never said by them at all. Their students observed a certain court-decision, and supposed upon that basis that the master held a given position upon the law. They then transmitted it in the form, "Rav says... Samuel says..." *as if* the men had actually so dictated. R. Ḥisda, in the next generation, however, reports that the master said no such thing, but that the students merely presumed it. They observed a practical decision and proposed a legal principle in the name of the master as basis for the decision. What is of special interest to us, however, is that we should never have known it, were it not for further analysis of the case.[1] But the cases of Yoḥanan undergo no such nearly-contemporary analysis. The reports are extremely limited. Extended discussion of the master's actions and words by his immediate disciples, so characteristic of later times, is rarely accorded to pre-70 figures.

At best, Yoḥanan's disciples reported his words, but they did not analyze or criticize them, unlike later disciples who analyzed the words of *their* masters. We simply do not know how most Yoḥanan-stories were originally redacted. Later rabbis analyze their contents, but Yoḥanan's immediate disciples almost never do so. We therefore have no certainty that things he supposedly said were actually spoken by him. Indeed, in the varying accounts of his escape from Jerusalem, we find in one a whole conversation, attributed to him and Vespasian, of which the other knows nothing. Someone, perhaps everyone, produced pseudepigraphic dicta, and that is all we shall ever know for certain.

Many speeches and conversations attributed to Yoḥanan in fact occur as part of narratives. They serve the purpose of the narrator, and cannot be thought to be part of an anterior tradition of Yoḥanan-sayings. In the comparison of the *Merkavah*-stories, for instance, we shall see speech-material obviously invented in later versions; that material includes not only conversations in direct discourse, but also blessings he supposedly invoked on various disciples, reports of his own dreams, and the like. Perhaps the earliest exegetical traditions

[1] See my *History of the Jews in Babylonia, II. The Early Sasanian Period* (Leiden, 1966), pp. 249ff.

contain words Yoḥanan actually spoke, or more likely, renditions of ideas he actually held in the conventional forms commonplace in midrashic collections. But the preserved sayings are not the same as the various sorts of logia attributed to Jesus, as we shall see.

v. Editorial Tendencies

Since most of Yoḥanan's reported sayings are preserved in a few large collections, one might be tempted to approach the problem of their authenticity from this side. Those stories or details which suited the *Tendenz* of the collections that preserved them would be obviously suspect. But no collection shows a specific *Tendenz* in the treatment of Yoḥanan. We know that Yoḥanan was subjected to criticism after his death, and probably during his lifetime as well, by his opponents. ʿAqiva's saying—if it *was* his—would reflect such opposition. But no document was edited from the viewpoint either of his friends or of his enemies. The saying cited in b. Giṭ. (V.ii.14) is not part of a collection edited to discredit Yoḥanan. It is cited quite tangentially, a comment interjected into an otherwise not unfavorable account.

Omissions are noteworthy, for it was largely by suppressing data that the rabbis expressed their opinion of their opponents. I think it very likely that numerous sayings of Yoḥanan were not merely lost or forgotten, but rather suppressed. The most striking instance concerns what he thought about the revolt of 66 and the conduct of the war. Apart from the contradictory stories of his escape from Jerusalem in 67, we know nothing. About a quarter of a century before then, he commented upon the destruction of a pagan altar in Yavneh, an event which necessitated the sending of the embassy to Gaius. We have some generalized counsels of caution, indicating that Yoḥanan said that the biblical regulations on draft exemptions were sensible. His sayings on the Temple as a source of peace and not war are most probably relevant to the "debate on the loyal sacrifices" which took place at the beginning of the revolt.

It would be unfair to him to suppose this was all he had to say at such a crucial time, when he was allegedly high in the councils of the Pharisaic party and of the Jerusalem administration as well. What he said and did his successors did not preserve. Nor did they report his actions. Perhaps he not only predicted, a long time earlier, that "Lebanon," meaning the Temple, would be destroyed, but actively opposed the war, and warned people that if they fought, they would lose. If so, were these wise counsels suppressed by his rival, the Hillelite Patriarch Gamaliel II, or by the later generations of Pharisees who, led by ʿAqiva, once again decided to rebel? And why were they then unable to wipe out also the memory of his exegetical prophecy and providential escape from Jerusalem? Or were these later inventions, for they first occur in Amoraic collections to begin with?

We know, similarly, only a few of his teachings and court actions at Yavneh, nine decrees in all. One must wonder whether these were the only actions he took after the war. Most of them dealt only with the appropriation for the synagogue of rites formerly reserved to the Temple, with a few details about receiving testimony about the New Moon, the proselyte's offering, fourth-year-fruits, and the like. That his teachings and acts at Yavneh were limited to the handful reported by rabbinic tradition is hardly reasonable. What is preserved of the legal record is clearly what the members of the court of Gamaliel II saw fit to recall. Yoḥanan probably envisaged a legal reconstruction of Judaism along lines which were subsequently modified. He may have proposed to declare in abeyance all those parts of the law which depended on the Temple for their performance or importance; modified those laws still useful to the synagogue; and rejected priestly privileges. Such a policy would have been unacceptable to the priests, and disappearance of other references to his enactments as legally valid *precedents*—for that is the issue—may have been the price Gamaliel II later had to pay to secure the priests' cooperation. But all of this is post-facto conjecture. Such conjecture is necessary because the literary sources reveal almost nothing of the opposition he must have met or of the viewpoints of groups that opposed him. Edited long after the great issues of Yoḥanan's day were settled, the sources contain only remnants of traditions handed on by opposing schools, and these occur mainly in legal matters and, even there, in a context of substantial agreement on basic political and social issues.

We have, as I said, almost no way of knowing what an editor thought of any great issue, whether legal, historical or theological, because, for the most part, we know very little about what he omitted, neglected, or suppressed. The only exception to this rule is the Mishnah, for we do have access to a rich body of Tannaitic data not included in it. But the Mishnah reveals nothing in particular about what its editor thought of Yoḥanan, who is cited 24 times. At least one of the citations, Sanh. 5.2 (III.i.15), refers to R. Yoḥanan as "ben Zakkai," which Allon plausibly took to be the name he bore within his opponents' traditions.[1] But numerous other sayings (e.g. Shab. 16.7, 22.3, III.i.1,2) refer to him respectfully and preserve important laws in his name. As an editor Judah the Prince did not reveal his opinions of Yoḥanan one way or the other. He had available many sayings, some formulated in a manner thought to be disrespectful. On the basis of his selections, we know only what he thought important for his *own* ends. From the rest of his work and from the stories about him, we know a good deal of his character and purposes, and we can guess what he would have thought of material he might have known but would not have chosen to include. But beyond such conjectures we can hardly go, and neither these, nor his perpetuation of certain stories about Yoḥanan, can enable us to evaluate the stories that have been preserved.

VI. TALMUDIC "HISTORIOGRAPHY"

Although traditions were accurately transmitted, they were not originally shaped by eyewitness observers or revised by historians. The rabbis did not produce critical, or any other kind of, history in the manner of Josephus or Tacitus. Rabbinic data are mainly legal and theological. Facts on men or events emerge only occasionally, and then for other than merely historical reasons. An example drawn from later times will be of interest.

> The story is told about R. Judah b. Bathyra, R. Mattiah b. Ḥeresh, R. Ḥananiah nephew of R. Joshua, and R. Jonathan, that they were going abroad, and when they reached Puteoli, they recalled Palestine. Their eyes filled up with tears...and they tore their clothes, and said, saying, "Dwelling in the land of Israel is considered equivalent to all the commandments in the Torah."
>
> (Sifré Deut. 80)

The four second-century rabbis did emigrate, but only R. Mattiah went to Italy. They left Palestine at different times. And they never returned. So the "story" reflects only the fact that several rabbis went abroad. It was told to make a homiletical point. No serious interest in facts characterizes the telling. From a historical viewpoint, it is a complete fabrication. One could duplicate this example many times. Philological fundamentalism offers a sterile approach for the historian.

Such examples are neglected when, as too often happens, it is supposed that once we have established a correct text of a rabbinic

[1] G. Allon, *Meḥqarim beToledot Yisra'el* (Tel Aviv, 1957), I, p. 273, n. 86.

work and properly interpreted it, then we know a set of historical facts. The facticity will be proportionately greater, the earlier the manuscript and the better its condition. So indeed it will, but these facts will concern *only* what the compiler of the text wished to tell us. Whether or not the original text was veracious is a question not to be settled by textual criticism.

VII. The Growth of the Normative Tradition

We shall begin our survey of the traditions by reviewing them according to the approximate chronological order of the Talmudic and midrashic collections in which they occur. As I said, that order implies nothing at all about the credibility or historical veracity of the sayings. Whether early and late, *none* is demonstrably an eyewitness account written down by a reliable observer. I may nonetheless suggest that sayings and stories clearly attributed to Tannaim are apt to be earlier than similar materials attributed to Amoraim, or not specifically assigned to any authority at all.

I cannot accept the unexamined opinion held in rabbinical circles, both scholarly and traditional, that all rabbinical material was somehow sent floating into the air, if not by Moses, then by someone in remote antiquity (the Men of the Great Assembly or the generation of Yavneh, for instance). It remained universally available until some authority snatched it down from on high, placed his name on it, and so made it a named tradition and introduced it into the perilous processes of transmission. By this thesis nothing is older than anything else: "There is neither *earlier* nor *later* in the Torah."

On the contrary, I suppose that in most instances, when a rabbi quoted a tradition, he did so, if he could, in the name of the authority from whom he had heard it. There are admittedly some important exceptions to this rule, for instance Judah the Prince's statements in the Mishnah stand without authority, because it was common knowledge that when he did not specify an authority he was quoting his teacher, R. Meir.[1] Anonymous statements in other major collections are similarly attributed, more or less reliably, to the major figures supposed to stand behind those collections. But apart from such cases, where a rabbi makes a statement without quoting his authority, we

---

[1] On this matter, see most recently Abraham Goldberg, "Vekulhu 'aliba' deRabbi 'Aqiva," *Tarbiẓ* 38, 1969, pp. 231-254.

must ask why. And the most likely suppositions are (1) it represents a conclusion which he himself reached by some process of reasoning from Scripture or observation of other traditions; or (2) he has forgotten from whom he heard it—in which case he probably does not consider it of great importance (or else he thinks it so important that he has convinced himself he must have heard it from somebody, though he never has); or (3) he heard it from somebody not worth citing—if so, he probably does not consider it authoritative; or (4) he has some special reason for omitting the name of the authority. Of these various reasons it seems probable that the first was by far the most common.

Hence it is important to see which sayings were said by earlier masters, which by later ones. We may thereby trace the growth of the traditions on Yoḥanan as some were invented, others taken up by the rabbis and made authoritative. Whether or not traditions about Yoḥanan were passed on for centuries until finally included in a given document, we do know for sure that traditions redacted earlier were approved of, or become *normative*, earlier. We can, in other words, be certain that a source appearing in an early Tannaitic midrash was *approved of* by the school which produced that midrash. We thereby gain some slight insight into what seemed important to men of a particular time and place to say about Yoḥanan or in his name. That is not much certainty, to be sure, but it provides a point of analysis hitherto widely ignored. Only at the end will the usefulness of this procedure become clear. I believe we shall likely gain a clearer notion of the growth of the authoritative or normative traditions than we now have.

That does not mean, as I said, that we shall have certain knowledge about the growth of all the Yoḥanan-traditions as a whole. But that is not important, for we can never have that and might as well not waste time trying to find out what the sources themselves do not contain. It is sufficient to know when and where things were first given the shape in which we now have them. That itself permits us to make consequential statements about the formation of the extant, authoritative legends on Yoḥanan ben Zakkai. So we can reliably trace the growth of the normative tradition, in the end the only one we have.

Nevertheless, we shall observe an important fact. The synoptic studies reveal time and again that versions of a story or saying appearing in later documents are demonstrably later than, and dependent upon, versions of the same story or saying appearing in earlier documents. This is important, for it shows that what comes late is apt to be late and what comes early is apt to be early. Admittedly, these are no more than probabilities—extrapolations from a small number of demonstrable cases to a large number in which no demonstration is possible. But at least there are grounds for such extrapolation, and this fact helps to justify the proposed order of operation in the present work. We must first trace the growth of the normative tradition, and then make use of the findings for the purposes of synoptic consideration. The two stages of study are kept separate. The third stage, the effort to relate developments in the normative tradition to the history of the Tannaitic and Amoraic schools, further depends upon the results reached in the first two parts of our work.

PART ONE

THE TRADITIONS IN HISTORICAL SEQUENCE

CHAPTER ONE

TANNAITIC MIDRASHIM

I. The School of R. Ishmael[1]

1. They were not satisfied to count from its building, so they had to count from its destruction, as it is said: *In the fourteenth year after the city was smitten* (Ez. 40:1). They were not satisfied to count according to their own era—so they had to count according to the era of others, as it is said: *In the sixth month, in the second year of Darius the king* (Hag. 1:15).

And thus it says: *If thou know not, O thou fairest among women* (Song 1:8), and it also says: *Because thou didst not serve... therefore shalt thou serve thine enemy* (Deut. 28: 47-48). Once R. Yoḥanan b. Zakkai was going up to Emmaus in Judea and he saw a girl who was picking barley-corn out of the excrements of a horse.

Said R. Yoḥanan b. Zakkai to his disciples, "What is this girl?"

They said to him, "She is a Jewish girl."

"And to whom does this horse belong?"

"To an Arabian horseman," the disciples answered him.

Then said R. Yoḥanan b. Zakkai to his disciples, "All my life I have been reading this verse and I have not realized its full meaning: *If thou know not, O thou fairest among women,*—you were unwilling to be subject to God, behold now you are subjected to the most inferior of the nations, the Arabs.

"You were unwilling to pay the head-tax to God, *a beqa a head* (Ex.

---

[1] On the division of the Tannaitic Midrashim between the schools of R. Ishmael and R. 'Aqiva, see Y. N. Epstein, *Mevo'ot leSifrut HaTannaim*, pp. 521ff., 550, 568, 588ff., 625ff. The Mekhilta of R. Ishmael in fact derives from his school. Epstein provides a number of proofs of that fact. The same is true of Sifré Numbers.

Similarly, Sifré Deut. 1-54 is from the Ishmaelean school, but no Yoḥanan-sayings occur in those segments. Sections 55 to 303 are of the school of R. 'Aqiva. Sifré Deut. 304 to 357, Epstein states, are not of the school of R. 'Aqiva. He later on definitely assigns them to the school of R. Ishmael (p. 634).

The Aqiban school produced Sifra, Sifré Deut. 55-303, Mekhilta of R. Simeon b. Yoḥai, and Sifré Zuṭa to Num. (p. 644). Sifra was edited not by Rav, but by R. Ḥiyya, Epstein says (p. 652).

38:26); now you are paying a head-tax of fifteen *sheqels* under a government of your enemies.

"You were unwilling to repair the roads and streets leading up to the Temple; now you have to keep in repair the posts and stations on the roads to the royal cities."

And thus it says: *Because thou didst not serve... therefore thou shalt serve thine enemy. Because thou didst not serve the Lord thy God with love, therefore shalt thou serve thine enemy with hatred; because thou didst not serve the Lord thy God when thou hadst plenty, therefore thou shalt serve thine enemy in hunger and thirst; because thou didst not serve the Lord thy God when thou wast well clothed, therefore thou shalt serve thine enemy in nakedness; because thou didst not serve the Lord thy God by reason of the abundance of all things, therefore shalt thou serve thine enemy in want of all things.*

What is the meaning of: *In want of all things?* They were out of their senses. Another Interpretation: *In Want of All Things*—They were deficient in the study of the Torah.

(Mekhilta of R. Ishmael, Baḥodesh I, ed. and trans. J. Z. Lauterbach, II, pp. 193-5)

Comment: The occasion for the sermon is spelled out in detail—Emmaus, girl picking barley corn, Arabian horseman. Yet the sermon itself exhibits no relationship to the story. Once the setting is completed, the sermon follows without much reference to it or its details. The girl hardly plays a role, except as a *mashal*. But "measure for measure" as the attribute of divine punishment is not peculiar to Yoḥanan. It appears in this very passage in the anonymous superscription. Further, the saying concerning the girl ends with the subjection to the Arabs. Afterward, a sermon is recorded, tacked on because "measure for measure" is to be demonstrated in other details. So we probably have here two separate elements, one depending on and relating to the girl, the other quite independent. This probably is confirmed by I.i.7, which is obviously another version of the story of the girl, but knows nothing of the appended sermon. See the comment there.

2(a). *For If Thou Lift Up Thy Sword upon it* (Ex. 20:25). In this connection R. Simon b. Eleazar used to say, "The altar is made to prolong the years of man and iron is made to shorten the years of man. It is not right for that which shortens life to be lifted up against that which prolongs life."

(b) R. Yoḥanan b. Zakkai says, "Behold it says: *Thou shalt build... of whole stones* (Deut. 27:6). They are to be stones that establish peace.

(c) "Now, by using the method of *qal vaḥomer*, you reason: The stones for the altar do not see nor hear nor speak. Yet because they serve to establish peace between Israel and their Father in heaven, the Holy One, blessed be He, said, *Thou shalt lift up no iron tool upon them* (ibid., v.5). How much the more then should he who establishes peace between man and his fellow-man, between husband and wife, between city and city, between nation and nation, between family and family, between government and government, be protected so that no harm should come to him."

(Mekhilta of R. Ishmael, Baḥodesh 11, ed. and trans. J. Lauterbach, II, p. 290)

Comment: This exegesis is not described as "in the manner of the *ḥomer*" but explicitly as a *qal vaḥomer*. I do not think, though, that *kemin ḥomer* means simply, "in the manner of an argument *a forteriori*," since other exempla of the *ḥomer* method contain no hint of an argument *a forteriori*.

Here the "whole stones" and the "iron" homilies are fused together. Elsewhere they appear as separate sayings. I.i.1 and I.ii.5 are both composites of sayings which may have been originally separate. I assume, therefore, that both Aqiban and Ishmaelean materials were based on some earlier data, now given pretty much as received but in a different, integrated context.

I.ii.1, the ʿAqiban version, substitutes *sons of Torah* for *peacemakers* who escape punishment; it omits the *altar*, and the *sword shortens life* becomes the *sword as a sign of punishment*. The *altar* does not prolong life but *atones* for Israel.[1]

I.ii.1 thus shows what the Aqiban party made of this midrash, which was none too palatable to them. The essential element was the exegesis on whole stones/peace. The function of the altar was that of making peace. Therefore peace-makers in this world perform the function of the altar—and more so! This is Yoḥanan's essential idea; the functions performed by the Temple and its instruments can be replaced by human virtues. So the *qal veḥomer* preserved in the Ishmaelean tradition I.i.2 and I.ii.5 is also originally from Yoḥanan, and the saying of Simeon b. Eleazar in I.i.2 shows an early development of Yoḥanan's idea in its original spirit: war is bad, peace is good.

The Aqibans therefore omitted the exegesis of peace/whole stones; revised the *qal veḥomer* to make the essential virtue *not* peace-making but study of the Torah; revised Simeon's saying to make both the sword and the altar symbols of the attributes of the divine nature—judgment and mercy, thus making the sword a good thing too; and attributed all of their revised complex to Yoḥanan. And they did an amazingly good job—their revised version looks so much like the original that the care-

[1] I owe this observation to Morton Smith.

less reader would think them nearly identical. It is only when one looks closely that he sees the reversal of the implications.

3. *His Ear. Through the ear-lap* (Ex. 21:6). And what is the reason that, of all the organs, the ear alone is to be pierced through? R. Yoḥanan b. Zakkai interpreted it *kemin ḥomer*; "His ear had heard the commandment: *Thou shalt not steal* (Ex. 20:13). And yet he went and stole. Therefore it alone, of all the organs, shall be pierced through."

(Mekhilta of R. Ishmael, Neziqin 2, ed. and trans. J. Z. Lauterbach III, p. 16)

Comment: The connection between stealing and being sold into slavery is clear: The man stole, but was unable to make recompense, and therefore was sold as a slave with the proceeds going to the injured party.

For a comparison of versions of this exegesis, see synoptic studies (XII.iii). This is the earliest and simplest exemplum.

4. *He shall pay five oxen* (Ex. 22:1). That is, four in addition to the one stolen. *And four sheep*. That is, three in addition to the one stolen.

R. Meir says, "Come and see how highly regarded labor is by Him who by his word caused the world to come into being. For an ox, which has to perform labor, one must pay fivefold. For a sheep, which does not perform labor, one pays only fourfold."

R. Yoḥanan b. Zakkai says, "God has consideration for the dignity of human beings. For an ox, since it walked with its legs, the thief pays fivefold. For the lamb, since he had to carry it on his shoulders, he pays only fourfold."

(Mekhilta of R. Ishmael, Neziqin 12, ed. and trans. J. Z. Lauterbach, III, p. 99)

Comment: Meir makes a similar point, but it is sufficiently different so no reference to Yoḥanan would have been called for. There is no parallel to this exegesis.

5(a). *If the Thief Be Found He Shall Pay Double* (Ex. 22:7). The thief pays double but the robber pays back only the principal. And what is the reason that the Torah made it severer for the thief than for the robber? R. Yoḥanan b. Zakkai says, "The robber regarded the servant like the Master. The thief honored the servant more than the Master.

(b) "The thief, as though such a thing were possible, regarded the Eye above as if it could not see, and the Ear as if it could not hear—just as when it is said: *Woe unto them that seek deep to hide their counsel from the Lord and their works are in the dark, and they say: 'Who sees us? and who knows us?'* (Is. 29:15). And it says: *And they say: 'The Lord will not see.'* (Ps. 94:7). And it also says: *For they say: 'The Lord has forsaken the land, and the Lord sees not'* (Ez. 9:9)."

(Mekhilta of R. Ishmael, Neziqin 15, ed. and trans. J. Z. Lauterbach III, p. 115)

Comment: The passage recurs in II.iii.8 as a *ḥomer*-exegesis. The several Scriptural citations there recur without change. I should imagine, though, that they mark a secondary development of the primary thought that the thief acts as if there is no God. Yoḥanan's original saying would have been the explanation of the law in the *ḥomer*-style, which here means, giving a rational reason for what seems an irrational law. Before the Ishmaelean Mekhilta was edited, the passage underwent some development, though Yoḥanan's own words could not have been changed much. The exegesis produces a whole story in ARNa, below, IV.i.11, and III.ii.1a, for his death-bed scene contains an identical homily. I therefore imagine that the early exegesis was taken up and given a dramatic setting. The Scriptural interpretation produced a whole speech, indeed a colloquy between Yoḥanan and the disciples; and the lemma here became the basis for a later story.

6(a). *This is the ordinance of the Torah* (Num. 19:1). Rabbi Eliezer says, "Here *ordinance* is stated, and later on likewise. Just as *ordinance* later on refers to white garments, so likewise here."

(b) His disciples asked Rabban Yoḥanan ben Zakkai, "In what garments is the [red] heifer [sacrifice] carried out?"

He said to them, "In golden garments."

They said to him, "But did you, our rabbi, not teach us 'in white garments'?"

He said to them, "If I have forgotten what my [own] eyes witnessed and my [own] hands did, how much the more so [have I forgotten] what I taught [you]!"

(c) And why such [assumption of ignorance on the master's part]? In order to sharpen disciples' [wits].

(d) And there are those who say it was Hillel, but *he* could not say "What my [own] hands did."

(Sifré Num. Ḥuqat #123, ed. Horovitz p. 151, l. 8-13)

Comment: The tale about Yoḥanan/Hillel is of slight historical value. A story which is told of two different men cannot confidently be told of either; it may at first have been anonymous. Yet it cannot be thought a complimentary story. It pictures a teacher who could not remember even what he had done, much less what he had taught. By contrast, stories were told about Yoḥanan's telling the Temple priests how to conduct *just* this ceremony (II.iii.12).

The addition, *why all this*, certainly does not belong to the original story. Without it, the story is about a teacher's forgetfulness. But with it, the teacher is excused and justified—his error was not really an error, but an act of kindness, to make the students believe that he could forget, just as they did.

To whom would it have been important to denigrate Yoḥanan or Hillel? Priests hostile to the Hillelite school of Pharisees, or to the decrees of Yoḥanan at Yavneh, or to both, would have found it agreeable. Disciples would have turned the hostile story into a favorable one by the addition. Indeed, the attribution to Hillel further suggests Yoḥanan was himself a priest, thus completely upsetting the original priestly assertion that Yoḥanan, a layman, was not a reliable teacher on priestly laws.

The tale is set into the context of Eliezer's teaching on the same subject. Since Eliezer was both a priest and a pupil of Yoḥanan, he is the person most likely to have heard the story the priests were telling of his teacher and to have made it over by the explanatory addition. We shall see a number of instances in which the sayings and doings of Yoḥanan are reported either directly by, or in the context of, Eliezer's circle; others clearly derive from Joshua's school. I think it evident that Yoḥanan-materials were preserved in Eliezer's and Joshua's schools, and doubtless were given their final form by the disciples of Yoḥanan's disciples, if not by Eliezer and Joshua themselves. In this instance, I may tentatively suggest that the "correction" of the hostile priestly story to produce a favorable view of Yoḥanan would have been introduced by Eliezer. However, Joshua's version (II.iii.13) is basically identical—apologetic addition, alternative assignment to Hillel, and all. Therefore either Joshua's version came from Eliezer, or Eliezer's from Joshua, or both from a common source.

Moreover, is it likely that either Eliezer or Joshua, immediate disciples of Yoḥanan ben Zakkai, would have hesitated as to whether the story was rightly told of Yoḥanan or of Hillel? It is not very likely. Therefore while the story may well have got its apologetic addition from Eliezer, the second addition, to the effect that it was also told about Hillel, must have been added by some still later collector and commentator, and some even later commentator must have inserted the whole, with both additions, into the collection of Joshua-materials from which the Tosefta drew. So we can trace six stages:

1. Sadducean story of a forgetful teacher of the law—who was also a high priest! The Sadducees were famous for their disrespect of their elders, so Josephus.
2. The Sadducean story was used against (a) Yoḥanan and (b) Hillel, though it does not fit either, since neither was a high priest.
3. Yoḥanan-story (b) was "corrected" by Eliezer's addition.

4. Eliezer's Yoḥanan-story was glossed by a collector who knew the Hillel story (d). A second glossator, perhaps very late, added the objection to the Hillel story.

5. Collector's-Eliezer's-Yoḥanan-story was inserted as a comment in a collection of Joshua-material.

6. Joshua's collector's-Eliezer's-Yoḥanan-story was used by the compiler of the Tosefta.[1]

7. The story is told of Rabban Yoḥanan ben Zakkai, that he was riding on an ass and his disciples were walking behind him. He saw a young girl gathering barley from under the hooves of Arab cattle. When she saw Rabban Yoḥanan ben Zakkai, she covered herself with her hair and stood before him, and said to him, "Rabbi, feed me."

He said to her, "Whose daughter are you?"

She replied, "The daughter of Naqdimon ben Gurion am I. But do you not remember that you witnessed my marriage-contract?"

Rabban Yoḥanan ben Zakkai said to his disciples, "I did [indeed] witness this [girl's] marriage-contract, and I read in it 'a thousand thousands of *dinarii* of gold of the house of her in-laws.' [Members] of the family of this girl did not enter the Temple mountain to bow down until linen carpets were spread under their feet. They would go in and bow down and joyfully return to their homes.

"And all my life I sought [the meaning of] this Scripture, but [now] have I found it: *If you do not know, O fairest of women, go in the tracks of the flock and pasture your kids* [gediyotayikh] *beside the shepherds' tents* (Song 1:8). Do not read your *kids [gediyotekha]* but your *bodies [geviyotayikh]*. While Israel does the will of the Omnipresent, no nation or tongue rules them, but when they do not, he gives them into the hand of a lowly nation, and not into the hand of a lowly nation but [even] under the feet of their cattle."

(Sifré Deut. #305, ed. Friedman, p. 129a)

Comment: The pericope is obviously a composite of two separate components. The first is the meeting with the girl. The second is the exegesis of Song 1:8, for which the meeting provides a setting. But the exegesis, without "All my life... now I have found it" could as well have stood by itself. I suspect that the exegesis preceded the story, that is, Yoḥanan made a comment on Song 1:8, that by a *read-not*, one learns that "while Israel does the will..." The reference of the Scripture to "fairest of women" then provoked the story about such a "fairest of women," a girl whose family, long ago enjoying close ties to Yoḥanan,

[1] The division into stages of development was contributed by Morton Smith.

ended up "going in the tracks of the flock." Without the Scripture, the detail about gathering barley from under the hooves of Arab cattle is meaningless and pointless. Hence I imagine it was invented to match the exegesis which, in final form, was to follow. If these suppositions are correct, then the account was originally composed of two elements, first the unhappy fate of Naqdimon's family, whom Yoḥanan had known; second, Yoḥanan's comments on Song 1:8. The former provided the life-setting for the exegesis—but only in the narrator's hands.

Now, however, this is a unitary account, unlike the story cited above, I.i.1. Here the girl is always in the center of things, and significant details of her life are invented. By pure coincidence she now turns out to be the daughter of the richest man of Jerusalem; her marriage contract was witnessed by Yoḥanan himself; and of course that makes her riches-to-rags story all the more pathetic and striking as an example for a sermon. The sermon now focuses upon the girl, and the proof texts always remain relevant to her. But the mode of exegesis is a *read-not*, rather than an exemplification of *measure for measure*: "If you do not know, then pasture your body..."

The point is somewhat different also. The account in I.i.1 stressed the master's reproach; this one by contrast contains the more general theological observation that by doing God's will, Israel will win her battles. The two stories thus show independent homiletic development of an original anecdote, of which the form is preserved more faithfully by I.i.1. The anecdote may have had its origin in some actual event, or may have been generated by Yoḥanan's exegesis of Song 1:8, which is clearly the essential element. The earlier version, I.i.1, supplies the detail about Emmaus, which may well be historical, since it seems unmotivated. Significantly, it has been dropped by I.i.7, and replaced by dramatic inventions (which would never have been forgotten had they been part of the original story!).

We have no way of determining which of the two versions was given its final form at an earlier date. Both the elaborate exegetical setting in which the anecdote has been placed by I.i.1 and the homiletical internal elaboration which it has undergone in I.i.7 are obviously second ary but hardly datable.

On the one hand, the simpler exegesis of one Scripture only may have antedated the proliferation of exegeses. On the other, both the selection of a single, particularly appropiate Scripture from the whole ready repertoire of possible proof texts *and* its association with a "historical" event may represent a later development of, and improvement upon, the more abundant version.[1]

---

[1] See Louis Finkelstein, *Mavo LeMassekhtot 'Avot ve'Avot deRabbi Natan* (N.Y., 1951), pp. 112-113. Finkelstein supposes that the story is based upon an event involving Yoḥanan, another involving Eleazar b. R. Ẓadoq. The report of the latter was influenced by Yohanan's story. This is on a par with the conservative New Testament commentaries which produce a different miracle for each occasion when parallel synoptic miracle stories are located in different places by different gospels.

8(a) *Moses was one-hundred-twenty years old* (Deut. 34:7). He was one of four who died at one-hundred-twenty years, and these are they: Moses, Hillel the Elder, Rabban Yoḥanan ben Zakkai, and R. ʿAqiva.

Moses was in Egypt forty years, in Midian forty years, and sustained Israel forty years.

Hillel the Elder came up from Babylonia at forty years of age, served the sages forty years, and sustained Israel forty years.

Rabban Yoḥanan ben Zakkai was in business forty years, served the sages forty years, and sustained Israel forty years.

R. ʿAqiva studied Torah forty years and sustained Israel forty years.

(b) Six pairs [lived] for an identical number [of years.] Rebecca and Kohath, Levi and Amram, Joseph and Joshua, Samuel and Solomon, Moses and Hillel the Elder, Rabban Yoḥanan ben Zakkai and R. ʿAqiva.

(Sifré Deut. #357, ed. Friedman p. 150a)

Comment: I am astonished at the pairing of Yoḥanan and ʿAqiva in a passage of supposedly Ishmaelean origin. Omission of the first forty years of ʿAqiva's life is striking; presumably the fact that he then was an ʿ*am ha*ʾ*areẓ* is regarded as beneath mention. But this must be secondary—presumably a matter of textual corruption in medieval transmission of the MSS, since the form of the saying obviously requires that three forty-year periods should have been specified. Ishmaelean tradents would have liked the opportunity to state plainly the facts about ʿAqiva's youth, but even so, the pairing with Yoḥanan is amazing. In any event, this story could not have been framed before the death of ʿAqiva. Ca. 150 A.D. would be a plausible date. By this time, the school of Ishmael was largely located in Babylonia and in any case exerted little or no influence in Palestine. Perhaps earlier disputes and the animosities they produced no longer meant much: the glorious martyrdom of ʿAqiva probably would have discouraged former tendencies to dispute with and criticize him.

The passage before us is clearly a composite of two *one-hundred-twenty-year* pericopae. The first lists four who lived for that period, the second lists twelve, including the original four. It is likely that the two components were framed separately, then brought together for purposes of compilation. Of the two, the second is the more succinct; the first develops the theme by selecting four more important figures and supplying the data of their life-stories. But the two elements do not seem to me to depend on one another, and perhaps originally they did not. I therefore cannot suggest which is earlier. The combinations of Moses and Hillel, Yoḥanan and ʿAqiva, appearing in both, reflect an identical tendency, as I said at the outset.

II. The School of R. ʿAqiva

1. This is what Rabban Yoḥanan ben Zakkai says, "What was the reason iron was prohibited more than all [other] metals [for use in building the tabernacle (Ex. 20:25)]? Because the sword is made from it, and the sword is a sign of punishment, but the altar is a sign of atonement. A sign [means] of punishment is removed from something which is a sign [means] of atonement.

"And is this not a matter of *qal veḥomer?* Stones, which neither see nor hear nor speak—because they bring atonement between Israel and their father in heaven, the Holy One blessed be he said [concerning them] *Thou shalt lift upon them no iron tool* (Deut. 27:5). Sons of Torah, who are an atonement for the world, how much the more so that none of all the harmful forces in the world should ever touch them!"

(Mekhilta of R. Simeon b. Yoḥai, Yitro 20:22,
ed. Epstein-Melamed pp. 157-8, 1. 29-31, 1-4)

Comment: We have two separate sayings. The first is Yoḥanan's, that metal is prohibited because the sword is made of metal and is a sign of punishment, while the altar is a sign of atonement. The second saying is the *qal veḥomer*, that as stones should not be injured because they bring atonement, so sons of Torah should all the more so be free of injury from harmful forces. The *qal veḥomer* has nothing to do with Yoḥanan's observation, and need not be directly attributed to him, though it occurs in all formulations of this passage. It seems to be a later development. For further discussion, see I.i.2.

2(a). And the story is told that Rabban Yoḥanan ben Zakkai was riding on an ass and going out of Jerusalem. R. Eleazar b. ʿArakh his disciple was walking behind him. He [R. Eleazar] said to him [Rabban Yoḥanan], "Rabbi, Teach me a chapter in the Works of the Chariot."

He replied, "Have I not taught you [plural], 'And Concerning the *Merkavah*, not with a single disciple [alone may one study] unless he is a sage and comprehends out of his own knowledge.' "

He said to him, "If not, give me permission that I may speak before you."

R. Eleazar b. ʿArakh was expounding [the Chariot] until fire was licking all around him. When Rabban Yoḥanan ben Zakkai saw that the fire was licking all around him, he descended from the ass and kissed him, saying to him, "Rabbi Eleazar b. ʿArakh, Happy is she who bore you, happy are you, O Abraham our father, that such a one has come forth from your loins."

(b). He [Rabban Yoḥanan] would say, "If all the sages of Israel were in one side of the scale and Rabbi Eleazar ben ʿArakh in the second side, he would outweigh them all."

(Mekhilta of R. Simeon b. Yoḥai, Mishpaṭim 20:1, ed. Epstein-Melamed pp. 158, 1. 8-17, and 159, 1.18-21)

Comment: 2b is tacked on, having nothing to do with the *Merkavah* story. It stands by itself. Several other examples of Eleazar's superiority are told. I do not know why it should have been important to the Aqibans to preserve Yoḥanan's praise of Eleazar. Perhaps their *Merkavah*-traditions depended on his, but it is more likely that ʿAqiva's *Merkavah* traditions come from Joshua (below III.iii.3). In that case it is all the more puzzling that Eleazar is represented as the chief *Merkavah*-disciple. Furthermore, Eleazar did not come to Yavneh, and probably had fallen from favor by the time of, if not before, Yoḥanan's death.[1] In other versions, the effort is made to transfer the *Merkavah*-tradition to Joshua and others. The present form of the story, speaking of both teachers in the third person and past tense, was almost certainly shaped by Eleazar's pupils (perhaps on the basis of what their master had told them, perhaps from wishful thinking or to glorify him). That it now stands in an Aqiban collection makes it likely that Eleazar's pupils after his death—how long we do not know—went over to the school of ʿAqiva.[2]

It is further to be supposed that the Aqibans preserved the *Merkavah* story pretty much as they received it, for, as I said, they could not have preferred an account praising Eleazar to one praising Joshua, ʿAqiva's *Merkavah*-teacher. The preservation is important as a reminder that ʿAqiva's school was by no means absolutely uniform or unified. Presumably as a center of nationalistic resistance to Rome it attracted and welcomed or at least tolerated a considerable variety of adherents, and each group brought in some traditions of its own. Therefore we should expect *a priori* that Aqiban material would be much more various than that from the Ishmaeleans, who had no such historical reason, or occasion, for accepting newcomers of other, now extinct, circles.

2a is the earliest version of the *Merkavah* incident. We shall see that

---

[1] See Louis Finkelstein, *Mavo*, pp. 41f. Finkelstein's view is that Eleazar went to Emmaus from Yavneh, and that therefore the Avot materials (below) as well as stories such as this were edited by a disciple, or a disciple of the disciples, of Yoḥanan before Eleazar's departure, "before his bitter fate of disappointing the hope of Yoḥanan that his name would be magnified in Torah became known. If so, these sages were still alive when the collection was written." I think it more reasonable to attribute the formulation of Eleazar materials to Eleazar's circle at Emmaus. Finkelstein notes that in ARNb, Yoḥanan's praise of Eleazar is corrected by Abba Shaul in *ʿAqiva's* name.

[2] Morton Smith provided the explanation for the inclusion of Eleazar's materials in the Aqiban collections.

many details are added in formations in both Talmuds. The *beraitot* of both are clearly Aqiban in origin.

3. *When ['asher] a prince sins* (Lev. 4:22). Rabban Yoḥanan ben Zakkai said, "Happy [*'ashré*] is the generation whose prince brings a sin offering for his unwitting transgression."

(Sifra Vayiqra, Parashah 5:1, ed. I. H. Weiss, p. 19b)

Comment: This is elsewhere listed as a *ḥomer*-exegesis, but in fact is merely a play on words. The saying may be read as 1) a post-70 lament at the destruction of the Temple and so of the possibility of bringing sin-offerings; 2) a post-44 lament at the restoration of Judea to government by procurators, after which there was no Judean "prince" to bring a sin-offering; 3) a pre-70 criticism of the Herodians for failing to bring sin-offerings. Of these, 1) contradicts Yoḥanan's concern after 70 to emphasize that virtues can satisfactorily substitute for the temple, and 2) is not consonant with Yoḥanan's willingness to accept Roman rule. It therefore seems more likely that the saying contains an implied criticism of rulers who do not bring sin-offerings either for accidental or for intentional sins. Hence it may derive from pre-70 Jerusalem. But if it does, it survived in a form so generalized that its original polemic has been removed.

4. *All that is in it shall render unclean.* (Lev. 11:33). Rabbi 'Aqiva says, "It does not say *is unclean*, but *shall render unclean*—to render unclean other objects, teaching, concerning the second loaf, that it renders the third unclean..."

Rabbi Joshua said, "Who will remove the dust from between your eyes, O Rabban Yoḥanan ben Zakkai, for you would say that another generation is destined to declare clean the third loaf, for which [exegesis] there is no Scriptural [proof] in the Torah, and behold 'Aqiva your disciple brings Scriptural [proof] from the Torah that it is unclean, for it is said, *And all that is in it will be unclean* (Lev. 11:33)."

(Sifra Shemini, Parasha 7:12, ed. I. H. Weiss, p. 54a)

Comment: It is natural for Aqibans to preserve a record of how Yoḥanan's outstanding student had conceded the superiority of 'Aqiva's exegetical method to Yoḥanan's. It is striking that 'Aqiva is called by the Aqibans "Yoḥanan's disciple." This is consistent with the preservation of several favorable accounts of Yoḥanan in the Aqiban circles. I think it is clear therefore that the Aqibans wanted to underscore their master's relationship to Yoḥanan, perhaps because of their master's political failure. Yoḥanan had advised against the first war; ʿAqiva backed the second, which led to disaster. Yet, the disciples would have stressed, the wisdom of the master was not lost upon his "disciple" ʿAqiva, who was not only a true heir to his master's prescience, despite his poor guess about Bar Kokhba, but also superior to the master in exegetical abilities. If that was the Aqiban's intent—and it is purely conjectural to suggest so—then Joshua's saying would have been useful. But standing by itself, Joshua's exclamation is ambiguous: It declares Yoḥanan had suspected that some day someone would say pretty much what ʿAqiva now maintained, but it says nothing of what Yoḥanan thought of the opinion. As to Yoḥanan's opinion, the parallel in II.i.11, which adds *to render unclean* to *no Scriptural proof* suggests that Yoḥanan would have approved the declaration of purity, whereas the version here is neutral, if not negative, in connotation.[1]

We cannot maintain that Joshua's Yoḥanan-materials reach us only, or chiefly, through the Aqiban school, Eliezer's from some other source (see I.ii.8). But, as we shall see, Eliezer's and Joshua's Yoḥanan-traditions certainly were at the outset edited in *their* respective schools and by *their* disciples. This passage would therefore represent a third stage in the process of transmission: 1. Actual event or saying; 2. Joshua's preservation of the tradition; 3. The Aqibans' rendition of Joshua's comment on ʿAqiva's exegesis. Clearly the teaching had to begin with something like this formulation:

> Rabban Yoḥanan ben Zakkai said, "The third loaf is [capable of rendering other loaves] unclean, though there are reasons to think the contrary."

An alternative (theoretical) formulation would be:

> Rabban Yoḥanan ben Zakkai said, "Some future generation is likely to declare the third loaf [incapable of transmitting] uncleanness."

In that form, or something like it, the teaching would probably have been handed on. But if this modest conjecture is correct, then it is noteworthy that no such saying actually *was* handed on in Yoḥanan's name in preserved materials. If one existed, it was suppressed, so the only exemplum we have is in the form as given here. The teachings of Yoḥanan reach us, therefore, through the medium not only (or chiefly) of his disciples, but also of the Aqibans (and others) later on, who chose to preserve only parts of Yoḥanan's disciples' teachings about their master, and to do so in forms different from the original ones. We shall later on see that *beraitot* went through a similar process.

5. Rabban Yoḥanan ben Zakkai says, "Behold it says, *[With] whole stones ['avanim shelemot] will you build the altar of the Lord your God* (Deut. 27:5)—Stones which make peace [*shalom*], and behold it is a matter of *qal veḥomer:* Stones which do not see and do not hear and do

[1] I owe this observation to Morton Smith.

not speak, because they bring peace between Israel and their father in heaven, Scripture says *You shall not lift up iron over them* (Deut. 27:6). A man who brings peace between a man and his wife, between one family and another, between one city and another, between one province and another, between one nation and another—how much the more so that punishment should not come near him!"

(Sifra Qedoshim, Pereq 10:4, ed. I. H. Weiss, p. 92b)

Comment: The exegesis is practically identical with I.ii.1. The Scriptures are different. There it is "why is iron prohibited" and here it concerns the play on words: "whole stones—stones which make peace." *Atonement* becomes *peace*, *sons of Torah* become *peacemakers*. The structure is otherwise the same; the thought is the same ("Peacemakers or those who atone for the world should come to no harm"). The details are somewhat different.

Yet the differences are not very considerable. I suspect that Yoḥanan would have said something about the altar/altar-stones in the form of a *qal veḥomer*. The context was Deut. 27:5 and 27:6. The play on words concerning the "whole stones" was dropped in I.ii.1, the stress on "iron" of all metals was omitted here.

Strikingly, the Ishmaelean version, I.i.2, follows I.ii.5; both versions elide the *whole stones* play on words and the *qal veḥomer* involving an iron tool. I should thus suppose that I.i.2 = I.ii.5. I.ii.1 differs, as I said, in omitting "whole stones" and stressing "iron." Both schools preserved an account exhibiting formal parallels (I.i.2 = I.ii.5), but the Aqibans alone preserved the other (I.ii.1), probably because they invented it.

Some anterior version was available to both schools, and that anterior version derived from circles close to Yoḥanan himself. In a period of less than a few decades between Yoḥanan's death and the formation of the schools of Ishmael and ʿAqiva, a group of Yoḥanan's disciples must have put into final form materials which were subsequently made use of by *both* schools.

This supposition is likely to be valid if the following conditions are also valid: (1) if both documents actually come from the schools to which they are attributed; (2), if the present form was edited ca. 200, if not somewhat earlier; and most important (3) if they were *not* expanded since that time. Then the story stands in both by 200 A.D. and was known to teachers in both schools. The common source of the story would have come substantially earlier than the founding of the two schools, ca. 100-120. In that case, as I said, the story is certainly part of the corpus of Yoḥanan-sayings edited by the time of Yavneh. But see below, p. 33, for alternative explanations.

We may safely go a step further and designate as Yavnean, *all* materials occurring in substantially similar form in materials ascribed to the two schools; as Ishmaelean, materials unique to that school, hence not necessarily later than Yavneh but probably from a circle at Yavneh not known or acceptable to the Aqibans; as Aqiban, materials unique to that school, within the same limitation. It would be tempting to suppose that materials unique to one or the other school were later than materials common to both, but the obvious imponderables prevent it.

It is consequential, since we have no documents edited at Yavneh, to recognize that within documents edited later on are materials which probably did come from Yavneh. But it is equally noteworthy that even the materials in the earliest collections have already undergone substantial development. Primitive logia, in which stories or sayings about Yoḥanan are transcribed close to when they happened or were actually stated, are unavailable. In general, the closest we can come to the man himself is through secondary materials based on Yavnean traditions.

6. When the Temple was destroyed, Rabban Yoḥanan ben Zakkai ordained that the entire Day of Waving [of the *ʿomer*] should be prohibited [for the eating of new produce].

(Sifra ʾEmor, Parasha 10:10, ed. I. H. Weiss, p. 100b)

Comment: See below, I.ii.7.

7. *And you will rejoice before the Lord your God seven days* (Lev. 23:40). But *not* in the provinces all seven [days].

And when the Temple was destroyed Rabban Yoḥanan ben Zakkai ordained (a) that the *lulav* should be taken in the countryside seven [days] as a memorial to the Temple and (b) that the entire Day of Waving should be prohibited [for the eating of new produce].

(Sifra ʾEmor, Pereq 16:9, ed. I. H. Weiss, p. 102b)

Comment: The first paragraph antedates the destruction of the Temple, and may perhaps be quite old. It is most plausibly seen as part of the ancient Pharisaic exegesis of Lev. 23:40: "*You will rejoice*... in the Temple, not in the provinces." The alteration of circumstances afterward required the inclusion of Yoḥanan's decree. But the Yoḥanan-passage has nothing to do with the preceding exegesis, and does not in any measure either relate to, or depend on it. In some old formulation of exegeses on Leviticus, the first paragraph would have stood pretty much as we have it, and we must also conclude that it was not thereafter altered, but only *supplemented* by new sayings.

Thus far we have only two of the [alleged] nine decrees of Yavneh. These two, concerning the "Day of Waving" and the carrying of the *lulav*, were neutral and offensive to no one. They dealt merely with problems of Temple liturgy in the interim. New produce obviously could be consumed, but the absence of the Temple ceremony meant that people must wait out the whole day on which it would have been performed. The *lulav* ceremony might be continued—but only as a memorial to the Temple, *not* as a usurpation of its prerogatives.

The Day of Waving decree was cited by itself, apart from the *lulav* one. The Day of Waving is tacked on in I.ii.7, but stands as the only element in I.ii.6. These are the only ones of the Yavnean decrees referred to in the Aqiban Tannaitic midrashim. In the Tannaitic midrashim from the school of Ishmael there are no references whatever to any decrees.

Now the decrees fit exactly the situation of Yavneh. They deal with matters which had to be settled at that time, and when we do begin to get traditions about them, they are unanimously referred to Yavneh and to Yoḥanan. It is thus indubitable that they come from there and from him. Their absence, therefore, from the Aqiban and Ishmaelean midrashim shows that these are not complete records of what was known and handed down in those schools. We must be cautious in using their silence to prove that teachings not mentioned were non-existent.

Similarly it is not improbable that there was from Yoḥanan's time on a tradition listing *all* his reforms. This is suggested by the way in which the Day of Waving decree is tacked onto the *lulav* decree in I.ii.7, although the two have no other connection than their common source. We should thus probably see both the reference to one reform in I.ii.6 and that to two reforms in I.ii.7 as mere excerpts from the list which is not completely reported until much later. To suppose that matters of general concern like these decrees were known only to one group of Yoḥanan's disciples, or that they were deliberately suppressed or kept secret by the others, is implausible. Therefore the explanation of their incomplete appearance prior to the Ushan period—and even afterward—must lie in the records for the earlier period, which were either themselves incomplete to begin with, or were incompletely preserved, or both.

8. *Righteousness, righteousness you will pursue* (Deut. 16:20): Go after a good court. After the court of Rabban Yoḥanan ben Zakkai and after the court of Rabbi Eliezer.

(Sifré Deut. #144, ed. Friedman, p. 103b)

Comment: This exegesis obviously derives from the school of Eliezer, which persistently linked Yoḥanan-stories with Eliezer's. It is important to observe that the Ishmaeleans also preserved an Eliezer-Yoḥanan sequence (I.i.6) which proves beyond doubt that *both* schools derived Yoḥanan-materials from his immediate disciple, Eliezer b. Hyrcanus.

But the preserved Eliezer-stories of the two schools are quite different, bearing no relationship to one another. I.i.6 pertains to a teaching on the priestly garb required for the heifer-ceremony, I.ii.8 to the excellence of the masters' courts (and this recurs in expanded form in a *beraita*, below, III.ii.24).

Presumably some principle of selection guided the two schools' respective choices of which Eliezer-Yoḥanan materials to redact, but the identifiable materials are too sparse to permit any conjecture on the operative criteria.

9. *And he said to them, "Hear O Israel... Which man fears and is faint hearted?"* (Deut. 20:3ff.). Why are all these things stated? So that the cities of Israel should not be desolated, according to the words of Rabban Yoḥanan ben Zakkai, "Come and see how much the Omnipresent pitied the honor of the creatures. On account of the man who was afraid and frail-hearted.

"When he returns [home], they will say, 'Perhaps he built a house? Perhaps he betrothed a wife?' And all of them have to bring their witness[es], except for the one who is afraid and frail-hearted. His witnesses are [right there] with him.

"He hears the sound of the clashing of shields and trembles, the sound of the neighing of horses and frets, the sound of the blowing of horns and is terrified. He sees the unsheathing of swords, and water runs down between his knees."

(Sifré Deut. #192, ed. Friedman, p. 110a)

Comment: I am not sure how one must punctuate this passage. It is possible that all that is attributed to Yoḥanan is "Why are all these things stated? So that... according to Yoḥanan." The "Come and see" exposition would be separate and anonymous. Alternatively, the latter passage may be attributed to Yoḥanan, as in Midrash Tannaim, I.iv.3. There the *so that* phrase is attributed to Judah the Prince.

We see here further indication that some of Yoḥanan's sayings about peace have made their way into the Aqiban Tannaitic midrashim. [On this, see I.i.2 and Epstein, *Mevo'ot*, p. 43]. In this instance, however, the inclusion may have been made by the Aqibans themselves, since the basic law stood in the Torah and had to be recognized, so they lost little by the inclusion of the exegesis, but they have probably appended the last paragraph, which is clearly contemptuous of the coward; contrast I.iv.3, where this paragraph is not added. It says only that the coward is favored because all others must bring witnesses to secure exemption, but he can testify of himself. The Aqiban school here takes up this ruling and asks, "How does he testify? What witnesses does he produce?" And they answer by listing the physical symptoms of cowardice, including involuntary urination. Consequently the coward is transformed from the class of the privileged to that of the ridiculous, and the exemption for cowardice is limited to those who actually produce these physical stigmata.[1]

In any event it stands to reason that Eliezer-Yoḥanan and Joshua-Yoḥanan materials occurring in Ishmaelean and Aqiban compilations come from Yavneh, probably after the deaths of the two major disciples, Ca. 100-150. See III.ii.24 for further comment.

iii. General Comments

The title *Rabban* is consistently used. All materials have been edited so that Yoḥanan's honorific is everywhere applied. That is important, because some materials call him "Ben Zakkai" as a term of derision. It is important, furthermore, because it proves beyond doubt that *all* early materials have been edited after it became customary to call Yoḥanan "Rabban." If it were supposed that materials from before that time, presumably the period of Yavneh, in fact were based upon eye-witness accounts, then the use of "Rabban" would indicate those very accounts were edited, or revised in this detail at least, long after many of them were written down.

Both schools obviously respected him. The Tannaitic Midrashim were edited ca. 200-250. The age was one in which the differences between ʿAqiva and the followers of Yoḥanan about Bar Kokhba and his holy war apparently had been forgotten, for it is practically impossible to locate any tendencies uniquely characteristic of either of the respective schools' treatment of Yoḥanan as an authoritative master.

The Ishmaelean school preserved two versions of Yoḥanan's exegesis of Song 1.8 (I.i.1,7), four exegeses in the manner of the *ḥomer* (I.i.2,3,4,5), a story about Yoḥanan as a teacher (I.i.6), and an account of four heroes who lived to one-hundred-twenty years (I.i.8)—including ʿAqiva. The Aqibans handed on four exegeses in the manner of the *ḥomer* (I.ii.1 [= i.2], 3,5,9), a *Merkavah*-mysticism story (I.ii.2), an account demonstrating Yoḥanan's disciple's recognition of ʿAqiva's exegesis over Yoḥanan's (I.ii.4), two decrees issued at Yavneh (I.ii.6, 7a,7b), and praise for the two men's courts.

The two schools had in common traditions on the *ḥomer*-expositions. For the Ishmaeleans, the *ḥomer*-exegeses were I.i.2, whole stones/iron; I.i.3, the ear that is pierced; I.i.4, the ox/lamb; I.i.5, the robber/thief. The Aqibans' materials included I.ii.1, iron, I.ii.3, the prince; I.ii.5,

---

[1] I owe this observation to Morton Smith.

whole stones/iron. In common therefore was I.i.2 = I.ii.1,5, and that alone. That does not mean the other *ḥomer*-exegeses, not held in common by the two schools, were redacted later than the Yavnean stage in the process of the formation of the traditions. On the contrary, I think that—like the Yavnean decrees, I.ii.9,—they are among the materials most likely to be attributed to Yoḥanan, probably even stated by him originally.

Parallels of midrashim from different schools may, as I argued above (I.ii.5), indicate the existence of a prior common source. However, there are two other possibilities which require specification. First, it may be that the parallels indicate posterior insertion in both midrashim from some outside source, not necessarily earlier than the two schools' traditions at all. Second, later scribal contamination of one midrash by insertion of material from the other may have taken place; or, similarly, one midrashic collection may have made reference to the other. This second possibility is especially likely if the material stands in the same place, either in exegesis of the same verse, or in the same contexts fore and aft, in both midrashim. I.i.2 and I.ii.1,5 manifestly provide exegesis of a common verse, Deut. 27:5-6. The Ishmaelean and Aqiban Mekhiltas (I.i.2, I.ii.1) obviously may have depended on one another, likely the latter on the former. But I.ii.5 concentrates on Deut. 27:5-6, while I.i.2 pertains to the parallel in Exodus. Hence the second possibility does not apply to this parallel.

We cannot come to firm conclusions, because the history of the texts is not known to us. We cannot be sure that the conditions specified above—(1) that the present text was *not* expanded since its editing in ca. 200 A.D.; (2) that the documents actually come from the schools to which they are attributed; (3) that the present form was in fact edited in ca. 200 A.D. and not many centuries later—we cannot be sure that these conditions have been met. So the conclusions advanced earlier must be regarded as tentative hypotheses. Still, regnant opinion is that posterior insertions were not made. Later scribal contamination of a substantial order did not take place; the documents actually did come from the schools to which they are attributed. I should suppose that I.i.2 = I.ii.5 probably does antedate the schools of Ishmael and ʿAqiva, were it not that I.ii.5 shows a *Tendenz* certain to be rejected by the Aqibans, and that they made over this material, in I.ii.1, to fit their own purposes. Consequently, I.ii.5 seems an example of later contamination—in this instance, contamination of an Aqiban midrash by insertion of an Ishmaelean pericope.

It may be that the Aqibans' greater interest in mysticism led to the preservation in their school, but not among the Ishmaeleans, of the story of Eleazar b. ʿArakh, whose students joined the Aqiban circle because they found it more congenial to their mysticism.

The condemnation of war and reproaches in its aftermath may likewise have been acceptable in the school whose master did not encourage the holy war of Bar Kokhba, but in any event ought to have been quite obnoxious to the one whose master did. Service of the Lord in love would have preserved the prosperity of the people, and the implied condemnation of war is present in the Ishmaelean stories about the Israelite girl.

Yoḥanan's decrees at Yavneh were not mentioned at all by the Ishmaeleans, but two of them were referred to by the Aqibans. We may partially account for this difference by the peculiar context in which the references are found, in the Sifra, on those Scriptural passages to which the decrees of Yavneh are actually relevant. I do not think we can suppose the Ishmaeleans suppressed Yoḥanan's legal record. But we do not know how they preserved it, for, in this case, we do not have their comments on Leviticus-laws.

Finally, that the Ishmaeleans preserved the story in which Yoḥanan and ʿAqiva are given the same life-span suggests that no one among the later Ishmaeleans was averse to saying praiseworthy things about ʿAqiva.

In all I think it has been proven that no *tendenz* concerning Yoḥanan *himself* characterized either school. Both preserved favorable, and more important, authoritative sayings and precedents. His legal role is, if anything, slightly greater among the Aqibans than among the Ishmaeleans, but the data are too sparse for that to matter much. Most important: *where the two schools differ in the sorts of stories they preserve about Yoḥanan, the reason for the difference is certainly found in the interests of the schools themselves, and not in their attitudes to Yoḥanan.*

What was the state of the Yoḥanan-tradition at this stage? These texts are primitive, in that they were not edited according to the principles of R. Judah the Prince. They contain several important details. First, Yoḥanan was somehow related to the destruction of Jerusalem. Second, he outlived it. Third, he probably regretted and opposed that war. These are the presuppositions of the story about the Israelite girl. Being "unwilling to be subject to God" was punished by the destruction and consequent suffering. What Yoḥanan thought such obedience consisted of is nowhere stated; knowledge of that was presumably taken for granted. What is important is that he was here placed into a specific historical context. This is striking, since few other sayings even suggest that he was involved in the events of 66-73. The reference in fixed form to what he decreed at Yavneh shows people knew that he was at Yavneh and made decrees there. But, by contrast, the rest of the stories do not pertain to any particular age or setting at all. In them Yoḥanan is an authority, but not a personality.

Conclusion: The main outlines of the Yoḥanan-tradition were vaguely present in the earliest stratum: the war, Yavneh, mysticism, *ḥomer*-exegesis. The war appears in Yoḥanan's reproaches in its aftermath, Yavneh in the two decrees; the *Merkavah*-story was told; and some of the *ḥomer*-exegeses occur in complete versions as well. Strikingly, we hear nothing about Yoḥanan's dramatic escape from Jerusalem. The Tannaitic Midrashim either had no knowledge of the escape, or chose to suppress it, or regarded it as unimportant. The first option seems unlikely—that Yoḥanan should not have told *some* story of his wartime movements, and that this story should not have been known to his disciples, is improbable. But it does not follow that the story he told is the one we have now. If it was the one we do have now, it could not have been thought unimportant. Its political, legal, and moral implications are obviously of extreme importance if Yoḥanan is taken as an authority and a model for his students. Also, if his story of his escape was the one we have now, we can easily understand why the Aqibans would have done their best to suppress it. That the Ishmaeleans should not have mentioned it is puzzling, but not decisive. We have seen that they also did not mention the Yavnean reforms. Accordingly we should suppose either that Yoḥanan told about his wartime adventures some colorless and inconsequential story, which was forgotten and replaced by the adventure now preserved; or that the preserved story is a more or less elaborated form of the original, but was not mentioned by the Aqibans because it did not suit their politics, nor by the Ishmaeleans—in the preserved material—for reasons we cannot now suggest. The persistence of a few details in all accounts—the escape in a coffin, the names of Naqdimon and others, the exegesis of Is. 10:34, and so forth—is hardly decisive, though it suggests that some single, primitive account containing these details *may* have been told before the fourth-century. But that does not bring us very close to the story Yoḥanan himself handed down.

IV. Midrash Tannaim

1. Why, in the verse *These are the laws and judgments which you will watch to do in the land all the days that you live* (Deut. 12:1) were the words "that you live" added? Hence Rabban Yoḥanan ben Zakkai would say, "If you have learned Torah, do not on that account take pride, for to this end were you created..."

(Midrash Tannaim, ed. Hoffman, p. 58)

Comment: This saying appears in Avot (below, II.i.18), but without the exegesis. It is generally characteristic of the Mishnah that laws are given without the underlying exegeses of Scriptures (if any), and that acounts for the difference between this formulation and the Mishnaic one. If so, this one is earlier, having been formulated before the editorial reforms of Judah the Prince, and not having been altered afterward. It would date, therefore, not much later than 150 A.D.

2. *You will surely destroy...* (Deut. 12:2). Hence Rabban Yoḥanan ben Zakkai would say, "Do not hastily destroy the altars of the gentiles, so that you do not have to rebuild them with your own hands. Do not destroy [altars] of mortar in order that they will not [come and] say to you to build them of stone, of stone—of wood..."

(Midrash Tannaim, ed. Hoffman, p. 58)

Comment: In the synoptic studies we shall compare this version with the one in ARNb Ch. 31, Schechter, p. 33b.

3. *And the officers shall... say, Who is the man who is faint-hearted* (Deut. 20:8ff.). On what account were all these things said? So that the cities of Israel would not be wastelands, according to Rabbi [Judah the Prince].

Rabban Yoḥanan ben Zakkai says, "Come and see how much the Omnipresent was concerned for the dignity of his creatures. On account of the fearful and faint-hearted [were these things said], for when he returns [home], they will say, 'Perhaps he built a house or planted a vineyard or betrothed a woman?' All have to bring witnesses, except for the faint-hearted, whose witnesses are [right there] with him."

(Midrash Tannaim, ed. Hoffman, p. 120)

Comment: For differences between this and the Aqiban tradition, see I.ii.9. Since the saying in this simpler form was known to both the

Ishmaelean and Aqiban schools—for it forms the basis of the Aqiban expansion—it perhaps would antedate the two schools and probably derive from Yavneh, if not earlier.

4. R. Joshua said, "...One time I went up to the Upper Market, to the Offal Gate which was in Jerusalem, and I found there Rabban Simeon ben Gamaliel and Rabban Yoḥanan ben Zakkai, seated with two scrolls unrolled before them. Yoḥanan a certain scribe was standing before them, pen and ink at the ready. They said to him, 'Write, From Simeon ben Gamaliel and from Yoḥanan ben Zakkai to our brethren who are in the Upper and Lower South, and to Shaḥlil, and to the seven provinces of the south, Peace. Let it be known to you that the fourth year has come, and still the sacred produce has not been burned. So hasten and bring five sheaves which are required for the Confession. We have not begun to write to you, but our fathers used to write to your fathers.' They said to him, 'Write a second letter, From Simeon ben Gamaliel and from Yoḥanan ben Zakkai to our brethren who are in the Upper and Lower Galilee and to Simonia and to 'Oved Bet Hillel, Peace. Let it be known to you that the fourth year has come, and still the sacred produce has not been burned. So hasten and bring olive heaps ['BYTY] which are required for the Confession. We have not begun to write to you, but our fathers used to write to your fathers.' "

(Midrash Tannaim, ed. Hoffman, pp. 175-6)

Comment: This is the sole source for the letters of Simeon and Yoḥanan. It is important to note that Joshua is the authority, indicating that Ishmaelean traditions come from him as well as from Eliezer.

5. *And your Torah to Israel.* About this matter, Agrippas the Hegemon asked Rabban Yoḥanan ben Zakkai, saying to him, "How many Torahs were given to you from heaven?"

He replied, "Two, one orally and one in writing."

He replied, "And is it said, And your *Torahs* to Israel?" He replied, "Even so, two, as it is said, *And Torot (TWRT) to Israel.*"

(Midrash Tannaim, ed. Hoffman, p. 215)

Comment: In Sifré Deut. #351, Ageniṭos asks Gamaliel the same question.

6. *And Moses was one hundred twenty years old* (Deut. 34:7)... He was one of four who lived one hundred twenty years, and these are they,

Moses and Hillel the Elder, Rabban Yoḥanan ben Zakkai and R. ʿAqiva.

Moses lived in Egypt forty years, Midian forty years, and served Israel forty years.

Hillel the Elder came up from Babylonia at forty years of age, served an apprenticeship with the sages for forty years, and served Israel forty years.

Rabban Yoḥanan ben Zakkai was in business forty years, served an apprenticeship to the sages forty years and served Israel forty years.

R. ʿAqiva studied Torah forty years and served an apprenticeship to the sages forty years and served Israel forty years.

Six pairs lived lifetimes of equal length, Rebecca and Kohath, Levi and Amram, Joseph and Joshua, Samuel and Solomon, Moses and Hillel the Elder, Rabban Yoḥanan ben Zakkai and Rabbi ʿAqiva.

(Midrash Tannaim, ed. Hoffman, p. 226)

General Comment: Hoffman provides no introduction to his edition of the *Midrash Tannaim*, and since, when he wrote *Zur Einleitung in den halachischen Midraschim* (Berlin, 1887) Midrash Tannaim, first published by Schechter, was unknown, he makes no reference to it there. J. N. Epstein (*Mevo'ot leSifrut haTannaim*, pp. 631-3) attributes it to the school of R. Ishmael.

We have already seen, in I.i.8, the Sifré Deut. #357 version of the account of the long lives of spiritual heroes. Here the only difference is the allegation that R. ʿAqiva studied Torah forty years, then served the sages another forty years. Since the copyists of Sifré Deut. deleted its reference to the first forty years, which on formal grounds *must* have stood in the primitive text, and since the reason for the deletion must have been that the facts reported were disagreeable, the laudatory report in Midrash Tannaim cannot represent the original tradition, but is almost certainly a "correction" of some statement reflecting the discreditable stories of ʿAqiva's early life. This indicates that we have both Midrash Tannaim and Sifré Deut. in independently censored forms, but the censors of both documents were friendly to ʿAqiva.

The Aqiban version of the draft-exemptions (I.ii.9, Sifré Deut. #192) is somewhat different from that in Midrash Tannaim, I.iv.3. To the question, "Why are all these things stated... should not be desolated," the first explanation, that it was to preserve the Jewish settlements in Palestine, is here explicitly attributed to R. Judah the Prince. Yoḥanan is thus left with the second explanation, to show God's concern for human dignity, and with the *ḥomer*-style exegesis about the frail-hearted's not having to bring witnesses to support his claim. The simple form of the exegesis given in Midrash Tannaim is presumably original. Sifré Deut. #192 has been developed to contradict the original purpose of the exegesis, as I said in I.ii.9. The brief formulation here omits the clashing of shields, neighing of horses, and various other vivid details.

The attribution of the first part to R. Judah the Prince provides a clearcut date, that is, no earlier than ca. 200 A.D. The anonymous form, I.ii.9, seems on the face of it earlier. Once a saying was attributed to a leading master, particularly one of the stature of R. Judah the Prince, it would not likely be given later on anonymously.

The whole passage is printed in Hoffman's edition in small type; he states that such materials are "already found in the Sifré with some variant readings." In this instance, the variants are of no small consequence.

The Ishmaelean material added here expands our earlier picture of their view of Yoḥanan at four points: first, the inclusion of the *Avot* saying about being created to study Torah, here appearing in an exeget-

Table
Ishmaelean and Aqiban Traditions in Halakhic Midrashim

	Ishmaelean		*Aqiban*
A.	I.i.1 ("Because you did not serve")		—
	I.i.2 (Whole stones/iron)	=	I.ii.1 '[Iron, I.ii.5 (Whole stones/ iron)] [1]
	I.i.3 (Ear pierced)		—
	I.i.4 (Oxen/sheep)		—
	I.i.5 (Thief/robber)		—
	I.i.6 (Heifer-garments), *Eliezer*		—
	I.i.7 (When Israel does will)		—
	I.i.8 (One-hundred-twenty-years)		—
B.	I.iv.1 (Created to study Torah)		—
	I.iv.2 (Altars of gentiles)		—
	I.iv.3 (Frail-hearted)	=	I.ii.9
	I.iv.4 (Letters) *Joshua*		—
	I.ii.5 (How many Torahs)		—
	I.iv.6 (One-hundred-twenty years)		—
	—		I.ii.2a (*Merkavah*)
	—		I.ii.2b (Praise of *Eleazar*)
	—		I.ii.3 (Prince sins)
	—		I.ii.4 (Third loaf, *Joshua*)
	—		I.ii.6 (Day of Waving)
	—		I.ii.7 (*Lulav*, Day of Waving)
	—		I.ii.8 (Good court, *Eliezer*)

$$\frac{\textit{Ishmaelean A}}{\text{I.i.8}} = \frac{\textit{Ismaelean B}}{\text{I.iv.6}}$$

[1] I.ii.5 is probably an interpolation in the Aqiban material, see I.i.2. Apart from that item, the two Aqiban parallels to Ishmaelean material *both* show militaristic revisions, marking them as secondary forms *vis-a-vis* the Ishmaelean. I.iv.6 has been censored by pro-Aqiban hands, as I said.

ical context; second, the teaching not to destroy pagan altars lest one have to restore them; third and most striking, the long account given by R. Joshua of the correspondence of R. Simeon ben Gamaliel and R. Yoḥanan ben Zakkai; and finally, the controversy-story with Agrippas the Hegemon.

Its relationship to the Aqiban material is as follows: I.iv.1: No equivalent; I.iv.2; No equivalent; I.iv.3, close parallel; I.iv.4, No equivalent; I.iv.5, No equivalent; I.iv.6, no equivalent in Aqiban material but repeated in Ishmaelean collections. The Midrash Tannaim stories therefore are mostly unique, and if Ishmaelean, as Epstein supposed, they represent a corpus of Ishmaelean traditions on Yoḥanan quite different from the corpus used in Mekhilta and Sifré. That is not in itself surprising, for just as great variations occurred within the Tannaitic movement as a whole, so within the several schools, various masters must have preserved separate and in some cases quite peculiar bodies of traditions. The hypothesis that within the Ishmaelean corpus are a number of subdivisions is illustrated in the table on page 39.

CHAPTER TWO

MISHNAH AND TOSEFTA

i. Mishnah Texts

1. One may [on the Sabbath] cover a lamp with a dish so that it shall not scorch a rafter, and [cover] animal droppings to protect a child, or a scorpion so that it shall not bite. R. Judah said, "Such a case once came before R. Yoḥanan b. Zakkai in 'Arav, and he said, 'I doubt whether one [who does so] is not liable to a Sin-offering.' "

(Mishnah Shab. 16:7, trans. Danby pp. 114-115)

2. A man may broach a jar to eat dried figs therefrom provided that he does not intend to make a utensil of it. One may not pierce the plug of a jar [on the Sabbath]. So R. Judah. But the Sages [or, R. Yosi] permit it.

One may not pierce it at the side; and if it was pierced already, a man may not put wax on it [on the Sabbath] since he would [need to] smooth it over.

R. Judah said, "Such a case once came before Rabban Yoḥanan b. Zakkai in 'Arav, and he said, 'I doubt whether he is not liable to a Sin-offering.' "

(Mishnah Shab. 22:3, trans. Danby, p. 119)

Comment: II.i.1 and II.i.2 exhibit identical form:
1. Sabbath law—cover lamp or scorpion with dish
—broach a jar to eat figs but not pierce plug of a jar.
2. R. Judah: Case came to Yoḥanan in 'Arav.
3. Yoḥanan's Decision. Liable to sin-offering.

Judah b. Ilai (ca. 120-180 A.D.), a disciple of 'Aqiva, and preserver of Eliezer b. Hyrcanus's traditions in Aqiban circles, cited Yoḥanan's case as precedent-setting support for his view. In II.i.1 no contrary view is stated.

We cannot guess at the original form of Yoḥanan's saying, if any, on Sabbath laws. It may be that a brief pericope existed, in which were preserved Yoḥanan's Sabbath-precedents. If so, it covered more Sabbath-laws than those pertaining to covering lamps and opening jars, which are not related and do not exhibit similar principles of law. But if such a collection of ʿArav-cases existed, it would have been formulated long before Judah b. Ilai, who perhaps merely alluded to, but did not *verbatim* cite its contents. We may assume it was originally from Eliezer's school, via the Aqibans. Ilai, Judah's father, studied with Eliezer.

In the light of other materials (e.g. II.i.4) we may suppose that the pericope began, "Once a case came before Yoḥanan... in which so-and-so had happened. Yoḥanan objected..." From such a tradition, Judah b. Ilai would have cited several cases which would originally have read, "He may be liable to a sin-offering." Judah would then have put the words back into direct discourse: "I doubt whether he is..."

All this is entirely conjectural, but represents one way in which the tradition on Yoḥanan's ʿArav-cases would have been revised in the generation preceding Judah the Prince's editing of the Mishnah. After Judah b. Ilai, the tradition obviously was not again revised; but preserved in the form Judah—but *not* Yoḥanan, or his ʿArav disciples (e.g. Ḥanina b. Dosa) or Eliezer—gave it.

Two facts emerge. First, Yoḥanan was regarded as a valid precedent for the generation of Usha, 140-180 A.D. Second, some of Yoḥanan's sayings were transmitted in coherent form by Judah b. Ilai.[1]

3. R. Judah said: "Ben Bukhri testified at Yavneh that if a priest paid the *sheqel* he committed no sin. Rabban Yoḥanan b. Zakkai answered: 'Not so! but rather, if a priest did not pay the *sheqel*, he committed sin; but the priests used to expound this scripture to their advantage, *And every meal offering of the priest shall be wholly burnt: it shall not be eaten* (Lev. 6:23). Since the ʿ*Omer* and the Two Loaves and the Showbread are ours, how can they be eaten?' "

(Mishnah Sheq. 1:4, trans. Danby, p. 152)

Comment: The colloquy of Ben Bukhri and Yoḥanan is reported now in direct discourse by Judah b. Ilai. It is striking that no response to Yoḥanan's ruling is included. Yoḥanan held that the priests should have paid the *sheqel* in the Jerusalem Temple, but did not do so because of an exegesis which he himself rejected, but here did not attempt to refute. In fact we do not know how he argued against the priestly exegesis; all we know is that he denied it was valid.

We cannot suppose that Yoḥanan had no response to make; he must have expounded the Scripture to the advantage of the Temple, rather than of the priests. I find it difficult to suppose Yoḥanan would have wanted the priestly exegesis to survive, his to be suppressed. But the Yavnean school took for granted that its pupils would know his exegesis and therefore merely cited his opinion, as an example of its application. Alternatively, since Judah's father, Ilai, was a disciple of the priest,

[1] See Epstein, *Mevoʾot*, p. 279, 295.

Eliezer b. Hyrcanus,[1] he may have learned the story from a reliable priestly source, in which it would have made Yoḥanan to go on to admit that he could not refute the priest's argument, an admission now dropped by his disciples.

4. Once, when they brought cooked food to Rabban Yoḥanan b. Zakkai to taste, and two dates and a pail of water to Rabban Gamaliel, they said, "Bring them up to the Sukkah." And [once] when they gave R. Ẓadoq less than an egg's bulk of food he took it in a towel and ate it outside the Sukkah and did not say the Benediction after it.

(Mishnah Suk. 2:5, trans Danby, p. 175)

Comment: Ẓadoq died very shortly after 70, Yoḥanan a little while later. It seems to me that this story pertains to Gamaliel I, and derives from the period between ca. 35 and ca. 50, rather than to Gamaliel II. But this is merely a guess. We know nothing about who finally edited it. Perhaps Gamaliel II would have received the story from the immediate disciples of Yoḥanan, who were with him in Jerusalem, and would have kept it alive as an example of the close associations between his grandfather and Yoḥanan, his predecessor and rival at Yavneh. But such conjecture seems to me neither persuasive nor very fruitful.

5(a). Beforetime the *lulav* was carried seven days in the Temple, but in the provinces one day only.

After the Temple was destroyed, Rabban Yoḥanan b. Zakkai ordained (a) that in the provinces it should be carried seven days in memory of the Temple; (b) also [he ordained] that on the whole of the Day of Waving (Lev. 23:11) it should be forbidden [to eat of new produce].

(Mishnah Suk. 3:12, trans. Danby, p. 177)

Comment: This same saying, verbally identical, has already appeared in I.ii.6, 7. It was evidently a fixed form, taken over by the later Aqibans from the earlier ones, and thence included by Judah the Prince in the Mishnah. It included only these two rules. In a second tradition, II.i.6-8, the two rules, which have nothing to do with one another, are repeated in the same form as part of a much longer list.

6. If a festival-day of the New Year fell on a Sabbath, they might blow the *shofar* in the Holy City but not in the provinces. After the Temple was destroyed Rabban Yoḥanan b. Zakkai ordained that they

[1] See Epstein, *Mevo'ot*, pp. 67-9. It was uncommon to cite Eliezer directly, Note also Epstein, p. 340.

might blow it wheresoever there was a court. R. Eliezer[1] said, "Rabban Yoḥanan b. Zakkai ordained it so only for Yavneh." They replied, "It is all one whether it was Yavneh or any other place wherein was a court."

In this also Jerusalem surpassed Yavneh, in that they could blow the *shofar* in any city that could see Jerusalem and that could hear [the *shofar* in Jerusalem] and that was near, and that was able to come, but at Yavneh they could blow it only in the court.

7. Before time the *lulav* was carried seven days in the Temple, but in the provinces one day only. After the Temple was destroyed, Rabban Yoḥanan b. Zakkai ordained that in the provinces it should be carried seven days in memory of the Temple; also [he ordained] that on the whole of the Day of Waving it should be forbidden [to eat of new produce].

8. Beforetime they used to admit evidence about the New Moon throughout the day. Once the witnesses tarried so long in coming that the Levites were disordered in their singing, so it was ordained that evidence could be admitted only until the afternoon offering. And if witnesses came from the time of the afternoon offering onwards, then this day was kept holy and also the morrow was kept holy. (a) After the Temple was destroyed Rabban Yoḥanan b. Zakkai ordained that they might admit evidence about the New Moon throughout the day.

(b) R. Joshua b. Qorḥa said, "Rabban Yoḥanan b. Zakkai ordained this also, that wheresoever the chief of the court might be, witnesses should go only to the place of assembly."

(Mishnah R. H. 4:1,[2]3,4, trans. Danby, pp. 192-3)

Comment: As in I.ii.7, II.i.6 may well begin with a law (in this case, a paraphrase of a law), antedating the destruction. It certainly pertains to that period, and Yoḥanan's decree is separate and distinct from it.

The dispute on the passage is important. It is clear that Eliezer (or Eleazar) would have read the law: After the Temple was destroyed, Yoḥanan ordained that they may blow it in Yavneh [*but no where else*].

---

[1] R. Rabbinovitz, *Diqduqé Soferim* (Repr. N.Y., 1960), Vol. V, p. 40a prefers the reading Eleazar, which appears in older printed versions and many manuscripts. Eleazar without further patronymics is normally Eleazar b. Shamu'a, a late student of 'Aqiva, who studied also with Joshua b. Hananiah. Epstein, *Mevo'ot*, pp. 159, 366, 371 also reads Eleazar.

That formulation did not survive. What survived was a record of Eliezer's rejection of the official form. Eliezer may be presumed to have known the master's intent.[1]

The underlying issue was obviously the significance of Yavneh. If Yavneh's court was really the equivalent of Jerusalem's Temple, then what was done in the Temple may be done in Yavneh; but just as outside the Temple, the *shofar* might not be sounded on the Sabbath, so outside of Yavneh likewise it was prohibited in the same circumstance.

The accepted opinion now rejected this view of Yavneh. That town as such had no special privilege. The blowing of the *shofar* was the symbol of the presence of the deity, and the deity was now present in the high court as formerly in the Temple. Therefore wherever the court is, there the *shofar* may be blown. This view would naturally have developed when the high court was compelled to move from Yavneh.[2] A further step would have been taken when the prerogative claimed by the high court was extended to, and claimed by, other courts. This may have been done by Aqibans in their opposition to Gamaliel II, or by the priests who, expecting the imminent reconstruction of the Jerusalem Temple, did not want to have trouble from a single surviving center of exceptional authority outside of the Temple.

Clearly Yoḥanan held otherwise, and Eliezer his disciple accurately reported his views. The reply to Eliezer is not, "Yoḥanan said..." but rather, "It is all the same." Presumably had the opposition held a tradition that Yoḥanan said such a thing, they would have cited it. Not having it, they simply confronted Eliezer with a statement of regnant opinion which could be defended as an exegesis of Yoḥanan's ruling (Why had he ruled that the *shofar* might be blown in Yavneh? Because the court was there. Therefore, had the court been elsewhere...).

This theory, however, raises the problem of what happened when Yoḥanan himself was forced to withdraw from Yavneh and went to Beror Ḥayil. One can hardly imagine his giving up the claim that what his court decided was the divine law—nor, therefore, the symbol of this claim, the blowing of the *shofar*. Perhaps no New Year's day fell on a Sabbath during his few years at Beror Ḥayil, and therefore he had no occasion to rule on the question. The failure to quote his exact words in an authoritative decree may be accounted for, therefore, by the theory that his exact words would *not* have said what the framers of the tradition wanted him to have said.

The *lulav*-Day of Waving saying is, as I have pointed out, another,

---

[1] If this is Eleazar b. Shamu'a, then the tradition would presumably have come to him via Joshua. While it would be more likely that a disciple, rather than the disciple of a disciple, would have known the master's intent, I do not think the substance of my interpretation is much affected by the possibility that it was not Eliezar b. Hyrcanus but rather Eleazar b. Shamu'a. On the contrary, if Eleazar b. Shamu'a learned the tradition from Joshua, it would render more plausible the conjecture that the rule derives from the dispute of Joshua with Gamaliel II.

[2] Morton Smith contributed this observation.

and entirely separate, formulation of Yoḥanan's ordinances. It too conforms to priestly policy, which explains its early acceptance into the normative tradition. Yavneh is not given special status, for "the provinces" here obviously include Yavneh. Likewise, the Yavnean court could do nothing to hasten the eating of the new produce on the Day of Waving. People simply had to wait out the whole day; no surrogate for the former Temple ritual was available. I.ii.7 does not begin "Beforetime," but is nevertheless a separate rule. This fact, plus the near identity of the wording of those two rules with those in I.ii.7 and II.i.5, strongly suggests that II.i.7 was originally an independent saying, identical with the other two, and has been slightly revised and used as a building block for the longer list. The longer list (II.i.6-8) is therefore not the original list of Yoḥanan's Yavnean decrees, but is a secondary composition, perhaps first put together by Rabbi Judah the Prince from reports of individual reforms, which were themselves fragments or reflections of the earlier list that may be presumed to have existed.

The witnesses on the New Moon's appearance might come at any time during the day. This ordinance seems to me least controversial of all. Since there was no sacrifice, there was no reason to preserve the former rule. I suspect that some earlier rule would have read, "Evidence may be admitted only until the afternoon offering." The little story explaining the rule would not have appeared as part of the official body of exegesis. Just as in I.ii.7, the law here appears without *beforetime*. In any event, Yoḥanan's later rule seems to me neutral and to have no bearing on the significance of his court in Yavneh. His disciples do not question the rule. They probably had no reason to do so.

Joshua b. Qorḥa, a disciple of Eleazar b. ʿAzariah, probably was a contemporary of Judah b. Ilai and Simeon b. Gamaliel. He cannot be assumed, therefore, to have had direct personal knowledge of Yoḥanan at Yavneh, still less of decrees issued by Yoḥanan. But we have no means of knowing exactly how he learned of the decree about the venue of testimony on the New Moon. It seems evident, though, that the ordinance pertained to some controversy at Yavneh, perhaps in the early years (if Yoḥanan actually said any such thing). In that case, the dispute concerned an absent chief of court, who could only have been Yoḥanan himself. Yoḥanan would have said, "Witnesses should continue to come to Yavneh, even though I myself am absent." At what point would such a ruling have been made? I assume it came when Yoḥanan had retired to Beror Ḥayil. Presumably people who favored his continued rule in Yavneh over the assumption of authority by Gamaliel II would have wanted to follow him with their testimony to Beror Ḥayil. Others might have held that since Yoḥanan was no longer present at Yavneh, the decree could not be issued by the Yavneans at all, wherever testimony had been delivered. Yoḥanan would have responded by saying that even though he—and others—might continue to regard himself as the exiled chief of the court of Yavneh, the decree of the New Moon must be issued at Yavneh and by its resident authorities. This conjecture depends upon the assumption, as I said, that Yoḥanan had actually made such a decree and that Joshua b. Qorḥa's information was accurate.

But if Joshua b. Qorḥa is attributing to Yoḥanan a decree he in fact *never* made, then the *sitz im leben* may well have been the rule of Gamaliel, troubled as it was by issues fought out in terms of decreeing the sacred calendar (b. Ber. 28a-b). Gamaliel may have wanted to maintain the witnesses should come where *he* was. Yavneh itself had *no* special importance apart from his presence. Such a view of the law would have served two parties: first, the priests who, as I said, wanted Yavneh to be regarded as a merely temporary, unimportant legal center; second, Gamaliel himself and those close to the Hillelite house, who wanted the importance of Yavneh to derive from the presence of the Hillelite patriarch, not from the collegium of masters assembled there. The opposition to such an alliance would have attributed to Yoḥanan the contrary view: it was not the presence of the Hillelite scion but of the collegium of masters that rendered Yavneh's court an important authority. The witnesses therefore should come to Yavneh *just* as they had earlier come to the Jerusalem Temple. But because the sacrifices were now no longer offered, they might give testimony any time during the day.

The Mishnaic formulation of the Yavnean ordinances thus includes the earlier Aqiban one, but goes far beyond it. The disciples of Yoḥanan probably played no part in this formulation. Eliezer b. Hyrcanus opposed the law given as Yoḥanan's opinion in II.i.6. II.i.7 certainly represents the Aqiban view, but we do not know whether the immediate disciples of Yoḥanan played a role in its authoritative promulgation. II.i.8 derives from a time when Yoḥanan was no longer in Yavneh; alternatively, it may come from the period immediately following his death. (If so, it would be attributable to R. Joshua b. Ḥananiah and his circle, involved in the struggle reported in b. Ber. 28a-b. But I am not prepared to suggest that Joshua b. Ḥananiah here actually reported the words of his master.) In any event the only authority associated with the teaching could not possibly have heard it from Yoḥanan himself, probably not from his immediate disciples either. In all, we cannot attribute the record of the Yavnean ordinances to Yohanan, who played no part in the formation of this pericope and would have rather different views of parts of the law, at least II.i.6.

9. There were two judges of civil law [financial cases] in Jerusalem, Admon and Ḥanan b. Abishalom. Ḥanan gave two decisions and Admon seven.

If a man went beyond the sea and his wife claimed maintenance, Ḥanan says, "Let her swear [to her claim] at the end [of the time] and let her not swear at the beginning."

But the Sons of the High Priests disputed with him and said, "Let her swear at the beginning and let her not swear at the end."

R. Dosa b. Harkinas decided according to their opinion.

R. Yoḥanan b. Zakkai said, "Ḥanan said well: let her swear only at the end."

10. If a man went beyond the sea and another rose up and maintained his wife, Ḥanan said, "His money is lost to him."

But Sons of the High Priests disputed with him and said, "Let him swear on oath how much he has expended and let him recover it."

R. Dosa b. Harkinas decided according to their opinion.

R. Yoḥanan b. Zakkai said, "Ḥanan said well: the man laid his money on the horn of the gazelle."

(Mishnah Ket. 13:1,2, trans. Danby, p. 262)

Comment: Like II.i.4, this little pericope pertains to the period before 70 A.D. Yoḥanan's opinion is tacked on at the end, but that does not mean his disciples did not preserve the story and give it its present formulation. Perhaps they did so in order to preserve evidence of Yoḥanan's position in relation to the authorities of the period before the destruction.

Yoḥanan says nothing about Dosa's judgment. Dosa was a contemporary of Yoḥanan (see Hyman, *Toledot Tannaim ve Amoraim* [London, 1910], I, p. 323) and lived to the Yavneh period. The point of the story is that Yoḥanan sided with the tradition of the lay-authorities against the priests, and Dosa with the priests against the laymen. Since the government of the city of Jerusalem before 70 was certainly in the hands of the High Priests, and marital and similar questions belong to religious law in any event, it is hard to believe that any lay judges of such questions existed there before 70. The story is most likely told by Yoḥanan's disciples to discredit the decisions of Dosa and the contemporary priestly party which appealed to them, or to which Dosa's disciples appealed. Within the Yavnean circle which preserved the tradition, it was of course unnecessary to declare explicitly that Yoḥanan was right. That was taken for granted. The form of the story, without any trace of direct address to either Dosa or Yoḥanan, argues against the notion that a confrontation between them lies behind the tradition.[1]

11. That same day R. ʿAqiva expounded, "*And every earthen vessel whereinto any of them falleth, whatsoever is in it conveys uncleanness* (Lev. 11:33): it does not say *is unclean* but *shall render unclean*, so that it makes other things unclean. This teaches that a loaf suffering second-grade uncleanness renders another unclean in the third grade." R. Joshua said, "Who will take away the dust from off thine eyes, O Rabban Yoḥanan ben Zakkai! for thou didst say that another generation

[1] See Y. N. Epstein, *Mevoʾot*, p. 20. I owe this comment to Morton Smith.

would declare the third loaf clean, for there is no verse in the Law to prove that it is unclean; and now does not thy pupil ‘Aqiva bring a verse from the Law to prove that it is unclean! for it is written, *Whatsoever is in it shall render unclean.*"

12. That same day R. Joshua b. Hyrcanus expounded, "Job served the Holy One, blessed is he, only from love, as it is written, *Though he slay me yet will I wait for him* (Job 13:15). Thus far the matter rests in doubt [whether it means] *I will wait for him* or *I will not wait*; but Scripture says, *Till I die I will not put away mine integrity from me* (Job 27:5) teaching that he acted from love." R. Joshua said, "Who will take away the dust from off thine eyes, O Rabban Yoḥanan ben Zakkai!—for all thy days thou didst expound that Job served the Holy One, blessed is he, only from fear, for it is written, *The man was perfect and upright and one that feared God and eschewed evil* (Job 1:1)—and has not Joshua, thy disciple's disciple, now taught us that he acted from love?"

(Mishnah Soṭ. 5:2,5, trans. Danby, p. 298, 299)

Comment: II.i.11 is the same as I.ii.4, with this difference. In I.ii.4, the saying of ‘Aqiva is formulated as a comment on Lev. 11:33: "*All that is in it*... R. ‘Aqiva says..." Here, the form is "*that same day*, R. ‘Aqiva expounded..." This difference is obviously to be explained by the context; the listing of things done on "that day" has required the minor revision of the superscription of the tradition to conform to the single form imposed for purposes of redaction. Otherwise, the passage is unaltered. I assume the Sifra version (I.ii.4) is older.

In any event, the same considerations spelled out above apply without modification. Yoḥanan made a statement of some kind on the third loaf. That statement was lost or suppressed. All we now have is the record of how Joshua approved ‘Aqiva's formulation of the law. Yoḥanan had long ago predicted just such a legal development. That formulation is purely Aqiban.

II.i.12 exhibits the same form. It seems possible that Joshua b. Ḥananiah's disciples formulated the master's traditions on Yoḥanan to conform to the new situation. But I think it more likely that some original saying existed, which was changed *not* by Joshua b. Ḥananiah's disciples, but by those of Joshua b. Hyrcanus himself. The saying would have been much as it stands before us, "Rabban Yoḥanan ben Zakkai expounded, Job served the holy one... for it is written." Joshua b. Hyrcanus was probably a disciple of R. ‘Aqiva, and so the entire passage has been edited from an Aqiban perspective on the events of "that day."[1]

[1] Ḥ. Albeq [Albeck,] *Seder Nashim* (Tel Aviv, Jerusalem, 1954), pp. 384-5, suggests that "on that day" may not always refer to the day on which Gamaliel II was deposed. In this particular instance, the meaning may be "On the day on which

13(a). When murderers became numerous, the rite of breaking the heifer's neck ceased. When Eleazar b. Dinai came (and he was also called Teḥinah b. Parishah) they changed his name to Son of the Murderer. (b) When adulterers became numerous, [the rite of] the bitter water ceased; and R. Yoḥanan b. Zakkai brought it to an end, for it is written, *I will not punish your daughters when they commit whoredom nor your daughters-in-law when they commit adultery, for they themselves [go apart with whores...]* (Hos. 4:14).

14. When R. Meir died there were no more makers of parables. When Ben Azzai died there were no more diligent students. When Ben Zoma died there were no more expounders. When R. Joshua died goodness departed from the world. When Rabban Simeon b. Gamaliel died the locust came, and troubles grew many. When R. Eleazar b. ʿAzariah died wealth departed from the Sages. When R. ʿAqiva died the glory of the Law ceased. When R. Ḥanina b. Dosa died the men of good deeds ceased. When R. Yosi Qaṭnuta died there were no more saintly ones. (And why was his name called Qaṭnuta? Because he was of the 'small' remnants of the saintly ones.) When Rabban Yoḥanan b. Zakkai died the splendor of wisdom ceased. When Rabban Gamaliel the Elder died, the glory of the Law ceased and purity and abstinence died. When R. Ishmael b. Phiabi died the splendor of the priesthood ceased. When Rabbi died, humility and the shunning of sin ceased.

(Mishnah Soṭ. 9:9,15, trans. Danby, pp. 304-306)

Comment: The tradition on Yoḥanan's authority in the Temple(II.i.13) which was sufficient to force the cessation of an old rite, would, if true, come from Yavneh. Then, as I said, it was important for Yoḥanan's disciples to report how influential he had been in the Temple. But if the passage did derive from Yavneh, it could not come from the same circles (Hillelite-priestly) who redacted his ordinances, for such a story as this would have been repugnant to the priestly part of the Hillelite-

---

ʿAqiva preached his sermon and was praised for it, he preached other sermons as well, and on that same day, other sermons were also preached..." *On that day* is used of other occasions in Shabbat 1:4, Tos. Pes. Chap. 4, with reference to the promotion of Hillel, and elsewhere. Albeq is led to this conclusion because of a difficulty in Rashi's commentary.

In any event, the fact that ʿAqiva's sermon occurs (II.i.11) without the *on that day* superscription is not taken into account by Albeq. His explanation of the language *On that day* here is therefore impossible.

Rabbi Robert Goldenberg kindly brought this matter to my attention; he is preparing a study of the *on that day* materials.

priestly alliance. We shall note a different formulation of (a), in which Yoḥanan simply records what *others* did. That formulation (II.iii.6) would be more agreeable to those also unwilling to preserve the story of Yoḥanan's unequivocal authority over the Temple, with the implication of renewed power when the Temple might be rebuilt. Judah the Prince selected this version (II.i.14) rather than the Toseftan one (II.iii.6), perhaps because the priests no longer had to be mollified, so the old Hillelite-priestly alliance ceased to influence the selection of traditions, and the authority of Hillel's disciple over the Temple rituals could be reported. These stories reflected a viewpoint on Temple matters held by the rabbinical party as a whole and preferable to any other—especially from the patriarch's perspective. The other tradition was thus relegated to the supplementary collection.[1]

But neither the patriarch's preference nor the rabbinical party's viewpoint is a guarantee of truth in a question of this sort, where their interests are involved. They were fully capable of inventing stories to justify their claim of an authority higher than the priests', and it is most probable that in II.i.13b we have such invention. Before the fall of the Temple the authority to abolish Temple rites was certainly vested in the high priest, and it is not likely that the high priest would have allowed a Pharisee to exercise it. In II.i.13 we have attempts to explain the disappearance of rituals long abandoned; for that of the heifer, the nickname of b. Dinai offered as an excuse; for that of the waters, the prophecy in Hosea 4:14; and Pharisaic interest credited the latter to Yoḥanan. Like II.i.14, therefore, II.i.13 probably derives from the latest stratum of Mishnaic materials.

II.i.14 refers to the death of R. Judah the Prince. The list it gives is in no apparent chronological order, but it may have as its basis a list beginning with Meir and going backward to Gamaliel I. If so, Ishmael b. Phiabi and R. Judah the Prince are later additions, and there must be several names out of order. The omission of Eliezer means nothing; the school of Joshua had long since been assimilated by the Aqibans, from whose school this redactor is descended. I doubt that an indepenent saying, "When Yoḥanan ben Zakkai died... ceased" circulated separately, along with other separate ones, until all were collected in a single tradition. It seems more likely that some later compiler put together a list of the worthies he most admired, with obviously hyperbolic statements reflecting the traditional virtue of each one.

15. The more a judge tests the evidence, the more is he deserving of praise. Ben Zakkai once tested the evidence even to the inquiring about the stalks of figs.

(Mishnah Sanh. 5:2, trans. Danby, p. 388)

[1] See Y. N. Epstein, *Mevo'ot*, p. 41. He regards II.i.13 as a late addition, and the Tosefta version, II.iii.6, as more reliable. He holds that Yoḥanan *edited* the *entire* pericope! See also pp. 400-401. For further discussion of Judah's motives, see XIII.ii.

Comment: This story about the virtue of "Ben Zakkai" speaks of him disrespectfully and tells of an event which may have originally been reported in derision. I should imagine those who first told stories about "Ben Zakkai" did not care much for him, and regarded his inquiry about fig-stalks as extreme and absurd, going far beyond what legitimate cross-examination would permit. But the story here serves as precedent for the very opposite view, "The more a judge tests the evidence, the more he is deserving of praise." "Ben Zakkai" had done right; there was nothing extreme in his actions, which indeed are exemplary.

The final redactors of the Mishnah, men of the school of Judah the Prince, obviously had a good opinion of Yoḥanan (as above, II.i.14). But in including older traditions, they did not always take the liberty of reformulating them. This one remained in its original, hostile form, probably because the discourtesy seemed trivial and the content was now declared creditable.

The likelihood is that "Ben Zakkai" materials were formulated while hatred of the master was intense, hence during his lifetime or shortly after his death. That they survived, with the appellation unchanged, to the time of Rabbi Judah the Prince, may be due either to the survival of priestly circles which remained hostile to Yoḥanan, or to the conservatism of the Oral Tradition, which tended to preserve unchanged whatever materials it had once accepted. Another possibility is that Yoḥanan may have been condemned among the more violently anti-Roman circles in the 130s, and these may have taken up and perpetuated contemptuous material originally circulated either by the priests or by the partisans of Gamaliel II.[1]

Since the "virtue" attributed to Yoḥanan is that of a judge in capital cases, and since Jewish courts supposedly lost the right to try capital cases long before Yoḥanan's mature years, it was only in the brief period from ca. 66 to ca. 68, when Yoḥanan remained in Jerusalem, that the event reported, *if* there was an event, could have taken place. As a municipal authority, part of the Pharisaic party included in the revolutionary coalition, Yoḥanan could have conducted a murder trial. His actions could thus have been observed by people who did not like him *and* who survived the destruction; and who later achieved considerable importance in Yavneh; and who were then able to launch their stories in the stream of legal transmission. These may have been Hillelite adherents, hostile priests, or both.[2]

16. R. Joshua [b. Ḥananiah] and R. Judah b. Bathyra testified that the widow of one who belonged to an *ʾIsah* family was eligible for marriage with a priest; [and] that the members of an *ʾIsah* family are qualified to bear testimony as to which [of themselves] is unclean or clean, and which must be put away and which may be brought near.

---

[1] I owe this observation to Morton Smith.
[2] See also Epstein, *Mevo'ot*, pp. 55-6.

Rabban Simeon b. Gamaliel said, "We accept your testimony, but what shall we do, for Rabban Yoḥanan b. Zakkai decreed that courts may not be set up concerning this. The priests would hearken to you in what concerns putting away but not in what concerns bringing near."

17. R. Joshua said, "I have received as a tradition from Rabban Yoḥanan b. Zakkai, who heard from his teacher, and his teacher from his teacher, as a *halakhah* given to Moses from Sinai, that Elijah will not come to declare unclean or clean, to remove afar or to bring nigh, but to remove afar those [families] that were brought nigh by violence and to bring nigh those [families] that were removed afar by violence."

(Mishnah ʿEd. 8:3,7 trans. Danby, pp. 435-6)

Comment: These two *on that day* accounts come from Joshua's school. Since Simeon b. Gamaliel II lived from ca. 120 to 180, his response cannot have been made directly to Joshua and Judah b. Bathyra, both younger contemporaries of Yoḥanan, but must be supposed, despite the use of the second person, to be a comment explaining his rejection of traditions handed down in their name. An alternative would suppose the speaker to be Simeon b. Gamaliel I, who probably died in the destruction before 70, and to attribute the colloquy to Jerusalem before 70. But this is difficult because the speaker refers to Yoḥanan's decision as one made in the past, irreversibly binding on him, and unknown to his "interlocutors." Now both Joshua and Judah b. Bathyra would presumably have known of Yoḥanan's ruling, and such a ruling would probably not have been considered binding by Simeon b. Gamaliel I, since he, and not Yoḥanan, was head of the Hillelite family before 70. Accordingly the later date is more probable, and the passage might be seen as evidence for the survival of important priestly circles, holding to their own legal traditions in spite of Pharisaic rulings, well down into the second half of the second century. However, in III.ii.15, the saying appears attributed to Gamaliel (II, of course). This is likely the correct attribution, and the date would therefore be ca. 100.

II.i.17 seems to me a reliable tradition. Joshua here quotes his master. The teaching is unequivocal, and since no teacher between Yoḥanan and Moses is assigned to the tradition, we may suppose Yoḥanan invented it.

The two sayings, though related in subject, are basically independent. II.i.16 is quite specific, legal, and utterly credible as far as Yoḥanan's decree is concerned. The reason given is down to earth and realistic. The ruling presumably dates from Yoḥanan's Yavneh period, where it would have been needed and politically wise. II.i.17 is *aggadah*, and has nothing to do with the legal question. Both may well be correct as to what they say of Yoḥanan—the only difficulty of II.i.16 is the "dramatic" form of presentation, and the same sort of dramatic address to a dead worthy is seen in the "who will take away the dust..." passages, I.ii.4, II.i.11-12.[1]

[1] Morton Smith contributed this comment.

18(a). Rabban Yoḥanan b. Zakkai received [the Torah] from Hillel and from Shammai. He used to say, "If thou hast wrought much in the Law claim not merit for thyself, for to this end wast thou created."

(b) Rabban Yoḥanan b. Zakkai had five disciples, and they are: R. Eliezer b. Hyrcanus, R. Joshua b. Ḥananiah, R. Yosi the Priest, R. Simeon b. Nathaniel, and R. Eleazar b. ʿArakh.

He used to describe their virtues as follows: "Eliezer b. Hyrcanus is a plastered cistern which loses not a drop; Joshua b. Ḥananiah—happy is she that bare him; Yosi the Priest is a saintly man; Simeon b. Nathaniel is fearful of sin; Eleazar b. ʿArakh is an everflowing spring."

(c) He used to say, "If all the Sages of Israel were in the one scale of the balance and Eliezer b. Hyrcanus in the other, he would outweigh them all."

(d) Abba Saul said in his name: "If all the Sages of Israel were in the one scale of the balance and with them Eliezer b. Hyrcanus, and Eleazar b. ʿArakh was in the other, he would outweigh them all."

19. He said to them, "Go forth and see which is the good way to which a man should cleave."

R. Eliezer said, "A good eye."

R. Joshua said, "A good companion."

R. Yosi said, "A good neighbor."

R. Simeon said, "One that sees what will be."

R. Eleazar said, "A good heart."

He said to them, "I approve the words of Eleazar b. ʿArakh more than your words, for in his words are your words included."

He said to them, "Go forth and see which is the evil way, which a man should shun."

R. Eliezer said, "An evil eye."

R. Joshua said, "An evil companion."

R. Yosi said, "An evil neighbor."

R. Simeon said, "He that borrows and does not repay. He that borrows from man is as one that borrows from God, for it is written, *The wicked borroweth and payeth not again but the righteous dealeth graciously and giveth*" (Ps. 37:21).

R. Eleazar said, "An evil heart."

He said to them, "I approve the words of Eleazar b. ʿArakh more than your words, for in his words are your words included."

(Mishnah Avot 2:8-9, trans. Danby, pp. 448-9)

Comment:[1] Of the four paragraphs of (18), the first two are part of the primitive structure of Avot, which seems to have first consisted of a genealogy of teachers and pupils, with one saying for each teacher. Paragraphs (b) and (c) are a first interpolation from the school of Eliezer b. Hyrcanus, whom they put first in the list of disciples and declare greatest of all. That this was the original tradition is strongly suggested not only by the importance of Eliezer in the rabbinic tradition generally, but also by the fact that the contrary sayings, which immediately follow, still reflect the original list with Eliezer at the head. The saying of Abba Saul (d) is clearly a counter to (c), as shown by the explicit inclusion of Eliezer in the lighter scale. It is obvious that the form of (c) is the original, and the form of (d) is a secondary and deliberate correction. The purpose of the correction—to replace Eliezer by Eleazar—is served also by (19), which, as remarked, reflects the original sequence of the disciples (Eliezer first), but contradicts it by turning it into a climax, so that the first is least and the last is greatest. The same hand which inserted this may have reversed the attributions of Eliezer and Eleazar in (18), since a flowing spring is better than a plastered cistern.

Paragraph (19) has itself been interpolated by the homiletic explanation of Simeon's saying, which clearly breaks the symmetry of the form and is unrelated to the original party-conflict. The downgrading of Eliezer ben Hyrcanus is probably a reflection of his ultimate disgrace and excommunication, and the sayings which put him first must have antedated these events. They surely will have come from his school and possibly would have surprised Yoḥanan. The sayings putting Eleazar first may both have come from Abba Saul. They are important evidence that Eleazar ben ʿArakh formed an influential school of his own after his early departure from Yoḥanan. After his own death his disciples evidently came to Yavneh and profited there by Gamaliel II's hostility to the memory of Yoḥanan and Eliezer's disgrace. R. Ṭarfon, the teacher of Abba Saul may have been among them. That any of this highly stylized material came from Yoḥanan himself is quite unlikely.

20. After the ʿ*Omer* had been offered, they used to go out and find the market of Jerusalem full of meal and parched corn, though this was not with the consent of the Sages. After the ʿ*Omer* was offered the new corn was forthwith permitted; but for them that lived far off, it was permitted only after midday.

After the Temple was destroyed, R. Yoḥanan b. Zakkai ordained that it should be forbidden throughout the Day of Waving.

R. Judah said, "Is it not forbidden in the Law, in that it is written, *Until this selfsame day?*" (Lev. 23:14). Why was it permitted to them that lived far off [immediately] after midday? Because they knew that the court would not be dilatory therewith."

(Mishnah Men. 10:5, trans. Danby, p. 506)

[1] All that follows is the contribution of Morton Smith.

Comment: The Day of Waving ruling appears without alteration. It is in fact *cited* from presumably earlier, already authoritative formulations. What is important here is that the whole pericope now derives from the time of Judah b. Ilai, the latest sage mentioned in the story.

It is equally striking that Judah b. Ilai has chosen to demonstrate Yoḥanan's decree (merely) conformed to the law of the Torah. I do not think the intention was hostile. What Judah b. Ilai emphasizes is that Yoḥanan's Yavnean decrees were not really alterations of Scriptural laws, but rather applications of them. Others may have contended the contrary. Yoḥanan at Yavneh had "changed" the Torah. This was bad, and Yavneh must be repudiated. Alternatively, this was good, and we too are able to "change" the Torah to conform to contemporary circumstances. Judah b. Ilai's position is that both positions are false. Yoḥanan had done nothing wrong at Yavneh—but he made no decree which revealed legal innovation. Yavneh provides no precedent for the latter group, and no excuse for repudiation by the former.

Judah b. Ilai received his traditions about Yoḥanan from his father, who was a disciple of Eliezer's circle. Hence I imagine his intent was to demonstrate the legal conservatism of Yoḥanan's decrees: Yoḥanan had only done what the Torah itself permitted. If so, we once again observe that the disciple's own attitudes have shaped their materials about Yoḥanan, their master.

The already formulated Day of Waving decree is now being cited, fully and without alteration, about three quarters of a century after it was first accepted in the normative tradition. This again suggests that some important materials were never altered after redaction. But, as we have seen, other equally significant legal sayings were certainly suppressed, or given forms different from what must have been their original one.

21. "The smallest remnants of earthenware vessels and the bottoms and sides [of broken vessels] that can stand without support [remain susceptible to uncleanness] if, [having when unbroken held] as much as a *log*, they can still hold enough [oil] to anoint the little finger [of a child]; or if, [having when unbroken held] from one *log* to one *se'ah*, they can still hold a quarter-*log*; or if, [having when unbroken held] from one to two *se'ahs*, they can still hold a half-*log*; or if, [having when unbroken held] from two to three or up to five *se'ahs*, they can still hold one *log*," so R. Ishmael.

But R. ʿAqiva says, "I would not prescribe any measure for [the unbroken] vessels; [but, rather, the rule should be]: The smallest remnants of earthenware vessels and the bottoms and sides [of broken vessels] that can stand without support [are still susceptible to uncleanness] if after having been as large as small cooking-pots, they can still hold [oil] enough to anoint the little finger [of a child]; or if after having been as large as Lydda jars, they can still hold a quarter-*log*; or if after having been of a size between Lydda jars and Bethlehem jars, they can still hold a half-*log*; or if after having been of a size between Bethlehem jars and large store-jars, they can still hold one *log*."

R. Yoḥanan b. Zakkai says, "The capacity of the fragments from large store-jars is two *logs;* the capacity of the bottoms of [broken] Galilean cruses and of little jars may be aught soever; but their [broken] sides are not susceptible to uncleanness."

(Mishnah Kel. 2:2, trans. Danby, p. 606)

Comment: This is the only Mishnaic formulation including Yoḥanan which conforms to the usual form of Mishnah-laws. It is striking, therefore, that Yoḥanan's opinion is still not a statement of law, but a mere description of the size of various jars. Only at the end does he give an opinion on the pertinent, moot point.

Ishmael had held that one measures the sherds, and determines their susceptibility of uncleanness on the basis of their size. ʿAqiva would not prescribe a specific measure, but would still hold broken sides may sometimes be susceptible to uncleanness. Yoḥanan's opinion is that broken bottoms of certain capacities are susceptible, but under no circumstances are broken sides susceptible.

Yoḥanan's opinion was thus rejected by the later masters, but still was preserved. It is equally noteworthy that the later masters made no reference to Yoḥanan's opinion, which, as elsewhere, was merely tacked on at the end. Just what function it was thus expected to have in the process by which the rabbis of the second century moved from legal traditions to legal decisions, I cannot say. Its preservation proves that some importance must have been attached to it. We may suppose that in its present form, his saying dates from the second half of the second century, that is, the period of Judah b. Ilai.

It seems clear that the generation of Usha, ca. 145 to 175, made a concerted effort to add to the Mishnaic tradition available teachings of Yoḥanan. These, however, were already complete and remained unaltered. We do not know who originally redacted them, or in what form they existed before inclusion in the Mishnah by Yosi b. Ḥalafta.[1] My guess is that they derive from Eliezer's school

The interest of the Ushans in Yoḥanan's Yavnean decrees is readily explained. They were in the process of issuing important decrees to cope with the crisis brought on in the aftermath of Bar Kakhba's war. Why they should have had special interest in Yoḥanan's ʿArav decrees is equally clear: they were located in Galilee, and apparently knew that he had spent some time there. Hence Judah b. Ilai reported what he had done in ʿArav. But why Ushans (Yosi) made certain to include Yoḥanan's purity rule I cannot say.

---

[1] Epstein, *Mevo'ot*, pp. 459ff. attributes *all* of Kelim to R. Yosi b. Ḥalafta!

22. A beam of a balance or a leveling-rod that contains a [secret] receptacle in which to load it with metal, or a carrying-yoke wherein is a [secret] receptacle for [stolen] money, or a beggar's cane that has a receptacle for water, or a stick that has a receptacle for a *mezuzah* and for pearls—these are susceptible to uncleanness.

And of all these Rabban Yoḥanan b. Zakkai said, "Woe is me if I speak of them and woe is me if I speak not of them."

(Mishnah Kel. 17:16, trans. Danby, p. 631)

Comment: The law would not have been changed had Yoḥanan's comment been omitted. As elsewhere, this addition seems to have been added by a school, or editor, whose view of Yoḥanan was most affirmative. We shall see (below II.iii.10) that this is merely a brief allusion to a longer saying of Yoḥanan. On the basis of the evidence provided by this passage we can come to no conclusions on the school or the time in which the passage was given its present form.

23. On that day... they voted and decided that Ammon and Moab should give Poorman's Tithe in the Seventh Year.

And when R. Yosi the son of the Damascene came to R. Eliezer in Lydda, he said to him, "What new thing had you in the House of Study to-day?"

He said to him, "They voted and decided that Ammon and Moab must give Poorman's Tithe in the Seventh Year."

R. Eliezer wept and said, "*The secret of the Lord is with them that fear him, and he will show them his covenant!* (Ps. 25:14). Go and tell them, 'Be not anxious by reason of your voting, for I have received a tradition from Rabban Yoḥanan b. Zakkai, who heard it from his teacher, and his teacher from his teacher, as a Halakhah given to Moses from Sinai, that Ammon and Moab should give Poorman's Tithe in the Seventh Year.' "

(Mishnah Yad. 4:3, trans. Danby, p. 783)

Comment: The *on that day* pericopae include Yoḥanan's disciples and their approval of decisions taken in Gamaliel's absence. It is as if the *on that day* materials stress not only the active approval of Yoḥanan's disciples on the occasion of Gamaliel's deposition, but even more important, their emphasis that everything done today merely serves to reaffirm the heritage of their master. Since Yoḥanan had been replaced at Yavneh by Gamaliel, who had now been replaced by the Aqibans, it was a pointed, important assertion. Yoḥanan, the founder of collaboration with Rome, was being made the sponsor and teacher of 'Aqiva, the backer of the revolt. Other material we have already seen reflecting Aqiban criticism of Yoḥanan suggests that this attempt to take over Yoḥanan for the war party was by no means wholly successful. Opponents of the war kept alive the memory of his genuine teachings and policy, and ʿAqiva and his followers reacted with hostility.

It is obvious that Yoḥanan originally said something like this:

"Ammon and Moab give Poorman's tithe in the Seventh year."

Alternatively, if Yoḥanan never said anything of the sort and the saying was falsely attributed to him, the original form may have been:

> Rabban Yoḥanan ben Zakkai in the name of his teacher, and his teacher in the name of his, as a law given to Moses at Sinai, said, "Ammon and Moab..."

Yoḥanan would hardly have said, "I heard from my teacher," without naming the teacher. Since Yoḥanan never does say in our preserved material, "I have heard from Rabbi X," and we have no sayings in the form "Rabban Yoḥanan ben Zakkai in the name of Rabbi X," it appears that appeal to prior authorities was not characteristic of Yoḥanan's teaching. He was a reformer and knew it, therefore based his reforms on his own understanding of the nature and implications of the Torah, not on tradition. While he might have said, "It is a law given to Moses on Sinai that...", he would *not* have said, "I heard from my [anonymous!] teacher that..." and in all sayings of this latter form, the form is spurious, though the legal content may be genuine.

At all events, the saying of Yoḥanan never survived in its original form. We should not know it had not Eliezer quoted it. And Eliezer quoted it only when he was able to do so—when Gamaliel II had temporarily fallen from power. We may suppose, therefore, that in that brief period it was possible to include in the official traditions sayings which formerly had been suppressed, or which the disciples had not previously been able to introduce into the corpus of accepted law. These sayings were not afterward suppressed again. Hence we have them, but only as quotations by later authorities, never in the form in which Yoḥanan had first uttered them.

It is further striking that Yohanan's name was expected to assure the revolutionary synod as to action it had already taken:

"Do not doubt you are right, for Yoḥanan said so."

This implies that, if Yoḥanan's opinion had been cited during the debate on the point, it would have carried weight. But it had not been cited. The assembly actually knew nothing of Yoḥanan's view. Therefore it had to vote on the issue. It was afterward reassured its vote was correct. We are expected to believe that Eliezer had kept his knowledge of Yoḥanan's teaching secret; he had not taught it publicly or even privately. But he had kept alive the memory of Yoḥanan's words, and when he at last was able, brought them to the attention of others who revered

Yoḥanan's memory, and therefore welcomed the assurance that he had agreed with them.

These facts raise the problem of the reason for such secrecy—of the excuse which could be found for such revelations of Yoḥanan's true teachings only some thirty years after his death. I suppose this reason, or excuse, lay in the political implications of the decision. The imposition of a modified form of Palestinian land-tax on Ammon and Moab implies the claim that they should be dependencies of the land of Israel.[1] The revolutionary government was staking out its territorial claims—claims which could only be realized over the dead bodies of the predominantly gentile inhabitants of Ammon and Moab. Yoḥanan was now "discovered" to have been a crypto-revolutionary. The content of the saying is thus as suspicious as its form, and both are probably fraudulent. When we add the facts that this secret teaching was revealed by Eliezer only at the end of his life, when he was in a state of excommunication, so that he never had an opportunity to deny the reported revelation at the actual consistory, the story becomes all the more incredible.

24. The Sadducees say, "We cry out against you, O ye Pharisees, for ye say, 'The Holy Scriptures render the hands unclean,' [and] 'The writings of Hamiram [Homeros] do not render the hands unclean.' "

Rabban Yoḥanan b. Zakkai said, "Have we naught against the Pharisees save this—for lo, they say, 'The bones of an ass are clean, and the bones of Yoḥanan the High Priest are unclean.' "

They said to him, "As is our love for them so is their uncleanness—[we have ruled them unclean so] that no man make spoons of the bones of his father or mother."

He said to them, "Even so the holy Scriptures: as is our love for them so is their uncleanness; [whereas] the writings of Homer, which are held in no account, do not render the hands unclean."

(Mishnah Yad. 4:6, trans. Danby, p. 784)

Comment: It is commonly supposed that this story comes from the period before 70, since after 70, the Sadducees were supposedly a negligible factor. Neither supposition is well grounded. Many Sadducees had been pro-Roman, so after 70 the contest between them and Yoḥanan's party for Roman support was probably sharp. Sadducean opinion was also preserved by Yoḥanan's priestly opponents, of whose importance after 70 we have already found several traces. Consequently, this dispute cannot be accurately dated.

---

1 Morton Smith contributed this observation.

Yoḥanan's argument is phrased in a highly formal structure as we shall see.

We cannot assume that the Sadducees were so stupid as this. II.i.3 showed the priests' skills were known among the sages. They would certainly have had some reply to Yoḥanan's remark. Their first argument is to be explained as a *reductio ad absurdum*—if human bones were not declared unclean, see what horrible consequences might follow! The Tosefta here, as occasionally elsewhere, contains only material supplementary to the Mishnah, so it supplies only Yoḥanan's counter *reductio ad absurdum*: if the Scriptures were not declared unclean, one might use old Torah-scrolls as bedding for his cattle (II.iii.16). This is important, not only because it completes the formal summary of the argument (a fact which proves it was originally part of the argument), but also because it thereby shows that in the present Mishnah text we have only an excerpt. Yoḥanan's counter argument has certainly been omitted, so other elements of the original dispute may have been omitted too.

This story is the first example we have seen of the genre of "how the master overcame the enemy by superior cleverness" stories. I should imagine that the picture of the Sadducees presented here, and below, III.i.22, would have been credible only long after they had passed from the scene. I therefore regard it as a late, not an early account. However, knowing the tendency of religious parties to vilify each other and their lack of concern for facts, I am by no means certain. The story may have been current in Pharisaic circles even before Yoḥanan's time, but this is equally uncertain. A *terminus ante quem* is provided by the polemic against the Sadducees, which points to a time when competition with them was still important, i.e. before ca. 130.

II. General Comments

We find the following kinds of Yoḥanan-traditions in the Mishnah:

1. *Stories* about legal opinions held, or decisions made, by Yoḥanan: II.i.1, i.2, told by R. Judah b. Ilai; III.i.3, told by R. Judah b. Ilai; II.i.4 (anonymous); II.i.5 ("Before time... after the Temple was destroyed); II.i.13 (anonymous); II.i.15 (anonymous), II.i.16, R. Simeon b. Gamaliel to R Joshua and R. Judah b. Bathyra; II.i.20 (anonymous—"After the Temple was destroyed..."); II.i.24 (anonymous);

2. *Stories* about decisions by others in which Yoḥanan's opinion is recorded: II.i.9,10 (decisions by judges of civil law in Jerusalem);

3. *Reports* of Yoḥanan's opinions by Yoḥanan's disciples given in context of later discussions: II.i.11,12 given by R. Joshua b. Ḥananiah

("Who will remove the dust..."); II.i.17, R. Joshua b. Ḥananiah ("I have received as a tradition");

4. *Praise* of Yoḥanan: II.i.14 (anonymous);

5. *Legal sayings in conventional Mishnaic form*: II.i.21 ("R. Yoḥanan b. Zakkai says...");

6. *Ethical discussions with students*: II.i.18,19 (Avot);

7. *Comments* by Yoḥanan on the law: II.i.22 ("And of all these Yoḥanan said...").

It is clear that most of the Mishnaic materials pertaining to Yoḥanan have been preserved in primitive forms, that is to say, in forms not usually used by R. Judah the Prince for the transmission of legal dicta. The commonplace form is, "Principle of law... Rabbi X says... Rabbi Y says..." Such a form appears only once, in II.i.21. The miscellaneous sayings (II.i.14, II.i.18-19, II.i.22) aside, practically all of the materials in fact are *stories*. These stories contain whatever legal opinions or decisions of Yoḥanan which were in fact preserved, nineteen of the twenty-four examples.

Yoḥanan's materials in the Tannaitic midrashim are not much different in form from those of others preserved in the same context. Here the contrary is the case. The revisions of traditional materials to conform to the editorial principles of laws taught by the Aqiban school and later on by Judah the Prince rarely affected Yoḥanan's sayings. Why this should have been the case I cannot say. It is clear both from these materials and from our earlier remarks that Aqibans (e.g. Judah b. Ilai) did preserve Yoḥanan's sayings and stories about him. It is equally evident that they had no negative intentions we can now discern. So we can hardly suppose a hostile attitude toward Yoḥanan led to suppression of some sayings and inattention to the editing of others. But the Aqibans did not preserve Yoḥanan's sayings according to conventions applied elsewhere. This would further suggest many of Yoḥanan's materials were given final form *before* the Aqiban revision of the normative forms for transmitting the tradition; hence much of the material probably derives from Yavneh, thus from Joshua and Eliezer.

The Yoḥanan ben Zakkai of the Mishnah differs from the Yoḥanan of the Tannaitic midrashim. Here he is a lawyer-judge, little more than that. He scarcely dealt with political or historical events. He judged cases (II.i.1,2,15). His exposition of Scriptures pertained chiefly to legal matters, such as whether priests pay the *sheqel* (II.i.3), and uncleanness laws (II.i.11). Stories *about* him illustrated legal principles, including the importance of eating in the *Sukkah* (II.i.14) and tithing (II.i.23). He issued important legal decrees, as at Yavneh (II.i.5,6,7,8,-20) and Jerusalem (II.i.9,10,13); with reference to marriage (II.i.16, 17) and to marriage-relationships involving property (II.i.9,10); and to uncleanness (II.i.21,22,24). Only a few sayings concerned *aggadic* subjects, such as the proper mode of service to God (II.i.12). The stories about his circle of disciples (II.i.18-19) find practically no echo at all in the Tannaitic midrashim.

The limited range of Yoḥanan's legal sayings might possibly be explained in terms of the narrow range of Pharisaic legal authority before and immediately after 70. But since the Pharisees presumably legislated for all aspects of the lives of their own members, it is likely that Yoḥanan's court at Yavneh handled a much wider range of cases. The traditions which have come down to us in Yoḥanan's name will be mainly those in which he introduced some innovation which subsequently prevailed. Less often he is remembered as an authority for a minority opinion preserved for reasons obscure to us, or an opinion or a question later disputed is falsely attributed to him, to invoke his authority for one or another side of the dispute. Since Pharisaic legislation was widely remodeled by ʿAqiva and Meir, it is presumable that in many cases Yoḥanan's opinions have been quietly dropped. We have no reason to suppose a wide selection of Yoḥanan's legal sayings existed at the middle of the second century but then was lost or suppressed.

What is most striking, however, is that we find practically *no* parallels of subject, story, or legal dicta between the Mishnah and the Tannaitic midrashim. There is, indeed, scarcely any relationship at all between the Tannaitic midrashim and the Mishnah so far as Yoḥanan is concerned. Specifically, I.i.1,2,3,4,5,6,7,8, I.ii.1,2,3,5,8,9 and I.iv.1,2,-3,4,5,6, exhibit no parallel at all, either in form, content, or even in general theme, in Mishnaic materials. We do not even find the same subjects treated in both cases.

I.ii.14 is the same as II.i.11 (the uncleanness of the third loaf). This is particularly important, because it shows that the character of the midrashic materials does not *eo ipse* exclude them from the Mishnah. I.ii.6,7a, and 7b are the same as II.i.5 and 7 (I.ii.7 = II.i,7, the *lulav* and Day of Waving). This further shows that some legal materials could and did prove useful in both documents. But by and large the Mishnah ignores the data of the Tannaitic midrashim.

It may be argued that the very purpose of the midrashic collections was different from that of the Mishnah, so the same materials ought not usually to have appeared in both, being inappropriate for either the one or the other. But it was certainly possible to phrase large segments of the midrashic materials in the Mishnaic form either as stories, as in the case of the bulk of the Yoḥanan-material in the Mishnah, or as apodictic laws, as in II.i.21, or as comments on the law, as in II.i.22. Homilies on the foolishness of Israel for not doing God's will in good times obviously could not prove useful to the editor of the Mishnah, even though we do find a few sermons in the Mishnah. But the "law" that one must pay heed to the dignity of human beings could easily have found a relevant place in discussions of legal penalties; likewise, the principle that the one who honors the Master as much as the servant is punished less severely. The law that the heifer-sacrifice is carried out in white garments certainly could have been included in Yoḥanan's name. The law about not teaching the *Merkavah* to a single disciple unless he is a sage is in fact quoted in the Mishnah. Why not, therefore, in Yoḥanan's name? Yoḥanan specifically claimed to have taught it to Eleazar, and solid grounds existed for thinking he had in fact taught it. "R. Yoḥanan b. Zakkai says, 'The *nasi* brings a sin offering for his unwitting transgression'" could have found a place in Mishnah Sanhedrin 1:1. The praise of Yoḥanan's court finds no echo in praise given to Yoḥanan in Mishnah Soṭ. 9:15. The draft-exemptions might well be included in a legal formulation, "R. Yoḥanan ben Zakkai says, 'The faint-hearted does not have to bring witnesses.' "

One might further argue that the Mishnah presents as laws Yoḥanan did teach only those original to him, or at least attributed to him. Hence the law about teaching the *Merkavah* was not assigned to Yoḥanan, because he merely cited a tradition "much older" than his own time. Of this older tradition Yoḥanan said nothing. One may have existed, but we can never know anything about those "traditions much older" than the age in which they were first given normative form. All we can and do know is that important laws were taught as sayings of Yoḥanan. These laws do appear in the Mishnah. With a few exceptions, they do not appear—in legal form—in the Tannaitic midrashim. Some of them, at least, might have been *given* legal form for inclusion in the Mishnah. The converse hardly needs argument. Mishnaic sayings and especially stories could easily have found their way into midrashic collections as stories or homilies (as the uncleanness of the third loaf did). It was a two-way street, but little seems to have moved on either side.

III. Tosefta Texts

1. The story is told that when R. Joshua went to Rabban Yoḥanan ben Zakkai to Beror Ḥayil, the villagers were bringing dates out to them. They said to him, "Are we required to tithe?" He said to them, "If we are remaining [here] we are obligated to tithe, otherwise we are not."

(Tos. Ma'aserot 2:1, ed. S. Lieberman, I, pp. 230-1)

Comment: The setting is Beror Ḥayil; the tradents, presumably Joshua's disciples. Yoḥanan gives a rule of law, plays no significant role otherwise. The rule of law is well known. A corpus of traditions deriving from Beror Ḥayil, as from Jerusalem and Yavneh, may have existed, including this story; I.i.8; as a *beraita*, III.ii.24. But those are the only clearcut examples. Both Joshua's and Eliezer's circles preserved Beror Ḥayil stories.

2. R. Joshua b. Qorḥa said, "These things did Rabban Yoḥanan ben Zakkai decree when the Temple was destroyed. When the house will be rebuilt—quickly in our days—these things will return to their former condition."

(Tos. R. H. 2:9, ed. S. Lieberman, II, p. 315)

(2a. R. Judah said, "These things did Rabban Yoḥanan ben Zakkai ordain [HNHYG] when the Temple was destroyed, and when the house will be rebuilt, these things will return to their former condition.")

(Tos. R. H. 2:3, ed. Zuckermandel p. 212 ls. 16-17)

Comment: The context is the sanctification of the New Moon. Immediately preceding is Simeon b. HaSegan's saying that if the witnesses to the appearance of the New Moon come after the Afternoon offering, the *shofar* should be sounded. Joshua b. Qorḥa's saying follows.

In fact, however, if we did not know the Mishnah (II.i.8), we should not have known the reference of R. Joshua b. Qorḥa's "these things." namely, receiving witnesses concerning the New Moon all day long. Lieberman's brief commentary (1.38) found it necessary to clarify this point, so the text of the Tosefta itself seemed to him unclear.

The saying of Joshua b. Qorḥa may originally have been, "R. Joshua said, 'R. Yoḥanan...ordained this also...These things did Rabban Yoḥanan decree... When the house will be rebuilt...'" R. Judah the

Prince selected only the first part for the Mishnah, leaving out the latter comment, which was thereupon included, without reference to its precise context, in the Tosefta (as II.iii.16).

But it is also noteworthy that Joshua's language is "these things." He may thereby have referred to the whole set of Yavnean ordinances, not merely the decree about testimony concerning the New Moon. Since Judah b. Ilai clearly regarded at least one of these ordinances as law, not merely temporary enactment, it was important to Joshua b. Qorḥa to state the contrary. But it may have seemed "obvious" to Judah the Prince that if the Temple would be rebuilt, then the several ordinances of Yavneh would be annulled.

Zuckermandel's reading is obviously inferior, and may be safely ignored.

I cannot see any motive for Judah's specific concern with testimony on the New Moon. On the other hand, as we noted above, the patriarch had every reason to want to keep the priests in their place, even after their place was the Jerusalem Temple in its restored state. Hence my guess is that Joshua's "these things" originally meant *everything* Yoḥanan had said and done at Yavneh. Rabbi Judah the Prince reduced the reference to witnesses on the New Moon. Having achieved primacy over the priesthood, the patriarch was by no means willing to give it up, either in the present, or in the forseeable future when the Temple would be rebuilt.

I do not suggest Joshua b. Qorḥa's saying represented a priestly viewpoint. It was a matter of piety on his part to assert that whatever had been done was merely temporary, "but of course we all hope for the restoration." The patriarch and his circle would have seen things more perceptively; they were preparing a law-code, not a collection of worthy sentiments. "Of course" we all hope for the rebuilding of the Temple, but that does not for one minute mean the old laws of priestly government will be restored—and certainly not by either the patriarchate or the rabbinate.

3. (a) [One may not teach... about the Chariot to a single individual unless he is a sage and understands from his own knowledge.] The story is told that R. Eleazar b. 'Arakh was driving the ass behind Rabban Yoḥanan ben Zakkai. He [Eleazar] said to him [Yoḥanan], "Teach me a chapter in the Works of the Chariot."

He [Yoḥanan] replied to him, "Have I not said to you, 'One may not teach about the Chariot to a single individual unless he is a sage and understands of his own knowledge.' "

He [Eleazar] said to him, "Give me permission, and I shall lecture before you."

Forthwith Rabban Yoḥanan ben Zakkai descended from the ass and covered himself with his cloak and the two of them sat on a stone under an olive tree and he [Eleazar] lectured before him.

(b) Then he [Yoḥanan] stood up and kissed him on his head and said, "Blessed is the Lord God of Israel who gave a son to Abraham our father who knows how to expound and to understand concerning the glory of our father who is in heaven. Some expound well but do not fulfill well; some fulfill well but do not expound well. But Eleazar ben ʿArakh expounds well and fulfills well.

"Happy are you, O Abraham our father, that Eleazar ben ʿArakh has come forth from your loins who knows how to expound and to understand concerning the glory of our father in heaven."

(c) R. Yosi b. R. Judah says, "R. Joshua lectured before Rabban Yoḥanan ben Zakkai. R. ʿAqiva lectured before R. Joshua. Ḥananiah b. Ḥakhinai lectured before R. ʿAqiva."

(Tos. Ḥag. 2:1-2, ed. Zuckermandel, pp. 233-4, ls. 25-7,1-7)

(d) The story is told that Rabban Yoḥanan ben Zakkai was riding on the ass, and R. Leazar b. ʿArakh was driving the ass from behind... [as above].

R. Leazar b. ʿArakh began to expound the works of the Chariot. Rabban Yoḥanan ben Zakkai descended from the ass, covered himself with his *tallit*, and the two of them sat on the stone under the olive and he lectured before him.

He [Yoḥanan] stood up and kissed him on his head and said, "Blessed is the Lord God of Israel who gave a son to Abraham our father who knows how to understand and to expound concerning the glory of his father in heaven. There are some who expound well but do not fulfill well, fulfill well but do not expound well. Leazar b. ʿArakh expounds well and fulfills well.

"Happy are you, O Abraham our father, that Eleazar b. ʿArakh has come forth from your loins, who knows how to understand and to expound in behalf of (*le*) his father in heaven."

(e) R. Yosi b. Judah says, "R. Joshua lectured before Rabban Yoḥanan ben Zakkai, R. ʿAqiva before R. Joshua, Ḥananiah b. Kinai before R. ʿAqiva.

(Ṭos. Ḥag. 2:1, ed. S. Lieberman, II, p. 380-1, ls. 1-15)

Comment: The differences between Zuckermandel's and Lieberman's texts are not substantial, and at the crucial points there are no variations at all. In the synoptic section (below, XI.iii) we shall compare the several *Merkavah* accounts. Here we may note that we have essentially three elements. First is the circumstance in which Eleazar gives his talk. Second is Yoḥanan's praise of the talk. Third is the saying that it was Joshua b. Ḥananiah, rather than Eleazar, who lectured for Yoḥanan and so formed the link in the chain of the *Merkavah*-tradition.

The obvious omission is the record of just what Eleazar said. This is, further, excluded in all versions of the *Merkavah*-event. Obviously, between 3a and 3b must have been a paragraph containing the content of the *Merkavah*-sermon, and this paragraph has been everywhere suppressed. But in I.ii.2, a substitute for it has been introduced—the miracles which begin to happen *before* the sermon. In II.iii.3 there is nothing; in I.ii.2 a miraculous fire appears; in III.i.4a, beside the fire we have dancing angels, singing trees, angelic approval, earthquakes, a rainbow, and a *bat qol.* This motif is not one which would have been dropped out. Its absence from the Mishnah might have been attributed to Judah the Prince's editing, but its absence here, from the Tosefta, is presumably a sign of a more primitive text.

3a and 3b are obviously to be attributed to Eleazar's pupils, for reasons stated above (I.ii.2).

3c derives from the Joshua-ʿAqiva line of Yoḥanan materials. In it Eleazar is *not* mentioned as having lectured for Yoḥanan. The *Merkavah*-doctrine came to ʿAqiva through Joshua, whose teaching was approved by Yoḥanan himself. None of the other disciples plays a part. Obviously, the Aqibans would have preferred this version. They however also chose to preserve the Eleazar one, but they were able to correct the "false" impression left by it that the official version of the *Merkavah*-mystery was known in Emmaus only. The *on that day* materials showed that earlier sayings of Yoḥanan were in fact suppressed in favor of later formulations, so it was not without precedent to do the same with the *Merkavah*-stories, which could have been retold by the Aqibans in a form more satisfactory to their master's teacher, Joshua. I am puzzled by their failure to do so.[1]

It seems that the central role attributed to Eleazar here and in a few other places must be based upon events before 70; but the account could have been framed afterward.

4. [R. Ṭarfon was criticized for receiving heave-offering from anyone on any day of the year. He replied], "May I bury my sons if I do not have a *halakhah* in my hands from Rabban Yoḥanan ben Zakkai

[1] My guess, as I said earlier, is that the disciples of Eleazar joined the Aqiban party and hence were able to insure the preservation of their master's traditions in the Aqiban corpus; but that did not prevent the Aqibans from giving their own view of what had happened.

who told me that you are permitted to receive heave-offering on the rest of the days of the year from everybody..."

(Tos. Ḥag. 3:33, ed. S. Lieberman, II, p. 393)

[4(a). Zuckermandel, p. 238 has, "law in my hands from Rabban Gamaliel Yoḥanan ben Zakkai," clearly an error. Similarly, p. 239, "*From what time* is it permitted for a man to receive..." should be deleted, leaving the reading as above.]

Comment: Yoḥanan's teaching about receiving heave-offering any time from anyone appears in no other source. Since Ṭarfon was probably about twelve or thirteen in 70, he must have been one of Yoḥanan's last pupils at Yavneh or Beror Ḥayil, when he would have been about twenty. But there is no reason to doubt Ṭarfon's statement.[1] Evidently some priests, such as Ṭarfon, did reconcile themselves to Yoḥanan's authority, and preserved his teachings as valid precedent. So Yoḥanan was able to impose his rules in part of the priesthood—that part which adhered to the rabbinical party to begin with.

5. ...R. Joshua said, "Who will remove the dust from your eyes, Rabban Yoḥanan ben Zakkai, for you would say that another generation is destined to declare the third loaf not susceptible of the capacity to receive uncleanness, for which there is no Scriptural [warrant] and does not your disciple R. ʿAqiva bring a Scripture from the Torah [to prove] that it is [capable of receiving] uncleanness..."

(Tos. Soṭ. 5:13, ed. Zuckermandel, p. 303, ls. 2-4.)

Comment: See above, I.ii.4 and II.i.11.

6. Rabban Yoḥanan ben Zakkai says, "When murderers multiplied, the [rite] of breaking the heifer's neck was annulled, for [the rite of] the breaking of the heifer's neck applies only in cases of doubt, but now murders are openly committed."

(Tos. Soṭ. 14:1, ed. Zuckermandel, p. 320, ls. 10-11)

Comment: The report as to the abolition of the heifer-ritual in the Mishnah (II.i.13) is anonymous and also gives no clear account of who

[1] See Epstein, *Mevo'ot* p. 51. On this basis, Epstein attributes the *whole* parallel pericope in the Mishnah to Yoḥanan!

did it. The atribution of the report to Yoḥanan in the present passage might be explained as confusion from II.i.13(b), but more probably the whole of the present passage is an independent version of the same basic tradition as that in II.i.13(a). The two forms have nothing in common except the essential fact. Yoḥanan there actually abrogated the rite. He merely reports it here. Earlier an exegesis is quoted to justify his action (Hos. 4:14). Here we find no exegesis, merely an observation on contemporary conditions which required the abrogation. Judah the Prince preferred the former version. Yoḥanan, representing the Pharisees, actually did wield great power in the Temple. He did not merely observe what the priests decided to do, but *told* them what to do.

As I said, the Tosefta account accords with what later priests would have preferred to remember. If and when the Temple is rebuilt, they did not want to face the meddling of the sages, let alone of the patriarchate. It was to Judah the Prince's advantage to teach as authoritative the version providing precedent for rabbinical, rather than priestly, rule in the Temple to come, and that, I think, is why he chose II.i.13 over this story.

7. His disciples asked Rabban Yoḥanan ben Zakkai, "For what reason did the Torah treat the thief more strictly than the robber?" He replied to them, "The robber regarded the honor of the slave as equal to the honor of his owner, while the thief paid more honor to the servant than to the master.

"It is as if the thief acted as though the eye which is on high does not see, and the ear as if it does not hear, as it is said, *Woe unto them that seek deep to hide their counsel from the Lord and their works are in the dark and they say, 'Who sees us and who knows us?* (Is. 29:15)."

"*They say, The Lord will not see and the God of Jacob will not understand* (Ps. 91:7)."

"*They say, The Lord does not see us, the Lord has forsaken the land* (Ez. 9:9)."

(Tos. B.Q. 7:1, ed. Zuckermandel, p. 357, ls. 19-25)

Comment: The analogical exegeses are entirely suppressed in the Mishnah; we have not got the slightest echo of Yoḥanan's teachings as exegete. Here, by contrast, we find the primitive formulation of I.i.5 with only minor modifications. In I.i.5 the form is a comment on the Scripture (Ex. 22:7). Here the form is "*his disciples asked*..." The Scriptures cited as proof-texts are identical. I imagine that the substance of the teaching underwent no significant changes. When it was used, the superscription (e.g., *His disciples asked*...) was altered to suit the context. Otherwise the tradition went in precisely as it was received. This conforms to our earlier observation (I.i.5).

8. Five things did Rabban Yoḥanan ben Zakkai say [teach] in the manner of a *ḥomer:*

(a) Why was Israel exiled to Babylonia rather than to all other lands? Because the house of Abraham was from there. To what may the matter be likened? To a woman who cuckolded her husband. Where does he send her? He sends her to her father's house.

(b) Of the first tablets it is said (Ex. 32:16), *And the tablets were the work of God*, but of the second, And the tablets were the work of Moses, as it is said (Ex. 32:16), *And the writing was the writing of God.* To what may the matter be likened? It is like a mortal king who betrothed a certain woman. He brings the scribe, the ink, the quill, the parchment, and the witnesses. If she cuckolded [him], she brings all. It is sufficient for her if the king [merely] gives her his signature.

(c) Behold it says, *When the prince sins* (Lev. 4:22)—Happy is the generation whose prince (*nasi*) brings a sin-offering for his unwitting offense.

(d) And it says (Ex. 21:6), *And his master will pierce his ear with an awl.* On what account was the ear [chosen] of all the limbs to be pierced? Because it heard from Mount Sinai, *For unto me are the children of Israel slaves, they are my slaves* (Lev. 25:55), yet it broke from itself the yoke of heaven and accepted the rule of the yoke of mortal man. Therefore Scripture says, "Let the ear come and be pierced, for it has not kept what it heard."

(e) Another matter, He did not wish to be enslaved to his master, let him come and be enslaved to his daughters.

(f) And it says, *An altar of stones, you will not lift up iron over them* (Deut. 27:5). On what account was iron [chosen] of all metals [as] the one to be tabooed? Because the sword is made from it. The sword is a sign of punishment, but the altar is a sign of atonement. Something which is a sign of punishment is removed from something which is a sign of atonement.

(g) And is this not a *qal veḥomer:* Stones, which do not see, hear, or speak—because they bring atonement between Israel and their father in heaven, Scripture says, *You should not lift up iron over them*, sons of Torah, who are an atonement for the world, how much the more so should none of all the demons touch them.

(h) And behold it says, *Whole stones should you [use to] build the altar of the Lord your God* (Deut. 27:6). Stones which bring peace between Israel and their father in heaven, the Omnipresent said, should be whole before me. Sons of Torah, who are complete before the world, how much the more so should they be complete before the Omnipresent.

(Tos. B.Q. 7:3-7, ed. Zuckermandel, pp. 357, ls. 30-38, 358, ls. 1-18)

Comment: This list of "five things" now consists of eight sections. The three interpolations are (c), (e), and (g), which are clearly not of the *ḥomer* form and also do not, except for (c), have the same framework as the rest. The present passage therefore is an expansion of an earlier list of the "five things." "Whether the expansion was made by the compiler of Tosefta, who found the list in his material, or whether he made the list and later copyists of the Tosefta expanded it, is uncertain; but the heading "five things" slightly favors the latter possibility. The "five things" originally listed items (a), (b), (d), (f) and (h), which certainly do not exhaust the *ḥomer*-exegesis. They are, rather, five such exegeses which were selected by the editor of the pericope. They were arranged in no apparent logical order, but were chosen to illustrate the *ḥomer*-exegeses. Some of the exegeses recur in numerous other documents, and when they do, they generally stand by themselves. There is no other exemplum of "the five things" cited in this order and in this context. (But the "nine decrees" of Yavneh exhibit the same enumerative form, presumably for mnemonic purposes.)

II.iii.8a and 8b are essentially alike in referring to the relationship of God and Israel according to the analogy of a marriage. They do not recur.

II.iii.8c is taken whole cloth from I.ii.3, the Aqiban tradition. But since its form shows it to be an interpolation in the present list, we cannot suppose that the whole "five things" version (or the enumerative style) is Aqiban. III.iii.8d has a parallel in the Ishmaelean tradition (I.i.3). However, in I.i.3, the Scripture that the ear heard was *You shall not steal* (Ex. 20:13) yet the man went and stole and consequently was sold into slavery. Here the ear heard *Unto me are the children of Israel slaves* (Lev. 25:55). This version is clearly that of the Aqibans, to whom the essential sin of the Jews was submission to foreign rule.[1] For the Ishmaeleans, on the contrary, the essential sin of the Jews was failure to keep the moral law. The Ishmaelean version is presumably that of Yoḥanan, the Aqiban one presents a pro-revolutionary revision. Another such revision, using the same proof text (Lev. 25:55) but interpreting it differently, appears in III.ii.18. Since the revision here is an essential part of the list of "five things," the list is an Aqiban or post-Aqiban construction. Thus the idea about the ear was preserved whole and in unvarying language, but it was assigned as an exegesis to various Scriptures. It would therefore seem that the foundation-stone of some pericopae was not a Scripture, but rather a particular teaching. The

[1] I owe this interpretation to Morton Smith.

verses of Scripture served as hooks by which alien ideas could be hung on the law.

III.ii.8f is cited by both Aqibans and Ishmaeleans (Ishmaelean: I.i.2= I.ii.5; Aqiban: I.ii.1); see the comment on I.i.2. Here we have the Aqiban version, agreeing with I.ii.1 against all others, so confirming our judgment above that the list is Aqiban or post-Aqiban. The *qal veḥomer* II.iii.8g is attached to the saying on iron which precedes it, just as it is to the same saying in I.ii.1, and presumably got into this list, where it is formally out of place, by contamination from that midrash. We listed it above as an interpolation, but it may have been taken over carelessly by the original compiler.

II.iii.8h, Whole stones, is the Aqiban version of the saying of which we have heard the Ishmaelean in I.i.2b-c and I.ii.5, and part of the Aqiban version in I.ii.1. Here again the agreement is closest to the Aqiban version; those who atone for the world and are consequently protected are not the *peacemakers* but the *sons of Torah*; see again I.i.2.

9. When the Temple was destroyed, Rabban Yoḥanan ben Zakkai decreed that the Day of Waving should be entirely prohibited [for the eating of new produce].

(Tos. Men. 10:26, ed. Zuckermandel, p. 529, ls. 4-5)

Comment: The Day of Waving stands as a separate teaching in Aqiban traditions (I.ii.6), and is not mentioned in Ishmaelean ones at all. I should therefore attribute II.iii.9 to Aqiban tradents.

10(a). Concerning all of these [objects which contain secret chambers] Rabban Yoḥanan ben Zakkai said, "Woe is me if I say, woe is me if I do not say [the law concerning them]. If I say, now I [find I am] teaching the deceivers how to deceive. But if I do not say, then I am impeding study [MWN' 'T HTLMWD], and I shall declare purities to be unclean."

(b) "Another explanation: that the deceivers should not say that the sages are not expert in their [nefarious] deeds."

(Tos. Kel. B.M. 7:9, ed. Zuckermandel, p. 586, ls. 27-30)

Comment: II.i.22 seems to allude to, perhaps even to depend upon, II.iii.10, which is the more detailed and complete version. Without II.iii.10 we should have no clear idea why Yoḥanan thought his choices were so unpleasant in II.i.22. Here we are told precisely what the unacceptable alternatives consisted of, surely a secondary explanation.

The longer saying might be the earlier one; the shorter may be a brief allusion to a well-known, antecedent account. The legal context is almost exactly the same. On the other hand, we have the short form of the saying, expanded with different explanations and in a different context, in III.ii.21. Therefore it seems most likely that the original saying was merely, "Woe is me if I speak, and woe if I do not speak." Which and how many of the applications and explanations are original is uncertain, but the best case can be made for the original reference to these purity rules. This does not exclude the possibility of original reference to other subjects too. Yoḥanan may have wanted to show that this dilemma occurs often in legal teaching. We have no way of dating, even attributing, the "Woe" sayings. We do not know what school originally formulated them, or when. Y.N. Epstein, *Mevo'ot*, p. 41, holds that the saying, "Concerning all of them, Yoḥanan said," indicates that, in fact, Yoḥanan is responsible for the editing of the entire pericope. This opinion requires no discussion.

11(a). His disciples asked Rabban Yoḥanan ben Zakkai, "One who searches—is he permitted to eat?"

He replied to them, "He may not eat."

They said to him, "You have taught us that he should eat."

He said to them, "Well spoken! A deed which my own hands have done and mine own eyes have seen, but I have forgotten—yet when my ears hear, how much the more so!"

(b) But it was not that he did not know, merely that he wanted to stimulate the disciples.

(c) And some say it was Hillel whom they asked, and not that he did not know, merely that he wanted to stimulate the disciples.

(d) R. Joshua says, "One who learns but does not do is like a man who sows but does not reap, and one who learns Torah but forgets [it] is like a woman gives birth and then buries."

(Tos. 'Ahilot 16:8, ed. Zuckermandel, p. 614 ls. 19-24)

Comment: See I.i.6 and II.ii.13. The story of the teacher caught giving a wrong answer has been developed, probably by the school of Joshua, as follows:

1. The enigmatic *and why all this* has been replaced by the explicit exoneration, *And it was not that he did not know*.

2. The full exoneration and explanation have been applied to Hillel as well as to Yoḥanan, this to achieve formal parallelism only.

3. The objection that Hillel could not have said, "What my own hands did" has been dropped, if it was even known to the source of the Tosefta form, for it looks like a secondary correction.

4. A saying of Joshua on the importance of practicing and remem-

bering what one learns has been added. All these changes are obviously secondary.

In this one instance (II.iii.11), this apologetic pericope has been attached to an error about Passover, not Temple law, perhaps because a ruling of Yoḥanan's in this matter had been "corrected" by later Pharisees.

Eliezer's story depended on the garments of the heifer sacrifice; Joshua's, on a purity-law. Joshua's leaves out the "Some say it was Hillel, but he could not say, 'What my [own] hands did.'" Obviously anyone could have been the object of this story. For Eliezer the priests' anti-Yoḥanan/Hillel story is turned into a favorable account. Here no echo of priestly hostility occurs. The context is entirely neutral. Joshua's school's way of coping with the priests' hostile story was therefore to revise the *setting* of the story, rather than merely adding *why all this* to change its point.

Eliezer's version must have been the earlier of the two to be given final form. At that time it was impossible to do more than explain away a story that seemed critical of Yoḥanan. Later on Joshua's disciples managed to "retell" the story of how Yoḥanan/Hillel had seemingly forgotten the law, but had done so purposely to sharpen the students' wits. Which law? A purity-law. The Temple setting is left out, and with it is suppressed the original, pointed polemic about Yoḥanan's inability to remember the very laws he also tried to force the priests to obey. Joshua's saying is not a criticism of Yoḥanan/Hillel, rather a comment on the sad fate of one who *really* forgets—something neither Hillel nor Yoḥanan had actually done at all.

12. And the story is told that a certain Sadduccee waited out his sunset and came to burn the [red] heifer. But Rabban Yoḥanan ben Zakkai learned of it. He came and placed his two hands on him and said to him. "My lord, high priest! How fitting are you to be high priest. Descend, immerse yourself once."

He descended and immersed himself and came up. After he came up, he [Yoḥanan] cut him on the ear.

He [the injured Sadducean] said to him, "Ben Zakkai—when I have time for you..."

He replied, "When you have time..."

Not three days passed before they put him into the grave.

His father came before Rabban Yoḥanan ben Zakkai, and said to him, "My son has time."

(Tos. Parah 3:8, ed. Zuckermandel, p. 632 ls. 18-22)

Comment: This story pertains to Temple times. A Sadducean priest intended to carry out the Sadducean purity-laws in burning the red-heifer, a very rare ceremony. Yoḥanan learned of it, rendered the priest unclean, ordered him to go through a purity-baptism and then to proceed to the sacrifice immediately, without awaiting sunset as Sadducean rules required. When the priest did what Yoḥanan told him to do, Yoḥanan mutilated him so he could not go on to carry out the ceremony even in accordance with the Pharisaic purity-laws after all. He threatened to get even with Yoḥanan later. Yoḥanan by a pun made of the threat a saying ominous of the speaker's death. And the priest died within a few days. His bereaved father is brought in at the end to suggest that the dead man was an only son and show the desolation of the family.

In spite of modern sympathies, it is quite unlikely that this was a story originally told by Sadducees to show Yoḥanan's implacability. First, there is no likelihood that these events or anything like them ever happened. That Yoḥanan should have dared to pollute a high priest in the preparations for a most important ceremony, that he should have had the opportunity to do so—since he was not a priest and had not access to the priests' area of the Temple,—and that he should have survived the action long enough for any conversation, all are alike incredible. Second, had he by any chance succeeded in polluting a high priest and getting out alive, the Sadducees should never have chronicled their discomfiture. The story must be seen therefore as a product of Yoḥanan's school—hardly of Yoḥanan himself—and of the most anti-priestly side of the school. Its purpose is to show how Yoḥanan was able to force the priests to observe Pharisaic law, to disqualify those who tried to resist him, and to bring down death on those who threatened him and ruin on their families. For this purpose the narrators were not troubled by the inconsistency that Yoḥanan disqualified the priest after forcing him to obey. His attempted disobedience merited both humiliation and disqualification. This party propaganda, glorifying Yoḥanan's legal authority, cleverness, and supernatural power, and glorifying the party in the person of its leader, was not intended to instruct the priests. It was intended to attract those who disliked priests —and who are said to have been many.[1] It may have been made up already in Yoḥanan's lifetime, but a later date is more likely, given the ignorance of the actual state of affairs before 70. The intense hostility to priests suggests a date before 130. Since the story first appears in the Tosefta, closer determination of the date is not possible.

13. His disciples asked Rabban Yoḥanan ben Zakkai, "The heifer—in what [garments] is [the rite] done?"

He replied, "In golden garments."

They said to him, "You have taught us, 'in white garments.' "

He said to them, "Well spoken! A deed which my [own] hands did and my own eyes saw I have forgotten, but when my ears heard, how much the more so."

[1] I owe this point to Morton Smith.

And it was not that he did not know, but he wanted to stimulate the disciples.

And some say it was Hillel whom they asked, and it was not that he did not know, but that he wanted to stimulate the disciples.

Rabbi Joshua says, "He who learns but does not do is like a man who sows but does not harvest..."

(Tos. Parah 4:7, ed. Zuckermandel, p. 633, ls. 22-27)

Comment: Here is Joshua's disciples' version of the heifer-ceremony story (II.iii.11, I.i.6). It is in fact identical to the Ishmaelean version (I.i.6) in all important details. I think it likely that the Ishmaelean version is what we have before us. Joshua's saying at the end applies equally well in II.iii.11 and II.iii.13. But the version in II.iii.11 obviously is different and separate; here it is merely a citation of the story in Sifré Num., with Joshua's subscription as an appropriate homily.

14. R. Eliezer said, "The story is told concerning Shemaʿyah of the village of ʿOtenai, who had in his hand *logs* full of water of sin [-offering], and he closed a door whose bolt was unclean [on account of] doubtful corpse-uncleanness. So he came and asked Rabban Yoḥanan ben Zakkai who said to him, "Shemaʿyah, Go and sprinkle your waters."

(Tos. Parah 10:2, ed. Zuckermandel, p. 638, ls. 32-34)

Comment: The comment is a dispute on technicalities of uncleanness-laws between Eliezer and Joshua. Eliezer states a law, then cites this story to prove he is right; Joshua replies with his view of the law, citing no story at all. This is the only example of a dispute between the two disciples in which a story of what the master had done is cited as authoritative. It is, of course, impossible to know when the supposed inquiry actually came to Yoḥanan, or how the account was finally put together. Perhaps it was while the Temple stood, when the waters of a sin-offering would have been available. Afterward, though, for a time some of the waters may have been preserved; purification-rites did not forthwith fall into disuse.

15. [On that day... they decreed that Ammon and Moab tithe poor-man's tithe in the seventh year...]

R. Eliezer said, "...do not doubt [the correctness of] your vote. I have a tradition from Rabban Yoḥanan ben Zakkai, who received it from the pairs, and the pairs from the prophets, and the prophets from

Moses as a law [revealed[to Moses at Sinai that Ammon and Moab tithe the poor-man's tithe in the seventh year."

(Tos. Yad. 2:16, ed. Zuckermandel, p. 683, ls. 16-26 [cited only in part])

Comment: See II.i.23.

16. Rabban Yoḥanan ben Zakkai said to them, "As to Sacred Scriptures—their preciousness [causes them to be susceptible to] uncleanness, so that people will not make them into mats for [their] cattle."

(Tos. Yad. 1:19/2:9, ed. Zuckermandel, p. 684, ls. 2-3)

Comment: See II.i.24. This is merely a fragment of the Mishnaic dispute-story. In Zuckermandel's text, it stands by itself; it is completely incomprehensible without reference to the Mishnah.

IV. General Comments

We find the following kinds of traditions:

1. *Stories* about legal opinions held, or decisions made, by Yoḥanan: II.iii.1 (story of decision); II.iii.2 (decree at Yavneh—witnesses); II.iii.9 (Yavneh-Day of Waving); II.iii.14 (uncleaness of sin-water);

2. *Reports of Yoḥanan's opinions given by Yoḥanan's disciples in the context of later discussions:* II.iii.4(Ṭarfon); II.iii.5 (R. Joshua); II.iii.15 (R. Eliezer);

3. *Legal sayings or reports in conventional form:* II.iii.6 (heifer-rite annuled);

4. *Legal traditions given in the context of teaching disciples:* II.iii.3 (*Merkavah*-teaching); II.iii.11 ("One who searches"); II.iii.13 (garments used in heifer ceremony);

5. *Comments by Yoḥanan on the laws:* II.iii.7 (robber/thief); II.iii.8;

6. *Analogical exegeses of the content of laws:* II.iii.7 (robber/thief); II.iii.8;

7. *Disputes with Sadducees:* II.iii.12 (red heifer ceremony); II.iii.16 (Sacred Scriptures unclean).

It is important to compare the materials preserved in the Tosefta with those in the Mishnah and the Tannaitic Midrashim. The following tables provide such a comparison.

Table

Tannaitic Midrashim compared to Tosefta and Mishnah

Mishnah	*Tosefta*	*Tannaitic Midrashim*
—	—	I.i.1 ("You were unwilling")
—	II.iii.8, v,vi	I.i.2 (Whole stones, & iron not to touch altar)
	II.iii.8d	I.i.3 (Slave's ear pierced)
—	—	I.i.4 (Oxen/sheep)
—	II.iii.7	I.i.5 (Robber/thief)
—	II.iii.13	I.i.6 (Red-heifer ceremony garments)
—	—	I.i.7 ("If you do not know")
—	—	I.i.8 (Moses was 120)
—	II.iii.8e	I.ii.1 (Iron not to touch altar)
—	II.iii.3	I.ii.2a (*Merkavah*)
—	II.iii.8c	I.ii.3 (Prince sins)
II.i.11	II.iii.5	I.ii.4 (Uncleanness of third loaf)
—	II.iii.8b	I.ii.5 (Whole stones)
II.i.5b, 7a, b, 20 20a, b	II.iii.9	I.ii.6 (Day of Waving)
II.i.5a, b (Lulav, Waving) 1.7a, b	II.iii.9 (Waving only)	I.ii.7 (*Lulav*, Day of Waving)
—	—	I.ii.8 (Go after good court)
—	—	I.ii.9 ("Frail-hearted")
II.i.18	—	I.iv.1 ("Created to study Torah")
—	—	I.iv.2 ("Do not destroy altars")
—	—	I.iv.3 ("Frail-hearted")
—	—	I.iv.4 (Letters)
—	—	I.iv.5 (Agrippas)
—	—	I.iv.6 (Moses was 120)

Table

Tosefta compared to Mishnah

Mishnah	*Tosefta*	
—	II.iii.1	(Villagers asked *re* tithing)
II.i.8	II.iii.2	(Witnesses to new moon)
—	II.iii.3	(*Merkavah*)
—	II.iii.4	(Ṭarfon *re* heave-offering)
II.i.11	II.iii.5	(Impurity of third-loaf)
II.i.13 (Yoḥanan decreed)	II.iii.6	(Murders multiplied—Yoḥanan reports decrees)
—	II.iii.7	(Robber/thief)
—	II.iii.8	(Five things)
II.i.5b; 20	II.iii.9	(Day of Waving)
II.i.22	II.iii.10	("Woe if I say")
—	II.iii.11	("One who searches")
—	II.iii.12	("Red heifer—when I have time")
—	II.iii.13	("Red heifer—in what garments")
—	II.iii.14	(Shema'yah)
II.i.23	II.iii.15	(Poor-man's tithe in Ammon)
II.i.24	II.iii.16	(Uncleanness of Scriptures—fragment only)

Table

Mishnah compared to Tosefta

Tosefta	*Mishnah*	
—	II.i.1	("I doubt whether he is not liable")
—	II.i.2	("I doubt whether he is not liable")
—	II.i.3	(Priests and *sheqel*)
—	II.i.4	(Yoḥanan and Gamaliel eat in Sukkah)
II.iii.9	II.i.5	(Day of Waving)
—	II.i.6	(Shofar-decree *re* Sabbath)
—	II.i.7	(*Lulav*)
—	II.i.8	(Witnesses)
—	II.i.9	(Judges of civil law)
—	II.i.10	(Judges of civil law)
II.iii.5	II.i.11	(Impurity of third loaf)
—	II.i.12	(Job served through love)
II.iii.6	II.i.13	(Murders multiplied)
—	II.i.14	(When Yoḥanan died, splendor of wisdom ceased)
—	II.i.15	(Ben Zakkai once tested)
—	II.i.16	(Priests hearken in what concerns putting away)
—	II.i.16	(Elijah will remove...)
—	II.i.18	("If you have wrought much")
—	II.i.19	("Go forth and see")
II.iii.9	II.i.20	(Day of Waving)
—	II.i.21	("Capacity of fragments... uncleanness")
II.iii.10	II.i.22	("Woe if I speak")
II.iii.15	II.i.23	(Poor-man's tithe in Ammon)
II.iii.16	II.i.24	(Uncleanness of Scriptures)

We have previously observed that the Tannaitic Midrashim have little in common with the Mishnah. It is now clear that whatever is included in both the Tannaitic Midrashim and the Mishnah occurs also in Tosefta, specifically: the uncleanness of the third loaf, the Day of Waving (with or without the *lulav*-decree). The only saying present in the Mishnah and Tannaitic Midrashim and absent in the Tosefta is the singular Avot-teaching about study of Torah.

On the other hand, numerous teachings in the Tannaitic Midrashim occur also in the Tosefta. Of twenty-two exempla in Tannaitic Midrashim, eleven have parallels of one kind or another in the Tosefta. As one would expect, the Tosefta and Mishnah have more in common than do the Mishnah and the Tannaitic Midrashim. Of sixteen exempla in the Tosefta, seven have parallels in the Mishnah. Yet the two collections do not seem so close when the Mishnah's twenty-four exempla are actually listed. The numerical relations are as follows:

Common to Mishnah and Tannaitic Midrashim only: 1
Common to Mishnah, Tannaitic Midrashim, *and* Tosefta: 3
Common to Mishnah and Tosefta only: 7
Common to Tannaitic Midrashim and Tosefta only: 11

The Mishnah-traditions stand apart, almost entirely isolated from the Tannaitic Midrashim, but only somewhat less so from the Tosefta. The Tosefta stands closer to the Tannaitic Midrashim than to the Mishnah.

These statistical judgments are not especially important by themselves. They help, however, to underline the substantial difference between the Yoḥanan of the Mishnah, on the one hand, and the Yoḥanan of the Tosefta and of the Tannaitic Midrashim on the other hand. The Mishnaic traditions on Yoḥanan cannot be thought to derive from other schools entirely. They are Aqiban—by definition. But they are different from other Aqiban materials. The same is so for the Ishmaelean traditions on Yoḥanan, which may be divided, though less strikingly, into two groups. Nor can we suppose that one set of materials is earlier than another. The following table makes it quite clear that the numerous traditions considered thus far derived in some earlier form from Eliezer and Joshua or from their schools; a few more came from Yavneh but cannot be attributed to the two chief disciples. No traditions can be attributed to Ḥanina b. Dosa, none to the others in Yoḥanan's Jerusalem circle (listed in Avot 2:9). If Judah the Prince selected his materials from a very wide range of possibilities, and if the Tosefta's editors thereupon collected much of what remained, we should have expected more examples of obvious relationships between sayings used in the Mishnah and longer sayings explicating, or at least related to, Mishnaic materials, preserved in the Tosefta. We found II.i.22/II.iii.10, II.i.24/II.iii.16 as two obvious instances. We shall see a few others in the Babylonian and Palestinian Talmudic *beraitot*. But in the main, as I have said, Mishnaic traditions normally do not depend upon, do not even allude to, other traditions. On the other hand, numerous close relationships exist between Toseftan and Tannaitic-Midrashic traditions. So we must regard the Mishnah's Yoḥanan as essentially a separate form of the Yoḥanan tradition and different from the Yoḥanan of the Tannaitic Midrashim and the Tosefta.

How does Yoḥanan emerge in the Tosefta? Yoḥanan was an important judge, to whom many inquiries were directed (II.iii.i, II.iii.14). His decrees at Yavneh were preserved (II.iii.2, II.iii.9), a point in common among all three Tannaitic collections. He was a great exegete. His *ḥomer*-exegeses are preserved in detail in the Tosefta (III.iii.7-8). His *Merkavah*-teachings were handed on to his student Eleazar and to Joshua as well (II.iii.3), a point in common with the Tannaitic midrashim, but not found in the Mishnah. His disciples preserved his teachings and reported them as authoritative. Ṭarfon appears in the Tosefta alone (II.iii.4). Eliezer (II.iii.15) and Joshua (II.iii.5) appear in the Tosefta, in the Tannaitic Midrashim, and in the Mishnah as well. Yoḥanan reported a decree concerning an important Temple rite (II.iii.6); the Mishnah has it that he made the decree himself. His legal teachings concerning uncleanness laws were important, as were his comments about handing them on to students (II.iii.10). He was a thoughtful, stimulating teacher (II.iii.11, II.iii.13). He engaged in vigorous struggles with the Sadducees (II.iii.12, II.iii.16), known to the Mishnah as well. To this point, we still have heard not a single word about his alleged escape from Jerusalem and journey to Vespasian's camp. We know nothing of the circumstances of the establishment of the Yavneh academy.

Table

Mishnaic and Toseftan Authorities for Yoḥanan-Materials

I. First Century

Disciples:

Eleazar b. 'Arakh: II.i.19, II.i.18 (Abba Shaul); II.iii.3a, 3b
Joshua b. Ḥananiah: II.i.11, II.i.12, II.i.16, II.i.17, II.iii.1, II.iii.3c (Yosi b. R. Judah); II.iii.5, II.iii.11, II.iii.13
Eliezer b. Hyrcanus: II.i.6, II.i.18 (first version); II.i.23

Yavneh-Ordinances: Gamaliel: II.i.5, II.i.6, II.i.7, II.i.8a
Joshua b. Qorḥa: II.i.8b = II.iii.2

Aqibans: II.iii.9
Ṭarfon: II.iii.4

II. *Second Century*

Judah b. Ilai: II.i.1, II.i.2, II.i.3, II.i.20
Joshua b. Qorḥa: II.i.8, II.iii.2
[*Second-half of second century or later:* I.ii.21]

Anonymous: II.i.4, II.i.9, II.i.10, II.i.13, II.i.14, II.i.15, II.i.21, II.i.21, II.i.22, II.i.24, II.iii.6, II.iii.7, II.iii.8, II.iii.10, II.iii.12

CHAPTER THREE

TANNAITIC MATERIALS IN THE *GEMAROT* OF PALESTINE AND BABYLONIA

I. Palestinian Talmudic Traditions Attributed to Tannaim

Traditions under consideration appear in the Palestinian Talmud and are introduced by TNY, TNYNN, and similar forms. We shall note in addition (III.i.4,5,6) that some materials not so designated certainly derive from Tannaitic sources. Of thirty-two paragraph references in Umansky, six contain Tannaitic materials. Of these, four are introduced by TNY (or variations thereof); the other items I have designated as "attributed to Tannaim" all report, in varying ways, traditions already familiar to us in earlier Tannaitic collections. In our synoptic studies, we shall see how these traditions have been changed from their earlier formulations.

1. TNY: The story is told that R. Joshua went after Rabban Yoḥanan ben Zakkai to Beror Ḥayil, and those villagers were bringing them fruit. Rabbi Joshua said to them, "If we are abiding here [for the night] we are liable to tithe, but if not, we are not liable to tithe."

(y. Demai 3:1)

Comment: R. Jonah introduces a comment on the Mishnah, which teaches that one may feed doubtful produce to travellers, saying it follows R. Joshua, who tells the story that follows. The story appears in II.iii.1. *Dates* become *fruit*. There, they asked whether they are obligated to tithe, and it is uncertain whether the reply is Joshua's or Yoḥanan's. Here only Joshua's *answer* to the (unasked) question appears.

2. TNY: The story is told that R. Joshua went after Rabban Yoḥanan ben Zakkai to *Benei* [sic] Ḥ*ayil*, and those villagers were bringing them fruit. R. Joshua said to them, "If we are abiding here [for the night], we are liable to tithe, but if not, we are not liable to tithe."

(y. Maʿaserot 2:2)

Comment: As above, III.i.1, and II.iii.1. The context is a discussion between R. Simeon b. Laqish and R. Yoḥanan, followed by an anonymous conclusion, "All agree concerning [merely] abiding for the night and permanent domicile that...." The story is then cited as an example of the former.

3. WHTNYNN: When the Temple was destroyed, Rabban Yoḥanan ben Zakkai decreed that [eating new fruit on] the entire Day of Waving is prohibited.

y. Ḥallah 1:1

Comment: The context is a discussion of whether the prohibition of new produce derives from a decree of the Scribes or from a law of the Torah. According to Tannaitic theory, it would have been possible for Yoḥanan to issue a decree concerning a Torah-law, but not to add to or alter a decree of the Scribes. R. Yosi b. R. Bun and R. Jeremiah in the name of R. Ḥiyya discuss the matter.

The Tannaitic teaching itself appears in II.ii.6, 7; II.i.5b, 7a, 7b, 20; II.iii.9. Clearly the Day of Waving rule continued to circulate as a separate teaching as well as in conjunction with the *lulav*-decree.

4. (a) The story is told that Rabban Yoḥanan b. Zakkai was going on the way riding on the ass, and R. Lazar b. ʿArakh was going after him.

He said to him, "Rabbi, Teach me a chapter in the Works of the Chariot."

He [Yoḥanan] said to him, "Have not the sages taught, *And not concerning the Chariot unless he is wise and understands from his own knowledge.*"

He said to him, "Rabbi, Give me permission that I may say something before you."

He said to him, "Speak."

When R. Lazar b. ʿArakh opened [his exposition of] the Works of Chariot, Rabban Yoḥanan ben Zakkai descended from the ass. He said, "It is not lawful that I should hear the Glory of my Creator and ride on an ass."

They went and sat under the tree and fire descended from heaven and surrounded them. The ministering angels danced before them as members of a wedding rejoice before a bridegroom.

One angel answered from the fire and said, "According to your words, O Lazar b. ʿArakh, so [indeed] are the Works of the Chariot."

Forthwith all the trees opened their mouths and sang a song, *Then shall all the trees of the forest sing for joy* (Ps. 96:12).

When R. Lazar b. ʿArakh finished [his exposition] in the Works of the Chariot, Rabban Yoḥanan ben Zakkai stood up and kissed him on his head and said, "Blessed is the Lord, God of Abraham, Isaac, and Jacob, who gave to Abraham our father a son who is a sage and understands [how] to expound the glory of our Father in heaven. Some expound well, but do not fulfill well, fulfill well, but do not expound well. Lazar b. ʿArakh expounds well and fulfills well.

"Happy are you, O Abraham our father, that Lazar ben ʿArakh has come forth from your loins."

(b) When R. Joseph the Priest and R. Simeon b. Natanel heard, they also began [to expound] the Works of the Chariot.

They said that it was the first day in the season of Ṭammuz, and the earth trembled and a rainbow appeared in a cloud, and a *bat qol* came forth and said to them, "Behold the place is vacant for you, and the dining couch [TRYQLYN] is spread out for you. You and your disciples are destined for the third heaven."

(y. Ḥag. 2:1)

Comment: The context is, as to be expected, the Mishnaic teaching, quoted (in italics) in the story itself, that one may not teach the *Merkavah*-mystery to ordinary, but only to especially well-qualified, disciples. The antecedent discussion includes a story told by Ḥiyya in the name of Judah [the Prince] about a student of Judah's who expounded the *Merkavah*-tradition contrary to Judah's wishes and was punished with various ailments. "This Torah is like two paths, one of light (fire), and the other of snow (cold). What should one do? Let him walk in between them." Then, "The story is told..." Afterward comes the story of Ben Zoma and R. Joshua, concerning the Creation-mystery, then the "four who entered Paradise."

The passage differs from I.ii.2 and II.iii.3 in the inclusion of the *Merkavah*-exposition attributed to two other disciples of Yoḥanan, Joseph the Priest and Simeon b. Natanel (the former appearing in II.i.18 as Yosi). This is the only instance in which the *Merkavah* mysteries are recited by disciples other than Joshua and Eleazar b. ʿArakh. In I.ii.2, only Eleazar is mentioned; in II.iii.3 and III.ii.13, Joshua is included in addition. As we have observed, the basic account about Eleazar is never suppressed, only supplemented. Further differences will be considered in the synoptic section (below pp. 249-254).

5. His disciples asked Rabban Yoḥanan ben Zakkai, "Why is this slave's ear pierced rather than any other of his limbs?"

He replied to them, "The ear which heard from Mount Sinai, *You will have no other Gods before me* (Ex. 20:3), yet broke from itself the yoke of the kingdom of heaven and accepted on itself the yoke of mortal man; the ear which heard before Mount Sinai, *For to me are the children of Israel slaves* (Lev. 25:55) yet went and acquired another master—therefore let the ear come and be pierced, for it has not observed what it has heard."

(y. Qid. 1:2)

Comment: The context is Tannaitic teaching (TNY) of Eliezer b. Jacob, who said that the slave is brought to the door, because by means of the door they will go from slavery to freedom. Then, "His disciples asked..." It may be that Yoḥanan's teaching has been added to the Tannaitic teaching of the school of Eliezer b. Jacob. I see no direct relationship to Amoraic discussants.

The passage occurs in II.iii.8d, where Lev. 25:55 is cited, Ex. 20:3 omitted; and I.i.3, where Ex. 20:13 (*You shall not steal*) is cited along with Lev. 25:55. We saw above, II.iii.8d, the difference between the Ishmaelean version and the Aqiban revision. The latter is here expanded by appeal to Ex. 20:3, Lev. 25:55. The Aqiban school has gone on to make obedience to gentiles a form of idolatry as well as misappropriation of sacred property.

6. *When a prince sins unwittingly* (Lev. 4:22). Rabban Yoḥanan ben Zakkai said, "Happy is he whose prince brings a sin-offering for his unwitting sin."

(y. Hor. 3:2)

Comment: The context is a discussion of the circumstances of bringing a sin-offering for an unwitting transgression. Yoḥanan's saying is cited by R. Ḥinnena at the conclusion of an exchange between R. Yoḥanan and R. Simeon b. Laqish, then R. Ḥisda and R. Hamnuna.

The passage is unchanged from its occurrences in I.ii.3 and II.iii.8.

II. Babylonian Talmudic Traditions attributed to Tannaim (Beraitot)

Traditions under consideration appear in the Babylonian Talmud, introduced by TNW RBNN, TNY, TNY', DTNN, and similar forms; or are attributed to Yoḥanan by Tannaitic authorities; or clearly are direct quotations from Tannaitic sources even though not so designated at all (III.ii.4,11,17 [with minor insertions], 18,19a,b). Of sixty page references in Umansky's list, twenty-nine contain Tannaitic materials.

1. TNW RBNN: (a) When R. Eliezer fell ill, his disciples went in to visit him.

They said to him, "Master, teach us the paths of life so that we may through them win the life of the future world."

He said to them, "Be solicitous for the honor of your colleagues, and keep your children from meditation, and set them between the knees of scholars, and when you pray, know before whom you are standing and in this way you will win the future world."

(b) When Rabban Yoḥanan ben Zakkai fell ill, his disciples went in to visit him. When he saw them, he began to weep. His disciples said to him:

"Lamp of Israel, pillar of the right hand, mighty hammer! Wherefore weepest thou?"

He replied, "If I were being taken today before a human king who is here today and tomorrow in the grave, whose anger, if he should be angry with me would not last forever, who, if he should imprison me, would not imprison me for ever, and who, if he should put me to death, would not put me to everlasting death, and whom I could persuade with words and bribe with money, even so I would weep. Now that I am being taken before the supreme King of Kings, the Holy One, blessed be He, who lives and endures for ever and ever, whose anger, if He should be angry with me, is an everlasting anger, who, if he should imprison me, will imprison me for ever, who, if He should put me to death, will put me to death for ever, and whom I cannot persuade with words or bribe with money—nay more, when there will be two ways before me, one leading to Paradise and the other to Gehinnom, and I do not know by which I shall be taken,—shall I not weep?"

(c) They said to him, "Master, bless us."

He said to them, "May it be [God's] will that you may fear God as much as you fear man."

His disciples said to him, "Is that all?"

He said to them, "If only [you can attain this]! You can see [how important this is], for when a man wants to commit a transgression, he says, 'I hope no *man* will see me.' "

(d) At the moment of his departure he said to them, "Remove the vessels so that they shall not become unclean, and prepare a throne for Hezekiah the king of Judah who is coming."

(b. Ber. 28b, trans. M. Simon, pp. 173-4)

Comment: The context is Mishnah-commentary. The *beraita* is preceded by another *beraita*; the two form the whole of the *gemara* on a Mishnah concerning a prayer of R. Neḥunya b. HaQaneh.

It is clear that the Yoḥanan-death-story was framed in Eliezer's school and in the context of Eliezer's death scene. In other formulations (IV.i.9 and V.i.11, 17), Eliezer tells the disciples to set a throne for Rabban Yoḥanan ben Zakkai, who is coming. In this instance, there is no homiletical relationship between Eliezer's last words and those of Yoḥanan. For a brief, exegetical form of the teaching in part c above, see I.i.5; and for the simpler, Palestinian-Amoraic version of part d, see V.i.11, 17.

Units (b), (c), and (d) are essentially separate. The weeping-scene could have stood independently, likewise the blessing and final saying. Perhaps originally the components were actually circulated as separate units, e.g. part (a), as the separate parallels to (c) and (d) suggest.

2. TNW RBNN: Once the son of R. Gamaliel fell ill. He sent two scholars to R. Ḥanina b. Dosa to ask him to pray for him. When he saw them, he [Ḥanina] went up to an upper chamber and prayed for him. When he came down he said to them, "Go, the fever has left him."

They said to him, "Are you a prophet?"

He replied, "I am neither a prophet nor the son of a prophet, but I learned this from experience: If my prayer is fluent in my mouth, I know that it is accepted; but if not, I know that it is rejected."

They sat down and made a note of the exact moment. When they came to R. Gamaliel, he said to them, "By the temple service! You were not a moment too soon or too late, but so it happened; at that very moment the fever left him and he asked for water to drink."

(a) On another occasion it happened that R. Ḥanina b. Dosa went to study Torah with R. Yoḥanan ben Zakkai. The son of R. Yoḥanan ben Zakkai fell ill. He said to him, "Ḥanina my son, pray for him that he may live."

He put his head between his knees and prayed for him and he lived.

(b) Said R. Yoḥanan ben Zakkai, "If Ben Zakkai had stuck his head between his knees for the whole day, no notice would have been taken of him."

Said his wife to him, "Is Ḥanina greater than you are?"

He replied to her, "No, but he is like a servant before the king, and I am like a nobleman before a king."

(b. Ber. 34b, trans. M. Simon, pp. 215-6)

Comment: The context is unrelated to the preceding discussion. Following is a passage beginning, *Ve'amar*, and R. Ḥiyya b. Abba said in the name of R. Yoḥanan a saying concerning appropriate objects of prayer. I therefore assume that the passage as it stands began with the *beraita* and then proceeded to Amoraic discussions on the same theme.

The passage was framed with reference to Gamaliel. But the origin must be in the circle around Ḥanina b. Dosa, which preserved memories of how the master had healed the children of the two greatest men of the day. That does not mean the *beraita* was formulated before 70 A.D. We do not know when it was given its final form or how the stories reached the Talmudic redactors.

Unit (b) is separate and additional. It is introduced to explain the dependence of Yoḥanan on Ḥanina's miracle, indeed to set into true perspective the nature of miracles. The first paragraph, "If ben Zakkai..." could have stood as the conclusion of the foregoing, and perhaps it did, provoking the fabrication of the colloquy between Yoḥanan and his jealous wife. The story is absolutely unique, and if it was developed as I have proposed, the development was completed before the story was finally redacted in this form.

3. TNW RBNN: Forty years before the destruction of the Temple the lot did not come up in the right hand, the red-strap did not become white, and the western light did not shine, and the doors of the *Heikhal* would open by themselves, until Rabban Yoḥanan ben Zakkai rebuked them, saying "*Heikhal, heikhal*, why do you yourself give the alarm? I know concerning you that you are destined in the end to be destroyed, for already has Zechariah b. ʿIddo prophesied concerning you, *Open, O Lebanan, your doors so that the fire may consume your cedars* (Zech. 11:1)."

(b. Yoma 39b)

Comment: The *beraita* is not related to the preceding discussion. It is followed, however, by the saying of R. Isaac b. Ṭavlai about why the Temple was called Lebanon; R. Zuṭra b. Ṭuvyah asks why it was called a forest. They therefore indicate the context in which the story was discussed. The Lebanon-prediction in fact parallels the story in Josephus, as discussed in my *Life of Yoḥanan ben Zakkai* (second edition), pp. 64-5. We have no hint as to who formulated the *beraita* or when it was shaped. This is the sole version in Yoḥanan's name.

4. The story is told that they brought to Rabban Yoḥanan ben Zakkai a dish to taste and to Rabban Gamaliel two dates and a pail of water, and they [both] said, "Bring them up to the Sukkah."

And it was taught [TNY] concerning this passage, "Not because the law is such, but because they wanted to be strict with themselves.

(b. Yoma 79a)

Comment: This citation of the Mishnah (II.i.4) is brought in connection with a saying of Rav Judah, to which this passage comes as an objection. The Tannaitic tradition on the passage, "Not because..." follows. That supplementary comment was possibly added in Tannaitic times and preserved along with the Mishnaic teaching. But I think it more likely that TNY here means that the Tanna of the Amoraic academy in which the Mishnah was under discussion made a further comment concerning the Mishnah when he recited it. It is an interjection, certainly not an integral part of the Mishnaic teaching. No one supposes the Mishnah was much altered after Judah the Prince published it. Alterations were effected by devices such as this. For a further instance of the same phenomenon, see III.ii.30=V.i.8, V.ii.21.

5(a). TNW RBNN: Hillel the Elder had eighty disciples, thirty of whom were worthy [to have] the Divine Spirit rest upon them, as [it did upon] Moses our master, thirty of whom were worthy that the sun should stand still for them [as it did for] Joshua the son of Nun, [and the remaining] twenty were ordinary. The greatest of them was Jonathan b. Uzziel, the smallest [least] of them was Yoḥanan b. Zakkai.

(b) They said of R. Yoḥanan b. Zakkai that he did not leave [unstudied] Scripture, Mishnah, Gemara, *Halakhah*, *Aggada*, details of the Torah, details of the Scribes, inferences *a minori ad majus*, analogies, calendrical computations, *gemaṭrias*, the speech of the Ministering Angels, the speech of spirits, and the speech of palmtrees, fullers' parables and fox fables, great matters or small matters. ("Great matters" mean the *Ma'aseh Merkavah*, "small matters", the discussion of Abbaye and Rava.) In order to fulfill what is said, *That I may cause those that love me to inherit substance, and that I may fill their treasuries.*

(c) And if the smallest [least] of them was so great, how much more so was the greatest?

(d) They said of Jonathan b. Uzziel that when he used to sit and occupy himself with the study of the Torah, every bird that flew above him was immediately burnt.

(b. Suk. 28a, trans. I. W. Slotki, pp. 123-4)

Comment: The section begins with a story about R. Eliezer's visit to Galilee and his emphasis on citing what he heard from his masters. There follows "They said about Rabban Yoḥanan ben Zakkai that he never talked about profane matters... and so did his disciple Eliezer behave after him." Then comes the *beraita* (a) before us about Hillel's disciples, ending with Yoḥanan. Finally comes a second pericope, "They said about Yoḥanan ben Zakkai..." as given here (b), concluding with a blessing of Yoḥanan, "That I may cause...", and followed by (c) the conclusion of the originally independent *beraita* about the Hillelites and an added saying about Jonathan. The original *beraita* obviously consists of (a) and (c). It has been broken up by the praise of Yoḥanan's thorough studies (b), which in its present form clearly comes from the later fourth-century Babylonian schools, and the sayings not introduced as Tannaitic have been added fore and aft.

The *beraita* about Eliezer, followed by a later saying about Yoḥanan and Eliezer must have been formed by descendents of Eliezer's school. To this the compiler of the talmudic passage added the complex a+b+c+d, which he found already extant as a whole, and which suited his purpose here because of its praise of Yoḥanan. But this praise of Yoḥanan was a later insertion to the complex. Its reference to Abbaye and Rava, if original, would point to a fourth-century Pumbedita-Moḥoza origin, but it is probably an explanatory gloss and therefore cannot be used to date the rest. However the rest interrupts the *beraita*, into which it has been inserted, and its reference to the speech of "ministering angels... spirits... trees" looks like a reminiscence of the later, elaborated form of the *Merkavah* story (III.i.4, II.iii.3). Even if it does not refer to that particular passage, it clearly reflects the late, thaumaturgic concept of Yoḥanan as opposed to the earlier mystical and legal one. Before its insertion the *beraita* (a) and (c) was pointedly and openly hostile to Yoḥanan.[1] But it supposed the recognition of Yoḥanan as a great authority of his time, because it used his greatness as a footstool for its hero, Jonathan b. Uzziel. It is therefore the creation of a mystic group in the late Tannaitic period which practiced some new form of speculative technique, distinctly different from the *Merkavah* tradition that went back to Yoḥanan, and which tried to justify itself by appealing to the shadowy ancient Jonathan and by declaring him the greatest of those disciples of Hillel, of whom Yoḥanan was only the least. The sort of stories this group went on to make up about its hero can be seen from specimen (d), now tacked on to the *beraita*. At some stage in the Amoraic tradition, (b) was inserted to remove the suggestion of contempt for Yoḥanan. The resultant complex b+c+d was also used elsewhere (III.ii.23, V.ii.7), and the last three elements appear alone without (b). Not all these passages contain the explanatory gloss about the discussion of Abbaye and Rava, so some would not be very late uses of a pericope, which by the fourth century was already circulating in form sufficiently fluid to be modified or explained.

6. TNW RBNN: There was a family in Jerusalem whose sons died at the age of eighteen. They came and informed Rabban Yoḥanan ben Zakkai. He said to them, "Perhaps you are of the family of Eli, concerning whom it was written, *And I shall cut off your strength and the*

[1] I owe the following analysis to Morton Smith.

strength of your father's house, so that there will not be an old man in your house (I Sam. 3:31). Go and busy yourselves in Torah and live."

They went and busied themselves in Torah and lived, and called that family *Rabban Yoḥanan* in his name.

(b. R.H. 18a)

Comment: The context is a discussion between Abbaye and Rava. Rava explains the teaching of I. Sam. 2:31, "By sacrifice and offering a sin is not atoned for, but by Torah it is atoned for." Abbaye replies, "By sacrifice and offering it is not atoned for, but it is atoned for by study of Torah *and* by doing deeds of lovingkindness." Then we are told that Rabbah and Abbaye were of the house of Eli, the former studied Torah and lived forty years, the latter also did good deeds and lived sixty years. The *beraita* follows. There can be no doubt that the *beraita* was cited by the Babylonian schools of the late fourth century, presumably Rava's in Maḥoza.

The original story relates to pre-70 Jerusalem. We have no idea who framed it, when, or how it was shaped. It reflects classical Pharisaic values, but no tendency of a particular circle or school. We shall note that the Pumbeditan school was responsible for the majority of points in the Babylonian *gemara* at which Yoḥanan's sayings were discussed, alluded to, or otherwise included in the *gemara*. This story obviously was important at Pumbedita, and I cannot think of a reason why it should not have been composed there to begin with. See below, III.ii.14.

7. TNW RBNN: At first they would profane [the Sabbath] for all [New Moons], but when the Temple was destroyed, Rabban Yoḥanan ben Zakkai said to them, "And do we now have a sacrifice [for the new moon, to justify profaning the Sabbath to receive testimony concerning the New Moon's appearance]?"

They decreed that one may not profane [the Sabbath] except for Nisan and Tishré alone.

(b. R.H. 21b)

Comment: The antecedent Mishnah reads, "One may profane the Sabbath [to bring testimony] concerning two months, Nisan and Tishré... and when the Temple was standing, they would profane the Sabbath [to bring testimony] concerning all of them." It is therefore clear that the Mishnah in fact is an anonymous formulation of the view actually put forward by Yoḥanan b. Zakkai in the *beraita* before us. We do not know how this Yavnean ordinance was handed on. The Mishnah, which of course abbreviates, gives only the decree, the *beraita* gives Yoḥanan's argument in its favor and then reports the decree a second time as a decision of Yoḥanan's court. The needless repetition of the decree is explicable as a consequence of insertion of an entire unit from a fixed form.

The *Gemara* is wholly anonymous, and therefore cannot be located in either Palestine or Babylonia or attributed to a particular circle of sages or school.

Compare II.i.8 for further Yavnean ordinances on receiving New Moon witnesses.

8. TNW RBNN: Once New Year fell on a Sabbath, and Rabban Yoḥanan ben Zakkai said to the Bné Bathyra, "Let us sound [the shofar]."

They said to him, "Let us debate."

He said to them, "Let us sound [it], and afterward let us debate."

After they sounded [the shofar], they said to him, "Now let us debate."

He said to them, "The horn has already been heard in Yavneh, and one does not reply [in debate] after an actual deed [= precedent]."

(b. R.H. 29b)

Comment: This *beraita* is a full account of the event referred to in the Mishnah (II.i.6). The Mishnah reports that when the Temple was destroyed, Yoḥanan decreed that the *shofar* might be sounded on a New Year which coincided with the Sabbath "wherever there was a court" or only in Yavneh (as above).

The encounter with the Bné Bathyra may be seen from two perspectives. From that of the Bné Bathyra, it is the story of a scoundrel. But from that of Yoḥanan's friends, it showed how, through cleverness, he overcame the claim of a potentially strong opposition group seeking to join Yavneh's councils. Unless we attribute all stories of Yoḥanan as a wily opponent to Yoḥanan's enemies, we shall have to assume this one derives from circles friendly to him.

But we do not know who they were. None of his immediate disciples plays a role. The passage as it stands refers to, and perhaps comes from, Yavneh.

It would not have been suppressed later on, I imagine, because Gamaliel II had no motive to suppress it. He clearly wanted as little opposition as possible from the sages, none at all from outsiders. Yoḥanan's success with the Bathyrans must have saved Gamaliel the need to struggle with them. What *they* might want to preserve as the record of Yoḥanan himself may not have interested him; what the synod said about Yoḥanan's authority in Yavneh greatly interested him.

Hence hostile stories of priestly origin about Yoḥanan could well be handed on under Gamaliel's auspices. Stories about Yoḥanan's strength, about the exclusion of priests from decision-making processes—these he was especially glad to transmit. This particular story may also have been preserved as an example of the legal principle involved (as well as of the particular ruling). Finally, stories of cleverness are preserved for their own sake (and sometimes invented for it). This is a well-known form of folk literature.

The context in the *gemara* is provided by discussion of the Scriptural origin of the rules about sounding the *shofar* on a New Year that coincides with the Sabbath. R. Levi b. Laḥma in the name of R. Ḥama b. R. Ḥanina offers Scriptural evidence. This is followed by Rava's question, "If Scripture prohibits it, then how was it justifiable in the Temple?" Rava's question is answered by exegeses irrelevant to our passage. The passage ends with Rava's explanation that it Scripturally is permitted, but the rabbis decreed against it. Yoḥanan thus supposedly annulled a rabbinical decree in order to increase the importance of the Yavnean school. Since the Pumbeditans were attempting to enhance the importance of the rabbinical school, it was an important assertion, much like Rava's similar teaching that a rabbinical disciple may allege apostacy to avoid paying unlawful taxes imposed by the exilarch. In both instances, the primacy of the Torah-academy would be asserted —even at the expense of the requirements of the Torah.

9. DTNN: When the Temple was destroyed Rabban Yoḥanan decreed that [eating the new fruit] would be prohibited for the entire Day of Waving.

(b. R.H. 30b)

Comment: R. Naḥman b. Isaac explains the legal theory of Yoḥanan. No other Amora appears in the discussion, the rest of which is anonymous. The context thus is probably late fourth-century Babylonia, presumably Maḥoza. The report of the law, however, is identical with that in the Tannaitic midrashim; see I.ii.6, 7 and comment on I.ii.7.

10. DTNN: When the Temple was destroyed, Rabban Yoḥanan ben Zakkai decreed that they might receive testimony concerning the New Moon all day long.

(b. Beẓ. 5a)

Comment: The context is Rabbah's observation, that since the enactment of Yoḥanan, the egg may be eaten on the second day of a festival. Abbaye said that Rav and Samuel both held the egg was prohibited. Rabbah replied, "I quote R. Yoḥanan b. Zakkai to you, and you tell me about Rav and Samuel!" There can be no doubt of the context: fourth-century Babylonia, probably Rabbah's school at Pumbedita. See II.i.8 for further comment.

11. R. Eliezer said, "Do not doubt your vote. I have a tradition

from Rabban Yoḥanan ben Zakkai who heard it from his master, and his master from his master, as a law to Moses at Sinai, that Ammon and Moab tithe the poor-man's tithe in the seventh year..."

(b. Ḥag. 3b)

Comment: The Mishnah (II.i.23) is here cited in a passage which is otherwise wholly anonymous. See II.i.23 and II.iii.15 for further comment.

12. TNY': R. Yoḥanan b. Zakkai said, "What answer did the *Bat Qol* give to that wicked one, when he said, *I will ascend above the heights of the clouds; I will be like the Most High* (Is. 14:14)?"

A *Bat Qol* went forth and said to him, "O wicked man, son of a wicked man, grandson of Nimrod, the wicked, who stirred the whole world to rebellion against Me by his rule. How many are the years of man? Seventy, for it is said: *The days of our years are three-score years and ten, or even by reason of strength fourscore years* (Ps. 90:10). But the distance from the earth to the firmament is a journey of five hundred years, and the thickness of the firmament is a journey of five hundred years, and likewise [the distance] between one firmament and the other.

"Above them are the holy living creatures: the feet of the living creatures are equal to all of them [together]; the ankles of the living creatures are equal to all of them; the legs of the living creatures are equal to all of them; the knees of the living creatures are equal to all of them; the thighs of the living creatures are equal to all of them; the bodies of the living creatures are equal to all of them; the necks of the living creatures are equal to all of them; the heads of the living creatures are equal to all of them; the horns of the living creatures are equal to all of them.

"Above them is the throne of glory; the feet of the throne of glory are equal to all of them; the throne of glory is equal to all of them. The King, the Living and Eternal God, High and Exalted, dwelleth above them.

"Yet thou didst say, *I will ascend above the heights of the clouds, I will be like the Most High!* Nay, *thou shalt be brought down to the nether-world, to the uttermost parts of the pit* (Is. 14:14)."

(b. Ḥag. 13a, trans. I. Abrahams, pp. 73-75)

Comment: The discussion of the firmaments includes a number of *beraitot* on the subject. Intervening are sayings of R. Simeon b. Laqish and R. Levi on the importance of study of Torah, but these sayings have nothing to do with the dominant theme. There follows a long anonymous discussion about heavenly creatures, ending in a saying of R. Aḥa b. Jacob that there is another heaven above the heads of the *ḥayyot*; finally comes a warning not to discuss such matters, derived from Ben Sira 3:21-2. Yoḥanan's *beraita* is thus loosely connected, if at all, with the material preceding it. A Mishnah-citation follows.

This saying, possibly in the *Shi'ur Qomah* tradition, thus stands entirely by itself, both without parallels elsewhere and unrelated to the material with which it is collected. We have no idea when or where it was first given its current shape. Since the story concerns a mystical tradition on the dimensions of God, we may suppose it somehow relates to the *Merkavah*-traditions as well. But that relationship, if any, is completely submerged, and there is no hint at what disciple learned this material and handed it on.

13. TNW RBNN: (a) Once R. Yoḥanan b. Zakkai was riding on an ass when going on a journey, and R. Eleazar b. 'Arakh was driving the ass from behind.

[R. Eleazar] said to him, "Master, teach me a chapter of the 'Work of the Chariot.' "

He answered: "Have I not taught you thus: *Nor [the work of] the chariot in the presence of one, unless he is a Sage and understands of his own knowledge?*"

[R. Eleazar] then said to him, "Master, permit me to say before thee something which thou hast taught me."

He answered, "Say on!"

Forthwith R. Yoḥanan b. Zakkai dismounted from the ass, and wrapped himself up, and sat upon a stone beneath an olive tree.

Said [R. Eleazar] to him: "Master, wherefore didst thou dismount from the ass?"

He answered, "Is it proper that whilst thou art expounding the 'Work of the Chariot,' and the Divine Presence is with us, and the ministering angels accompany us, I should ride on the ass!"

(b) Forthwith, R. Eleazar b. 'Arakh began his exposition of the 'Work of the Chariot', and fire came down from heaven and encompassed all the trees in the field; [thereupon] they all began to utter [divine] song. What was the song they uttered?—*Praise the Lord from the earth, ye sea-monsters, and all deeps... fruitful trees and all cedars... Hallelujah* (Ps. 147:7,9,14).

An angel [then] answered from the fire and said, "This is the very 'Work of the Chariot.'"

(c) R. Yoḥanan b. Zakkai rose and kissed him on his head and said, "Blessed be the Lord God of Israel, Who hath given a son to Abraham our father, who knoweth to speculate upon, and to investigate, and to expound the 'Work of the Chariot.' There are some who preach well but do not act well, others act well but do not preach well, but thou dost preach well and act well.

"Happy art thou, O Abraham our father, that R. Eleazar b. ʿArakh hath come forth from thy loins."

(d) Now when these things were told R. Joshua, he and R. Yosi the priest were going on a journey.

They said, "Let us also expound the 'Work of the Chariot.'"

R. Joshua began an exposition.

Now that day was the summer solstice. The heavens became overcast with clouds, and a kind of rainbow appeared in the cloud, and the ministering angels assembled and came to listen like people who assemble and come to watch the entertainments of a bridegroom and bride.

(e) R. Yosi the priest went and related what happened before R. Yoḥanan b. Zakkai, and [the latter] said, "Happy are ye, and happy is she that bore you; happy are my eyes that have seen thus. Moreover, in my dream, I and ye were reclining on Mount Sinai, when a *Bat Qol* was sent to us, [saying], 'Ascend hither, ascend hither! [Here are] great banqueting chambers, and fine dining couches prepared for you; you and your disciples and your disciples' disciples are designated for the third heaven.'"

(f) But is this so? For behold it is taught: R. Yosi b. R. Judah said, "There were three discourses: R. Joshua discoursed before R. Yoḥanan b. Zakkai, R. ʿAqiva discoursed before R. Joshua, Ḥanania b. Ḥakinai discoursed before R. ʿAqiva;"—whereas R. Eleazar b. ʿArakh he does not count!—One who discoursed [himself], and others discoursed before him, he counts; one who discoursed [himself], but others did not discourse before him, he does not count.

But behold there is Ḥananiah b. Ḥakinai before whom others did not discourse, yet he counts him!—He at least discoursed before one who discoursed [before others].

(b. Ḥag. 14b, trans. I Abrahams, pp. 88-90)

Comment: The pericope stands as a comment on the Mishnaic teaching cited in its midst. It is related in theme to other materials in the same section, mainly discussions of Ezekiel's vision. Immediately preceding, however, is a saying about the destruction of Jerusalem, and in fact there is no direct connection between the *Merkavah-beraita* and the foregoing material. There follows the Tannaitic story (TNW RBNN) of the four who entered Paradise. The context therefore is a disconnected set of sayings pertinent in some way to mystical visions of God. The usual careful, dialectical argument is utterly absent (except at the end). It is a collection of *beraitot*, not a *gemara* in the usual sense. It could indeed have been put together in pretty much its present form in Tannaitic times, and then included by Talmudic editors as a complete and final Tannaitic tradition. If so, it was shaped in the Aqiban schools, where 'Aqiva's prowess in mystical speculation and mystical experience was celebrated.

The story is in many details dependent upon, but an expansion of, the earlier *Merkavah*-account, with the striking additions of units (e) and (f). Part (e) is only a picturesque piece of late speculation on the rewards of the saints, but (f) shows that there were people anxious to discredit Eleazar and therefore persons claiming their practices derived from him. The attack is based on the alleged lack of any tradition about his disciples.

The *beraita* as a whole is thus a composite, indeed a kind of *Merkavah*-encyclopaedia.

14. TNW RBNN: There was a certain family in Jerusalem whose sons would die at the age of eighteen. They came and told Rabban Yoḥanan ben Zakkai. He said to them, "Perhaps you are of the family of Eli, as it is said (I Sam. 3:31) *And your strength and the strength of your father's house shall I cut off, so that there will not be an old man in your house.* Go and busy yourselves in Torah and live."

They went and busied themselves in Torah and lived, and called that family *Yoḥanan* in his name.

(b. Yev. 105a)

Comment: See above, III.ii.6. The context here is identical to III.ii.6. Abbaye and Rabbah discuss expiation of sin through Torah and/or lovingkindness; Rabbah lived forty years, Abbaye sixty. The passage is introduced as a commentary on I. Sam. 3:14, following an allusion to that Scripture on the part of R. Samuel b. Ammi. It seems to me likely, therefore, that the Amoraic discussion of Rabbah and Abbaye and the *beraita* concerning Yoḥanan were conjoined in the second half of the fourth century as a single unit of tradition, then used in the two separate passages as pertinent.

15. TNY: Rabban Gamaliel said to them, "We should accept your testimony, but what shall we do, for Rabban Yoḥanan ben Zakkai decreed not to call a court into session on this matter, for the priests listen to you to drive away but not to bring near."

(b. Ket. 14a)

Comment: Abbaye and Rava discuss the opinion of R. Joshua as revealed in this teaching. The context is therefore the middle of the fourth-century, in Pumbedita. See II.i.16 for further comment.

16. It once happened that R. Yoḥanan b. Zakkai left Jerusalem riding upon an ass, while his disciples followed him, and he saw a girl picking barley grains in the dung of Arab cattle. As soon as she saw him she wrapped herself with her hair and stood before him.

"Master," she said to him, "feed me."

"My daughter," he asked her, "who are you?"

"I am," she replied, "the daughter of Naqdimon b. Gorion."

"My daughter," he said to her, "what has become of the wealth of your father's house?"

"Master," she answered him, "is there not a proverb current in Jerusalem: *The salt of money is diminution?*" (Others read: Benevolence.)

"And where [the Master asked] is the wealth of your father-in-law's house?"

"The one," she replied, "came and destroyed the other."

"Do you remember, Master," she said to him, "when you signed my *ketuvah?*"

"I remember," he said to his disciples, "that when I signed the *ketuvah* of this [woman], I read therein 'A million gold denarii from her father's house besides [the amount] from her father-in-law's house.' "

Thereupon R. Yoḥanan b. Zakkai wept and said, "How happy are Israel. When they do the will of the Omnipresent no nation nor any language-speaking group has any power over them; but when they do not do the will of the Omnipresent, he delivers them into the hands of a low people, and not only in the hands of a low people but into the power of the beasts of a low people."

(b. Ket. 66b, trans. I. W. Slotki, p. 405)

Comment: The story, already familiar from I.i.1, I.i.7, is here embellished with more dramatic dialogue and the detail about the danger of miserliness to the wealth of a cheapskate. It otherwise is close to I.i.7.

The context is sayings by R. Ashi about the prescribed allowances owing to a wife. There follows R. Judah's saying in the name of Rav that Naqdimon b. Gurion granted his wife four hundred gold coins for her perfume basket. Then comes this *beraita*, followed by further discussion about Naqdimon's charity, all anonymous; then a *beraita* of Eleazar b. R. Ẓadoq about that same "daughter," this time barley grains among the horses' hoofs at Akko. Afterward, the subject changes. Thus the subject of Naqdimon's daughter is introduced by Rav Judah in the name of Rav, and the collection of *beraitot* pertinent to her was probably made in the early part of the fourth century, in Pumbedita.

It was afterward introduced by R. Ashi's discussion of the pertinent Mishnah to which it was originally attached.

17. R. Dosa b. Harkinus said, "R. Yoḥanan ben Zakkai said [it according to your opinion], 'Well has Ḥanan spoken. He placed his coins on the horn of a deer!' "

(b. Ned. 33b)

Comment: The citation of the Mishnah comes in the context of a discussion of Ḥanan's views by R. Hoshaia and Rava. The following discussion then analyzes the views of Rava and R. Hoshaia, but is of Saboraic origin. Rava comes somewhat later than R. Hoshaia, a Palestinian, so presumably he was offering a comment on R. Hoshaia's comment on the Mishnah. The rest then derives from Rava's school, middle-fourth-century Pumbedita-Maḥoza.

18. Rabban Yoḥanan ben Zakkai would expound this Scripture in the manner of a *ḥomer*, "Why was the ear different from all the limbs in the body? The Holy One blessed be he said, 'The ear heard my voice on Mount Sinai when I said, *For to me are the children of Israel slaves* (Lev. 25:55) and not slaves to slaves, and yet this one went and acquired for itself a master, [therefore] let it be pierced!' "

(b. Qid. 22b)

Comment: In II.iii.8d, Lev. 25:55 is cited; in I.i.3, Ex. 20:13 is cited. This version is therefore akin to the Toseftan one, using Lev. 25:55. But it is an independent tradition. Not only does it omit the lemma (Ex. 21:3) given in II.iii.8d—this might be explained as mere abbreviation—but it phrases the introductory question differently, and shows a different exegesis of the basic proof text. In II.iii.8d, the thought is that the Israelite sinned by exchanging the yoke of God for that of men. Here his sin is disregard of his divine election, which destined him to be a slave (of God) but not the slave of a slave (man). Both interpretations are potentially revolutionary, the latter, with its description of gentiles as slaves, expecially so; both therefore are presumably Aqiban revisions of Yoḥanan's original saying (see II.iii.8d).

The context is a string of *beraitot* on the laws (Ex. 21, Lev. 25 and elsewhere) on treating slaves. No Amoraic authorities play a part in the passage, which is, as above, not really *gemara* at all, but a Tannaitic collection inserted into the *gemara* without modification, comment, or legal discussion.

19(a). His disciples asked Rabban Yoḥanan ben Zakkai, "Why did the Torah deal more stringently with the thief than the robber?"

He said to them, "This one equated the honor of the slave to the honor of his owner, but that one did not equate the honor of the slave to the honor of his owner [but held the slave's honor higher].

(b) "He [the thief] acted as though the eye which is below does not see, and the ear which is below does not hear.

"So it is said, *Woe unto those who go deep to hide their counsel from the Lord* (Is. 29:15) and it is written (Ps. 94:7) *The Lord will not see*, and it is written (Ezek. 9:9), *For they say, 'The Lord hath forsaken the earth and the Lord seeth not.'* "

(c) R. Yoḥanan ben Zakkai said, "See how great is the importance attached to the dignity of man. In the case of an ox, which walks away on its own feet, the payment is five-fold, but the sheep, which the thief had to carry on his shoulder, requires a four-fold indemnity."

(b. B.Q. 79b)

Comment: The context is a collection of Tannaitic sayings about thieves, the dignity of labor, respect for royalty (divinity), and the like. Immediately following is a Mishnah. The first preceding remark which is pertinent to Yoḥanan's is R. Yoḥanan's and R. Abbahu's definition of a robber, based on II Sam. 23:21 and Jud. 9:25. Then comes "His disciples asked..." If the collection was originally Palestinian, we have no way of knowing when or how it reached Babylonia, or in what school it was originally related to Amoraic discussions.

The sayings are familiar, deceptively so. III.ii.19a presents as a story what I.i.5(a) presents as exegesis. It omits the essential rule which stands as the beginning of III.ii.19 and preserves only the explanation. The wording and structure of the explanations differ in the two texts—evidently we have here records of independent traditions concerning the same saying. This may be true even of II.iii.19b, by comparison with I.i.5b, though here the differences are only in the connective formulae used. III.ii.19c, which here follows above, while in I.i.4 it precedes, has also minor differences of wording, but substantial identity of content. See also II.iii.7 and the comments there.

20. (a) *TNY'*: Rabban Yoḥanan b. Zakkai said to his disciples: "My sons, what is the meaning of the verse, *Righteousness exalteth a nation, but the kindness of the peoples is sin* (Prov. 14:34)."

(b) R. Eliezer answered and said: "*Righteousness exalteth a nation*:" this refers to Israel of whom it is written, *Who is like thy people Israel, one nation in the earth* (II Sam. 7:23)? *But the kindness of the peoples is sin*: all the charity and kindness done by the heathen is counted to them as sin, because they only do it to magnify themselves, as it says, *That they may offer sacrifices of sweet savour unto the God of heaven, and pray for the life of the king and his sons* (Ezra 6:10)."

(c) But is not an act of this kind charity in the full sense of the word, seeing that it has been taught: "If a man says,—I give this *sela* for charity in order that my sons may live and that I may be found worthy of the future world, he may all the same be a righteous man in the full sense of the word?"—There is no contradiction; in the one case we speak of an Israelite, in the other of a heathen.

(d) R. Joshua answered and said: "*Righteousness exalteth a nation*: this refers to Israel of whom it is written, *Who is like thy people Israel, one nation in the earth? The kindness of peoples is sin*: all the charity and kindness that the heathen do is counted sin to them, because they only do it in order that their dominion may be prolonged, as it says, *Wherefore O king, let my counsel be acceptable to thee, and break off thy sins by righteousness, and thy iniquities by showing mercy to the poor, if there may be a lengthening of thy tranquillity* (Dan. 4:27)."

(e) Rabban Gamaliel answered, saying: "*Righteousness exalteth a nation*: this refers to Israel of whom it is written, *Who is like thy people Israel* etc. *And the kindness of the peoples is sin*: all the charity and kindness that the heathen do is counted as sin to them, because they only do it to display haughtiness, and whoever displays haughtiness is cast into Gehinnom, as it says, *The proud and haughty man, scorner is his name, he worketh in the wrath of pride* (Prov. 21:24), and *wrath* connotes *Gehinnom*, as it is written, *A day of wrath is that day* (Zeph. 1:15)."

(f) Said Rabban Gamaliel: "We have still to hear the opinion of the Modiite."

(g) R. Eliezer the Modiite says: "*Righteousness exalteth a nation*: this refers to Israel of whom it is written, *Who is like thy people Israel, one nation in the earth. The kindness of the peoples is sin*: all the charity and kindness of the heathen is counted to them as sin, since they do it only to reproach us, as it says, *The Lord hath brought it and done according as he spake, because ye have sinned against the Lord and have not obeyed his voice, therefore this thing is come upon you.*"

(h) R. Neḥuniah b. HaQaneh answered saying: "*Righteousness exalteth a nation, and there is kindness for Israel and sin for the peoples.*"

(i) Said R. Yoḥanan b. Zakkai to his disciples: "The answer of R. Neḥuniah b. HaQaneh is superior to my answer and to yours, because he assigns charity and kindness to Israel and sin to the heathen."

(j) This seems to show that he also gave an answer; what was it?

(k) As it has been taught (DTNY'): R. Yoḥanan b. Zakkai said to them: "Just as the sin-offering makes atonement for Israel, so charity makes atonement for the heathen."

(b. B.B. 10b, trans. M. Simon, pp. 50-51)

Comment: This is a thoroughly garbled *beraita*, for reasons given in my *Life*, 2nd ed., pp. 246-249.

The context is a long series of sayings about proper forms of charity, predominately *beraitot* of R. Meir, a story about R. 'Aqiva, R. Judah b. R. Shalom citing a story about Yoḥanan (below, p. 152); R. Papa's foot slipped and he was endangered, thus he realized he might have neglected to give charity; then a *beraita* concerning Eliezer b. R. Yosi; R. Judah b. Ilai; R. Dosethai b. R. Yannai. Several sayings by R. Abbahu on charity, with a reference to the martyrs of the Roman suppression of Bar Kokhba's war, followed by the *beraita* cited here, complete the passage.

But who shaped the materials as we now have them is not at all clear to me. Immediately following is the story of Ifra Hormiz's gift of four hundred dinarii to R. Ammi, then to Rava, then *beraitot* about other charitable individuals. The context is clear, therefore: charity and martyrdom.

The basic element here is III.ii.20k, Yoḥanan's saying which served as a basis for his cooperation with the Romans.[1] This was of course unacceptable to the Aqibans and those who carried on the Aqiban tradition of uncompromising hostility to the gentiles and utter condemnation of them. Therefore they invented a framework (III.ii.20a-j), modeled on II.i.18-19, which would make Yoḥanan confess that his own saying was inferior to one which contradicted it. Whether or not they had any genuine sayings of Yoḥanan's pupils to serve their purposes is a question the present text does not suffice to answer. At all events they had four exegeses of Prov. 14:34 explaining that the kindness of the gentiles is sin, because they do it for a bad purpose, and they assigned the first two of these (III.ii.20b-d) to Eliezer and Joshua, following the pattern of II.i.18f. III.ii.20c is a late gloss which interrupts the

[1] Morton Smith contributed the following analysis.

completed form. Then they left the pattern and assigned the third (III. ii.20e) to Rabban Gamaliel II in order to contradict stories of his cooperation with the Romans and make him appear a supporter of their side (which he certainly was not). To give an appearance of veracity to this attribution, they attached to it III.ii.20f, a cliché in which Rabban Gamaliel asks the advice of Eliezer the Modiite, and attributed the fourth of their exegeses to this Eliezer (III.ii.20f). All these exegeses, however, were unsatisfactory to them because by "explaining" why "the kindness of gentiles is sin" they admitted its existence. Therefore they preferred the exegesis attributed to Neḥuniah b. HaQaneh, and probably attributed correctly since he is an obscure figure who does little to attract a false attribution, III.ii.20h. This exegesis attributes both the righteousness and the kindness of Prov. 14:34 to Israel and leaves only the sin to the gentiles. That this is an absurd misreading of the text did not, of course, disturb anyone in the least. So it was this exegesis that Yoḥanan was made to declare best of all, III.ii.20i! This misrepresentation of Gamaliel II shows that the main structure cannot be earlier than ca. 130; the use of the model now in II.i.18 and the neglect of most of Yoḥanan's traditional students suggest a date considerably later, perhaps ca. 180. It should not be too late because the motives of the Aqiban school and the desire to have Yoḥanan and Gamaliel II as sponsors are still dominant. About 150 is likely for the whole construction; it is one of the many pieces which show the survival of the resolutely anti-Roman exegesis through the generations after Bar Kokhba, in spite of the official policy of reconciliation practiced by the restored patriarchate. The gloss (c) will of course be still later.

21. TNW RBNN: The strike may not be made thick on one side and thin on the other. One may not strike with a single quick movement, for striking in this manner causes loss to the seller and benefits the buyer. Nor may one strike very slowly, because [this] is disadvantageous to the buyer and beneficial for the seller. Concerning all these [sharp practices of traders], R. Yoḥanan b. Zakkai said, "Woe to me if I should speak [of them], knaves might learn [them]; and should I not speak, the knaves might say, 'the scholars are unacquainted with our practices' [and will deceive us still more]."

(b. B.B. 89b, trans. I. W. Slotki, p. 368)

Comment: The Mishnah concerns weights and measures. Several anonymous *beraitot* are cited about weights, balances, and so on. Immediately following this passage, R. Samuel b. R. Isaac says that Yoḥanan actually did decide to speak of them, basing his decision on Hos. 14:10, *For the ways of the Lord are right and the just do walk in them, but transgressors stumble therein.* At the very least, therefore, we may be sure the *beraita* was subjected to discussion in the circle of R. Samuel b. R. Isaac. For further comment, see II.i.22, III.iii.10.

22(a). R. Huna said in the name of Rab, "Anyone, even a prince in Israel, who says that a daughter is to inherit with the daughter of the son, must not be obeyed; for such [a ruling] is only the practice of the Sadducees."

(b) DTNN: On the twenty-fourth of Ṭevet we returned to our [own] law; for the Sadducees having maintained [that] a daughter inherited with the daughter of the son, R. Yoḥanan b. Zakkai joined issue with them.

(c) He said to them, "Fools, whence do you derive this?"

And there was no one who could say a word in reply, except one old man who prated at him and said, "If the daughter of his son, who succeeds [to an inheritance] by virtue of his son's right, is heir to him, how much more so his daughter who derives her right from himself!"

He read for him this verse, "*These are the sons of Seir the Horite, the inhabitants of the land: Lotan and Shobal and Zibeon and Anah* (Gen. 36:20) and [lower down] it is written, *And these are the children of Zibeon: Aiah and Anah!*"

(d) But this teaches that Zibeon had intercourse with his mother and begat Anah. Is it not possible that there were two [called] Anah? Rabbah said: I would say something which King Shapur [could] not have said;—and who is he?—Samuel; others say [that it was] R. Papa [who] said: I would say something which King Shapur [could] not have said—and who is he?—Rava. "Scripture says: *This is Anah*, [implying]: The same Anah that was [mentioned] before."

(e) He said unto him, "O, master, do you dismiss me with such [a feeble reply]?"

He said to him, "Fool, shall not our perfect Torah be as [convincing] as your idle talk! [Your deduction is fallacious for] the reason why a son's daughter [has a right of inheritance is] that her claim is valid when there are brothers, but can the same be said of the [deceased's] daughter whose right [of inheritance] is impaired when there are brothers?"

(f) Thus they were defeated. And that day was declared a festive day.

(b. B.B. 115b-116a, trans. I. W. Slotki, pp. 475-6)

Comment: The context is a Mishnah on inheritance law. The *gemara* opens with a *beraita* discussed by Abbaye. Then this passage follows, with the interjections by Rabbah, R. Papa, Rava. It is clear that the *beraita* has been subjected to close discussion in fourth-century Babylonia, with the comments being added in the schools of Pumbedita (Abbaye, Rava, Rabbah) and then Nersh (R. Papa).

The Sadducean-dispute stories derive from a time when the party could be credibly described as consisting of a few bumbling old men, hence late in the second century at the earliest. Otherwise it is a deliberate misrepresentation, indeed a fraud, and while misrepresentations are not uncommon, I think it likely that the framers of the *beraita* here described matters as they saw them, hence anachronistically attributing the conditions of the later day to an earlier time no longer actually known to them. In other words, the account of the dispute as it now stands is a late composition with a yet later insertion (d). The original tradition was probably (b)+(f), which would report a dispute in the Yavneh period, a time when the Pharisaic law could have prevailed and a public celebration of the victory been decreed—both matters practically incredible before 70. If this interpretation is correct, the record is of some importance as indicating an attempt by Yoḥanan to enlist even Sadducean support for the Yavnean institution; had it been an exclusively Pharisaic project there would have been no reason to dispute with Sadducees, nor would a "victory"—if such a dispute had occurred—have been a matter for any surprise or celebration. But if there was an attempt to make it a national legal assembly, and serious discussions with some Sadducees took place, with both sides bound to abide by the results, then celebration of a Pharisaic victory on an important point would be understandable.

The report (b+f) has now been expanded by insertion of the pseudo-dramatic dialogue (c+e). This dialogue is quite out of touch with the original situation. No one discusses in such fashion—and it probably dates, as argued above, from the late second century. At most it may be based on a correct tradition as to the arguments and proof texts used on both sides. The last step was insertion of the gloss (d), which may provide a terminus ante quem for the rest of the structure.

23. TNW RBNN: Hillel the Elder had eighty disciples. Thirty of them deserved that the divine presence shall rest upon them as [upon] Moses our teacher. Thirty of them deserved that the sun shall stand [still] for them as [for] Joshua the son of Nun. Twenty were of an average character. The greatest of them was Jonathan b. Uzziel; the least of them was R. Yoḥanan b. Zakkai...

(b. B.B. 134a, trans. I. W. Slotki, p. 563)

Comment: Earlier (III.ii.5), I included the whole Amoraic discussion of the *beraita*. Here the materials are no different. The *beraita* is split by the "It was said of Yoḥanan...", with the late fourth century interjections, then concludes with "It was told of Jonathan b. Uzziel," as above. The context is stories about Jonathan b. Uzziel. I do not know how the whole passage was shaped. I think it is clear, though, that the late fourth-century masters after Abbaye and Rava, presumably in Pumbedita-Maḥoza, discussed the passage and were responsible for its current form.

24(a). TNW RBNN: *Justice, justice shalt thou follow* (Deut. 16:20). Seek a good court, [such as] the court of Rabbi Eliezer in Lud, the court of Rabban Yoḥanan ben Zakkai in Beror Ḥayil.

(b) TNW RBNN: *Justice, justice shalt thou follow* (Deut. 16: 20). Follow the scholars to their academies: R. Eliezer to Lud, R. Yoḥanan b. Zakkai to Beror Ḥayil, R. Joshua to Peqiʿin, Rabban Gamaliel to Yavneh, R. ʿAqiva to Bené Beraq, R. Matthew to Rome, R. Ḥananiah b. Teradion to Sikhnin, R. Yosi b. Ḥalafta to Sepphoris, R. Judah b. Bathyra to Nisibis, R. [Ḥananiah nephew of] R. Joshua to the Exile, Rabbi [Judah the Prince] to Bet Sheʿarim, the Sages to the Chamber of the Hewn Stones.

(b. Sanh. 32b)

Comment: See I.ii.8, where III.ii.24a appears in identical form. The context is a set of *beraitot* on Deut. 16:20. Preceding Amoraic authorities discussing the topical Mishnah are Rava, R. Papa, and R. Ashi. Opinions of R. Simeon b. Laqish are cited.

III.ii.24a clearly derives from Eliezer's school, and must be included in the corpus of Eliezer-Yoḥanan stories. That it sends Yoḥanan to Beror Hayil and says nothing of the court in Yavneh—which certainly continued to exist after Yoḥanan went to Beror Ḥayil!—indicates that it came from Eliezer's school at a time when the relations with Yavneh were bad and the school was emphasizing the double use of "justice" in Deut. 16:20 and the use of follow (pursue) there as indications that justice was not to be found in the one central court but must be sought in the two courts of the great scholars who had separated themselves from Yavneh, and whom the lovers of justice should pursue. III.ii.24b deliberately misunderstands this by making III.ii.24a merely the beginning of a list of great scholars who had courts in various places, and leading the list back to the central court of the Hillelite house under Rabbi [Judah the Prince]. Therefore this *beraita* must have been framed after the turn of the third century, as an expansion and correction of the preceding. The author, unknown, was certainly an adherent of the patriarchal court.

25. TNYʾ: The story is told that Rabban Yoḥanan ben Zakkai inquired [in a murder trial] concerning the stems of the figs.

(b. Sanh. 41a)

Comment: The discussion begins with a saying of R. Joseph replying to a statement by Rammi b. Ḥama. Once "Ben Zakkai" is mentioned the (anonymous) editor proceeds to discuss the question of how Yoḥanan ben Zakkai could have been called "ben Zakkai"; identical *beraitot*, except that in each, Yoḥanan is called by a different name, are cited. Since the "Ben Zakkai" materials are cited in connection with R. Joseph's citation of "Ben Zakkai's" opinion, we may assign this discussion to R. Joseph's school, early fourth-century Pumbedita.

For further comment, see II.i.15. Here the Mishnaic form has been "corrected" by insertion of "Rabban Yoḥanan" to show proper respect to the master. It therefore comes later than II.i.15. If the editors of the Mishnah had known this form, they would certainly not have preferred the disrespectful one.

26. TNW RBNN: *When a prince sins* (Lev. 4:22). Rabban Yoḥanan ben Zakkai said, "Happy is the generation whose prince brings a sacrifice for his unwitting sin."

(b. Hor. 10b)

Comment: Immediately following, Rabbah disputes the interpretation of Yoḥanan. We may take it for granted, then, that he discussed Yoḥanan's *beraita*, and assign the context to mid-fourth-century Babylonia, presumably Pumbedita-Maḥoza. For further comment, see I.ii.3, II.iii. 8c, III.i.6.

27. Thereupon R. Mordecai said to R. Ashi, "Thus said R. Shisha the son of R. Idi, 'It had to be stated only according to Ben Bukhri's view, DTNN:' " R. Judah said, "Ben Bukhri testified at Yavneh that a priest who paid the *sheqel* has committed no sin."

Rabban Yoḥanan b. Zakkai said to him, "Not so, but rather a priest who did not pay the *sheqel* has committed a sin. The priests, however, used to expound the following verse to their advantage, *And every meal-offering of the priest shall be wholly burnt; it shall not be eaten* (Lev. 6:16) since the *'Omer*-offering and the Two Loaves and the Showbread are ours, how can they be eaten?"

(b. Men. 21b, trans. Eli Cashdan, pp. 139-40)

Comment: The context is perfectly clear. Rabina, R. Ashi and R. Mordecai discuss who supplies the salt for the meal-offering. The citation of Ben Bukhri's argument with Yoḥanan therefore takes place in Sura at the start of the fifth century. For further comment, see II.i.3.

28. Rabbah said, Whence do I arrive at this view? Because we have learnt (TNN): R. Judah said, "Ben Bukhri testified at Jabneh that a priest who paid the *sheqel* has committed no sin."

Rabban Yoḥanan b. Zakkai said to him, "Not so, but rather a priest who did not pay the *sheqel* has committed a sin. The priests, however, used to expound the following verse to their advantage, *And every meal-offering of the priest shall be wholly burnt, it shall not be eaten* (Lev. 6:16). Since the *ʿOmer*-offering and the Two Loaves and the Showbread are ours, how can they be eaten?"

(b. Men. 46b, trans. Eli Cashdan, p. 281)

Comment: The context now is Rabbah's citation of the Ben Bukhri dispute. Abbaye, R. Joseph, and Rabbah participate in the subsequent discussion. The citation therefore is by late fourth-century Pumbeditan-Maḥozan tradents.

29. All may evaluate, even priests, Levites and Israelites. But that is self-evident?—Rabbah said: This is necessary in view of the opinion of Ben Bukhri, DTNN: R. Judah said, "Ben Bukhri testified at Yavneh that any priest who paid the *sheqel* does not thereby commit a sin."

R. Yoḥanan b. Zakkai said to him, "Not so! But a priest who does not pay the *sheqel* commits a sin. The priests, however, used to explain the following verse to their advantage: *And every meal-offering of the priest shall be wholly made to smoke; it shall not be eaten* (Lev. 6:16). Now, [they argued] since the *ʿOmer* and the two loaves and the showbread are ours, how could they be eaten?"

(b. ʿArakh. 4a, trans. Leo Jung, pp. 14-15)

Comment: The law here is different, the masters the same. Here the issue concerns the Mishnaic teaching that all may evaluate objects devoted to the Temple, priests, Levites, and Israelites. Rabbah argues that the law is not self-evident, citing III.ii.29 as given. Abbaye and Rava participate in the subsequent discussion. The citation is therefore by late fourth-century Pumbeditan-Maḥozan masters.

30. TNY: A convert who converts in this time [after the destruction of the Temple] must bring his bird offering, a quarter of silver. R. Simeon said, "Rabban Yoḥanan ben Zakkai annuled [the requirement] because of [the possibility of] disorder."

(b. Ker. 9a)

Comment: See V.i.8, V.ii.21. I am not certain that the *beraita* consisted of more than the opening phrase, with the saying of R. Simeon appended later on. I therefore have listed the material a second time in the Amoraic collections, though one might well suppose it belongs to the Tannaitic ones, for a Tanna here refers to a decision of Yoḥanan.

III. General Comments

The Palestinian Talmudic traditions attributed to Tannaim in every case have parallels in the Tosefta, in four of six instances in the Babylonian *beraitot* as well, but in only one instance in the Mishnah (Day of Waving). The analogical exegeses, well known to us in Tannaitic midrashim, recur, along with the *Merkavah*-vision. The story about Joshua and the villagers is already known. So in fact the Palestinian Talmudic traditions of Tannaitic origin contain absolutely nothing we have not already seen; they contribute only to the perpetuation, not to the development of the Yoḥanan-legend.

The Babylonian *beraitot* are entirely another matter. Numerous *beraitot* are new, unparalleled (III.ii.1,2,3,5,6,7,12,14,20,22,23,24); further *beraitot* constitute quite different versions of Mishnaic laws (e.g. III.ii.8; III.ii.25; II.i.6; III.i.15). The new information includes the death scene, the story of Ḥanina ben Dosa's healing powers, the ominous opening of the Temple doors, the story about Hillel's disciples, the family who died young until Yoḥanan told them what to do, exegeses on "Righteousness exalteth a nation," and "I will ascend." The Sadducean dispute about the inheritance of the daughters is added to the tradition. Praise of the righteousness of Yoḥanan's court in Beror Ḥayil first occurs here.

In all, the legend of Yoḥanan is greatly augmented by the Babylonian *beraitot*. His relationship to Hillel is reemphasized, presumably as a criticism of hereditary Davidic rulers. His control of the Temple is given new dimensions. His exegeses are enriched by allusion to his opinion of the Romans—something we have not heard before—and his struggles with the Sadducees, mentioned in the Mishnah and Tosefta, are further enhanced.

Mishnaic teachings recurring in Amoraic discussions include Yoḥanan's and Gamaliel's meal in the Sukkah; blowing the *shofar* on the New Year that coincides with the Sabbath; receiving New Moon testimony all day long; the priests hearken too little to allow us to set up courts to rule on their marriages; the judges of civil law rule with Yoḥanan's approval; and the dispute with Ben Bukhri about the priests' *sheqel*. A further version of the "Woe" saying occurs.

In common with the Tosefta, the Palestinian Talmud, but not the Mishnah, are the *Merkavah*-traditions, as well as several analogical exegeses. The Yoḥanan of the Babylonian Talmud thus constitutes not only a resume of almost all earlier themes, but also a far fuller, more detailed portrait.

The Amoraim who cite, or are quoted in the context of citations of, Yoḥanan are mainly Pumbeditans of the third (Rav Judah) and fourth centuries (Rabbah, R. Joseph, Abbaye, Rava) and their disciples and successors at Maḥoza and Nersh (R. Naḥman b. Isaac, R. Papa). R. Ashi, of fifth century Sura, is further involved in two sayings. Thus of the twenty-two identifiable contexts in which Yoḥanan-Tannaitic-traditions occur, sixteen are from third and fourth century Pumbedita and related schools, two from fifth century Sura. To put it negatively, third century Babylonian Amoraim seem *never* to have discussed Tannaitic traditions about Yoḥanan ben Zakkai. Interest in Yoḥanan-traditions was concentrated in Pumbedita in the years of its independence from the exilarch, that is, from 295 to ca. 350, the times of Rav Judah, Rabbah, Abbaye, and the first part of Rava's rule, until the school was moved by the exilarch to Maḥoza, the exilarch's capital. During that half-century, Pumbedita sought its own funds and tried to keep clear of exilarchic interference. Further comments on this striking fact must await consideration of Palestinian and Babylonian Amoraic traditions on Yoḥanan.

Table

Palestinian Talmudic Traditions attributed to Tannaim

Pal. Tal.	*Tan. Mid.*	*Mishnah*	*Tosefta*	*Bab. Tal.*
III.i.1 (Joshua, tithing)	—	—	II.iii.1	—
III.i.2 (Joshua, tithing)	—	—	II.iii.1	—
III.i.3 (Day of Waving)	I.ii.6, 7	II.i.5b, 7a, 7b, 20	II.iii.9	III.ii.8
III.i.4 (*Merkavah*)	I.ii.2	—	II.iii.3	III.ii.13
III.i.5 (Slave's ear)	I.i.3	—	II.iii.8d	III.ii.18
III.i.6 (Prince sins)	I.ii.3	—	II.iii.8c	III.ii.26

Table

Babylonian Talmudic Traditions attributed to Tannaim

Bab. Tal	*Tan. Mid.*	*Mishnah*	*Tosefta*	*Pal. Tal*
III.ii.1 (Death scene)	—	—	—	(V.i.11)
III.ii.2 (Ḥanina)	—	—	—	—
III.ii.3 (Temple doors)	—	—	—	—
III.ii.4 (Yoḥanan and Gamaliel eat in Sukkah)	—	II.i.4	—	—
III.ii.5 (Hillel's disciples)	—	—	—	—
III.ii.6 (Family died young)	—	—	—	—
III.ii.7 (New Moon testimony on Sabbath)	—	—	—	—

Bab. Tal.	*Tan. Mid.*	*Mishnah*	*Tosefta*	*Pal. Tal.*
III.ii.8 (Shofar on New Year/ Sabbath)	—	II.i.6	—	—
III.ii.9 (Day of Waving)	I.ii.6, 7	II.i.5b, 7a, 7b, 20	II.iii.9	II.i.3
III.ii.10 (New Moon testimony all day long)	—	II.i.8	—	—
III.ii.11 (Poor-man's tithe)	—	II.i.23	II.iii.15	—
III.ii.12 ("I will ascend")	—	—	—	—
III.ii.13 (*Merkavah*)	I.ii.2a	—	II.iii.3	III.i.4
III.ii.14 (Family died young)	—	—	—	—
III.ii.15 (Priests hearken in what concerns putting away)	—	II.i.16	—	—
III.ii.16 ("You were unwilling")	I.i.1/I.i.7	—	—	—
III.ii.17 (Judges of civil law)	—	II.i.9/10	—	—
III.ii.18 (Slave's ear pierced)	I.i.3	—	II.iii.8d	III.i.5
III.ii.19a (Robber/thief)	I.i.5	—	II.iii.7	—
III.ii.19 (Dignity)	I.i.4	—	—	—
III'ii.20 ("Righteousness exalteth a nation")	—	—	—	—
III.ii.21 ("Woe if I speak")	—	II.i.22	II.iii.10	—
III.ii.22 (Sadducees: Daughter inherits)	—	—	—	—
III.ii.23 (Hillel's disciples)	—	—	—	—
III.ii.24 (Follow righteousness)	I.ii.8	—	—	—
III.ii.25 (Stems of figs)	—	II.i.15	—	—
III.ii.26 (Prince sins)	I.ii.3	—	II.iii.8c	III.i.6
III.ii.27 (Priests and *sheqel*)	—	II.i.3	—	—
III.ii.28 (Priests and *sheqel*)	—	II.i.3	—	—
III.ii.29 (Priest and *sheqel*)	—	II.i.3	—	—
III.ii.30 (Convert)	—	—	—	—

CHAPTER FOUR

AVOT DERABBI NATAN

Goldin observes that the relationship of ARN to the Mishnah tractate Avot is much like that of the Tosefta to the Mishnah. It was compiled between the seventh and the ninth centuries, but the latest authority quoted is of the Tannaitic age; the language, teachings, and idiom are "typical of what we find in Tannaite sources." Therefore, Goldin concludes, "the composition of the contents of ARN cannot be much later than the third or following century, or at the utmost shortly thereafter" (p. xxi). I have placed ARN materials between Tannaitic and Amoraic traditions on Yoḥanan, at the chronological point that seems to Goldin most likely.

i. Texts

On acts of loving-kindness: how so? Lo, it says, *For I desire mercy and not sacrifice* (Hos. 6:6). From the very first the world was created only with mercy, as it is said, *For I have said, The world is built with mercy; in the very heavens Thou doest establish Thy faithfulness* (Ps. 89:3).

Once as Rabban Yoḥanan ben Zakkai was coming forth from Jerusalem, Rabbi Joshua followed after him and beheld the Temple in ruins.

"Woe unto us!" Rabbi Joshua cried, "That this, the place where the inquities of Israel were atoned for, is laid waste!"

"My son," Rabban Yoḥanan said to him, "be not grieved; we have another atonement as effective as this. And what is it? It is acts of loving-kindness, as it is said, *For I desire mercy and not sacrifice*" (Hos. 6:6).

(ARN, Chap. four, trans. Goldin, p. 34, Schechter ARNA, p. 11a)

Comment: The story pertains to the Yavneh period and presumably derives from Joshua's circle. No other disciples are mentioned, even though in other Yavnean materials, Eliezer plays a considerable role. The occasion of the visit to Jerusalem is not explained; the likelihood is that the visit is invented to provide a setting for the sermon on Hos.

6:6. The story is unique; no other exegesis of Hos. 6:6 is attributed to Yoḥanan; no parallel or remotely similar account exists.

Why should Joshua's school have wanted to stress the unimportance of the Temple cult? It is clear, for one thing, that Joshua encouraged people to avoid excesses of mourning; b.B.B. 60b contains the story of his argument with those who would not eat meat or drink wine. The point there is that one cannot permit himself unlimited mourning. Here, as I said, the additional teaching is that the Temple really does not matter so much as do deeds of compassion.

My guess is that the issue to which this story is addressed is the effort to rebuild the cult by means of a new war. In his old age Joshua opposed the gathering enthusiasm preceding the Bar Kokhba war. A story such as this one would serve to stress two principles. First, Israel does not depend on Temple cult for reconciliation with God. Therefore efforts to recover Jerusalem cannot be justified on the grounds of divine will. God wants no such thing. Second, by indirection, the story underlines the results of the first war. The Temple was destroyed once, and Joshua, among the disciples of Yoḥanan, *was* one of the mourners for Zion. He cannot therefore be accused of indifference, but rather must be followed because of his wisdom.

But if, as is possible, the story was invented later on, then the exegesis would have been fabricated for much the same purposes, and then attributed to Yoḥanan and his great disciple. It would not have been addressed to the Bar Kokhba period, but rather to some later time, when the hope for rebuilding the Temple had to be tempered by the realities of the day. And if, furthermore, the issue was not whether to rebuild the Temple, but rather, how to assess the relative importance of sacrifice against acts of lovingkindness, then a theological issue has set the stage for the exegesis, placed into an invented context. The difficulty in accurately dating ARN prevents us from reaching firm conclusions about these, and related, questions.

2. (a) Now, When Vespasian came to destroy Jerusalem he said to the inhabitants, "Fools, why do you seek to destroy this city and why do you seek to burn the Temple? For what do I ask of you but that you send me one bow or one arrow, and I shall go off from you?"

They said to him, "Even as we went forth against the first two who were here before thee and slew them, so shall we go forth against thee and slay thee."

When Rabban Yoḥanan ben Zakkai heard this, he sent for the men of Jerusalem and said to them, "My children, why do you destroy this city and why do you seek to burn the Temple? For what is it that he asks of you? Verily he asks naught of you save one bow or one arrow, and he will go off from you."

They said to him, "Even as we went forth against the two before him and slew them, so shall we go forth against him and slay him."

Vespasian had men stationed inside the walls of Jerusalem. Every word which they overheard they would write down, attach (the message) to an arrow, and shoot it over the wall, saying that Rabban Yoḥanan ben Zakkai was one of the Emperor's friends.

(b) Now, after Rabban Yoḥanan ben Zakkai had spoken to them one day, two and three days, and they still would not attend to him, he sent for his disciples, for Rabbi Eliezer and Rabbi Joshua.

"My sons," he said to them, "arise and take me out of here. Make a coffin for me that I might lie in it."

Rabbi Eliezer took hold of the head end of it, Rabbi Joshua took hold of the foot; and they began carrying him as the sun set, until they reached the gates of Jerusalem.

"Who is this?" the gatekeepers demanded.

"It's a dead man," they replied. "Do you not know that the dead may not be held overnight in Jerusalem?"

"If it's a dead man," the gatekeepers said to them, "take him out."

(c) So they took him out and continued carrying him until they reached Vespasian. They opened the coffin, and Rabban Yoḥanan stood up before him.

"Art thou Rabban Yoḥanan ben Zakkai?" Vespasian inquired; "tell me, what may I give thee?"

"I ask naught of thee," Rabban Yoḥanan replied, "save Yavneh, where I might go and teach my disciples and there establish a prayer [house] and perform all the commandments."

"Go," Vespasian said to him, "and whatever thou wishest to do, do."

(d) Said Rabban Yoḥanan to him, "By thy leave, may I say something to thee?"

"Speak," Vespasian said to him.

Said Rabban Yoḥanan to him, "Lo, thou art about to be appointed king."

"How dost thou know this?" Vespasian asked.

Rabban Yoḥanan replied, "This has been handed down to us, that the Temple will not be surrendered to a commoner, but to a king; as it is said, *And he shall cut down the thickets of the forest with iron, and Lebanon shall fall by a mighty one*" (Is. 10:34).

It was said: No more than a day, or two or three days, passed before messengers reached him from his city (announcing) that the emperor was dead and that he had been elected to succeed as king.

(e) A catapult was brought to him, drawn up against the wall of Jerusalem. Boards of cedar were brought to him which he set into the catapult, and with these he struck against the wall until he made a breach in it. A swine's head was brought and set into the catapult, and this he hurled toward the (sacrificial) limbs which were on the altar.

It was then that Jerusalem was captured.

(f) Meanwhile Rabban Yoḥanan ben Zakkai sat and waited trembling, the way Eli had sat and waited; as it is said, *Lo, Eli sat upon his seat by the wayside watching; for his heart trembled for the ark of God* (I Sam. 4:13). When Rabban Yoḥanan ben Zakkai heard that Jerusalem was destroyed and the Temple was up in flames, he tore his clothing, and his disciples tore their clothing, and they wept, crying aloud and mourning.

(ARN, Chap. four, trans. Goldin, pp. 35-7, ARNb, ed. Schechter, Chap. 6, p. 10a)

Comment: This is the first escape story. It is highly developed and full of literary artifice. Part (a) sets the stage. Vespasian was not asking for much, merely for signs of submission. The Jewish zealots were overconfident. Yoḥanan tried to save the city, but the zealots would hear of no such thing. Part (a) ends with the detail, important later on, that Vespasian had heard of Yoḥanan. Including the detail at just this point is artful, for it invites the reader to go on and prepares him for the climax.

Part (b) then shows that Yoḥanan's escape was not treason, but in fact was directly caused by the zealots' intransigeance (illustrated in [a]). The details of the escape, with a coffin, against the opposition of the gatekeepers, who had to be outwitted by the disciples—these details again show the work of a highly skilled narrator. The tension of the actual escape is stressed. Yoḥanan did not merely climb over a wall. His escape required courage and careful planning, culminating in the tense moment at the gate itself.

Part (c) continues to heighten the tension. Having escaped, the disciples went directly to their master's counterpart. Vespasian, having been informed of Yoḥanan's dependability, could credibly receive him. Presumably hearers would have been astonished at the Roman general's availability had not an earlier detail prepared them to expect it. Yoḥanan's modest request then provides the etiology for the Yavneh school. How did it all begin? In this interview with Vespasian, Yoḥanan obtained a charter.

Part (d) is an additional and separate colloquy. It is not tacked on, but rather included as an integral part of the story. Yoḥanan's prescience once again is demonstrated, this time in most dramatic fashion. His knowledge of Scripture permitted him to see what others did not suspect, namely Vespasian's coming rise to power. And, with appropriate drama, word came to verify Yoḥanan's prediction.

Part (e) is not integral to the story, yet, having been included, enhances it. Jerusalem fell at the precise moment that a pig's head landed on the altar. The conclusion is appropriate. It refers to the capture of the earlier sanctuary. We have already seen other Tannaitic materials in which Eli plays a part. Yoḥanan had shown how to overcome the curse of Eli's family. I do not think the detail is hostile to Yoḥanan; he is not compared to Eli; his disciples are not denigrated as were Eli's sons. It is simply that two obviously comparable moments in Israelite history are brought into juxtaposition. Afterward the Scripture is not subjected to rabbinic exegesis, as in the instance of II Kings 25:9. Indeed, no rabbinical exegesis is permitted to impede the course of the narrative. The quite natural conclusion is that Yoḥanan mourned for the Temple.

Apart from (e), no element seems tacked on or drawn from an earlier corpus of materials. The whole passage is a smooth, polished narrative —something uncommon in other Tannaitic materials, though common enough in materials transmitted by Rav Judah in the name of Rav, to mention one example.

It is clear that this story serves several important polemical purposes. First and most important, it counters the accusations that Yoḥanan was a traitor with the opposite claim, that the zealots were over-confident fools, whose only accomplishment was to cause the destruction of the Temple. It was not Yoḥanan's "treason" that was responsible for the disaster. And the zealots were not only foolish, but also incompetent, for the master succeeded in outwitting them. Second, the origins of Yavneh are made clear. Whatever others thought, the fact was that Yavneh came about through the wise policy of Yoḥanan *vis à vis* the Romans. Any other policy would not have led to even this much continued Jewish freedom. But Yavneh was to be a center for study of the law, not for the subversion of Roman rule. Third, Yoḥanan's prescience is underscored. Not only did he predict the coming destruction, but he knew it through his study of Torah, not through some lucky guess or magical hocus-pocus. It was the sage through Torah who would predict the future, not the prophet or messiah proclaiming his own visions or revelations from heaven. Yet Yoḥanan was a loyal Jew, like any other mourner for Zion. Assertions to the contrary were patently false.

The chief figures, apart from Yoḥanan, were Eliezer and Joshua, whose circles preserved much material on Yoḥanan. The other disciples are ignored. We are not told how they escaped from the city. Perhaps some of them did not. But Eleazar b. ʿArakh certainly did, and his absence is noteworthy. Indeed, he never appears in materials shaped by Eliezer's and Joshua's schools, though the Aqibans do make use of Eleazar's mystical materials without altering them in crucial details. We do not know how Eleazar's circle told the story of the escape, but we may be absolutely certain that this is not its account.

The story obviously dates from a time after Yavneh was well-established, after Eliezer and Joshua had achieved pre-dominance in the formation of Yoḥanan-traditions, hence presumably well after Yoḥanan's death. But a date of ca. 90 A.D. must be a *terminus a quo*. It would be difficult to argue that so complete and artistic an account was shaped at about the same time as the primitive and episodic *ḥomer*-materials, for instance.[1] If the items already noted do come from Eliezer's and Joshua's schools, then it seems likely this story comes from a far later time.

Who would have told it? One possible setting would be the period before the Bar Kokhba War, when the peace-party would have been eager to remind the messianists about an earlier messianic struggle. But I think an even more likely setting would be *after* the Bar Kokhba War, when the bitter issue of collaboration with Rome was once again raised. We know that some of the sages were totally opposed to the patriarch's collaboration. Others, who did the patriarch's work, such as Eliezer b. R. Simeon b. Yoḥai and Ishmael b. R. Yosi b. Ḥalafta, supposedly were the subject of rebukes from Elijah, and similarly hostile stories were told about them. Telling the old story of how rabbinical government actually began, of why the zealots should be dismissed because of the hopelessness of their cause and the foolishness of their behavior, underlining the source of the collaborationists' wisdom, in Scripture itself, finally making it clear that the collaborationists shared the sentiments of the nation as a whole—making these points would have been particularly important in the last half of the second century and especially at the patriarchal court.

If, therefore, Goldin is correct in assigning the materials of ARN to the early third-century, then I should suppose this story comes from the final period in the compilation of ARN and serves the interests of the patriarchate itself. I imagine, too, that the beautiful artistry of the account is no accident. I doubt that previously fixed sayings are included here; earlier traditions on the escape were not circulated at all, because the escape-story probably was not part of the corpus of Yoḥanan-sayings beforehand. Therefore the person who framed this story was free to do as he liked, in the absence of earlier, well-known sayings or details (with the possible exception of the reference to *Lebanon* as the Temple). The narrator therefore was able to make up a single, unitary account. Otherwise, as I said, the marks of an earlier transmission of one detail or another would be apparent.

---

[1] Indeed, Is. 10:34 contains an echo of the "iron on the altar" exegesis. *He shall cut down the thickets of the forest with an iron*—and the "forest" is none other than Lebanon, meaning the Temple. Iron is supposed to be tabooed, as a sign of punishment, and contact of iron with the altar forms the substance of an important *ḥomer*-exegesis, as we have seen. Perhaps the earlier exegesis on Deut. 27:5-6 (I.i.2; I.ii.1,5; II.iii.8e; II.iii.8f) underlay the selection of Is. 10:34 as a counterpoint; it may be that the elaborate use of Is. 10:34 was to begin with provoked by the reference to iron. This, to be sure, is pure conjecture, but it would help to relate later to earlier Yoḥanan materials.

Yet even though we do not discern already-established components, we cannot deny that earlier elements may well have been available and may have been incorporated in this account. It is possible that separate traditions about an escape in a coffin, an exegesis of Is. 10:34, an interview with Vespasian, and the like actually existed, and were finally unified in the story as we have it. But because of the polished style of the author, we may suppose it *is* an author, not merely an editor, who created this account.

3. What were the beginnings of Rabbi Eliezer ben Hyrcanus?

(a) He was twenty-two years old and had not yet studied Torah. One time he resolved, "I will go and study Torah with Rabban Yoḥanan ben Zakkai."

Said his father Hyrcanus to him, "Not a taste of food shalt thou get before thou hast plowed the entire furrow."

He rose early in the morning and plowed the entire furrow (and then departed for Jerusalem).

(b) It is told: That day was the eve of the Sabbath, and he went for the Sabbath meal to his father-in-law's. And some say: He tasted nothing from six hours before the eve of the Sabbath until six hours after the departure of the Sabbath.

(c) As he was walking along the road, he saw a stone; he picked it up and put it in his mouth. And some say: It was cattle dung. He went to spend the night at a hostel.

Then he went and appeared before Rabban Yoḥanan ben Zakkai in Jerusalem—until a bad breath rose from his mouth. Said Rabban Yoḥanan ben Zakkai to him, "Eliezer, my son, hast thou eaten at all today?"

Silence.

Rabban Yoḥanan ben Zakkai asked him again.

Again silence.

Rabban Yoḥanan ben Zakkai sent for the owners of his hostel and asked them, "Did Eliezer have anything to eat in your place?"

"We thought," they replied, "He was very likely eating with thee, master."

He said to them, "And I thought he was very likely eating with you! You and I, between us, left Rabbi Eliezer to perish!"

(Thereupon) Rabban Yoḥanan said to him, "Even as a bad breath rose from thy mouth, so shall fame of thee travel for thy mastery of the Torah."

(d) When Hyrcanus his father heard of him, that he was studying

Torah with Rabban Yoḥanan ben Zakkai, he declared, "I shall go and ban my son Eliezer from my possessions."

It is told: That day Rabban Yoḥanan ben Zakkai sat expounding in Jerusalem and all the great ones of Israel sat before him. When he heard that Hyrcanus was coming, he appointed guards and said to them, "If Hyrcanus comes, do not let him sit down,"

Hyrcanus arrived, and they would not let him sit down. But he pushed on ahead until he reached the place near Ben Ẓiẓit Hakkeset, Naqdimon ben Gorion, and Ben Kalba Shavu'a. He sat among them trembling.

It is told: On that day Rabban Yoḥanan ben Zakkai fixed his gaze upon Rabbi Eliezer and said to him, "Deliver the exposition."

"I am unable to speak," Rabbi Eliezer pleaded.

Rabban Yoḥanan pressed him to do it, and the disciples pressed him to do it. So he arose and delivered a discourse upon things which no ear had ever before heard. As the words came from his mouth, Rabban Yoḥanan ben Zakkai rose to his feet and kissed him upon his head and exclaimed, "Rabbi Eliezer, master, thou hast taught me the truth!"

Before the time had come to recess, Hyrcanus, his father, rose to his feet and declared, "My masters, I came here only in order to ban my son Eliezer from my possessions. Now, all my possessions shall be given to Eliezer my son, and all his brothers are herewith disinherited and have naught of them."

ARN Chap. six, trans. Goldin, pp. 43-4

Comment: Like most ARN exempla, this story is a finished, artful account. Its elements are clear. Part (a) relates the ploughing story; it recurs in various ways, but invariably includes the fact that suddenly, while at work, Eliezer decided to go to Jerusalem. It serves, further, to explain (b), why Eliezer had nothing to eat. The climax is (c), Yoḥanan's saying that "just as your breath was foul, so will your Torah travel from your mouth and be noteworthy." The image must have been more attractive then than it is now. Part (d) is a combination of the disinheritance story and Yoḥanan's blessing; they fit naturally together, however, and we need not imagine they were once separate and distinct. The great men of Jerusalem were, I suppose, sufficiently well known to be included in stories emanating from different schools and serving different purposes. We do not have to conclude that Naqdimon, Ben Kalba Shabu'a, and Ben Ẓizit Hakeset[1] were names routinely used in

[1] On the contrary, the appearance of the three men in several, unrelated stories—the escape, the exegeses of Song 1:8 (*If you do not know*...) and elsewhere—

Eliezer's school but not elsewhere, or that their appearance would mark a story as derived from Eliezer's circle.

The story obviously comes from Eliezer's school, and I see no reason to doubt it was shaped fairly early. But I have no clear notion about what provoked its formulation as we now have it, nor are there earlier versions.

4. And he that does not attend upon the sages deserves to die: what is that? The story is told:

There was once a certain man of Bet Ramah who cultivated a saintly manner. Rabban Yoḥanan ben Zakkai sent a disciple to examine him. The disciple went and found him taking oil and putting it on a pot-range, and taking it from the pot-range and pouring it into a porridge of beans.

"What art thou doing?" the disciple asked him.

"I am an important priest," he replied, "and I eat heave offering in a state of purity."

The disciple asked, "Is this range unclean or clean?"

Said the priest, "Have we then anything in the Torah about a range being unclean? On the contrary, the Torah speaks only of an *oven* being unclean, as it is said, *Whatsoever is in it shall be unclean*" (Lev. 11:33).

Said the disciple to him, "Even as the Torah speaks of an oven being unclean, so the Torah speaks of a range being unclean, as it is said, *Whether oven or range for pots, it shall be broken in pieces, they are unclean* (Lev. 11:35)." The disciple continued, "If this is how thou hast been conducting thyself, thou hast never in thy life eaten clean heave offerings!"

ARN Chap. twelve, trans. Goldin, p. 71
(ARNb, 27, ed. Schechter, p. 28b)

Comment: This is a formulation completely separate from the Joshua-Aqiban account about Lev. 11:33 ("Who will remove the dust from between your eyes, O Rabban Yoḥanan ben Zakkai", I.ii.4, II.i.11, II.iii.5). In this version, 'Aqiva plays no part. But the Aqiban rule of

---

establishes a strong *prima facie* case that in the very earliest Yoḥanan-traditions were references to his relationships with the leading upper-class families of Jerusalem. These evidences are, moreover, not all late, as in the origins of Eliezer and the escape stories, but to the contrary appear in the very earliest stratum of the normative tradition. Naqdimon may well have been cited from the first occurrences, but I do not see how the others would have been. My guess is that the historical Yoḥanan ben Zakkai actually did have close ties with these families.

law is taken for granted, that is, the range is unclean, and does transmit uncleanness. That, however, is still not the point of the story at all; it is indeed peripheral. What is important is that the oven *is* unclean and so is the range, and anyone who supposes the range is not capable of transmitting uncleanness is in error. Hence the Aqiban rule of law is unimportant here, and plays no role in the formulation of the story.

The important point is that self-important priests do not really know the cleanness-laws at all, but have to learn from Yoḥanan and his disciples how to keep those very Temple-laws. In its present form, the story is part of the anti-priestly polemic. It is important to note that this polemic was preserved in Joshua's school. I do not know when the story was formulated in its present form. Since Joshua is the central figure, and since the Aqiban interpretation of Lev. 11:33 plays no part, I suppose the story *may* come from a time before ʿAqiva's rule was enunciated, for afterward it is difficult to see how it could have been excluded or utterly ignored. So it is at least possible that the story comes from Joshua's school and was not afterward revised. But this must remain a mere possibility.[1]

5. Rabban Yoḥanan ben Zakkai took over from Hillel and Shammai.

(a) Eighty disciples had Hillel the Elder. Thirty of them were worthy to have the Shekhinah rest upon them as upon Moses, our master, but their generation was unworthy of it. Thirty of them were worthy to intercalate the year, and twenty were middling. The greatest of them all was Jonathan ben Uzziel; the least of them all was Rabban Yoḥanan ben Zakkai.

(b) They tell of Rabban Yoḥanan ben Zakkai that he did not neglect Scripture or Mishnah, Gemara, Halakha, Agada, or Supplements, the subtleties of Scripture or the subtleties of the Scribes, or any of the Sages' rules of interpretation—not a single thing in the Torah did he neglect to study, confirming the statement, *That I may cause those that love me to inherit substance, and that I may fill their treasuries* (Prov. 8:21).

(c) He used to say, "If thou hast wrought much in thy study of Torah, take no credit for thyself, for to this end wast thou created: for men were created only on condition that they study Torah."

(d) Five disciples did Rabban Yoḥanan ben Zakkai have, for each of whom he had a name.

Eliezer ben Hyrcanus he called "plastered cistern which loses not a drop, pitch-coated flask which keeps its wine."

---

[1] See Finkelstein, *op. cit.*, p. 152.

Joshua ben Ḥananiah he called "threefold cord not quickly broken."

Yosi the Priest he called "The generation's saint."

Simeon Ben Nathanel he called "Oasis in the desert which holds on to its water."

And Eleazar ben ʿArakh he called "Overflowing stream and ever-flowing stream whose waters ever flow and overflow"—confirming the statement, *Let thy springs be dispersed abroad, and courses of water in the streets* (Prov. 5:16). Happy the disciple whose master praises him and testifies his gifts!

(e) He used to say, "If all the sages of Israel were in one scale of the balance and Rabbi Eliezer ben Hyrcanus were in the other scale, he would outweigh them all."

Abba Saul says in his name, "If all the sages of Israel were in one scale of the balance, and even if Rabbi Eliezer ben Hyrcanus were with them, and Rabbi Eleazar ben ʿArakh were in the other scale, he would outweigh them all."

(f) Rabban Yoḥanan said to them, "Go out and see which is the good way to which a man should cleave so that through it he might enter the world to come."

Rabbi Eliezer came in and said, "A liberal eye."

Rabbi Joshua came in and said, "A good companion."

Rabbi Yosi came in and said, "A good neighbor, a good impulse, and a good wife."

Rabbi Simeon (came in and) said, "Foresight."

Rabbi Eleazar came in and said, "Wholeheartedness toward Heaven [and wholeheartedness toward the commandments] and wholeheartedness toward mankind."

Said Rabban Yoḥanan to them, "I prefer the words of Rabbi Eleazar ben ʿArakh to your words, for in his words your words are included."

(g) He said to them, "Go out and see which is the evil way which a man should shun, so that he might enter the world to come."

Rabbi Eliezer came in and said, "A grudging eye."

Rabbi Joshua came in and said, "An evil companion."

Rabbi Yosi came in and said, "An evil neighbor, an evil impulse, and an evil wife."

Rabbi Simeon came in and said, "Borrowing and not repaying; for he that borrows from man is as one who borrows from God, as it is said, *The wicked borroweth, and payeth not; but the righteous dealeth graciously, and giveth*" (Ps. 37:21).

Rabbi Eleazar came in and said, "Mean heartedness toward Heaven and mean heartedness toward the commandments and mean heartedness toward mankind."

And Rabban Yoḥanan said to them, "I prefer the words of Rabbi Eleazar to your words, for in his words your words are included."

(h) When Rabban Yoḥanan ben Zakkai's son died, his disciples came in to comfort him. Rabbi Eliezer entered, sat down before him, and said to him, "Master, by the leave, may I say something to thee?"

"Speak," he replied.

Rabbi Eliezer said, "Adam had a son who died, yet he allowed himself to be comforted concerning him. And how do we know that he allowed himself to be comforted concerning him? For it is said, *And Adam knew his wife again* (Gen. 4:25). Thou too, be thou comforted."

Said Rabban Yoḥanan to him, "Is it not enough that I grieve over my own, that thou remindest me of the grief of Adam?"

Rabbi Joshua entered and said to him, "By thy leave, may I say something to thee?"

"Speak," he replied.

Rabbi Joshua said, "Job had sons and daughters, all of whom died in one day, and he allowed himself to be comforted concerning them. Thou too, be thou comforted. And how do we know that Job was comforted? For it said, *The Lord gave, and the Lord hath taken away; blessed be the name of the Lord*" (Job 1:21).

Said Rabban Yoḥanan to him, "Is it not enough that I grieve over my own, that thou remindest me of the grief of Job?"

Rabbi Yosi entered and sat down before him; he said to him, "Master, by thy leave, may I say something to thee?"

"Speak," he replied.

Rabbi Yosi said, "Aaron had two grown sons, both of whom died in one day, yet he allowed himself to be comforted for them, as it is said, *And Aaron held his peace* (Lev. 10:3)—silence is no other than consolation. Thou too, therefore, be thou comforted."

Said Rabban Yoḥanan to him, "Is it not enough that I grieve over my own, that thou remindest me of the grief of Aaron?"

Rabbi Simeon entered and said to him, "Master, by thy leave, may I say something to thee?"

"Speak," he replied.

Rabbi Simeon said, "King David had a son who died, yet he allowed himself to be comforted. Thou too, therefore, be thou comforted. And how do we know that David was comforted? For it is said, *And David comforted Bath-Sheba his wife, and went in unto her, and lay with her; and she bore a son, and called his name Solomon* (II Sam. 12:24). Thou too, master, be thou comforted."

Said Rabban Yoḥanan to him, "Is it not enough that I grieve over my own, that thou remindest me of the grief of King David?"

Rabbi Eleazar ben ʿArakh entered. As soon as Rabban Yoḥanan saw him, he said to his servant, "Take my clothing and follow me to the bathhouse, for he is a great man, and I shall be unable to resist him."

Rabbi Eleazar entered, sat down before him, and said to him, "I shall tell thee a parable: to what may this be likened? To a man with whom the king deposited some object. Every single day the man would weep and cry out, saying, 'Woe unto me! when shall I be quit of this trust in peace?' Thou too, master, thou hadst a son: he studied the Torah, the Prophets, the Holy Writings, he studied Mishnah, Halakhah, Aggadah, and he departed from the world without sin. And thou shouldst be comforted when thou hast returned thy trust unimpaired."

Said Rabban Yoḥanan to him, "Rabbi Eleazar, my son, thou has comforted me the way men should give comfort!"

(i) When they left his presence, Rabbi Eleazar said, "I shall go to Emmaus, a beautiful place with beautiful and delightful waters."

But they said, "We shall go to Yavneh where there are scholars in abundance who love the Torah."

Because he went to Emmaus—a beautiful place with beautiful and delightful waters—his name was made least in the Torah. Because they went to Yavneh—where there are scholars in abundance who love the Torah—their names were magnified in the Torah.

ARN Chap. fourteen, trans. Goldin, pp. 74-78
(ARNb, ed. Schechter, p.29a-b, ch. 31, pp. 33b.)

Comment: Both the Avot materials and those of ARN before us include substantial sources from Eleazar's circle. It is simply incredible that Joshua's or Eliezer's disciples would have preserved an account using their masters, as well as Yosi and Simeon, merely as foils for the brilliance of Eleazar and for Yoḥanan's praise of his sayings. Here, by contrast, (d), (e), (f), (g), and (h) are all pericopes in which Eleazar stands at the climax. Only (i) contradicts the former accounts, probably coming from circles hostile to Eleazar and eager to denigrate his importance. But the former materials were, as usual, uncorrected later on.

Part (a) is known to us in *beraitot* (III.ii.5). But the *they say of* segment (b) is reformulated in late fourth-century Pumbedita-Maḥoza, as we have seen. Hence (b) is either earlier than the Babylonian version or has been inserted later on; but if the latter is the case, then the direct references to Abbaye and Rava have been omitted in favor of generalized references to subtleties and rules of interpretation. My guess is that the former alternative is more likely. The *beraita* here omits the references to Jonathan b. Uzziel included in other versions.

Part (c) appears, as we saw, as an exegesis, along with a teaching of Judah the Prince. Perhaps the saying in this form derives from before his time.

Part (d) lists the whole of the Jerusalem circle in its conventional, fixed order and form. In fact, (d) through (h) are all exemplifications of that form, and materials have manifestly been forced to conform to it. But the origins of the words of praise are unclear. We cannot suggest that Eleazar's circle assigned to Yoḥanan various mild compliments, so that the "overflowing stream" would standout. In fact no complimentary epithet seems to me necessarily superior to any other. If the order were different, and if the secondary exegeses (Prov. 5:16) were omitted, Eliezer or Joshua, Simeon or Yosi—any one of them might have come as a climax without necessitating the inclusion of more enthusiastic praise. Hence I am not forced to conclude Eleazar's circle was responsible for the particular epithets, and I think it likely Yoḥanan himself said them. Eleazar's school then made it clear that he was superior to the others.

Part (e) is the most striking. Yoḥanan could not have praised Eliezer and also Eleazar. One or the other had to be "worth all the rest." Clearly, Abba Saul's saying presupposes the earlier one *and* corrects it. So in its current form, Abba Saul's saying in Yoḥanan's name must come later.

But consideration of Eleazar's biography suggests otherwise. Eleazar, it is generally believed, did not accompany Yoḥanan to Yavneh; he went to Emmaus instead. In Part (i) the departure took place after the master's death, which would suggest he first loyally went to Yavneh. But as we have seen, Eleazar's name is elsewhere omitted from Yavnean materials, until Aqiban times. I think it likely he did not go to Yavneh at all. If he did, he played no part in the formulation of Yavnean traditions; and that seems highly unlikely. Hence it is most probable that he was not there to begin with. Part (i) puts a good face on matters. He never abandoned the master until death. But (i) still is not an account from Eleazar's circle.

If Eleazar did not go to Yavneh, then anything favorable Yoḥanan said about him would have had to be formulated in Jerusalem before 70 and preserved afterward at Emmaus. I think it unlikely that at Yavneh, Yoḥanan would have said the (absent) Eleazar is superior to the (present) Joshua and Eliezer; but if he had said so, it is not likely that Eliezer or Joshua would have been glad to preserve the saying.

Hence whatever Yoḥanan actually said—and this we do not know—the praiseworthy references to Eleazar do not come from Yavneh and probably do not date from that period either. They certainly come from Emmaus, and probably were brought to Yavneh by Eleazar's students after the master's death. If this is so, then the original saying would have been, "If all the sages of Israel were in one scale of the balance, and Rabbi Eleazar b. ʿArakh were in the other scale, he would outweigh them all." Such a saying would have been unacceptable to Eliezer's disciples, and they revised it as we now have it; Abba Saul corrected *their* tradition, but he still did not produce the suppressed, original one. I do not know why Joshua's students did not invent something of the same sort. The greatest likelihood is that they did not know these materials at all. Eliezer's disciples preserved them and handed them on to the Aqibans, who made no substantial changes afterward. Eleazar's materials were likewise preserved by the Aqibans, for reasons noted earlier (I.iii.2a, II.iii.3, III.i.4).

Parts (f) and (g) clearly derive from Eleazar's circle. The order conventional in Eleazar's materials is strictly followed. But here, the content does reflect the form, for Eleazar's words really do contain the general principle merely illustrated by the discrete examples brought by the lesser disciples.

Part (h) refers, most likely, to the Jerusalem years, for Yoḥanan's son is never mentioned in Yavneh or afterward, and I think the context makes it clear that he died young. This account presents a formidable contrast to the earlier ones (f) and (g), for it is extended, literary, and elegant. Perhaps Eleazar's circle gave it its current form; but if not, I cannot guess who would have wanted to tell the story or for what purpose.

Part (i) obviously is tacked on by other disciples, presumably Eliezer's, to show that despite the favorable traditions herein cited, still Eleazar came to naught, while their names were "magnified" in Torah. Since the preceding materials hardly demonstrate that Eleazar's name was "made least in Torah," the final account (i) must be understood as separate and unrelated, a hostile subscription to a collection which otherwise is manifestly favorable to Eleazar.

I cannot account for the obscurity of Yosi and Simeon. They appear in some of the *Merkavah*-versions, hence were known to and regarded as valid precedent by the Aqibans. But their disciples, if any, did not succeed in forcing the inclusion of the master's materials in any substantial collection available to us. It is at least possible that neither survived the destruction of Jerusalem and hence had no influence on the shaping of Yavnean materials. It is also possible that they were at Yavneh, *but* that their disciples afterward faded from the scene. I think the former more reasonable. If so, *Merkavah*-materials in which they occur must derive from Jerusalem before the destruction. Since those materials consist merely of a reference to the alleged participation of the masters in *Merkavah* speculations, it is not a far-fetched suggestion.

See above, II.i.18 for further discussion of the *Avot*-form.

6. (a) He would say, "Do not destroy their altars, so you do not have to rebuild them with your own hands. Do not destroy [altars] of mortar so they do not say to you, "Rebuild them of stone."

(b) "If a sprout is in your hands and they say to you, 'Behold the Messiah!'—Come and plant your sprout and afterward go and receive him. And if the young men say to you, 'Let us go and build the Temple,' do not listen to them. But if the elders say to you, 'Come and let us destroy the Temple,' listen to them. For the building of youths is destruction, but the destruction of elders is building. Proof of the matter is Rehoboam b. Solomon."

(c) He would say, "Keep the children from pride and separate them from the householders, for householders keep men far from matters of Torah."

(d) He would say, "For three sins householders are given over to the government, because they lend on interest, and because they preserve mortgages which have already been paid, and because they pledge charity publicly but do not give it, and because they remove the yoke from themselves and place the yoke and the tax on the poor and impoverished and wretched. And concerning them Scripture says, *Cursed is he who does not carry out the teachings of this Torah* (Deut. 27:26)—these are the householders."

ARNb Chap. thirty-one, ed. Shechter pp. 33b-34a

Comment: Chap. 31 of ARNb begins with Yoḥanan as Hillel's and Shamai's disciple. There follows the saying about man's being to made study Torah, as an exegesis of Deut. 30:20, much as in I.iv.i. Then there is a collection of "He used to say" materials: (a), (b), and (c) as given here. Part (d) is represented in IV.i.8, below.

Part (d), like (a), (b), and (c), may not be attributed to Yoḥanan at all. Goldin omits the passages from his ARN, and I know of no parallel sources which attributed these sayings to Yoḥanan; (c) and (e) are especially problematical, for they do occur, but *not* in Yoḥanan's name. Since here they are not, in fact, explicitly attributed to Yoḥanan, except, perhaps, inferentially, it is difficult to know whether *anyone* actually thought he said them.

7. (a) One time as Rabban Yoḥanan ben Zakkai was walking in the market place, he saw a girl picking up barley grains from under the feet of Arab cattle. "My child," he asked her, "who are thou?" She did not answer.

Again he asked her, "My child, who art thou?" But she would not answer.

Finally she said to him, "Wait one moment." She covered herself with her hair and sat down before him. "Master," she said, "I am the daughter of Naqdimon ben Gorion."

"My child," he asked, "the wealth of thy father's house, where is it?"

"Master," she replied, "is this not how the proverb goes in Jerusalem: 'Your wealth will keep if you don't keep it.' "—And some say: ('Your wealth will keep) if you give alms.'

"And your father-in-law's," he asked, "where is that wealth?"

"Master," she said, "the one went down and dragged the other down with it."

(b) Thereupon Rabban Yoḥanan ben Zakkai said to his disciples, "All my life I've read this verse, *If thou know not, O thou fairest among women, go thy way forth by the footsteps of the flock* (Song 1:8), and not understood what is meant, and now I come along and learn what the meaning is: That Israel has been surrendered to the meanest of peoples, and not merely to a mean people but to their cattle dung!"

(c) Moreover, she said to him, "Master, dost thou remember when thou didst sign my marriage deed?" "Indeed!" he answered. "By the Temple service!" he exclaimed to his disciples, "I signed this girl's marriage deed, and it read, 'A million gold *denar* in Tyrian *denar*.' In the prosperous days of the household of this girl's father, they did not go from their home to the Temple unless woolen carpets were laid for them to walk on!"

ARN Chap. seventeen, trans. Goldin, pp. 88-89

Comment: Parts (a) and (b) are already familiar to us (I.i.1, 7). The sermon and the setting are integrally related, though some details are absent (see synoptic section, below, pp. 237-240). The account is evidently the Ishmaelean version, without significant omission. Part (c) is tacked on as an additional detail, preserved in connection with Naqdimon's daughter. For further comment, see I.i.7.

8. (a) Rabbi Ḥanina ben Dosa says, "He whose fear of sin takes precedence over his wisdom, his wisdom shall endure; but he whose wisdom takes precedence over his fear of sin, his wisdom shall not endure: as it is said, *The fear of the Lord is the beginning of wisdom* (Ps. 111:10)."

He used to say, "He whose works exceed his wisdom, his wisdom shall endure; but he whose wisdom exceeds his works, his wisdom shall not endure: as it is said, *We will do and study* (thereafter) (Exod. 24:7)."

(b) Rabban Yoḥanan ben Zakkai was asked, "If one is wise and fears sin, what is he like?"

He replied, "Lo, that's a craftsman with the tools of his craft in his hand."

"If one is wise but does not fear sin, what is he like?"

"Lo, that's a craftsman without the tools of his craft in his hand," he replied.

"If one fears sin but is not wise, what is he like?"

He replied, "He is no craftsman, but the tools of the craft are in his hand."

ARN, Chap. twenty-two, trans. Goldin, p. 99

Comment: Yoḥanan's saying (b) is different from that of his disciple Ḥanina. Ḥanina praised both fear of sin over wisdom, and works over wisdom. Yoḥanan praised wisdom and fear of sin alike; but fear of sin *without* wisdom is foolish, for the tools are there, but ability to use them is absent. The editor clearly recognized the antiphonal relationship between Ḥanina's and Yoḥanan's sayings, but that does not show he knew Ḥanina was Yoḥanan's disciple. We cannot suppose the passage originally began in Ḥanina's school, for the school would hardly demonstrate that their master had taught differently from *his* master. Hence I imagine the sayings existed separately until brought into juxtaposition by the editor of ARN.

I have no way of guessing at who might have wanted the passage to appear in its present form, or who would have formulated Yoḥanan's saying.

9. In his last hours Rabban Yoḥanan ben Zakkai kept weeping out loud. "O master," his disciples exclaimed, "O tall pillar, light of the world, mighty hammer, why art thou weeping?"

Said he to them, "Do I then go to appear before a king of flesh and blood—whose anger, if he should be angry with me, is but of this world; and whose chastising, if he should chastise me, is but of this world; whom I can moreover appease with words or bribe with money? Verily, I go rather to appear before the King of kings of kings, the Holy One, blessed be He—whose anger, if He should be angry with me, is of this world and the world to come; whom I cannot appease with words or bribe with money! Moreover I have before me two roads, one to Paradise and one to Gehenna, and I know not whether He will sentence me to Gehenna or admit me into Paradise; and of this the verse says, *Before Him shall be sentenced all those that go down to the dust, even he that cannot keep his soul alive*" (Ps. 22:30).

He said, "Clear the house of uncleanness and prepare a throne for Hezekiah, king of Judah."

ARN, Chap. twenty-five, trans. Goldin, pp. 105-107

Comment: The death scene, already familiar in III.ii.1 (=V.i.11) cannot in this form be attributed to any school, age, or context. In its present form it is fully developed, highly literary.

The detail about Hezekiah's throne is added, which would seem to suggest he looked forward to the imminent coming of the messianic scion. But we cannot suppose that someone later on wanted to stress Yoḥanan's expectation that the messiah would soon come; contrast IV.i.6b above.

In any event, Eliezer's school certainly shaped the parallel versions, and probably this one too, for the Hezekiah-throne is included to serve as a parallel to Eliezer's orders about a throne for Yoḥanan.

II. General Comments

Some of the materials clearly derived from, or relate to, schools of major disciples, particularly IV.i.1,4 = Joshua; IV.i.2, 3,5c,9= Eliezer; IV.i.5,d,e,f,g,h = Eleazar. But we cannot assert that ARN traditions were shaped as early as the end of the first century. I am confident that IV.i.7 is fairly early in its primary form, though the current, developed version is not necessarily so. Apart from the points at which the Mishnah *Avot* is actually cited in IV.i.5, three exempla exhibit significant parallels to earlier collections: IV.i.7, as I just said; Hillel's disciples; and the death scene in IV.i.9. Other material sometimes shows slight connections, as IV.i.4 and the passage on Lev. 11:33.

Despite these parallels, ARN greatly increases the Yoḥanan-legend, particularly IV.i.1 and IV.i.2. These passages are crucial to any account of Yoḥanan, and they first occur, as I said, in this last of all (supposedly) Tannaitic formulations of Yoḥanan-materials. I doubt that the escape story existed earlier. I know no grounds to suppose the exegesis on Hos. 6:6 did either. Even though Joshua appears in both, and Eliezer in the former, we cannot imagine that they gave the materials their current and final form. Indeed, until ARN, we have not had the slightest hint of an escape from Jerusalem. Nor do we have any reference to ideas Yoḥanan may have entertained about the Temple's relationship to deeds of lovingkindness. These both are innovations in the tradition. Other materials, particularly the disciple-stories emanating from Eleazar's circle, simply expand upon what we already had, or, as in the beginnings of Eliezer, the death scene, and *if you do not know*, mostly add a few minor details to an existing account.

Table

ARN Compared to Earlier Tannaitic Materials

ARN	*Tan. Mid.*	*Mishnah*	*Tosefta*	*Pal. Tan.*	*Bab. Tan.*
Iv.i.1 (Lovingkindness)	—	—	—	—	—
Iv.i.2 (Escape)	—	—	—	—	—
IV.i.3 (Eliezer's beginnings)	—	—	—	—	—
IV.i.4 (Range unclean)	—	—	—	—	—
IV.i.5a (Hillel's disciples)	—	—	—	—	III.ii.24
Iv.i.5b (Did not neglect)	—	—	—	—	—
IV.i.5c (Study Torah)	I.iv.1	II.i.18	—	—	—
Iv.i.5d,e (Five disciples)	—	—	—	—	—
Iv.i.5f,g (Good, evil way)	—	—	—	—	—
Iv.i.5h (Death of son)	—	—	—	—	—
Iv.i.5i (Emmaus)	—	—	—	—	—
IV.i.6a-c,e (Do not destroy, sprout, keep children, three sins)	I.iv.2 (= IV.i.6a)	—	—	—	—
IV.i.7 (*If you do not know*)	I.i.1,7	—	—	—	III.ii.6
Iv.i.8 (Wise, fears sin)	—	—	—	—	—
IV.i.9 (Death)	—	—	—	V.i.11	III.ii.1

Table

Authorities who cite, or are cited in connection with, Yoḥanan

IV.i.1	(Lovingkindness, not sacrifice)—Joshua
IV.i.2	(Escape)—Eliezer, Joshua
IV.i.3	(Beginning of Eliezer)—Eliezer
IV.i.4	(Heave-offering in state of purity)—Anonymous (Joshua)
IV.i.5	(Disciples)—Eliezer, Joshua, Yosi, Simeon b. Nathanel *Eleazar b. 'Arakh* (3)
IV.i.6	(Do not destroy)—Anonymous
IV.i.7	(If you do not know)—Anonymous
IV.i.8	(Wise and fears sin)—Ḥanina b. Dosa
IV.i.9	(Death)—Anonymous (Eliezer)

CHAPTER FIVE

AMORAIC TRADITIONS

I. Palestinian Talmud

1. The *tefillin* of Rabban Yoḥanan ben Zakkai did not move from him either in summer or in winter, and so did R. Eliezer his disciple after him.

y. Ber. 2:3

Comment: The context is stories about how great authorities had worn their *tefillin*. Mentioned in this connection are R. Yannai and R. Yoḥanan.

The saying itself clearly follows the "Yoḥanan did... and so did Eliezer his disciple after him" model. There is no sign, however, that the pericope was originally formulated as a *beraita* in Tannaitic times. While all the *beraitot* considered above are in good Mishnaic Hebrew, this saying is in Aramaic. It may be a reformulation of an earlier teaching, but we have no hint as to where and how it was revised, or for what purpose.

2. Rabbi ʿUlla said, "Eighteen years he was settled in ʿArav (ʿBYD HWY HY[T]B BHDʾ ʿRB), and there came to him only these two cases. He said, 'Galilee, Galilee, you have hated [Or: You hate] the Torah. Your end is to work in chains.' "

y. Shab. 16:8

Comment: The saying of ʿUlla is attached to the Mishnah about a case before Yoḥanan in ʿArav. No other authorities are mentioned in this context.

ʿUlla's saying contains two elements, first, the assertion that only these two cases came to Yoḥanan, second, the "quotation" of his curse. In fact, in connection with ʿArav all we have are the cases; I have supposed that in addition Ḥanina b. Dosa's studies with Yoḥanan took place in ʿArav (see *Life*, 2nd ed., pp. 47-53), but no talmudic source explicitly says so. Hence all ʿUlla knew were in fact the cases cited in Mishnah Shabbat. But the attribution to Yoḥanan of a curse of the Galileans is ʿUlla's alone. It appears nowhere else. The language is Aramaic, while all Yoḥanan-sayings are cast into good Mishnaic Hebrew. The likelihood is that the saying is pseudepigraphic, and that ʿUlla is responsible for it. He may have taken a famous maxim and put it into Yoḥanan's mouth.

3. [Mishnah: After the destruction of the Temple, Rabban Yoḥanan ben Zakkai decreed concerning the *Lulav* and the Day of Waving.] And did Rabban Yoḥanan ben Zakkai decree against a teaching of the Torah?

y. Suk. 3:11

4. [Mishnah: In this matter too Jerusalem was superior to Yavneh, (regarding) the sounding of the Shofar on the New Year which falls on the Sabbath only in the court of the town.] And did Rabban Yoḥanan ben Zakkai decree against a teaching of the Torah?

y. R.H. 4:2

5. [Mishnah: Re *Lulav*]
And did Rabban Yoḥanan ben Zakkai decree against a teaching of the Torah...

y. R.H. 4:3

Comment: V.i.3 is set into an anonymous discussion, in which the Mishnah about Yoḥanan's *lulav* and Day of Waving decrees is cited. V.i.4 appears in an anonymous discussion, in which the Mishnah about sounding the *Shofar* on the New Year coinciding with the Sabbath is cited. V.i.5 relates to the *lulav*-decree mentioned in the Mishnah. No authorities are cited in, or in connection with, the discussion.

It is therefore clear that in the Palestinian Amoraic schools Yoḥanan's decrees were analyzed in terms of their legal character. Did they set aside laws deriving from the Torah, or laws promulgated by the Scribes? We do not, as is clear, have any idea who raised the issue, or how the question was first provoked, then formulated.

6. [Mishnah: R. Judah said, "Ben Bukhri testified in Yavneh, 'Any priest who gives the *sheqel* does not sin.' "]

(a) Gemara: R. Berekiah said, "This is the reason of Rabban Yoḥanan b. Zakkai..." R. Ṭavi in the name of R. Hamnuna said, "So do the sages answer R. Yoḥanan..."

(b) R. Judah and R. Neḥemiah, one said... The other said... The one who said...supports [the view of] R. Yoḥanan b. Zakkai... The one who said...supports the view of Ben Bukhri.

(y. Sheq. 1:3)

Comment: R. Berekiah gives a reason for Yoḥanan's ruling, namely, that all twelve tribes should give the *sheqel*, thus including the priests. R. Ṭavi in R. Hamnuna's name provides a reply to R. Judah's opinion. R. Judah's and R. Neḥemiah's disagreement follows; it is clear that the editor has tried to show the same moot issue divides Yoḥanan and Ben

Bukhri and the two later Tannaim as well. But the "One who says..." construction is not Judah's and Neḥemiah's; indeed, we do not know what position either Tanna took. V.i.6b is therefore anonymous so far as the Amoraic context is concerned.

Where Yoḥanan's teachings appeared in the Mishnah, they were discussed by the Palestinian Amoraim and included in their *gemara* at appropriate places. We hardly need to suppose that some special interest in Yoḥanan himself underlay the discussions of V.i.3-6, for it is evident that Mishnah-study, involving inquiry into legal principles, not study of Yoḥanan's sayings for their own sake, provoked the discussions.

7. R. Joshua b. R. Neḥemiah in the name of R. Yoḥanan ben Zakkai said, "Because they transgressed the Ten Words, let each one give ten gerahs."

y. Sheq. 2:3

Comment: The saying of Joshua b. R. Neḥemiah is introduced by a dispute between R. Judah and R. Neḥemiah concerning the reason for giving a half-*sheqel* (=ten *gerahs*). R. Joshua's saying in Yoḥanan's name follows. Afterward come still other reasons, this time provided by R. Berekiah and R. Levi in the name of R. Simeon b. Laqish, then by R. Pinḥas in the name of R. Levi.

R. Joshua b. R. Neḥemiah's citation of Yoḥanan thus appears in the context of a pericope about the ten *gerahs*=half-*sheqel*. The pericope stands as a unit.

We have no idea how R. Joshua b. R. Neḥemiah knew Yoḥanan's teaching, which is in the manner of the *ḥomer*-exegeses; if he made it up himself, we do not know why he attributed it to Yoḥanan.

8. TNY: A convert who converts in this time [after the destruction of the Temple] must bring his bird-offering a quarter [coin] of silver.

R. Simeon said, "Rabban Yoḥanan ben Zakkai annulled [the requirement] because of [the possibility of] disorder."

y. Sheq. 8:4

Comment: R. Simeon is presumably R. Simeon b. Yoḥai. If so, the *beraita* beginning TNY was shaped before his time, and he amended it by saying that long before, Yoḥanan had ruled, to the contrary, that no offering whatever would be required from the convert. That ruling exists only in this form; it nowhere appears in the Yavnean materials. I do not know how R. Simeon knew Yoḥanan's ruling, assuming that he did. He was 'Aqiva's disciple, so it is possible that he learned the tradition from his master, and his master from Joshua or Eliezer. But if so, no indication of a chain of tradition is given here, and I doubt that any existed.

It is possible that the *beraita* consisted only of the words immediately following the superscription TNY, and that it was constructed in its current form later on, perhaps even in early Amoraic times. For that reason I have not listed the tradition as *certainly* Tannaitic in origin; see III.ii.30. But one might have just as well assumed that the TNY-sentence and R. Simeon's correction of it were put together as early as the last third of the second century. Since the saying occurs in no Tannaitic collection, I think the former possibility more likely.

The context is a citation of R. Simeon b. R. Simeon b. Judah; there follows the *beraita* cited here; then a confirmatory *beraita*. No other names are mentioned in this context.

For discussion of the law, see my *Life* (second edition, p. 210).

9. R. Joshua b. Levi said, "*And he burned the house of the Lord* (II. Kings 27:9)—This refers to the Temple. *And the house of the king*—This refers to the palace of Zedekiah... *And every great house he burned in fire* (II Kings 25:9)—This is the school-house of Rabban Yoḥanan ben Zakkai, for there they would teach the great deeds of the Holy One, blessed be he."

y. Meg. 3:1

Comment: Joshua b. Levi's exegesis of II Kings 25:9 is interrupted by a saying in the name of Pinḥas in the name of Hosha'ayah, but it is clear that the exegesis of II Kings 25:9 is in fact entirely Joshua's. He is therefore the Amora who refers to Yoḥanan. The exegesis requires no direct knowledge of Yoḥanan or his times, and I do not think Joshua had any. What is noteworthy is the importance *to* Joshua b. Levi of explaining "every great house" in terms of Yoḥanan's school.

10. When Rabban Yoḥanan ben Zakkai wanted rain to fall, he would say to his barber, "Arise, go before the Temple [saying] that my master wants a haircut and has no power to undergo the anguish [of a fast]." Forthwith rain would fall.

y. Ta'anit 3:11

Comment: The antecedent discussion does not relate to Yoḥanan's saying. That which follows tells a similar story about R. Adda b. Aḥva. The story about Yoḥanan is not attributed to any authority. We do not know where it came from; it appears only here.

11. Rabbi Jacob b. Idi in the name of R. Joshua b. Levi said, "Rabban Yoḥanan ben Zakkai, when dying, gave orders, saying, 'Clear out the courtyard on account of the [coming corpse-] unclean-

ness and set up a throne for Hezekiah, king of Judah.' Rabbi Liezer his disciple, when he was dying, gave orders saying, 'Clear out the courtyard on account of [coming corpse-] uncleanness and prepare a throne for Rabban Yoḥanan ben Zakkai.' "

y. Soṭ. 9:16

Comment: The context is stories about what happened when various ancient authorities died. Jacob b. Idi in the name of Joshua b. Levi tells a tale which was formulated in Tannaitic times, probably, to begin with, in Eliezer's school. But he does not attribute the story of Tannaitic sources, rather to Joshua b. Levi. It is clear that Joshua b. Levi was responsible for important Palestinian Amoraic materials on Yoḥanan.

For the relationship between Joshua's version and the Tannaitic ones, see below, synoptic studies (pp. 223-226).

12. Eighty pair[s] of disciples did Hillel have. The greatest among them was Jonathan ben Uzziel, the youngest, Rabban Yoḥanan ben Zakkai.

One time he [Hillel] fell ill and all of them came in to visit him. Rabban Yoḥanan ben Zakkai took his place in the courtyard [outside].

He said to them, "Where is the youngest among you, for he is the father of wisdom and the father of the [coming] generations, and one hardly needs to say, the greatest among you?"

They replied, "Behold, he is in the courtyard [outside]."

He said to them, "Let him come in."

When he came in, he [Hillel] said to them, "*To cause those who love me to inherit substance, and their treasuries will I fill.* (Prov. 8:15)."

y. Ned. 5:6

Comment: The *Gemara* begins with a comment by R. Yoḥanan apparently on the Mishnah, "It is discerned that this one is a disciple of a sage." There follows "Eighty pairs..." Then again, "And R. Yoḥanan said, 'It is discernable that this one is a disciple of a sage.'" Afterward R. Yosi b. R. Bun discusses Jonathan b. Uzziel and how his father vowed he would have no pleasure from his possessions; the antecedent Mishnah deals with such vows. Hence the context is provided by Yoḥanan and Yosi b. R. Bun.

It is clear that the Hillel-*beraita* is before us, but the *beraita* is not introduced as such, and further, no authority quotes it. It stands by itself, then provokes Yoḥanan's comment.

For a comparison of this version with the Babylonian *beraita*, see below, synoptic studies (pp. 223-226).

13. R. Ba said, "At first each one would ordain his own disciples, for instance, Rabban Yoḥanan ben Zakkai ordained Rabbi Liezer and Rabbi Joshua, and R. Joshua ordained R. ʿAqiva, and R. ʿAqiva ordained R. Meir and R. Simeon."

y. Sanh. 1:2

Comment: R. Ba's statement stands by itself, with no relationship to what precedes. The tradition dates, at the earliest, from the generation following ʿAqiva, presumably from Meir's school. It is followed by the story of ʿAqiva's arrangements in his own academy, in good Mishnaic Hebrew. We have no clear idea of how R. Ba concluded that ordination began with Yoḥanan. No earlier evidence pertained to the issue.

14. Agenṭos the *Hegemon* asked Rabbi Yoḥanan ben Zakkai, "*The ox will be stoned and also its master will die* (Ex. 21:29). [What has the ox done to be liable to the death-penalty?]"

He replied, "The accomplice of a brigand is like a brigand [also culpable]."

When he [the *Hegemon*] left, his disciples said to him, "Rabbi, this one you have driven away with a reed, but what will you reply to us?"

He replied to them, "It is written, *The ox will be stoned and also its master will die*—The death of the ox will be like the death of its master, for the death of the master was tied to the death of the ox. Just as the master [is tried by a process of] careful investigation [of the testimony against him] and in a court of twenty-three [judges], so the death of the ox will [come about through a trial characterized by] careful investigation [of the testimony against him] and in a court of twenty-three [judges]."

y. Sanh. 1:2

Comment: The context is a discussion about the stoning of the ox; R. Yosi b. R. Bun and R. Abbahu discuss the matter. Then "Agenṭos the *Hegemon*..." This is a disciple-story following the pattern in which an outsider asks a question, Yoḥanan replies, then the disciples say the reply is unsatisfactory, and Yoḥanan offers a completely different answer. The exoteric doctrine generally does answer the question; the esoteric doctrine does not. In this instance, for example, the esoteric doctrine explains the Scripture, showing that the biblical requirement is simply for a full-dress trial for the ox. But the original question of the gentile is ignored: Why should the ox be tried at all?

We do not know how such stories were framed. Presumably the narrator places himself with the circle of disciples, or otherwise he would not know what Yoḥanan said to them. But the reply is so patently irrelevant to the difficulty that one might wonder whether the narrator was friendly to Yoḥanan or not. I suppose he was, and that the technicalities of Scriptural exegesis did interest him, as they did Yoḥanan and the disciples. It is probably not a story to demonstrate Yoḥanan's incompetence as defender of the faith. But whatever the narrator's intent, we have not got the slightest notion of how he claimed to know what Yoḥanan said or did; or what provoked him to invent this account.

15. Antoninus the *Hegemon* asked Rabban Yoḥanan ben Zakkai, "In general [when numbered all together] they were found wanting, but in detail [when added up one by one] they were found excessive."

He said to him, "Those three hundred extras were the firstborn sons of the priesthood, and the holy [coin] cannot fulfill the obligations of the holy [tribe]."

y. Sanh. 1:4

Comment: No Amoraim are related, so far as I can tell, to the citation of this story.

In fact it is a fragment of an account more fully provided in Num. R. 3:14, cited below. The reference is to Num. 3:39 and 4:9. But Num. R. 3:14 does not contain a reference to Yoḥanan, let alone to a conversation with "Antoninus." The passage as we have it seems to allude to a more complete account. I have no idea who framed it, how it lost all the details so as to remain a mere outline. The full account is contained in Num. R. 4:9. Num. R. 3:14 is as follows:

> *At the command of the Lord, by their families, all males from a month old and upward, were twenty and two thousand* (Num. 3:39). You will find that the tribe of Levi, in the detailed numbering, consisted of twenty-two thousand and three hundred. For there were three families—Gershon, Kohath, and Merari. Now if you take each family separately and compute the figures in it—seven thousand and five hundred, eight thousand and six hundred for Kohath, six thousand and two hundred for Merari—the total for all amounts to twenty-two thousand and three hundred. Yet when the Levites are counted all together, their numbers are given as twenty-two thousand; where were the three hundred? The detailed numbers were in fact given in order to make known how many there were in each family. But a sum total of twenty-two thousand, a reduction of three hundred from the real figure, is given because this numbering was in order to compare them with the number of first born for the purposes of redeeming the firstborn Israelites. He deducted from their number three hundred who were firstborn belonging to the Levites, because one firstborn cannot redeem another firstborn. For this reason there are twenty-two thousand and three hundred in the numbering of the families, and twenty-two thousand in the total used for the redemption of the firstborn Israelites.

Num. R. 3:14, trans. J. J. Slotki, pp. 93-4.

16. Antoninus the *Hegemon* engaged in polemics with Rabban Yoḥanan ben Zakkai: "Either your teacher Moses was an embezzler or he was inexpert in keeping accounts, for it is written, [*The silver of those of the community who were recorded came to one hundred talents and 1,775 sheqels by the sanctuary weight] a half-sheqel a head [half-a-sheqel by the sanctuary weight, for each one who was entered in the records]* (Ex. 31:25-6). Now if you reckon the *centenarius* as one hundred *libras*, Moses misappropriated one sixth [of the silver], and if you reckon the *centenarius* at sixty *libras*, as is normal, he misappropriated one half."

[The regular talent was sixty *minas*, or fifteen hundred *sheqels*, or three thousand half *sheqels*. Thus, 600,000 in all. But Scripture states that approximately one hundred talents were reported. Therefore half the silver was *not* reported. At one hundred *minas* to the talent, the misappropriation would have amounted to one sixth of the silver, since at that rate a talent was equal to twenty-five hundred *sheqels*, five thousand half-*sheqels*. Thus 100 × 5,000 = 500,000, which leaves the silver collected for 100,000 people unreported. For the population, see Ex. 31:26].

Rabban Yoḥanan ben Zakkai replied, "Moses our teacher was a trustworthy treasurer and expert in keeping accounts. And," he continued, "Is it not written, *And the copper from the wave-offering was seventy talents and twenty-four hundred sheqels* (Ex. 38:29)? Observe that these twenty-four hundred *sheqels* amount to ninety-six *libras* [One *libra* is twenty-five *sheqels*] and yet Scripture did not convert them into *libras* [which would have been convenient.]"

[This is taken as proof that these *libras* did not have the usual weight of twenty-five sheqels each, but twice that weight, which was the standard of the sanctuary. Otherwise they would have been converted. Now if the sanctuary weight was indeed twice the regular standards, Moses misappropriated nothing whatsoever.]

To this the *Hegemon* countered, "[The reason Scripture did not convert the *sheqels* into *libras* is] that the *centenarii* do not amount to a talent. But if you insist that they do, [I maintain that Scripture was interested only in the round total of seventy talents and therefore did not convert the relatively small amount of twenty-four hundred *sheqels*.] Moses thus misappropriated half."

[At sixty *libras* per *centenarius*, twenty-four hundred *sheqels* would amount to one talent and nine hundred forty *sheqels*. At one hundred *libras* per *centenarius*, twenty-four hundred would not amount to a full talent, which would be twenty-five hundred *sheqels*.]

Rabban Yoḥanan ben Zakkai replied, "Is it not written, *And of the one-thousand seven-hundred-seventy five [sheqels] he made hooks for the posts* (Ex. 38:28). You observe that these *sheqels* amount to seventy-one *libras*, yet Scripture reported them specifically as *sheqels* [and did not convert them into *libras*.]"

[The *Hegemon* repeated his earlier objection] saying to Rabban Yoḥanan ben Zakkai, "It is because the *centenarii* did not amount to a talent. Moses was [consequently] guilty of misappropriation."

[At one hundred *libras* per *centenarius*, twenty-five hundred *sheqels* would amount to a full talent, and here we have only one thousand seven-hundred-seventy-five.]

Yoḥanan ben Zakkai argued further, "Is it not written, *The sheqel is twenty gerah, and twenty and twenty five and fifteen sheqels are one mina for your purposes* (Ezek. 45:12). The Holy One, blessed be he, ordained a talent of twice the regular weight."

[The usual *mina* (= *libra*) amounts to twenty-five *sheqels*, but the sanctuary weight of a *mina* in the Torah was fifty *sheqels*. In Ezekiel's time, ten *sheqels* were added, making sixty.]

The *Hegemon* finally conceded, "Verily, [Moses your teacher] was a trusted treasurer and expert in keeping accounts."

y. Sanh. 1:4, translated by Baruch A. Levine

Comment: Compare the approximately parallel account in b. Bekh. 5a, cited below V.ii.20. The context is as above, that is, no Amoraim report the story; none is cited in connection with it.

17. Rabbi Jacob b. Idi in the name of R. Joshua b. Levi said, "Rabban Yoḥanan ben Zakkai, when he was dying, said, 'Clear the house on account of the [corpse-] uncleanness, and set up a throne for Hezekiah king of Judah.' Rabbi Liezer his disciple when he was dying said, 'Clear out the house on account of the [corpse-] uncleanness, and set up a throne for Rabban Yoḥanan ben Zakkai.' "

y. A.Z. 3:1

Comment: As in V.i.11, the Amoraic context is clear. For further discussion, see above III.ii.1, V.i.11, 17.

18. [Behold the shadow of the Temple may not be used for pleasure]. But Rabban Yoḥanan ben Zakkai [was] sitting and teaching in the shadow of the Temple.

y. A.Z. 3:11

Comment: The context is anonymous. Attached to the Mishnah is a discussion in the name of R. Ḥisda that it is permitted to make use of the shadow of the Temple, but not the shadow of the Temple itself. There follows the story as we have it, beginning "and/but Rabban Yoḥanan..." Then comes a statement of R. Abin in the name of the "rabbis of that place" [Babylonia] on a legal principal concerning corpse uncleanness, and making no reference to Yoḥanan's action. Hence the story seems unrelated to the discussion that follows; the antecedent discussion is quite germane, but anonymous. I imagine, therefore, that Ḥisda's saying did not include reference to Yoḥanan's action. The parallel is below, V.ii.3.

II. Babylonian Talmud

1. They said concerning Rabban Yoḥanan ben Zakkai that no man ever preceded him [in saying] *Shalom*, even a gentile in the marketplace.

b. Ber. 17a

Comment: The context is a list of "favorite sayings" (pearls) of various Amoraim; Abbaye praises subtlety in fear of heaven; then it is said that one should try to maintain good relations with everyone. Yoḥanan is cited as an example. Immediately following is a saying of Rava, then of Rav. I think it probable, therefore, that Yoḥanan's saying was placed into the context as an illustration of Abbaye's.

We shall consider the *They said concerning Yoḥanan*... form in the synoptic studies, below (pp. 221-223).

2. A certain two students were seated before Hillel and one of them was Rabban Yoḥanan ben Zakkai—and they tell [that they were seated] before Rabbi [Judah the Prince] and one of them was Rabbi Yoḥanan.

One said, "On what account do they cut grapes in cleanness but do not harvest olives [MWSQYN] in cleanness" and the other said, "...in uncleanness."

He [Hillel/Judah] said, "I am certain that this one is going to teach instruction in Israel," and the days were not many until he [actually] did teach instruction in Israel.

b. Pes. 3b

Comment: The passage begins with R. Huna's saying in Rav's name in R. Meir's name, that one should teach students in refined speech. Rav's students, then Hillel's (or Rabbi Judah the Prince's) are cited as examples; finally comes a similar story of three priests. The whole passage therefore probably derives in final form from R. Huna's school.

As to the content, it cannot antedate R. Judah the Prince. The likelihood is that Yoḥanan b. Nappaḥa and Yoḥanan b. Zakkai are confused, likewise Judah the Prince and Hillel. The story can have no direct pertinence to Yoḥanan's life, but probably illustrates the way in which his name was used as an example of the good disciple. While the Amoraic context seems clear, we cannot conclude that the story was framed in Huna's school; it may have come from early third-century Palestine.

3. Abbaye said [to Rava]... Because it was taught [TNY']. They said concerning Rabban Yoḥanan ben Zakkai that he would sit in the shadow of the Temple and expound all day long.

b. Pes. 26a

Comment: Abbaye here cites a *beraita*-formulation of the same tradition as V.i.18; but the language here is good Mishnaic Hebrew; in the Palestinian Talmud's version, in Aramaic. The context clearly is fourth-century Pumbedita. The Palestinian, Aramaic form is certainly earlier than the Babylonian, Hebrew one. The *beraita* probably does not come from Tannaitic times at all, but presumably from the Tanna of Pumbedita in Abbaye's day.

4. Come and hear: For R. Yoḥanan b. Zakkai said, "What answer did the *Bat Qol* give that wicked man [Nebuchadnezzar] when he asserted, '*I will ascend above the heights of the clouds; I will be like the Most High?*' (Is. 14:14) A *Bat Qol* came forth and rebuked him: 'Thou wicked man, son of a wicked man, descendant of the wicked Nimrod, who incited the whole world to rebel [*himrid*] against Me during his reign! How many are the years of man? Seventy years; and if by reason of strength, eighty years, for it is said, *The days of our years are threescore years and ten, or even by reason of strength fourscore years* (Ps. 90:10). Now from earth to heaven is a five hundred years' journey, the thickness of heaven is a five hundred years' journey, and between the first heaven and the next lies a five hundred years' journey, and similarly between each heaven—*Yet thou shalt be brought down to the nether-world, to the uttermost parts of the pit* (Is. 14:15)." This is [indeed] a refutation.

b. Pes. 94a-b, trans. H. Freedman, pp. 504-5

Comment: The passage begins with Rava's saying that the world is six thousand parasangs in diameter, the thickness of the firmament is one thousand parasangs. A number of teachings are then cited in the "come and hear" form. Among these is Yoḥanan's, which appears in more complete form as a *beraita* in b. Ḥag. 13a (III.ii.12). We shall compare these versions in the synoptic studies below (pp. 253-254). It is striking that the *beraita* is not cited, but briefly paraphrased.

5. [CITATION OF MISHNAH: The story is told that they brought to Rabban Yoḥanan ben Zakkai to taste... and they said, "Bring them up to the Sukkah."]

b. Suk. 26b

Comment: The Mishanh is cited in the Gemara, then, "Shall we say this is a refutation of R. Joseph and Abbaye?"

6. They said concerning R. Yoḥanan b. Zakkai that during his life he never uttered profane talk, never walked four cubits without Torah and *tefillin*, nor was any man earlier than he in the school house. He never slept or dozed in the school house. He did not meditate in dirty alleys. He did not leave anyone in the school house when he left. No one ever found him sitting in silence, but only sitting and learning. No one but he himself ever opened the door to his disciples. He never in his life said anything which he had not heard from his teacher. Except on the eve of Passover and on the eve of the Day of Atonement, he never said, "It is time to arise from the studies of the school house." So did his disciple R. Eliezer behave after him.

b. Suk. 28a

Comment: The context is a series of *beraitot* pertinent to R. Eliezer. This tradition is clearly edited in Eliezer's school, but it is not cited as a *beraita*. There is no Amoraic context. V.i.1 includes, in Aramaic, the Palestinian version of the detail about the *tefillin*. It is certainly earlier than this account, and perhaps the *they said* form was intended as a catchall for many kinds of sayings about Yoḥanan's way of living, of which only a few—such as this one and that about teaching in the Temple's shadow—occur in Palestinian traditions.

7. SEE ABOVE, b. Suk. 28a (cited in full, III.ii.6).

Comment: The *beraita* about Hillel's disciples is interrupted by "They said of Yoḥanan," including the explanation of "small matters" as discussions of Abbaye and Rava. Hence the Amoraic setting is clear: fourth-century Pumbedita-Maḥoza.

8. Rabbi Merion said in the name of R. Joshua b. Levi, and some say that it was a tannaitic tradition (TNY'LH) of Rabbah b. Meri in the name of Rabban Yoḥanan ben Zakkai, "Two date-palms were in the valley of Ben Hinnom and smoke went up between them," and this is [the matter concerning which] we have learned [TNY] 'the thorn-palms of the iron mountain are valid,' and this is the gate of Gehenna."

b. Suk. 32b

Comment: In the current form, several authorities are involved in the tradition, which we cannot attribute to Yoḥanan. However, what is important is that Abbaye is cited in the preceding passage, which immediately concerns the thorn palms of the Iron Mountain.

9. R. Naḥman b. Isaac said, "Rabban Yoḥanan ben Zakkai [follows] the reasoning of R. Judah [*Re* Mishnah on *Lulav*]."

b. Suk. 41a

Comment: It is obvious that Naḥman b. Isaac provided the context for the discussion of Yoḥanan's ruling.

10. [R. Eliezer had fourth-year fruit and wanted to give it to the poor. His disciples informed him that his colleagues had already permitted using the fruit for any purpose.] "Who are his colleagues? Rabban Yoḥanan ben Zakkai."

b. Suk. 31b

Comment: The anonymous reference to the "colleagues" is clearly an interjection not originally found in the teaching concerning Eliezer. But we do not know when it was introduced, or by whom.

11. [Mal. 3:5: *And I will come near to you to judgment, and I will be a swift witness against the sorcerers and against the adulterers and against false swearers and against those that oppress the hireling in his wages.*]

Rabbi Yoḥanan ben Zakkai said, "Woe unto us that the Scripture weighed against us light [sins] as much as heavy ones."

b. Ḥag. 5a

Comment: The context is sayings of Yoḥanan b. Nappaḥa and R. Simeon b. Laqish concerning various sorts of sins. Yoḥanan b. Nappaḥa is reported to have wept when reading Mal. 3:5. Then comes Yoḥanan's comments on the same verse, though in this context, the verse is not cited. Yoḥanan's saying thus depends upon the antecedent one of Yoḥanan b. Nappaḥa. The following comment is that of Simeon b. Laqish.

12. And Rabban Yoḥanan ben Zakkai does not [raise] questions on the severe side...

b. Soṭ. 29b

Comment: The context is a discussion of Yoḥanan's prediction concerning the third loaf. No Amoraim are cited in connection with the reference to Yoḥanan's reasoning.

13. [The priests are not permitted to go up wearing their sandals to the platform (to bless the people)]. And this is one of the nine decrees which Rabban Yoḥanan ben Zakkai decreed.

b.Soṭ. 40a

Comment: R. Ashi then provides the reason for Yoḥanan's ruling. The antecedent discussion concerns the priestly benediction in general, but not Yoḥanan's rule in particular.

14. R. Yoḥanan said, "What is illustrative of the verse, *Happy is the man that feareth always, but he that hardeneth his heart shall fall into mischief?*" (Prov. 28:14). The destruction of Jerusalem came through Qamẓa and Bar Qamẓa; the destruction of Ṭur Malka came through a cock and a hen; the destruction of Bethar came through the shaft of a leather.

(a) The destruction of Jerusalem came through Qamẓa and Bar Qamẓa in this way. A certain man had a friend Qamẓa and an enemy Bar Qamẓa. He once made a party and said to his servant, "Go and bring Qamẓa." The man went and brought Bar Qamẓa. When the man [who gave the party] found him there, he said, "See, you tell tales about me; what are you doing here? Get out."

Said the other, "Since I am here, let me stay, and I will pay you for whatever I eat and drink."

He still said, "No," and he took him by the hand and put him out.

Said the other, "Since the rabbis were sitting there and did not stop him, this shows that they agreed with him. I will go and inform against them to the Government."

He went and said to the Emperor, "The Jews are rebelling against you."

He said, "How can I tell?"

He said to him, "Send them an offering and see whether they will offer it [on the altar]."

So he sent with him a fine calf.

While on the way he made a blemish on its upper lip, or as some say on the white of its eye, in a place where we [Jews] count it a blemish but they do not. The Rabbis were inclined to offer it in order not to offend the Government.

Said R. Zekhariah b. Abqulas to them, "People will say that blemished animals are offered on the altar."

They then proposed to kill Bar Qamẓa so that he should not go and inform against them, but R. Zekhariah b. Abqulas said to them, "Is one who makes a blemish on consecrated animals to be put to death?"

R. Yoḥanan thereupon remarked: "Through the scrupulousness of R. Zekhariah b. Abqulas, our House has been destroyed, our Temple burnt and we ourselves exiled from our land."

(b) He [the Emperor] sent against them Nero the Caesar. As he was coming he shot an arrow towards the east, and it fell in Jerusalem. He shot towards all four points of the compass, and each time it fell in Jerusalem.

He said to a certain boy, "Repeat to me [the last] verse of Scripture you have learnt."

He said, "*And I will lay my vengeance upon Edom by the hand of my people Israel.*" (Ezek. 25:14)

He said, "The Holy One, blessed be He, desires to lay waste his House and to lay the blame on me."

So he ran away and became a proselyte, and R. Meir was descended from him.

(c) He then sent against them Vespasian the Caesar who came and besieged Jerusalem for three years. There were in it three men of great wealth, Naqdimon b. Gorion, Ben Kalba Shavu'a and Ben Ẓiẓit Hakeset.

Naqdimon b. Gorion was so called because the sun continued shining for his sake.

Ben Kalba Shavu'a was so called because one would go into his house hungry as a dog *[kelev]* and come out full *[save'a]*.

Ben Ẓiẓit Hakeset was so called because his fringes [*ẓiẓit*] used to trail on cushions [*keset*]. Others say he derived the name from the fact that his seat [*kisé*] was among those of the nobility of Rome.

One of these said to the people of Jerusalem, "I will keep them in wheat and barley."

A second said, "I will keep them in wine, oil and salt."

The third said, "I will keep them in wood."

The Rabbis considered the offer of wood the most generous, since R. Ḥisda used to hand all his keys to his servant save that of the wood, for R. Ḥisda used to say, "A storehouse of wheat requires sixty stores of wood [for fuel]."

These men were in a position to keep the city for twenty-one years.

(c) The *biryoni* [*zealots*] were then in the city. The Rabbis said to them, "Let us go out and make peace with them [the Romans]."

They would not let them, but on the contrary said, "Let us go out and fight them."

The Rabbis said, "You will not succeed."

They then rose up and burnt the stores of wheat and barley so that a famine ensued.

(d) Martha the daughter of Boethius was one of the richest women in Jerusalem. She sent her man-servant out saying, "Go and bring me some fine flour." By the time he went it was sold out.

He came and told her, "There is no fine flour, but there is white [flour]."

She then said to him, "Go and bring me some."

By the time he went, he found the white flour sold out. He came and told her, "There is no white flour, but there is dark flour."

By the time he went it was sold out. He returned and said to her, "There is no dark flour, but there is barley flour."

She said, "Go and bring me some." By the time he went, this was sold out.

She had taken off her shoes, but she said, "I will go out and see if I can find anything to eat."

Some dung stuck to her foot, and she died.

Rabban Yoḥanan b. Zakkai applied to her the verse, *The tender and delicate woman among you, which would not adventure to set the sole of her foot upon the ground* (Deut. 28:5).

Some report that she ate a fig left by R. Ẓadoq and became sick and died.

R. Ẓadoq observed fasts for forty years in order that Jerusalem might not be destroyed, [and he became so thin that] when he ate anything, the food could be seen [as it passed through his throat.] When he wanted to restore himself, they used to bring him a fig, and he used to suck the juice and throw the rest away.

When Martha was about to die, she brought out all her gold and silver and threw it in the street, saying, "What is the good of this to me," thus giving effect to the verse, *They shall cast their silver in the streets* (Ezek. 7:19).

(e) Abba Sikra the head of the *biryoni* in Jerusalem was the son of the sister of Rabban Yoḥanan b. Zakkai. [The latter] sent to him saying, "Come to visit me privately."

When he came he said to him, "How long are you going to carry on in this way and kill all the people with starvation?"

He replied, "What can I do? If I say a word to them, they will kill me."

He said, "Devise some plan for me to escape. Perhaps I shall be able to save a little."

He said to him, "Pretend to be ill, and let everyone come to inquire about you. Bring something evil-smelling and put it by you so that they will say you are dead. Let then your disciples get under your bed, but no others, so that they shall not notice that you are still light, since they know that a living being is lighter than a corpse."

He did so, and R. Eliezer went under the bier from one side and R. Joshua from the other.

When they reached the door, some men wanted to put a lance through the bier. He said to them, "Shall [the Romans] say, 'They have pierced their master?' "

They wanted to give it a push.

He said to them, "Shall they say that they pushed their master?"

They opened a town gate for him and he got out.

(f) When he reached the Romans he said, "Peace to you, O king, peace to you, O king."

He [Vespasian] said, "Your life is forfeit on two counts, one because I am not a king and you call me king, and again, if I am a king, why did you not come to me before now?"

He replied, "As for your saying that you are not a king, in truth you are a king, since if you were not a king, Jerusalem would not be delivered into your hand, as it is written, *And Lebanon shall fall by a mighty one. Mighty one* [is an epithet] applied only to a king, as it is written, *And their mighty one shall be of themselves*, and *Lebanon* refers to the Sanctuary, as it says, *This goodly mountain and Lebanon* (Deut. 3:25). As for your question, why, if you are king, I did not come to you till now, the answer is that the *biryoni* among us did not let me."

He said to him, "If there is a jar of honey round which a serpent is wound, would they not break the jar to get rid of the serpent?"

He could give no answer.

R. Joseph, or as some say R. ʿAqiva, applied to him the verse, *[God] turneth wise men backward and maketh their knowledge foolish* (Is. 44:25). He ought to have said to him, "We take a pair of tongs and grip the snake and kill it, and leave the jar intact."

(g) At this point a messenger came to him from Rome saying, "Up, for the Emperor is dead, and the notables of Rome have decided to make you head [of the State]."

He had just finished putting on one boot. When he tried to put on the other, he could not. He tried to take off the first but it would not come off. He said, "What is the meaning of this?"

R. Yoḥanan said to him, "Do not worry: the good news has done it, as it says, *Good tidings make the bone fat* (Prov. 15:30). What is the remedy? Let someone whom you dislike come and pass before you, as it is written, *A broken spirit drieth up the bones* (Prov. 17:22)."

He did so, and the boot went on.

He said to him, "Seeing that you are so wise, why did you not come to me till now?"

He said, "Have I not told you?"

He retorted, "I too have told you."

(h) He said, "I am now going, and will send someone to take my place. You can, however, make a request of me, and I will grant it."

He said to him, "Give me Yavneh and its sages, and the chain of Rabban Gamaliel, and physicians to heal R. Ẓadoq."

R. Joseph, or some say, R. ʿAqiva, applied to him the verse, *[God] turneth wise men backward and maketh their knowledge foolish.* "He ought to have said to him, 'Let them off this time.' He however thought that so much he would not grant, and so even a little would not be saved."

(i) How did the physicians heal R. Ẓadoq? The first day they let him drink water in which bran had been soaked; on the next day, water in which there had been coarse meal; on the third day, water in which there had been flour; so that his stomach expanded little by little.

b. Giṭ. 55b-56b, trans. M. Simon, pp. 254-260.

Comment: This is a completely different version of the escape story from the one in IV.i.2. It is difficult to attribute the entire account to R. Yoḥanan, who introduces it. In fact R. Yoḥanan's statement ab-viously is not the center of interest. Yoḥanan b. Zakkai suddenly enters the account in part (d), as if his role were already well-known, and then he becomes the focus of interest with the reference to Abba Sikra. Either R. ʿAqiva or R. Joseph criticizes the interview with Vespasian, far more likely R. Joseph.

I have presented the opening part of the story to indicate the variety of materials mixed up in this context. Indeed we have a collection of stories somehow related to the destruction of Jerusalem. The latest authority mentioned in the whole collection is R. Joseph, so I should imagine that the passage as we now have it comes from some time after his death (ca. middle of the fourth century). But its elements may have existed in some earlier form, to be sure. Parts (a), (b), and (c) do not pertain to Yoḥanan at all. They have no relationship to what follows, except, in a general way, as accounts of the approach of war and the later degradation of the rich men of Jerusalem.

Yoḥanan appears in part (d) only by indirection. We hear an echo of his sermon, by now famous, I suppose, with respect of Naqdimon's daughter; but the Scripture cited here (Deut. 28:57) is not found in the earlier materials. Presumably whatever he said about Naqdimon's daughter applied equally conveniently to Boethius's. "Yoḥanan applied the verse" is clearly an after-thought, tacked on, presumably because of the more famous passage cited above (I.i.1, 7, etc.).

Yoḥanan-material is inserted beginning with part (e). It is quite separate and distinct from what precedes, as I said. Whether or not it was invented in the period of, or after, R. Joseph is hardly clear. As it stands, the detail of being carried out as a corpse is expanded; likewise the colloquy at the gate. Otherwise there are only few connections with the ARN account (of which more below, synoptic studies, pp. 231-236): Is. 10:34, escape in a coffin, interview with the emperor, then to Yavneh.

Part (f) is entirely without Amoraic markings, except for the criticism of R. Joseph or, some say, ʿAqiva. The key proof-text, Is. 10:34, recurs.

Part (g) is a separate and distinct passage as well. Then part (h) returns to the interview with Vespasian, and Yoḥanan makes his request for Yavneh.

This version of the escape seems to me less literary, and much more composite, episodic, and folkloristic than ARN. I have not copied the later sections, the entry of Titus into the story, and so forth.

Abraham Weiss (*ʿAl Ha Yeẓirah HaSifrutit shel HaAmoraim* [N.Y., 1962], pp. 261-3) assigns the whole passage considered here to R. Yoḥanan b. Nappaḥa, on the basis of the superscription. The entire account, he says, is an expansion of Yoḥanan's introduction. The whole is Palestinian; Babylonian comments are brief and episodic, notes rather than complete sayings. The pericope, he feels, is a literary unity.

As I said at the outset, the saying of R. Yoḥanan does not relate to the bulk of the material; the story of Qamẓa and Bar Qamẓa to which he alludes is completed at the end of (a), and afterward is never mentioned again. Hence all we can really attribute to R. Yoḥanan is part (a) —*if* that. It also is possible that R. Yoḥanan referred to a well-known story, but did not tell it; the editor or compiler of the pericope then supplied the story to which R. Yoḥanan referred. In any event, upon that basis it seems dubious to assign the whole corpus of destruction-materials either to R. Yoḥanan or to Palestinian schools. We do not know where the materials were originally framed or how they were put together; but they certainly do not seem to be to have been composed as a literary unity, or anything approaching a single, smooth account such as Weiss's attribution would lead us to expect.

15. R. Judah, son of R. Shalom preached as follows: "In the same way as a man's earnings are determined for him from New Year, so his losses are determined for him from New Year. If he finds merit [in the sight of Heaven], then, 'deal out thy bread to the poor'; but if not, then, he will 'bring the poor that are outcast to his house.' "

A case in point is that of the nephews of Rabban Yoḥanan b. Zakkai. He saw in a dream that they were to lose seven hundred *denars* in that year. He accordingly forced them to give him money for charity until only seventeen *denars* were left [of the seven hundred]. On the eve of the Day of Atonement the Government sent and seized them.

R. Yoḥanan b. Zakkai said to them, "Do not fear [that you will lose any more]; you had seventeen *denars*, and these they have taken."

They said to him, "How did you know that this was going to happen?"

He replied, "I saw it in a dream."

"Then why did you not tell us?" they asked.

"Because," he said, "I wanted you to perform the religious precept [of giving charity] quite disinterestedly."

b. B.B. 10a, trans. M. Simon, p. 46

Comment: The context is clearly Judah b. R. Shalom's sermon. The story about Yoḥanan and his nephews is told in Aramaic and in no way conforms to the usual Tannaitic forms.

I do not know how Judah knew the story—if he did not invent it. I have no clear idea where it was first told, when, why or by whom. Perhaps Judah made it up for use in his sermon.

16. It was said of R. Yoḥanan b. Zakkai that his studies included Scriptures, Mishnah, *Gemara*, *Halahot*, *Aggadot;* the subtle points of the Torah and the minutiae of the Scribes; the inferences from minor to major and the [verbal] analogies; astronomy and geometry; washer's proverbs and fox fables; the language of the demons, the whisper of the palms, the language of the ministering angels and the great matter and the small matter.

The 'great matter' is the manifestation of the chariot [*Merkavah*] and the small matter is the arguments of Abbaye and Rava.

Thereby is fulfilled the Scriptural text, *That I may cause those that love me to inherit substance and that I may fill their treasuries* (Prov. 8:15). Now, if the least among them [was] so, how great must have been the greatest among them.

It was related of Jonathan b. Uzziel [that] when he sat and studied the Torah, every bird that flew over him was burned.

b. B.B. 134a, trans. I. W. Slotki, pp. 563-4

Comment: See V.ii.7. It is noteworthy that Prov. 8:15 appears apart from Hillel's death-scene. I suspect the death-scene was shaped after this Scripture entered the repertoire of exegetical conventions concerning Yoḥanan.

17. [Re Day of Waving]. R. Naḥman b. Isaac said, "Rabban Yoḥanan ben Zakkai [follows] the reasoning of Rabbi Judah..."

b. Men. 68b

Comment: See V.ii.9.

18. From the eighth of the same until the close of the Festival [of Passover], during which time the date for the Feast of Weeks was reestablished, fasting is forbidden. For the Boethusians held that the Feast of Weeks must always be on the day after the Sabbath.

But R. Yoḥanan b. Zakkai entered into discussion with them saying, "Fools that you are! whence do you derive it?"

Not one of them was able to answer him, save one old man who commenced to babble and said, "Moses our teacher was a great lover of Israel, and knowing full well that the Feast of Weeks lasted only one day, he therefore fixed it on the day after the Sabbath so that Israel might enjoy themselves for two successive days."

[R. Yoḥanan b. Zakkai] then quoted to him the following verse, "*It is eleven days' journey from Horeb unto Kadesh-Barnea by the way of Mount Seir* (Deut. 1:2). If Moses was a great lover of Israel, why then did he detain them in the wilderness for forty years?"

"Master," said the other, "is it thus that you would dismiss me?"

"Fool," he answered, "should not our perfect Torah be as convincing as your idle talk! Now one verse says, *Ye shall number fifty days*, (Lev. 23:16) while the other verse says, *Seven weeks shall there be complete* (Lev. 23:15)

"How are they to be reconciled? The latter verse refers to the time when the first day of the Festival of Passover falls on the Sabbath, while the former to a time when the first day of the Festival of Passover falls on a weekday."

b. Men. 65a-b, trans. Eli Cashdan, pp. 385-6.

Comment: The passage is introduced by a citation from the fasting-scroll. Before it are Tannaitic citations of the same document; afterward come other Tannaitic sayings. There is no Amoraic context at all. We do not know how the story was first formulated or what evidence the tradent had for attributing the event to Yoḥanan.

19. [Day of Waving]: Rabbis of the school of R. Ashi *re* "Rabban Yoḥanan ben Zakkai [follows] the reasoning of Rabbi Judah."

b. Men. 68b

Comment: See V.ii.9.

20. (a) Qunṭroqes the prince asked Rabban Yoḥanan ben Zakkai, "In the detailed record of the numbering of the Levites you find the total is twenty-two thousand three hundred, but in the summary you only find twenty-two thousand (Num. 3:39). Where did the other three hundred go?"

He replied, "The remaining three hundred were first-born [Levites] and a first-born cannot cancel the holiness of a first-born." What is the reason?

Abbaye said, "Because it is sufficient for a first-born [Levite] to cancel his own holiness.

(b) And again he asked, "With reference to the collection of the money [*sheqels*] you count two hundred and one *kikkar* and eleven *manehs* for Scripture says, *A beqa for every man, that is, half a sheqel after the sheqel of the Sanctuary* (Ex. 38:26). On the other hand, when the money was given, you find only one hundred *kikkar*, for it is written, *And the hundred talents of silver were for casting* (Ex. 38:26). Was Moses your master a thief or a swindler or a bad arithmetician? He gave half, took half, and did not return a complete half."

He replied, "Moses our teacher was a trustworthy treasurer and a good arithmetician, only the sacred *maneh* was double the common one."

R. Aḥi argued, "What was his [Qunṭroqes's] difficulty?..."

b. Bekh. 5a

Comment: The context is sayings about first-born, firstlings, and so forth. However I see no close relationship between the story about Yoḥanan and the antecedent materials. Since Abbaye appears in the middle of the story, we may readily assign the account as we have it to his school. R. Aḥi follows with further discussion of the problem raised by Qunṭroqes; then R. Ḥisda.

In V.i.15 and 16 the themes are the same, but here the texts are clearer, better developed and fully articulated. We cannot on that account assume the Babylonian versions are both later and dependent on the Palestinian ones, though that is a clear possibility.

21. TNW RBNN: A convert at this time must separate a quarter for his bird-offering. R. Simeon said, "Already has Rabban Yoḥanan ben Zakkai annulled it on account of [possible] disorder." b. Ker. 9a

Comment: The *beraita* is introduced in a selection of Tannaitic materials on converts and their obligations. Following is a comment of Idi b. Gershom in the name of Adda b. Aḥva, that R. Simeon's saying in fact is the law. See III.ii.30 and V.i.8.

III. General Comments

Since we have already reviewed Palestinian Amoraic references to Tannitic materials, we cannot be surprised to find so little in common between Palestinian Amoraic traditions and Tannaitic ones. Yet it is still striking that we have only a few expanded versions of earlier materials, particularly the death scene (V.i.11, 17 = III.ii.1 and IV.i.9) and Hillel's disciples (V.i.12). That would suggest that it was possible for Palestinian Amoraim to make use of earlier materials. In fact, however, they barely make reference to them, except when they are cited fully and completely in their earlier form.

Of the seventeen unduplicated Palestinian Amoraic items, none even refers to anything in the Tannaitic Midrashim, Mishnah, or Tosefta.

It seems to me that all materials considered in V.i.1-18, excluding V.i.8, V.i.12, and V.i.11,17, probably are inventions of Palestinian Amoraim. The tradition on Yoḥanan's wearing his *tefillin* winter and summer may have begun in a circle of Eliezer's followers, to be sure, but I think it more likely that the stories of Yoḥanan's intense devotion to study "and so did Eliezer after him" provided a model for this new detail about wearing *tefillin* all the time "and so did Eliezer after him." Perhaps the school of Yannai and Yoḥanan (b. Nappaḥa) regarded Yoḥanan b. Zakkai as a significant authority, but on this basis we can hardly say so.

ʿUlla's tradition on ʿArav is unique, unverifiable, and probably his own fabrication.

It is clear that only a few of Yoḥanan's legal sayings provoked careful study in Palestinian schools, particularly V.i.3,4,5 and 6, all on the same principle. No other context reveals close attention to what Yoḥanan actually said; all other exempla merely are sayings or stories about the master. The ten *gerahs* saying (V.i.7) is part of a series of explanations of the same Scripture, all in the name of Palestinian Amoraim. Inclusion of a saying attributed to Yoḥanan in such a list is certainly an anomaly. I see no clear connection between this *homer*-exegesis and any other, before or afterward.

V.i.8, on the convert's offering, may well be a Tannaitic formulation, as I said.

The exegesis of II Kings 27:9, applying the Scripture to the burning of Yoḥanan's [*bet-*] *midrash*, is certainly Joshua b. Levi's. V.i.10, about rain-making, is typical of Palestinian Amoraic accounts. It stands by itself, with no connection to anything said before or afterward. R. Ba's tradition about ordination is similar. While we know R. Ba said it, we do not know his basis, let alone precedents.

The several *defender-of-the-faith* stories, which we shall compare to one another below (synoptic section, XII.i), here make their first appearance. I suppose some contemporary disputes would have aroused interest in earlier settings; obviously, Yoḥanan's life at Yavneh would have provided a useful context in which to place such stories. Yet no story says Yavneh was the setting. But why a tradent, or a group of tradents, would have shaped a whole series of exegeses of various unrelated Scriptures in terms of *defender-of-the-faith* stories is simply unknown to me. V.i.14, 15 and 16 have no close relationship to one another. The names of the disputants differ (Antoninus, Antonius, Agentos), and, as we shall see, other Amoraic dispute-stories are no more closely tied to one another. I therefore presented the anonymous exegesis (Num. R. 3.14, in V.i.15) to illustrate *other* ways in which the same exegesis comes down to us. V.i.18 recurs in V.ii.3, but in Hebrew, and in the *They said about Yoḥanan*... form. It may be that the Palestinian Talmud version is older; only later did the more polished rendition, in Hebrew, take shape.

Much of the new Babylonian Amoraic material concerns Yoḥanan's life and personality. The setting of the sayings is not always apparent; we do not know how they were shaped. But as a group they are more literary and polished than anything in the Palestinian Talmud. Thus V.ii.1,2,3,6,7,15 all enrich the portrait of Yoḥanan's youth. Further, an echo of the *beraita* about Nebuchadnezzar's boast recurs, in abbreviated but elegant style, in V.ii.4. Some of Yoḥanan's sayings are subjected to close legal analysis, in V.ii.5,9,10,12,17,19, and 21.

A new exegesis occurs (V.ii.11); likewise another dispute-story, this time presented as commentary on the Fasting-Scroll, but *not* specified as a *beraita* (V.ii.18). The *defender-of-the-faith* stories (V.ii.20) appear in a clear and fluent text.

The Babylonian escape story is the only element which is literarily inferior to what has gone before. It is a mass of scarcely related traditions, only partly tied to one another, not at all carefully edited, and, by contrast to ARN, *not* centered on Yoḥanan; they are broken up by interjections and parenthetical remarks, with numerous digressions as well.

The Babylonian Amoraic material has little in common with earlier, Tannaitic data, but is not so remote from it as the equivalent Palestinian accounts. Thus the numerous references to his life are consistent with Tannaitic materials, if not identical with them. There are few items which stand completely apart and isolated from the whole rest of of the Yoḥanan-legend.

Table

Palestinian Amoraic Traditions Compared to Tannaitic Materials

Pal. Tal.		*Tan. Mid.*	*Mishnah*	*Tosefta*	*Bab. Tal.*	*ARN*
V.i.1	(Tefillin)	—	—	—	—	—
V.i.2	(Oh Galilee)	—	—	—	—	—
V.i.3	(Did Yoḥanan decree against teaching of Torah)	—	—	—	—	—
V.i.4	(Did Yoḥanan decree against teaching of Torah)	—	—	—	—	—
V.i.5	(Did Yoḥanan decree against teaching of Torah)	—	—	—	—	—
V.i.6	(Discussion of Yoḥanan's view on priestly *sheqel*)					
V.i.7	(Ten *gerahs*)	—	—	—	—	—
V.i.8	(Yoḥanan annuled convert's offering)	—	—	—	V.ii.10	—
V.i.9	(House of king)	—	—	—	—	—
V.i.10	(Rain-making)	—	—	—	—	—
V.i.11	(Death scene)	—	—	—	III.ii.1	IV.i.9
V.i.12	(Hillel's disciples)	—	—	—	V.ii.7	—
V.i.13	(Ordination)	—	—	—	—	—
V.i.14	(Ox stoned)	—	—	—	—	—
V.i.15	(Census)	—	—	—	V.ii.20	—
V.i.16	(Moses as accountant)	—	—	—	—	—
V.i.17	(= V.i.11)					
V.i.18	(Shadow of temple)	—	—	—	V.ii.3	—

Table

Babylonian Amoraic Traditions Compared to Tannaitic Materials

Bab. Tal.		*Tan. Mid.*	*Mishnah*	*Tosefta*	*Pal. Tal.*	*ARN*	*Bab.*
V.ii.1	(Greeted every-one)	—	—	—	—	—	—
V.ii.2	(Clean language)	—	—	—	—	—	—
V.ii.3	(Shadow of Temple)	—	—	—	V.i.18	—	—
V.ii.4	(Ascend to heights)	—		—	—	—	III.ii.
V.ii.5	Citation of Mishnah						
V.ii.6	(Always wore tefillin etc.)	—	—	—	V.i.1	—	—
V.ii.7	(Hillel's disciples)	—	—	—	V.i.12	IV.i.5	III.ii.24
V.ii.8	(Thorn-palms)	—	—	—	—	—	—
V.ii.9	(Naḥman b. Isaac discusses Yoḥanan's reasoning on *lulav*)						
V.ii.10	(Who are his colleagues)	—	—	—	—	—	—
V.ii.11	(Light/heavy sins)	—	—	—	—	—	—

Bab. Tal.		Tan. Mid.	Mishnah	Tosefta	Pal. Tal.	ARN	Bab.
V.ii.12	(Discussion of Yoḥanan's reasoning about the uncleanness of third loaf)						
V.ii.13	(Nine decrees)	—	—	—	—	—	—
V.ii.14	(Escape story)	—	—	—	—	IV.i.2	—
V.ii.15	(Nephews lose money)	—	—	—	—	—	—
V.ii.16	(Studied widely)	—	—	—	—	—	III.ii.24
V.ii.17	Discussion of Yoḥanan's reasoning on *lulav* (as V.ii.9)						
V.ii.18	(Boethusian dispute on date of weeks)	—	—	—	—	—	—
V.ii.19	As V.ii.9, 17						
V.ii.20	(Census of Levites)	—	—	—	V.i.15-16	—	—
V.ii.21	(Convert's offering)	—	—	—	V.i.8	—	—

Table

Amoraic authorities who cite, or are cited in connection with, Yoḥanan ben Zakkai; and the Language of Amoraic Materials in the Palestinian Talmud

Authorities		*Language of Pericope*
V.i.1:	Yannai, Yoḥanan (Eliezer)	Aramaic
V.i.2:	'Ulla	Aramaic
V.i.3:	—	Hebrew
V.i.4:	—	Hebrew
V.i.5:	—	Hebrew
V.i.6:	Berekiah, Ṭavi. Hamnuna [Judah, Neḥemiah]—Anonymous	Aramaic-Hebrew
V.i.7:	[R. Judah, R. Neḥemiah]—Joshua b. R. Neḥemiah [Berekiah, Levi—Simeon b. Laqish, Pinḥas—Levi]	Hebrew
V.i.8:	[Simeon b. Yoḥai]	Hebrew
V.i.9:	Joshua b. Levi	Hebrew
V.i.10:	Adda b. Aḥva	Aramaic
V.i.11:	Jacob b. Idi—Joshua b. Levi	Direct quotations: Hebrew Narrative: Aramaic
V.i.12:	Yoḥanan—Yosi b. R. Bun	Hebrew

CHAPTER SIX

SOME LATER MIDRASHIM

1. Genesis Rabbah

Genesis Rabbah dates from the time of the Palestinian Talmud (Strack, p. 218), ca. 350-400; Waxman places it ca. 500.

1. *And the Lord God created from the earth every beast of the field* (Gen. 2:19). They asked before R. Yoḥanan b. Zakkai, "It has already been written, *Let the earth bring forth each living soul according to its species* (Gen. 1:24). So what does Scripture [mean to] say, *And the Lord God created from the earth?*"

He said to them, "The former verse refers to creation, the latter to gathering together, as you read, *When you shall mass (taẓur) against a city a long time in making war against it*" (Deut. 20:19).

Gen. R. 17:4, ed. Theodor-Albeck, p. 155

Comment: The form "They asked before" is not found in Babylonian sources, which instead use "His disciples asked..." The play on words [YẒR/ẒR] serves to explain the repetition of the Creation-legend. The passage is anonymous; we do not know how, when, or by whom it was shaped. It does not occur earlier.

2. *And the eyes of both of them were opened* (Gen. 3:7). R. Judan in the name of R. Yoḥanan ben Zakkai, and R. Berekhiah in the name of R. ʿAqiva [compared it to] a villager who was passing in front of a glass-worker's store, before which was set a basket full of cups and cut-glass. He swung his staff and broke them.

[The glass-worker] arose and grabbed him, saying, "I know that I cannot claim redress from you, but come and I shall show you how much good you have destroyed."

Thus he [God] showed them how many generations they had destroyed.

Gen. R. 19:6, ed. Theodor-Albeck, p. 175

Comment: The confusion of attributions of exegeses to Yoḥanan and ʿAqiva tells us the story in this form could not have come into existence while the disciples of ʿAqiva were still available, for they would certainly have known what was to be attributed to their master, what to the earlier one. In fact, Judan and Berekhiah are the first authorities for this exegesis, which does not occur earlier.

3. R. Joshua commenced his discourse in the name of R. Levi, *The wicked have drawn out the sword* (Ps. 37:14).

(a) The story is told that R. Liezer's brothers were ploughing in the flat-land but he was ploughing on the mountain. His ox fell and was broken. It was for his own good that his ox was broken.

(b) He would eat clods of earth until a bad smell came out of his mouth. They went and told Rabban Yoḥanan ben Zakkai that the breath of R. Eliezer is hard [to take]. He said to him, "Just as the breath of your mouth became foul for the sake of Torah, so will the breath of your story go from one and of the world to the other."

(c) After some days his father came up to disinherit him from his property, and found him sitting and expositing and the great men of the state were sitting before him: Ben Ẓiẓit HaKeset and Naqdimon b. Gurion and Ben Kalba Shavuʿa.

(d) And he was expounding this verse, "*The wicked have drawn out the sword and have bent the bow*—alludes to Amraphel and his companions. *To cast down the poor and the needy*—to Lot. *To slay such as are upright in the way*—this is Abraham. *And their sword shall enter their own heart* (Ps. 37:15), as it is written, *And he fought against them by night, he and his servants, and he killed them* (Gen. 14:15).

(e) His father said to him, "I came, my son, only to disinherit you, now, behold, all my possessions are given to you as a gift."

He replied, "Behold they are *ḥerem* to me, but divide them equally among my brothers."

Gen. R. 42:1, ed. Theodor-Albeck, pp. 398-9

Comment: The story of Eliezer's beginnings is here increased by part (d). For that purpose, parts (c) and (e) are separated from one another. But otherwise the elements we have earlier observed all recur without much variation. Part (a), the ploughing story, is standard, but here is enhanced by the homily, "It was for his own good..." Part (b) omits the details about his having no funds, pretending to eat at the hostel, and so forth. The disinheritance story is routine, but omits the references to having to force Eliezer to give an exposition. Eliezer's reply to his father in part (e) makes no reference to Scriptural teachings that gold and silver belong to God.

In all, the story is not much different from those seen earlier. It shows a few marks of development, but some omissions are noteworthy. We have no idea how it was included in Gen. R. Its superscription would lead us to suppose R. Levi assigned it to the exposition of Ps. 37:14-15/ Gen. 14, and this explains the location of the story in this particular section of Gen. R. The detail that he was expounding Ps. 37:14 when his father came to Jerusalem may therefore have been added by the school of R. Levi, for it appears nowhere else.

4. *In that day the Lord made a covenant with Abraham* (Gen. 15:18).

R. Judah [in the name of] R. Yoḥanan ben Zakkai and R. ʿAqiva: One said, "This world he showed to him."

The other said, "This world and the world to come he showed to him."

Gen. R. 44:21, ed. Theodor-Albeck, pp. 444-5

Comment: As in VI.i.2, we see a tendency in later Palestinian schools to confuse teachings of ʿAqiva and those of Yoḥanan. In this case, still another solitary exemplum contains no hint as to when and where the passage was originally framed. We do not know which R. Judah is involved here, or whether it is the same as R. Judan above.

Perhaps the earlier tendency to pair Yoḥanan with ʿAqiva led the later Palestinian schools to suppose unnamed traditions might be attributable to "the one or the other" as a unit.

5. *And Joseph dwelt in Egypt... And Joseph lived a hundred and ten years* (Gen. 50:22). These six pairs lived an equal length of time: Rebecca and Kohath, Levi and Amram, Joseph and Joshua, Samuel and Solomon, Moses and Hillel the Elder, Rabban Yoḥanan ben Zakkai and R. ʿAqiva.

Moses lived in the palace of Pharaoh forty years, in Midian forty years, and served all Israel forty years. Hillel the Elder came up from Babylonia aged forty years, and served [as a disciple of] the sages forty years, and served Israel forty years.

Rabban Yoḥanan ben Zakkai spent forty years in business, studied Torah forty years, and served Israel forty years.

R. ʿAqiva lived as an ignorant man forty years, studied forty years, and served Israel forty years.

Gen. R. 100:10, ed. Theodor-Albeck, p. 1295.

Comment: This is now a standard text, cited without much alteration when the length of life of Joseph is mentioned, just as it appeared in connection with Moses's life in earlier versions.

II. Lamentations Rabbati

Lamentations Rabbati dates from the time of the Palestinian Talmud (Strack, p. 219); Zunz places it in ca. 650. It depends on Genesis Rabbati, so is somewhat later than that collection.

1. *Even every great man's house* (II Kings 25:9): i.e. the academy of Rabban Yoḥanan b. Zakkai. Why does he call it 'great house'? Because there he taught the praise of the Holy One, blessed be He. Since they sinned, they were exiled; and since they were exiled, Jeremiah began to lament over them, '*How sitteth solitary.*'

Lam. R. Proem #12, trans. A. Cohen, p. 18

Comment: The exegesis of II Kings 25:9 recurs without change.

2. (a) *Her adversaries are become the head* (Lam. 1:5). R. Hillel b. Berekiah said, "Whoever undertakes to vex Israel becomes a chief." What is the ground [of R. Hillel's statement]?

Her adversaries are become the head. You find that before Jerusalem was destroyed no province was held in any esteem; but after Jerusalem was destroyed Caesarea become a metropolis.

Another interpretation of her *adversaries are become the head:* this refers to Nebuchadnezzar; *her enemies are at ease*, this refers to Nebuzaradan.

Another interpretation of *her adversaries are become the head:* this refers to Vespasian; *her enemies are at ease*, this refers to Titus.

(b) For three and a half years Vespasian surrounded Jerusalem, having four generals with him: the general of Arabia, of Africa, of Alexandria, and of Palestine. With regard to the general of Arabia two teachers differ as to his name, one declaring that it was Killus and the other Pangar. In Jerusalem there were four councillors, viz. Ben Ẓiẓit, Ben Gorion, Ben Naqdimon, and Ben Kalba Shavu'a. Each of them was capable of supplying food for the city for ten years.

There was also there Ben Baṭṭiaḥ, the nephew of R. Yoḥanan b. Zakkai, who was appointed in charge of the stores, all of which he burnt.

When R. Yoḥanan b. Zakkai head of this, he exclaimed, "Woe!"

It was reported to Ben Baṭṭiaḥ, "Your uncle exlaimed 'woe!' "

He sent and had him brought before him and asked, "Why did you exclaim 'woe!'?"

He replied, "I did not exclaim 'woe!' but 'wah!' "

He said to him "You exclaimed 'wah!'? Why did you make that exclamation?"

He answered, "Because you burnt all the stores, and I thought that, so long as the stores were intact, the people would not expose themselves to the dangers of battle."

Through the difference between 'woe' and 'wah', R. Yoḥanan b. Zakkai escaped death; and the verse was applied to him, *The excellency of knowledge is that wisdom preserveth the life of him that hath it* (Qoh. 7:12).

(c) Three days later R. Yoḥanan b. Zakkai went out to walk in the market-place and saw how people seethed straw and drank its water; and he said [to himself], "Can men who seethe straw and drink its water withstand the armies of Vespasian?"

He added, "I have come to the conclusion that I must get out of here."

He sent a message to Ben Baṭṭiaḥ, "Get me out of here."

He replied, "We have made an agreement among ourselves that nobody shall leave the city except the dead."

He said, "Carry me out in the guise of a corpse."

R. Eliezer carried him by the head, R. Joshua by the feet, and Ben Baṭṭiaḥ walked in front.

When they reached [the city gates, the guards] wanted to stab him.

Ben Baṭṭiaḥ said to them, "Do you wish people to say that when our teacher died, his body was stabbed!"

On his speaking to them in this manner, they allowed him to pass. After going through the gates, they carried him to a cemetery and left him there and returned to the city.

(d) R. Yoḥanan b. Zakkai came out and went among the soldiers of Vespasian. He said to them, "Where is the king?"

They went and told Vespasian, "A Jew is asking for you."

He said to them, "Let him come."

On his arrival he exclaimed, "*Vive domine Imperator!*"

Vespasian remarked, "You give me a royal greeting, but I am not king; and should the king hear of it, he will put me to death."

He said to him, "If you are not the king, you will be eventually, because the Temple will only be destroyed by a king's hand, as it is said, *And Lebanon shall fall by a mighty one* (Is. 10:34)."

They took and placed him in the innermost of several chambers and asked him what hour of the night it was, and he told them. They subsequently asked him what hour of the day it was, and he told them. How did R. Yoḥanan b. Zakkai know it? From his study.

(e) Three days later Vespasian went to take a bath at Gophna. After he had bathed and put on one of his shoes, a message arrived, and it was announced to him that Nero had died, and the Romans had proclaimed him king. He wished to put on the other shoe, but it would not go on his foot.

He sent for R. Yoḥanan and asked, "Will you not explain to me why all these days I wore two shoes which fitted me, but now one fits and the other does not?"

He answered, "You have been informed of good news, because it is written, *A good report maketh the bones fat* (Prov. 15:30)."

He inquired, "What must I do to get it on?" He replied, "Is there anybody whom you hate or who has done you wrong? Let him pass in front of you and your flesh will shrink, because it is written, *A broken spirit drieth the bones* (Prov. 17:22).

(f) Then they began to speak to him in parables, "If a snake nested in a cask, what is to be done with it?"

He answered, "Bring a charmer and charm the snake, and leave the cask intact."

Pangar said, "Kill the snake and break the cask." [Then they asked,] "If a snake nested in a tower, what is to be done with it?"

He answered, "Bring a charmer and charm the snake, and leave to tower intact."

Pangar said, "Kill the snake and burn the tower."

R. Yoḥanan said to Pangar, "All neighbors who do harm, do it to their neighbors; instead of putting in a plea for the defence you argue for the prosecution against us!"

He replied, "I seek your welfare; so long as the Temple exists, the heathen kingdoms will attack you, but if it is destroyed, they will not attack you."

R. Yoḥanan said to him, "The heart knows whether it is for *ʿaqqel* or *ʿaqalqalot*."

(g). Vespasian said to R. Yoḥanan b. Zakkai, "Make a request of me and I will grant it." He answered, "I beg that you abandon this city of Jerusalem and depart."

He said to him, "Did the Romans proclaim me king that I should abandon this city? Make another request of me and I will grant it."

He answered, "I beg that you leave the western gate which leads to Lydda, and everyone who departs up to the fourth hour shall be spared."

After Vespasian had conquered the city, he asked him, "Have you any friend or relative there? Send and bring him out before the troops enter." He sent R. Eliezer and R. Joshua to bring out R. Ẓadoq.

They went and found him in the city gate. When he arrived, R. Yoḥanan stood up before him.

Vespasian asked, "You stand up before this emaciated old man?"

He answered, "By your life, if there had been [in Jerusalem] one more like him, though you had double your army, you would have been unable to conquer it."

He asked, "What is his power?"

He replied, "He eats one fig and on the strength of it teaches at one hundred sessions in the academy."

"Why is he so lean?" he inquired.

He answered, "On account of his numerous abstinences and fasts."

Vespasian sent and brought physicians who fed him on small portions of food and doses of liquid until his physical powers returned to him.

His son Eleazar said to him, "Father, give them their reward in this world so that they should have no merit with respect to you in the world to come."

He gave them calculation by fingers and scales for weighing.

(i) When Vespasian had subdued the city, he assigned the destruction of the four ramparts to the four generals, and the western gate was allotted to Pangar. Now it had been decreed by Heaven that this should never be destroyed because the *Shekhinah* abode in the west. The others demolished their sections but he did not demolish his.

Vespasian sent for him and asked, "Why did you not destroy your section?"

He replied, "By your life, I acted so for the honor of the kingdom; for if I had demolished it, nobody would [in time to come] know what it was you destroyed; but when people look [at the western wall], they exclaim, 'Perceive the might of Vespasian from what he destroyed!' "

He said to him, "Enough, you have spoken well, but since you disobeyed my command, you shall ascend to the roof and throw yourself down. If you live, you will live; if you die, you will die." He ascended, threw himself down and died.

Thus the curse of R. Yoḥanan b. Zakkai alighted upon him.

Lam. R. 1.5.31, trans. A. Cohen, pp. 100-105

Comment: Part (a) is unrelated to the story that follows. Hence we cannot attribute the entire account to Hillel b. Berekiah. But if not, then we have no idea how the extended story of Yoḥanan's escape was formed, for no earlier authority is mentioned throughout. The absence of the exclamations of R. Joseph/ʿAqiva, "He should have said," combined with the correction to conform to the criticism, is incontrovertible evidence that the story is later than that in b. Giṭ. 56a. Hence it must be dated no earlier than the fifth century. Lam. R. probably is no earlier than ca. 400-450, if this story is not a later addition to the compilation. But the Arab role suggests a post-Islamic date.

Part (b) introduces the four generals, with chief reference to the Arab general Pangar. Later on, Pangar takes an important role. Part (b) likewise contains new information, this time about Yoḥanan's nephew, Ben Baṭṭiaḥ. The burning of the stores, which by now was well known, is thus tied to Yoḥanan's escape. Before this, the escape had nothing to do with the burning of the stores, but now is provoked by that event. Yoḥanan's cleverness is underlined, for he knew how to prevaricate when necessary. This is not criticized, but regarded as the "excellency of knowledge." In Part (c), the immediate motive for the escape is spelled out. The people had nothing to eat, therefore would be too weak to fight. Knowing on the basis of his own observation—not through exegesis of Is. 10:34—that the city would fall, Yoḥanan determines to escape. He consults his nephew about it. The two disciples are intruded without introduction. They are already a well known part of the story. But the narrator's focus remains on Ben Baṭṭiaḥ, who manages the problem of the guardians at the gates. He is then ceremoniously returned to the city. So Yoḥanan is clearly related to a leading zealot, but had no influence or power in the revolutionary councils. Indeed, he was suspect and had to lie to defend his own life.

The encounter with Vespasian is similar to that in b. Giṭ. 56a. Vespasian knows nothing about Yoḥanan ("A Jew is asking for you"), but after predicting Vespasian would be emperor, is given a hearing. The well-known exegesis of Is. 10:34 is now introduced. There follows a new detail, about Yoḥanan's ability to tell time on the basis of his study. What this means is that he repeated memorized sayings in cadence, and knew pretty well how long it took to say them. Hence he could tell time without seeing the light.

Part (e) likewise amplifies the story of Vespasian's swollen feet. Yoḥanan through his knowledge of Torah is able to solve the mystery and heal the emperor. Part (f) is wholly new. Pangar reappears, now as the clever "sage of the gentiles." Pangar's wisdom is used for Israel's disadvantage, and the new Balaam is therefore to be given his comeuppance. Part (g) returns to the thread of the encounter, left off with part (d). Vespasian, knowing his visitor's sagacity and grateful for the information of his coming enthronement, asks what he can do. Yoḥanan replied, as Joseph/ʿAqiva said he should, but then asks only for free egress for refugees. But after the capture of the city by Vespasian (Titus in unknown in the Yoḥanan materials), Yoḥanan is able to rescue Ẓadoq, who thereupon becomes the focus of interest. Part (i) refers to the "curse of Yoḥanan" on Pangar. This was hinted at in "The heart knows.."

It would be difficult to explain details of this story in terms of contemporary conditions. We do not know what school produced it, or what masters were responsible for either forming or accepting the story into the tradition. It would be fruitless, therefore, to speculate on what life-situation lay behind the intrusion, for instance, of Yoḥanan's relationship to Ben Baṭṭiaḥ, the new "sage of the gentiles" in the form of Pangar, the magical wisdom of the master in telling time, and similar matters. If some motive shaped tendencies in the account formerly not seen by us, we have not got the slightest way to locate it.

III. Pesiqta de Rav Kahana

Pesiqta de Rav Kahana is dated by Zunz in 700, by Theodor in 800 (Strack, p. 211), by Waxman (I, p. 140) as "seventh-century Palestinian."

1. *Righteousness exalts a nation and the lovingkindness of the nations is sin* (Prov. 14:34). R. Eliezer and R. Joshua and the rabbis.

R. Liezer says, "*Righteousness exalts*—refers to Israel. But *the lovingkindness of the nations is a sin*—The lovingkindnesses are sins for the nations, for they take pride in them."

R. Joshua says, "*Righteousness exalts*—refers to Israel. *But lovingkindness of the nations is a sin*—It is a source of pleasure for the nations of the world when Israel sins, for they go and subjugate them [Israel, on that account]."

Rabban Gamaliel says, "*Righteousness exalts*—refers to Israel. *But lovingkindness of the nations is a sin*—The lovingkindness which the nations of the world do is a sin for them, for so Daniel says to Nebuchadnezzar, *And your sin remove by means of righteousness* (Dan. 24:4)."

R. Leazar b. ʿArakh says, "*Righteousness exalts a nation and mercy*—these are Israel, But Sias—these belong to the nations of the world."

Rabban Yoḥanan ben Zakkai said, "I prefer the words of Leazar b. ʿArakh to your words, for he places righteousness and mercy upon Israel and sins, upon the nations of the world."

Pesiqta deR. Kahana, ed. Mandelbaum, pp. 20-21

Comment: In the synoptic studies we shall consider the several stories of Yoḥanan's exegesis of Prov. 14:34. The passage before us is anonymous. Yoḥanan is not introduced until the end. Up to that point, it is a case of several sages divided on the interpretation of a Scripture.

The *Avot*-form is alluded to, but not perfectly followed, for Gamaliel intervenes in the normal pattern, and the other members of the Jerusalem circle are omitted.

The passage follows with teachings in Prov. 14:34 in the name of Abin b. R. Judah, Neḥuniah b. HaQaneh and others, but the saying of Yoḥanan ends a complete unit. See above, II.i.18.

2. R. Joshua b. R. Neḥemiah in the name of Rabbi Yoḥanan ben Zakkai said, "Because Israel transgressed against the Ten Words, therefore each one of them must bring ten *gerahs*."

Pesiqta deRav Kahana, ed. Mandelbaum, p. 32

Comment: As above, V.i.7.

3. A certain gentile asked Rabban Yoḥanan ben Zakkai, "These things which you do appear to me like some sort of sorcery. You bring a calf, slaughter it, and burn it, mash it, take its dust, and when one of you becomes unclean by reason of corpse-uncleanness, you sprinkle on him two or three drops and you say to him, 'You are purified.'"

He said to him, "Has a wandering spirit ever entered you?"

He replied, "No."

He said to him, "But have you ever seen someone else into whom a wandering spirit has entered?"

He said to him, "Yes."

He said to him, "And what do you do?"

He said to him, "You bring branches, make smoke under him, throw water on him, and it flees."

He said to him, "Should not your ears hear what your mouth speaks? So it is with this spirit. It is the spirit of uncleanness, as it is written, *And also with the prophets and with the spirit of uncleanness* (Zech. 13:2)."

When he went out, his disciples said to him, "Rabbi, this one you have driven away with a reed, but what will you reply to us?"

He said to them, "By your lives! The corpse does not [really] render unclean, nor does the water [really] purify, but [the whole matter is] the decree of the Holy One, blessed be he. The Holy One, blessed be he, says, 'A decree have I decreed, an ordinance have I ordained, and you are not free to transgress my decree. *This is the ordinance of the Torah* (Num. 19:1).'"

Pesiqta deR. Kahana, ed. Mandelbaum, p. 74

Comment: This story first occurs now, but it several times recurs in still later sources. We have no idea about its origins or primary setting. The idea of the students that Yoḥanan had an esoteric as well as an exoteric doctrine is already familiar, but until now has been applied mainly to exegesis of Scriptures in disputes with gentiles. It was perfectly natural to extend the supposition from exegetical disputes to other sorts of encounters, and that is what I suppose took place. It is noteworthy, though, that the concept of an esoteric doctrine never pertains to teachings given to disciples or disputes with other Jews. On the contrary, the Sadducee-dispute stories contain no hint that Yoḥanan taught something to his disciples which he did not reveal to Sadducees, or replied to his disciples in a manner different from his replies to Sadducean opponents. In relationships to other Jews, therefore, the tradition reports no esoteric/exoteric distinction whatever.

4. *And all the houses of Jerusalem and the great house he burned in fire* (II Kings 25:9). And why does he call it "the great house?" But this is the school house of Rabban Yoḥanan ben Zakkai, where they would teach the great deeds of the Holy One blessed be he.

Pesiqta deR. Kahana, ed. Mandelbaum, p. 76

Comment: As above, V.i.9, VI.ii.1.

5. Rabban Yoḥanan ben Zakkai said, "We find that the day and the night are [both] called day, as it is written, *And there was evening, and there was morning, one day* (Gen. 1:5).

Pesiqta deR. Kahana, ed. Mandelbaum, p. 126

Comment: There is no sign of the context of this saying, which is unrelated to what precedes. Joshua b. R. Neḥemiah afterward provides another proof-text for the same proposition, but makes no remark about Yoḥanan's proof.

IV. Pesiqta Rabbati

This collection is dated by Zunz in 845 (Strack, p. 213). Braude places it in Palestine in the seventh century, possibly the sixth.

1. A heathen asked Rabban Yoḥanan ben Zakkai, saying, "The things you Jews do appear to be a kind of sorcery. A heifer is brought, it is burned, is pounded into ashes, and its ashes are gathered up. Then when one of you gets defiled by contact with a corpse, two or three drops of the ashes' mixture are sprinkled upon him, and he is told, 'You are cleansed!' "

Rabban Yoḥanan asked the heathen, "Has the spirit of madness ever possessed you?"

He replied, "No."

"Have you ever seen a man whom the spirit of madness has possessed?"

The heathen replied, "Yes."

"And have you not seen what is done to the man?"

[The heathen replied], "Roots are brought, they are made to smoke under him, water is splashed upon him, until the spirit flees."

Rabban Yoḥanan then said, "Do not your ears hear what your mouth is saying? A man defiled is like a man possessed of a spirit. This spirit is a spirit of uncleanness, and Scripture says, *And I will cause the prophets of the spirit of uncleanness to pass out of the Land* (Zech. 13:2)."

Now when the heathen left, Rabban Yoḥanan's disciples said, "Our master, you thrust off that heathen with a mere reed of an answer, but what reply will you give us?"

Rabban Yoḥanan answered, "No matter how it appears, the corpse does not defile, nor does the mixture of ash and water cleanse. The truth is that the rite of the Red Heifer is a decree of the Lord. The Holy One, blessed be He, said: 'I have set down a statute, I have issued a decree. Thou art not permitted to transgress My decree.' "

Pesiqta Rabbati, #14, ed. and trans. Braude, p. 291

Comment: As I noted (Vi.iii.3), this is now a popular story. The account is practically identical in all versions. Minor differences occur only because the translators are different.

2. R. Yoḥanan ben Zakkai explained away the apparent contradiction, saying, "We find in Scripture that the day and the night together are spoken of as a day, as is said *And there was evening and there was morning, one day* (Gen. 1:5)."

Pesiqta Rabbati, #17, ed. and trans. Braude, p. 367

Comment: See VI.iii.5.

3. His disciples asked R. Yoḥanan ben Zakkai, "Why of all his organs is the ear of the Hebrew slave [who refuses to accept his freedom] pierced through?"

He replied, "The ear which heard on Mount Sinai, *I am the Lord thy*

God, who brought thee out of the land of Egypt, out of the house of bondage (Exod. 20:2), yet took upon itself the yoke of sovereignty under flesh and blood—the ear which heard before Mount Sinai, *Thou shalt have no other gods before Me*, is now the ear of a man who went and got another master for himself. Therefore let the ear come and be pierced through because it did not heed what it heard. In a bygone time Israel were servants of servants. From now on they are servants of the Holy One, blessed be He: *For unto Me the children of Israel are servants; they are My servants whom I brought forth out of the land of Egypt* (Lev. 25:55)."

Pesiqta Rabbati, #21, ed. and trans. Braude, p. 452

Comment: As we have now observed in almost all later midrashic compilations, the passage is not introduced by an authority, but is simply cited. The several previous versions are, as we shall see, now conflated into a single unitary account in the "His disciples asked..." form.

v. Tanḥuma

J. Z. Lauterbach (*JE* xii, p. 45) states that the Buber Tanḥuma collection "is even older than Ber. R., which quotes several of its decisions." It was edited in the fifth century, before the completion of the Babylonian Talmud, to which work it nowhere refers.

1. [This is an elaborate account of the origins of R. Eliezer b. Hyrcanus. The passage in which R. Yoḥanan ben Zakkai appears is as follows:]

He [Eliezer[came into Jerusalem as a poor man. He saw Rabban Yoḥanan ben Zakkai sitting and teaching Torah, with the disciples seated before [studying] a chapter. When they had completed a chapter, he taught them *haggada*, and afterward *Mishnah*. He [Eliezer] entered and sat near Rabban Yoḥanan ben Zakkai.

He stayed with him two or three Sabbaths. He came to speak against the students [in argument], and they smelled the breath of his mouth, which was foul. And they kept away and did not say so.

Once again he came to speak, and they hid from him and did not say anything, and still a third time [it happened]. Rabban Yoḥanan ben Zakkai learned that the smell of his mouth was not from a bad thing which he had in his mouth, but because of hunger, for he had eaten nothing.

Rabban Yoḥanan ben Zakkai said to his disciples: "By your lives!

You stick to the matter and find out about the affairs of this disciple, if it is on account of hunger. What is he eating?"

They went throughout Jerusalem and asked the inn-keeper, "Is a *ḥaver* a guest here?"

They said no.

Finally they came to a certain woman [and asked the same thing] and she said yes.

"Does he have anything here?" She said to them, "He has a single sack."

[They found out he was eating dirt and told Yoḥanan].

Tanḥuma par. Lekh Lekha #10

Comment: This version of the beginnings of Eliezer contains an elaborate account of the foul-breath story, as well as other details already familiar in earlier versions. The exegetical setting is the same as Ber. R. (VI.i.3).

2. A star-worshipper asked Rabban Yoḥanan ben Zakkai, "These things which you do look like a kind of sorcery. They bring a calf and burn it and mash it and take its dust, and if one of you becomes unclean [on account of] corpse uncleanness, they sprinkle on him two or three drops and say to him, "You are clean."

He said to him, "Has a wandering spirit ever entered you?"

He said, "No."

He said to him, "Perhaps you have seen a man into whom a wandering spirit has entered?"

He said to him, "Yes."

He said to him, "And what do you do for him?"

He said to him, "They bring twigs and smoke them and place water on [the fire] and it [the spirit] flees."

He said to him, "Let your ears hear what you bring out of your mouth. This is an unclean spirit, as it is written, *And also the prophets and a spirit of uncleanness I shall cause to pass from the land* (Zech. 13:2). They sprinkle the waters on it, and it flees."

After he went out his disciples said to him, "This one you have driven away with a reed, but what will you say to us?"

He said to them, "By your lives! It is not the corpse which renders unclean, nor the waters which purify, but it is a decree of the king of the kings of kings. The Holy One has said, 'An ordinance have I ordained for you, a decree have I decreed, and you are not permitted to transgress my decree, as it is written, *This is the decree of the Torah* (Num. 19:1)."

Tanḥuma par. Ḥuqat #26

Comment: There is no significant variation between this and the versions already considered.

3. *And the great house he burned in fire* (II Kings 25:9). Why does he call it the great house? This is the school house of R. Yoḥanan ben Zakkai, where they would teach the great deeds of the Holy One, blessed be he.

Tanḥuma par. Ḥuqat, #28

Comment: See VI.ii.1.

4. *Then I will draw near to you for judgment, and I will be a swift witness against the sorcerers, against the adulterers, against those who swear falsely, against those who oppress the hireling in his wages, the widow, and the orphan, against those who thrust aside the sojourners, and do not fear me, says the Lord of hosts* (Mal. 3:5).

"Woe unto us on account of the day of judgment—woe unto us on account of the day of retribution, for the Scripture has compared those who upset justice to all the worst sins. Therefore the Holy One blessed be he warned, '*You will not pervert justice.*' "

Tanḥuma par. Shofeṭim #7

Comment: See above, V.ii.11.

5. The evil Hadrian, when he had conquered Jerusalem, was puffing himself up and saying, "I have overcome Jerusalem by my own might."

Rabban Yoḥanan ben Zakkai said, "Do not puff up. If it was not [decreed] from heaven, you would not have conquered."

What did Rabban Yoḥanan do? He took him and brought him into a cave and showed him buried Amorites, and one of them was eighteen *amot* high.

I said to him, "When we had merit, all these fell into our hands. Now you have ruled over us by means of our *own* sins." Yet is it not written, *And I have driven out the Amorites from before you* (Amos 2:96)? By what merit? By merit of the Torah which you received, which begins, *I am the Lord your God* (Ex. 20:2)—In behalf of the "I"—I destroyed the Amorites from before you.

Tanḥuma Additions to Deut. #7

Comment: This is a strange, garbled account, which first occurs here. The reference to Hadrian contains the echo of Yoḥanan's saying about Is. 14:14-5. But that passage is not quoted. The passage moves from third-person reference to Yoḥanan, "What did he do," to "I said to him." In any event the passage illustrates how late tradents would invent their own accounts of Yoḥanan's dealings with Roman generals. We have no idea who invented it or what circumstances (if any) provoked him to do so.

VI. Qohelet Rabbah

Strack states (p. 221), "The late date of this midrash becomes clear from the fact that the tractate Aboth and even several of the smaller tractates... are referred to by name." But Strack does not say what he means by "a late date." Theodor (*JE* vii, p. 529) gives no precise date either. We may assume, at any rate, that the work comes long after the editing of the Babylonian Talmud.

1. Simeon of Siknin was a shrewd man, and he used to dig wells, trenches, and caves in Jerusalem. He said to R. Yoḥanan b. Zakkai, "I am as great a man as you."

"How is that?" he asked, to which he replied, "I work on behalf of the public as well as you."

"If a man comes to you for a decision or with an inquiry, you tell him to drink from a certain well whose waters are pure and cold. Or if a woman questions you concerning her ritual impurity, you tell her to immerse herself in a certain well whose waters cleanse."

The rabbi thereupon applied this verse to him, *And be ready to hearken: It is better than when fools give sacrifices, for they know not that they do evil* (Qoh. 4:17).

Qoh. R. 4.17.1, trans. A. Cohen, pp. 125-6

Comment: This story occurs no wher eelse, and there is no allusion of any kind in exegeses of Qoh. 4:17 to Yoḥanan's interest in that particular Scripture. I imagine the story is a complete invention of a period long after living traditions about Yoḥanan ceased to circulate in unedited form.

2. *There is an evil which I have seen under the sun* (Qoh. 6:1).

R. Samuel b. Ammi said, "This refers to the devices of cheats; e.g. one who adulterates wine with water, oil with the juice of glaucion, honey with the juice of the wild strawberry, balsam with ass's milk, myrrh with gum, aromatic leaves with vine-leaves, brine with red coloring matter, pepper with vetch, or uses a weight-beam which is longer on one side than the other [to give false measure]."

Concerning all these R. Yoḥanan b. Zakkai remarked, "Woe is me if I say it, and woe is me if I do not say it. If I say it, there is the danger that cheats will learn what to do; and if I do not say it, the cheats may assert, 'The Sages are unacquainted with our actions.' "

Finally, he did say it, *For the ways of the Lord are right* (Hosea 14:10).

(Qoh. R. 6.1.1. trans. A. Cohen, p. 158)

Comment: The citation of Yoḥanan is tacked on to Samuel b. Ammi's statement. In fact it serves equally well for any sort of list of cheaters' devices and schemes, and was cited without regard to its original context. We cannot say Samuel b. Ammi was responsible for the addition of Yoḥanan's *woe* saying. We do not know how it was added, but we may be sure that by now, it was merely a conventional citation.

3. Three councillors were in Jerusalem, viz., Ben Ẓiẓit Hakeset, Naqdimon b. Gorion and Ben Kalba-Shavu'a, each of whom was capable of supplying food for the city for ten years. Ben Baṭṭiaḥ, nephew of R. Yoḥanan b. Zakkai, was appointed in charge of the stores, as chief of the zealots in Jerusalem, and he arose and burnt the storehouses.

When R. Yoḥanan b. Zakkai heard of this he exclaimed, "Woe!"

It was reported to Ben Baṭṭiaḥ, "Your uncle exclaimed 'Woe!' "

He sent and had him brought, and asked, "Why did you exclaim 'Woe!'?"

He replied, "I did not exclaim 'Woe!' but 'Weh!' because so long as the precious stores were intact the people would not jeopardize their lives in battle."

Through the difference between 'woe and 'weh' R. Yoḥanan escaped death; and the verse was applied to him, *The excellency of knowledge is that wisdom preserveth the life of him that hath it.* (Qoh. 7:12).

Qoh. R. 7.12.1, trans. A. Cohen, p. 193

Comment: For the purposes of exegesis of Qoh. 7:12, the burning of the stores is cited, but without the further materials given in VI.ii.2. But VI.vi.3 clearly depends upon VI.ii.2b.

4. *Let thy garments be always white; and let thy head lack no oil* (Qoh. 9:8).

(a) R. Yoḥanan b. Zakkai said, "If the text speaks of white garments, how many of these have the peoples of the world; and if it speaks of good oil, how much of it do the peoples of the world possess! Behold, it speak only of precepts, good deeds, and Torah."

(b) It has been taught: Repent one day before your death. R. Eliezer was asked by his disciples, "Rabbi, does any man know when he will die, so that he can repent?"

He answered them, "Should he not all the more repent today lest he die the day after, and then all his days will be lived in repentance. For that reason it is said, *Let thy garments be always white* (Qoh. 9:8)."

Qoh. R. 9.7.1, trans. A. Cohen, pp. 235-6

Comment: Yoḥanan's comment is followed by a long parable of Judah the Prince, "To what may this be likened?" Bar Kappara and Isaac b. Kappara then offer a second parable. Part (b) follows Eliezer's comment on the same verse. In some early version, therefore, parts (a) and (b) may well have been handed on in Eliezer's school, as a composite exegesis of Qoh. 9:8. It may well be that Judah the Prince and his circle added a fitting parable for the exegesis. But in the form before us, the whole account is much too late to have been preserved unchanged from the end of the second century onward; in any event we do not have the slightest reference to Yoḥanan's treatment of Qoh. 9:8 in an earlier document.

VII. Numbers Rabbah

Numbers Rabbah is dated by Zunz in ca. 900, by Waxman in ca. 1100.

1. This was the very question which the general Agentus put to R. Yoḥanan b. Zakkai. He said to him: "Moses, your teacher, was either a thief or else did not know arithmetic."

Said he to him, "Why?"

"Because," answered Agentus, "there were twenty-two thousand first-born and an additional two hundred and seventy-three, and the Omnipresent commanded that the Levites should redeem the first-born. Reckon twenty-two thousand of the Levites against twenty-two thousand firstborn. Now there were still three hundred Levites over and above the twenty-two thousand, as is calculated in detail in the first numbering. For what reason did these surplus three hundred Levites not redeem the two hundred and seventy-three firstborn who were over and above the twenty-two thousand firstborn? For we find that those two hundred and seventy-three gave five *sheqels* each! And furthermore, why is it that when he sums up the number of Levites at the end he deducts three hundred of them from the original number? Ergo, did he not suppress them from the correct number only so that those two hundred and seventy-three firstborn might each give five *sheqels* to his brother Aaron? Or was he perhaps unable to do arithmetic?"

R. Yoḥanan said to him, "He was no thief, and he knew how to do arithmetic. But there is one thing he whispered to me that I should tell you."

Said he to him, "Say it."

R. Yoḥanan b. Zakkai said to him, "You are able to read, but cannot expound, the Scripture. He [Moses] thought: Those twenty-two thousand Levites will redeem the twenty-two thousand firstborn, but there will still remain of the Levites another three hundred, and of the firstborn another two hundred and seventy-three. Now those three hundred of the Levites were firstborn and firstborn cannot redeem a firstborn, so when he summed up their number he omitted them, because they were firstborn."

Thereupon he took his leave of him.

Num. R. 4.9, trans. J.J. Slotki, pp. 105-6

Comment: See above, V.i.15, V.ii.20. As usual, we have no idea how this account was shaped.

2. An idolater asked R. Yoḥanan b. Zakkai, "These rites that you perform look like a kind of witchcraft. You bring a heifer, burn it, pound it, and take its ashes. If one of you is defiled by a dead body, you sprinkle upon him two or three drops and you say to him: 'Thou art clean!' "

R. Yoḥanan asked him, "Has the demon of madness ever possessed you?"

"No," he replied.

"Have you ever seen a man possessed by this demon of madness?"

"Yes," said he.

"And what do you do in such a case?"

"We bring roots," he replied, "and make them smoke under him, then we sprinkle water upon the demon and it flees."

Said R. Yoḥanan to him, "Let your ears hear what you utter with your mouth! Precisely so is this spirit a spirit of uncleanness; as it is written, *And also I will cause the prophets and the unclean spirit to pass out of the land* (Zech. 13:2). Water of purification is sprinkled upon the unclean and the spirit flees."

When the idolater had gone R. Yoḥanan's disciples said to their master, "Master! This man you have put off with a mere makeshift, but what explanation will you give us?"

Said he to them, "By your life! It is not the dead that defiles nor the water that purifies! The Holy One, blessed be He, merely says: 'I have laid down a statute, I have issued a decree. You are not allowed to transgress My decree, as it is written, *This is the statute of the law* (Num. 19:2).' "

Num. R. 19:8, trans. J. J. Slotki, pp. 757-8

Comment: See above, VI.iii.3, VI.v.2.

VIII. Deuteronomy Rabbah

Deuteronomy Rabbah is dated by Waxman at 900; Zunz presented the same date.

1. It is related that once a Gentile put a question to R. Yoḥanan b. Zakkai, saying: "We have festivals, and you have festivals; we have the Calends, Saturnalia, and Kratesis, and you have Passover, Pentecost, and Tabernacles. Which is the day whereupon we and you rejoice alike?"

R. Yoḥanan b. Zakkai replied, "It is the day when rain falls." For it is said, *The meadows are clothed with flocks; the valleys also are covered over with corn; they shout for joy, yea, they sing'* (Ps. 65:14). What follows immediately on this? *A Psalm. Shout unto God, all the earth* (Ps. 66:1).

Deut. R. 7:7, trans. J. Rabbinowitz, p. 139

Comment: This "defender-of-the-faith" story occurs nowhere else. The Roman holidays are accurately named, which would suggest that the story was shaped at a time when those days were still known and observed, presumably before the end of Roman rites in Palestine. But I do not know when that would have taken place, or how the story circulated before its inclusion in this late collection.

IX. Song of Songs Rabbah

This midrash is "not of the talmudic period," but how late it is to be dated I cannot say. For our purposes its date is not essential.

1. *And at our doors are all manner of precious fruits* (Song 7:14). Members of the school of R. Shila and the Rabbis gave different explanations of this.

Members of the school of R. Shila said, "It is like the case of a virtuous woman to whom her husband [on going away] left only a few articles and little money for her expenses; yet when he returned she was able to say to him, 'See what you left me and what I have saved up for you. Nay, I have even added to what you left.' "

The Rabbis compare it to the case of a king who had an orchard which he handed over to a tenant. What did the tenant do? He filled some baskets with the fruit of the orchard and put them at the entrance of the orchard. When the king passed and saw the goodly show, he said, "All this fine fruit is at the entrance of the orchard; then what must be in the orchard itself!"

So in the earlier generations there were the Men of the Great Synagogue, Hillel, Shammai and Rabban Gamaliel the Elder; in the later generations R. Yoḥanan b. Zakkai, R. Eliezer, R. Joshua, R. Meir, and R. 'Aqiva and their disciples; how much the more! And of these it says, *New and old which I have laid up for thee, O my beloved.*

Song R. 7:14.1, trans. M. Simon, pp. 301-302

Comment: Here is a very late allusion to Yoḥanan and his disciples; it is striking that they are referred to as "what was in the orchard itself." One may hear an echo of the "Four who entered paradise" and the mystical doctrines of Yoḥanan. But Eleazar is absent; no mystical teachings are attributed to Gamaliel the Elder.

x. Midrash on Psalms

Braude sees the collection as concluded in the thirteenth century, but says it contains materials from "as early as the third century." The sole passage referring to Yoḥanan is, of course, familiar from much earlier documents.

1. Once R. Yosi the son of the Damascene went to Lud to pay his respects to R. Eliezer. R. Eliezer asked R. Yosi: "What new thing happened today in the house of study" R. Yosi replied, "The Sages voted and decided that those Jews owning fields in Ammon and Moab be required to set aside, from crops raised in the seventh year, another tithe for the poor."

Thereupon R. Eliezer said to R. Yosi: "Yosi, stretch out the hands, and lose thy sight."

R. Yosi stretched out his hands and lost his sight.

But then R. Eliezer wept and said, "*The secret of the Lord is with them that fear Him*," and told R. Yosi: "Go back to the house of study and say to them, 'Have no fear as to the rightness of your decision; I hold a tradition from Rabban Yoḥanan ben Zakkai who heard his master say, and whose master heard his master say, and who in the name of Moses at Sinai heard say that this is the law: Jews owning fields in Ammon and Moab are required to set aside, out of crops raised in the seventh year, another tithe for the poor.' "

When R. Eliezer had calmed himself, he prayed: "May it be the will of our Father in heaven that the eyes of Yosi see again." And his eyes saw again.

Midrash on Psalms 25, ed. and trans. Braude, p. 355

Comment: See above II.i.23, III.iii.15.

xi. Scholion to Megillat Ta'anit

Lichtenstein (*HUCA* viii-ix, pp. 257ff) places the Scholion in "post-Talmudic times" (p. 259); it probably dates, in its present form, in the thirteenth century. Two of the three Yoḥanan-passages are copied from the Babylonian Talmud; the third appears here only.

1. A Boethusian said to Rabban Yoḥanan ben Zakkai, "Moses loved Israel and knew that Pentecost is only one day. He therefore established it for them after the Sabbath, so that they would have two days off."

Rabban Yoḥanan ben Zakkai attended to him, saying to him, "*It is an eleven day journey from Horev to Mount Seir to Kadesh Barnea* (Deut. 1:2). If Moses loved them, why did he keep them in the wilderness forty years?"

He said to him, "Behold you are ridiculing us."

He said to him, "Biggest fool in the world! Let not our whole Torah be like your idle speech."

He said to him, "Do you thus dismiss me?"

He said to him, "No. One Scripture says, *Seven complete weeks will there be* (Lev. 23:15), and another says, *You will count fifty days* (Lev. 23:16). How? If the festival falls on the Sabbath, one counts fifty days. And when you read, *And you will count for yourselves from the day after the*

Sabbath, [the meaning is], from the day *after* the first day of Passover."

Megillat Ta'anit Scholion, ed. Lichtenstein, *HUCA* viii-ix, p. 325 [68-9].

2. The Sadducees were making judgments according to their own laws, saying, "The daughter inherits with the son's daughter." Rabban Yoḥanan ben Zakkai said, "How do you know?"

Not a single one knew how to bring proof from the Torah except for one who was mumbling in his presence, saying to him, "If the son's daughter, who inherits on account of her father [inherits], who inherits on my account inherits me—the daughter who inherits from me [directly]—how much the more so!"

Rabban Yoḥanan ben Zakkai recited for him the following Scripture, "*And these are the sons of Seir the Horrite, dwellers in the Land of Lotan, Shuval and Zibeon and Anah* (Gen. 36:20), and one Scripture says, *He is Anah who found the hot springs in the wilderness when he was pasturing the asses of Zibeon his father* (Gen. 36:24). But this teaches that Zibeon had intercourse with his mother and fathered from her Anah."

He said to him, "Behold, you ridicule us."

He said to him, "Idiot! Let not the words of our Torah be like your idle chatter."

He said to him, "With this do you dismiss me?"

He said to him, "If the daughter of my son, who inherits right along with the brothers [should inherit], will you say the same of my daughter, who does *not* inherit right along with the brothers? It is logical that she should not inherit me."

The day that he vanquished them they made into a holiday.

Megillat Ta'anit Scholion, ed. Lichtenstein, *HUCA* viii-ix, p. 334 [78].

3. The Sadducees were saying that they should eat the meal-offering accompanying the ox. Rabban Yoḥanan ben Zakkai said, "How do you know?"

They did not know how to bring proof from the Torah, except one who was mumbling in his presence, saying, "Because Moses loved Aaron, he said, 'Let him not eat meat all by itself, but let him eat fine flour with the meat, like a man who says to his friend, 'Here is meat, here is savory.' "

R. Yoḥanan ben Zakkai recited for him, "*And they came to Elam and there were twelve wells of water and seventy date-palms* (Ex. 15:27)."

He said to him, "What has one thing to do with the other?"

He said to him, "Idiot! Let not our whole Torah be like your idle chatter. Is it not already written, *The holocaust will be for the Lord, and its meal-offering and drink-offering will be for a pleasant odor, a fire-offering to the Lord* (Lev. 23:18)." Megillat Ta'anit Scholion, ed. Lichtenstein, *HUCA* viii-ix, p. 338 [82].

Comment: VI.xi.1 appears in b. Men. 65a, VI.xi.2 in b. B.B. 115a, and VI.xi.3 here alone. The first two are in *beraitot*, and the third is modeled after them; but we do not know its origin.

xii. General Comments

The later midrashic materials differ from the Amoraic ones in a number of respects. First and most striking, no later Talmudic authority is ever cited; materials appear without superscription, are inserted in the appropriate exegetical context, but are never related to a particular master, school, or setting. Second, when older materials are used, they are rarely much changed from earlier appearances. They are cited, sometimes garbled, but never reworked in any significant or creative way. I have, to be sure, omitted the obviously pseudepigraphic materials in *Pirqé de Rabbi Eliezer*, which are quite original, but have nothing to with the Yoḥanan-legends.

Materials already familiar include VI.i.3 (Eliezer's origins), = VI.v.1; VI.iii.1 (Righteousness exalts a nation) in a new formulation; VI.iii.2 (Ten *gerahs*); VI.iii.4 (the burning of Yoḥanan's great house in Jerusalem) = VI.v.3 A new version of the escape-story occurs in both an earlier and a later formulation (VI.ii.2, VI.vi.3). Strikingly new legends include the encounter with Simeon of Sikhnin (VI.vi.1), the exegesis on white garments (VI.vi.4), the dismissal of the efficacy of the red heifer (VI.iii.3, VI.v.2, VI.vii.2). We also have two dispute-stories, one old, the other new (VI.vii.1, VI.viii.1).

The summary table shows the relationships between later midrashic and earlier Talmudic materials. Here we conclude our survey of the growth of the Yoḥanan-legend. Later midrashic collections contain nothing of interest, for they do not relate to the living tradition at all. When they cite from earlier materials, it is verbatim. Where they differ from earlier documents, they cannot be supposed to indicate some new revision of, or element in, a legend not yet in final form. Rather they supply materials quite unrelated to the earlier tradition, indeed standing in no synoptic relationship whatever. Their lateness and independence together suggest they are, if not pseudepigraphic, at least historically fictitious.

Table

Later Midrashic Materials in Relationship to Earlier Documents

		Tan. Mid.	*Mishnah*	*Tosefta*	*Pal.Tan.*	*Bab. Ber.*	*Pal. Tal.*	*Bab.Tal.*	*ARN*
VI.i.1	(Create/ Gather)	—	—	—	—	—	—	—	—
VI.i.2	(Eyes opened)	—	—	—	—	—	—	—	—
VI.i.3	(Eliezer's origins)	—	—	—	—	—	—	—	IV.i.3
Vi.i.4	(Covenant with Abraham)	—	—	—	—	—	—	—	—
VI.i.5	(One-hundred-twenty)	I.iv.6	—	—	—	—	—	—	—
VI.ii.1	(Great house)	—	—	—	—	—	V.i.9	—	—
VI.ii.2	(Escape)	—	—	—	—	—	—	V.ii.14	IV.i.2
VI.iii.1	(Righteousness exalts a nation)	—	—	—	—	III.ii.20	—	—	—
VI.iii.2	(Ten *gerahs*)	—	—	—	—	—	V.i.7	—	—
VI.iii.3	(Hocus-pocus	—	—	—	—	—	—	—	—
	of heifer)	—	—	—	—	—	—	—	—
VI.iii.4	(Great house)	—	—	—	—	—	V.i.9	—	—
VI.iii.5	(Day/night both called day)	—	—	—	—	—	—	—	—
VI.iv.1	(Hocus-pocus of heifer)	—	—	—	—	—	—	—	—
VI.iv.2	(Day/night both called day)	—	—	—	—	—	—	—	—
VI.iv.3	(Slave's ear pierced)	I.i.3	—	II.iii.8d	III.i.5	III.iii.18	—	—	—
VI.v.1	(Eliezer's origins)	—	—	—	—	—	—	—	IV.i.3
VI.v.2	(Hocus-pocus of heifer)	—	—	—	—	—	—	—	—
VI.v.3	(Great house)	—	—	—	—		V.i.9	—	—
VI.v.4	(Mal. 3.5. Woe unto us on account of judgment)	—	—	—	—	—	—	V.ii.11	—
Vi.v.5	(Yoḥanan and Hadrian)	—	—	—	—	—	—	—	—
VI.vi.1	(Simeon of Sikhnin)	—	—	—	—	—	—	—	—
VI.vi.2	(Woe if I say it)	II.ii.22	II.iii.10	—	—	—	—	—	—
VI.vi.3	(Yoḥanan and.. Ben Battiaḥ, see VI.ii. 2b-c)	—	—	—	—	—	—	—	—
VI.vi.4	(Let garments be always white)	—	—	—	—	—	—	—	—

		Tan. Mid.	*Mishnah*	*Tosefta*	*Pal. Tan.*	*Bab. Ber.*	*Pal. Tal.*	*Bab. Tal.*	*ARN*
VI.vii.1	(Moses not good at arithmetic)	—	—	—	—	—	V.i.11, 17	V.ii.20	—
VI.vii.2	(Hocus-pocus of heifer)	—	—	—	—	—	—	—	—
VI.viii.1	(We have festivals and you have festivals)	—	—	—	—	—	—	—	—
VI.ix.1	(Fruit of orchard)	—	—	—	—	—	—	—	—
VI.x.1	(Ammon pays tithe, poor man's tithe)	—	II.iii.23	II.iii.15	—	III.ii.11	—		—
VI.xi.1	(Date of Pentecost)	—	—	—	—	—	—	V.ii.18	—
VI.xi.2	(Daughter inherits with the son's daughter)	—	—	—	—	II.ii.22	—	—	—
VI.xi.3	(Priests eat the meal-offering)	—	—	—	—	—	—	—	—

Table

Amoraic Authorities who cite, or are cited in connection with, Yoḥanan in Later Midrashim

VI.i.1	—	VI.v.2	—
VI.i.2	Judan, Berekhiah	VI.v.3	—
VI.i.3	—	VI.v.4	—
VI.i.4	R. Judah	VI.v.5	—
VI.i.5	—	VI.vi.1	—
VI.ii.1	—	VI.vi.2	(Samuel b. Ammi)
VI.ii.2	(Hillel b. Berekhiah)	VI.vi.3	—
VI.iii.1	—	VI.vi.4	—
VI.iii.2	Joshua b. R. Neḥemiah	VI.vii.1	—
VI.iii.3	—	VI.vii.2	—
VI.iii.4	—	VI.vii.1	—
VI.iii.5	—	VI.ix.1	—
VI.iv.1	—	VI.x.1	—
VI.iv.2	—	VI.xi.1	—
VI.iv.3	—	VI.xi.2	—
VI.v.1	—	VI.xi.3	—

PART TWO

SYNOPTIC STUDIES

CHAPTER SEVEN

INTRODUCTION

The purpose of the following studies is to compare several versions of the same saying or event.[1] These studies are different from New Testament synopses, for while the Jesus-material was eventually edited into coherent accounts, the Yoḥanan-data were left in the discrete and unrelated state in which they were originally redacted. As I said earlier, we have no "life of Yoḥanan ben Zakkai" produced in antiquity. The first complete, coherent "life" was mine. The Yoḥanan-materials are therefore to be compared to the isolated, episodic state of the equivalent ones about Jesus *before* the evangelists compiled their gospels.

But here too an important, obvious difference must be noted. Jesus-sayings and stories *have* been reworked to suit the purposes of the evangelists, and in considerable measure New Testament scholarship has succeeded in showing what these purposes were. In the case of Yoḥanan, the pericopae and logia were probably not subjected to a similar, comprehensive editing. I doubt that anyone ever tried to relate one group of stories to another, or the whole to some larger legal or theological purpose. Hence the "synoptic problem" of Jesus and that of Yoḥanan hardly relate to one another. It might be countered that the gospels are not really "lives" or biographies of Jesus, but rather assemblages of Jesus-materials in ways different from biographies produced in late antiquity. Apollonius of Tyana's life by Philostratus and the Gospel according to Luke, for example, are different; if one is a "life," the other is something else. But however one categorizes the gospels, Yoḥanan-stories and sayings have never been shaped into anything like a "gospel" at all, and that is the main point.

We do not, for example, have to uncover what the original units of the Yoḥanan-materials consisted of, for they lie here spread out before us. In some instances we observe composite units, but the components are readily discerned. For the most part, isolated sayings or composite stories attributed to, or concerning, Yoḥanan are all we have. Some

[1] I have not paid attention to items which appear in only one version. Such singletons do not lend themselves to synoptic inquiry.

longer accounts cannot easily be broken down with certainty into their originally separate, component parts. The sophisticated editor who shaped the ARN materials, for example, has obliterated the marks of those earlier traditions which he may have now reworked and improved. The escape story in b. Giṭ 56a (V.ii.14) represents a striking contrast. But by and large I have not found it possible certainly to establish the primary units, or even the historical settings, definitively to show whether materials belong to a primary or secondary tradition, or finally to demonstrate what was the product of editorial activity and what is "raw" and "primitive," therefore possibly older and more "reliable." I cannot propose a general theory for distinguishing traditional from invented materials. Still, as I said, we already have the individual units of a tradition in a highly fluid state. These units never were set into a fixed form established with reference to Yoḥanan's life and teachings. Quite to the contrary, the *framework* into which the units are set is invariably *irrelevant* to Yoḥanan himself, and directly reveals little, if anything, of the opinion of the compilers of the several documents concerning him.

If, therefore, the task of form-criticism is "to rediscover the origin and history of the particular units and thereby to throw some light on the history of the tradition before it took literary form,"[1] then the work before us cannot be called form-criticism, and this for two reasons. First, as I have stressed, we already *have* the Yoḥanan-tradition in, if not oral, at least pre-literary form, except for ARN. As to the "oral" form, I do not see how we can usefully speculate on what is not now before us. Those who hold the bulk of the sayings was memorized and then written down will argue that the tradition as we have it *is* the "oral" form. Those who suppose the sayings were preserved both in memory and in some sort of unofficial notes will not agree there ever was a truly "oral" form at all. In either case the tradition was never given the elegant literary form of the Gospels—so, ironically, part of the task is done. The other part seems to me impossible. Second, the discovery of the origin and history of the particular units before us is probably not accessible through present methodology; all I have been able to offer are conjectures, some more plausible than others. New Testament form-critics claim to isolate the life-situation which provoked, or gave rise to, various tales. The

[1] M. Dibelius quoted approvingly by R. Bultmann, *History of the Synoptic Tradition*, trans. John Marsh (Oxford, 1963), p. 4.

typical situation is the life of the Christian community. In the case of all rabbinical materials, without exception or qualification, the life-situation is the rabbinical academy and its political, legal, and theological concerns. But having said that, we have not gained much. Just as "the Christian community" has become too one-dimensional a category to accommodate all we know about various Christian communities, so "the rabbinical academy" is an abstraction, obscuring, and not illuminating, the varieties of academies, the richness of rabbinical opinion, the breadth of concern of masters in schools in two countries and five centuries. And, as we have already learned, it is not always possible, and generally is impossible, to attribute the creation of a given saying or story to a particular school or sage. Practically none of the later midrashim preserves traces of the origins or authorities who first quoted Yoḥanan or told stories about him. What is old is conventional and stereotyped, merely *cited*. But what is new is enigmatic.

Synoptic studies are nonetheless necessary. They permit us to follow the history of sayings, stories, and biographical details through several documents. We cannot hope to produce "the original form" of a piece of narrative, to offer absolutely certain judgments on primary and secondary elements. But the most elementary task of collection and comparison has never been done, and that is the best reason—and not hope of "revolutionary" results—to do it. We can, after all, hardly proceed with confidence to the analysis of a story, even for our limited purposes, until we have all the versions of it in view and know which details of each can be attributed to the collectors and editors who handed it down, and which *may* be "original."

We shall use the simplest, most obvious categories I can think of. These derive from the theme or subject-matter of the data, and from obvious key-words or central themes within each category. The entire corpus may first be conveniently divided into categories natural to talmudic literature. These obviously are legal materials, exegetical sayings, biographical and historical tales. Natural subdivisions present themselves according to forms, or types of sayings and stories, as I just said. Talmudic and cognate literature is primarily legal, secondarily exegetical, and lastly historical. But these divisions are set forth merely to serve our convenience, and it is within them that the important formal and substantive distinctions will have to be drawn.

New Testament form-critics have used very different categories, but when these are reviewed, they turn out to be nothing more than the natural divisions produced by the materials of the synoptic gospels, for instance divisions into sayings of Jesus and narrative materials. They further derive from earlier literary-critical studies of Greek literature. Bultmann divides the sayings into conflict and didactic sayings, biographical apophthegms; dominical sayings: logia (Jesus as the teacher of wisdom), prophetic and apocalyptic sayings, legal sayings and church rules, 'I' sayings, similitudes. The narrative material is divided into miracle stories (healing, nature-miracles), and historical stories and legends.

Sayings of Yoḥanan could, to be sure, be similarly analyzed through whatever direct discourse is attributed to him. But such a procedure would be misleading. It would produce the false supposition that equal weight is to be attached to all sayings given in direct discourse. It is one thing to regard legal sayings, beginning, "Rabban Yoḥanan ben Zakkai says..." as relatively reliable attributions. Sayings in the context of narratives, on the other hand, obviously are shaped by the needs of the narrative, not by what, if anything, Yoḥanan actually said, or even by what, if anything, people *supposed* Yoḥanan actually said. Most narrative discourse is invented. Hence collectively treating direct-discourse sayings as a unity would confuse. The sayings do not constitute a single and unified fabric of traditions. Conflict-stories are not shaped around something Yoḥanan said, but rather around principles dividing the Sadducees and Pharisees. Yoḥanan serves as a spokesman, not as an independent figure. Yoḥanan never refers to his own life or upbringing, so biographical apophthegms do not exist, though much biographical material occurs in other forms. Some logia do exist and are important, to be sure, but they are framed in the form of stories, and more commonly still, of discourses with disciples in which the master actually says very little. It would be pointless, for example, to study the words, "I prefer the words of Eleazar b. 'Arakh..." or "Ḥanan spoke well" as wisdom-logia. Prophetic sayings occur as exegeses and only as such. Legal sayings are important in the context of legal literature; they do not stand by themselves. We have no 'I' sayings, no miracle stories, no healings.

The primary difference derives not only from the materials, but, self-evidently, from the two men's personalities, characters, and roles in their respective communities. No rabbi was so important to rabbinical Judaism as Jesus was to Christianity. None prophesied as an independent authority. None left a category of 'I' sayings, for none had the prestige to do so. Legal sayings are in no way comparable in form or context, let alone *content*. Similitudes generally are common property, rarely claimed as the creation or invention of the master who used them.

As I said, my primary categories serve merely as convenient means of blocking out the materials according to theme. The really useful categories can be shaped only in the context of the data, cannot be imposed upon the traditions, but must arise from peculiarities of style.

CHAPTER EIGHT

LEGAL SAYINGS AND STORIES

I. "Conventional" Sayings

1. In legal sayings the form "Rabban Yoḥanan ben Zakkai says..." appears only twice.

We find it in Mishnah Kelim 2:2 (II.i.22). All other Yoḥanan-materials in the Mishnah appear as, or in the context of, stories. Judah the Prince generally imposed the form:

1. Abstract statement of law
2. Dispute about a point of law
    a. Opinion of Rabbi Peloni
    b. Opinion of Rabbi Almoni
    or
    Opinion of "the Sages."

Materials appearing in contemporary documents (e.g. Tosefta) and later ones as well (e.g. Babylonian *beraitot*) have likewise *not* been revised to follow that standard form. It would be inviting to suppose that once Yoḥanan's legal sayings were fixed, they were not thereafter changed, and therefore continued in their *earlier*, pre-Aqiban or *later*, pre-Judahite versions.[1]

2. "Rabban Yoḥanan ben Zakkai says" occurs, second, in Tos. Soṭ. 14:1 (II.iii.6). There, however, he does not lay down a law, but reports an event, "When murderers multiplied." This saying is followed by others also *reporting* what happened when adulterers, hedonists, sorcerers, seers, and others multiplied, but in subsequent cases the reports are not attributed to Yoḥanan. In Mishnah Soṭ. 9:9, the report about what happened when murderers multiplied appears without

[1] In the following tables, I have used — to indicate the absence of a detail appearing in the left-hand column in the other accounts, and " " to indicate recurrence of a detail in exact, or almost exact, form, later on. To signify the replacement of a single word by another, I have italicized the variant word.

variation, *except* that Yoḥanan's name is omitted. On the other hand, we have, "When adulterers multiplied, [the rite of[the bitter water ceased, and Rabban Yoḥanan ben Zakkai abrogated it," with an accompanying proof-text (Hos. 4:14).

The two traditions differ as follows:

Mishnah	*Tos.*
1. Murderers	1. *Yoḥanan* said, Murderers
2. *Yoḥanan* abrogated bitter waters	2. Bitter waters *were abrogated*

We cannot suppose Judah the Prince had reason deliberately to omit Yoḥanan's name in Mishnah #1, for he included it in Mishnah #2. The compilers of the Tosefta did the exact opposite. Judah also excluded the hedonists, sorcerers, seers, and others.

It is difficult to draw any conclusions about these related, yet differing traditions. I do not know which of the traditions on the murderers and adulterers came before the other, or why Yoḥanan's name was variously suppressed or highlighted. Indeed, Judah the Prince thought Yoḥanan exercised authority in the Temple sufficient to abrogate one rite, but did not know about, or did not report, a similar action concerning another rite. Obviously, no opinion on Yoḥanan may be adduced, then attributed to an editor, on the basis of what appears in either document. Judah's preference in #2 reflects his concern that the priests not resume the government of the Temple in time to come. So his selection was purposeful, not random (II.iii.6).

The conventional form, "Rabbi Yoḥanan ben Zakkai says/said a law" in any event is remarkably uncommon in legal contexts. What is common is stories of various sorts, attributions of indirect discourse, and the like. Yoḥanan's legal sayings have evidently not been reworked according to the normal editorial standards of the Mishnah.

II. Woe if I say it

1. The formula *Woe if I say it* appears in Mishnah Kelim 17:6 (II.i.22) and Tos. Kelim B.M. 7:6 (II.iii.10). The laws in question concern identical objects. But the Mishnah version ends, "These *are* susceptible to uncleanness." The Tosefta holds, "All are *not* susceptible to uncleanness *unless* they [are used to] serve their [own] purpose." Then, in both documents, follows: And concerning all of them Yoḥanan says, "Woe is me if I speak of them, woe is me if I do not

speak of them." Yoḥanan's saying is thus attached to two different laws about the same objects. In fact it has no intimate relationship to the decided law at all.

It is probably an independent *lemma*, for it is added in a completely different context in the Bab. *beraita* b. B.B. 89b (III.ii.21) *not* about cleanness rules, but about the sharp practices of traders. The saying here is expanded and now is made to relate to the *substance* of the law. Laws concerning the making and use of weights and measures are followed by, "Woe is me if I speak, woe is me if I do not speak. If I speak, knaves may learn; but if not, knaves will say, the sages do not know our practices." This is followed by the Amoraic form, "The question was raised, Did Yoḥanan finally speak of them or not?" Samuel b. R. Isaac said that he did, citing Hos. 14:10.

The lemma finally is cited in Qoh. R. 6:1:1 (Vi.vi.2), concerning *neither* purity laws *nor* weights and measures, but adulterating wine with water, honey with juice, and so forth. Then, "Concerning all of these," Yoḥanan said his saying, and "finally he did say it, *For the ways of the Lord are right* (Hos. 14:10)." The last form is clearly a tertiary development, now of the *beraita*. Since it was decided that Yoḥanan spoke of the deceitful practices—whatever they were—in the later version, it is simply related that he decided to speak of them, and Hos. 14:10 is cited as a proof-text, not to show his having done so, but to justify his action.

Three facts are clear. First, Yoḥanan's saying, "Woe if I say it" is independent of the context of law in which it is cited. It is used in the earliest documents with reference to the same legal issue, *but* to conflicting decisions; in the later documents it is used in completely unrelated legal materials. Therefore, as I said, it has nothing to do with the law in question, but serves as a subscription—a stock-phrase.

Second, the saying undergoes striking development from the Mishnah-Tosefta to the Babylonian *beraita*. It is expanded with an *explanation* of his dilemma. In the latest of all versions, that augmented form is further expanded by the inclusion of his decision to speak his mind, but the reference to Samuel b. R. Isaac is dropped. Now his saying so is an integral part of the story. We see that the anonymous character of the later *midrashic* compilations applies not only to the framework of the pericopae, but also to their contents.

Third, and most important, the *woe*-saying in the earliest documents is simple, and then clearly undergoes development in the *beraita* and still further development afterward. This proves that the earlier documents *do* contain the more primitive materials. What appears later on (at least in this instance) is not a saying derived from olden times but only now redacted. It is, rather, a saying which has undergone development from the earlier to the later documents. This may be obvious, but is nonetheless important. It is claimed that it makes no difference for the "historicity" or antiquity of a saying whether it appears early or late. As to historicity, we now can say nothing. But as to antiquity, it is clear what that appears in a document edited at an earlier date in fact is earlier than what we find in a compilation of a later date. This further strongly suggests that *beraitot* come later in the formation of the tradition than the Tannaitic Midrashim, Mishnah, and Tosefta, and were given their final form in Amoraic times, that is after the Mishnah was redacted, perhaps even in the generation of Amoraim which discussed the cited *beraita*. These conclusions, however, cannot be everywhere applied. As we shall see, some materials which both appear in later sources and seem to be later formulations of a tradition do appear to be simpler, less fully developed and articulated, than equivalent versions in earlier sources which seem to be earlier formulations. No fixed laws may be adduced that what is elaborated is therefore later than what is simple and less detailed. Each case requires its own analysis, and only at the end will we see which is the more common rule.

III. Further Subscriptions

1. *Ḥanan spoke well* occurs three times, in Mishnah Ket. 13:1 (II.i.9) and 13:2 (II.i.10), and in b. Ned. 33b (III.ii.17). In the last-named, the saying is unaltered from Mishnah Ket. 13:2. The form is as follows:

1. Abstract point of law (*re* marriage-contracts)
2. Ḥanan says
3. The sons of the high priests disagree
4. R. Dosa b. Harkinas said
5. Rabban Yoḥanan ben Zakkai said, Ḥanan spoke well
6. Reason: a. Let her swear
   b. The man has laid his money

Yoḥanan's saying is not integral to the law, but has been added to an already-formulated saying. Like the *woe*-lemma, *Ḥanan spoke well* in both cases stands independently of the law under discussion and requires secondary explanation or elaboration ("Let her swear at the end," "the man laid his money on the horn of the gazelle").

2. In two instances, R. Judah [b. Ilai] reports, "A story/case [*Ma'aseh*] came before Rabban Yoḥanan ben Zakkai in 'Arav, and he said, 'I doubt whether he is not liable to a sin-offering.' " These are Mishnah Shab. 16:7 and 22:3 (III.i.1,2). The contexts are different and unrelated, first, covering with a dish a lamp, animal droppings, a scorpion; second, broaching a jar to eat dried figs, piercing the plug of a jar, or covering it with wax. But the rules of law in both instances concern covering or closing up on the Sabbath.

The form *Ma'aseh be/ve* (below, section iv) bears a different meaning from *Ma'aseh* as used here. R. Judah reports the event, and *ma'aseh* hence means *case*. When a story or case is cited for purposes of illustration of a law without attribution to a particular master, *ma'aseh be/ve* means, *the story is told concerning / that*.

R. Judah's story is independent of the preceding rule of law. Perhaps an abstract saying of Yoḥanan would have read:

1. They may cover
   a. example
   b. example
   c. example
2. Rabban Yoḥanan ben Zakkai says, "They may not cover..." or, "I doubt they may cover... and if they do, they are liable..."

But that formulation has not come down to us, may not have come down to R. Judah b. Ilai, and may not have existed. What he apparently received was a story of a court-decision made by Yoḥanan in such a case as was covered in the Mishnah. But Yoḥanan probably ruled *contrary* to the Mishnah; at any rate, he was in doubt as to whether the law permitting covering in certain instances was valid.

The story of R. Judah is indirectly referred to, apparently anonymously, in the Palestinian *gemara: And a scorpion so that it shall not bite*. A case came before Rabban Yoḥanan ben Zakkai in 'Arav and he said...R. 'Ulla said, "Eighteen years..." (as above, V.i.2). I think it more likely that Judah's story is cited without attribution to him because the Mishnah is merely *alluded* to, not completely quoted. In fact, until Rabbi 'Ulla's saying, we have simply an abbreviated citation of the Mishnah, nothing more. We should have reproduced it as follows:

...And a scorpion so that it shall not bite... A case came...

Hence we cannot regard the Palestinian Gemara's "version" as separate and distinct. In the Babylonian Talmud (b. Shab. 121b-122a, 146a-146b), Yoḥanan's ruling is not referred to.

The subscriptions conform to no formula. "Woe if I say it," "Ḥanan spoke well," and "R. Judah said, A case came..." have in common only one trait. They are all appended to abstract formulations of laws, and the antecedent materials in no way reflect either Yoḥanan's opinion or the fact that he held a contrary opinion ("But Rabban Yoḥanan ben Zakkai says..."). We may assume that the several sorts of subscriptions existed independently of the laws as finally formulated In all three instances, the Mishnah's redactor made use of that independent corpus of sayings in the construction of the Mishnah. But we do not know why, or when, the Yoḥanan-subscriptions were added. What is clear, however, is that they originally existed by themselves, but I have no idea on the primary form or shape of such a corpus of Yoḥanan-sayings and cases. Since the subscriptions have nothing to do with one another, we cannot suppose they originally constituted a single collection and later were divided into segments in the Mishnah. Nor do the subscriptions suggest that Yoḥanan compiled his own law-book, based on existing collections but with his decisions and additions as well. We have no evidence, furthermore, that Yoḥanan commented on an extant, early form of the Mishnah as we have it, or even of individual mishnaic segments. The subscriptions are an enigma.

IV. The Story is Told

Several matters of law are introduced by *ma'aseh ve-* [+ verb] or *ma'aseh be-* [+ noun] (depending on whether the following word is a verb or a subject). The first is Mishnah Suk. 2:5 (II.i.4), which is cited in b. Yoma 79a (III.ii.4) without alteration. However, when the Mishnah is cited in the Gemara, it is accompanied by *VeTNY 'alah*, "Not because the law is so, but because they wanted to be more strict with themselves." This "tannaitic" amendment of the Mishnaic story need not be thought to derive from Tannaitic times. It may well be the Tanna of the Babylonian Amoraic school who possessed a further tradition on, or has been instructed to interpret, the Mishnah, so that the actual law is as specified. That is to say, *VeTNY 'alah* may mean, "The academy's Tanna taught concerning the Mishnah..." In any event, we see that the Mishnah is accurately quoted in the context of the Gemara. This can be explained in two ways. First, the actual quotation in academic discussion was accurate. Second, the Mishnah was merely alluded to, but when quoted for the purposes of redaction, it was copied verbatim from the published Mishnah. The latter alternative seems more likely, but the difference between the two is not very great.

The second instance occurs in Mishnah Sanh. 5:2 (II.i.15), "The story is told that Ben Zakkai tested the evidence by inquiring about the stalks of figs." This "story" is an illustration of the superscription, "The more a judge tests the evidence, the more he is deserving of praise." What follows is quite unrelated to the story. A *beraita* identical in all respects but one appears (b. Sanh. 41a, (III.ii.25) as follows: "The story is told that *Rabban Yoḥanan* ben Zakkai tested..." As we noted, the story has thus been handed on in two forms, the "Ben Zakkai" one, which later on seemed hostile or dishonorable, and the consequent, polite "Rabban Yoḥanan ben Zakkai" of the Mishnah comes first. The substance of the story is identical in both versions. I imagine that whatever hostile circles originally told stories about "Ben Zakkai" told more than this one. But all others—if they were preserved—have already been corrected.

The *ma'aseh be/ve* form is standard, and serves the editor of a document as a means to link a pre-existing story to his context. In both instances, without *ma'aseh be/ve*, the story would be perfectly smooth and clear, "They brought cooked food...", "Ben Zakkai tested..." The words therefore are probably editorial superscriptions. We cannot say, however, that any particular editor's editorial procedures were characterized by the use of *ma'aseh*, for it is standard and appears in all sorts of documents. It should therefore be regarded as commonplace, not peculiar either to a school or to Yoḥanan.

A third legal *ma'aseh* occurs in y. Demai 3:1 (III.i.1). The story is told concerning Joshua that he went after Yoḥanan to Beror Ḥayil, and the villagers brought them fruit. Joshua told them if they are staying here for the night, they must tithe. In y. Ma'aserot 2:2 (III.i.2) Beror Ḥayil becomes Bene Ḥayil. Otherwise the passages are practically identical; only the order of the words *we* and are *obligated* are reversed in the latter passage.

In Tos. Ma'aserot 2:1 (II.iii.1), the form is altered. There we find, *The story is told that R. Joshua went* (Ma'aseh shehalakh). *Fruit* of the Palestinian Talmudic versions becomes *figs*. Before R. Joshua gives his instructions, *they said to him*, *Are we obligated to tithe?* The Tos. version omits *here*. The concluding clause in the Talmudic versions is, "If we are staying here, we are obligated to tithe, and if we are not staying here, we are not obligated to tithe." The Tos. version concludes, "If we are staying, we are obligated to tithe, and if not, we are *free* [from the obligation] to tithe."

The Palestinian Talmudic Tannaitic version is therefore more general (fruit/figs); omits the setting for Joshua's teaching ("Are we obligated?") but merely gives his ruling; and phrases his instructions *If so, then obligated*, *if not*, *then not obligated*, while the Tos. phrases them, *If*, *so*, *then obligated*, *if not*, *then free*. The most striking difference, therefore, is the inclusion of the question raised by the villagers. Without it, the instructions of Joshua make no sense, indeed have no context.

One might argue that the Palestinian Talmudic versions, being simpler, are older than the Toseftan one. On the other hand, in this instance we may have in the Talmudic versions a defective, therefore, probably later version of the earlier and more perfect account in the Tosefta. We certainly cannot claim whatever is more complete is augmented, therefore also later, and whatever is full of lacunae is more primitive, therefore older.

I must admit, though, that had the Toseftan version appeared in the Palestinian Talmud, and vice versa, I should have been prone to interpret matters otherwise. And, further, what seems to me as the more perfect version, because of the inclusion of the villagers' question, may be an improvement on the earlier, less clear account. I therefore find it impossible to come to a secure opinion.

v. His Disciples Asked

1. The form is used of two unrelated legal questions, in Sifré Num. 123 (I.i.6) = Tos. Parah 3:7 (II.iii.13) and Tos. ʾAhilot 16:8 (II.iii.11). It is as follows:

a. His disciples asked R. Yoḥanan ben Zakkai...
b. He said to them [a wrong answer]...
c. They said to him, You have taught us...
d. He said to them, Well said, and a deed which my hands did...
e. Not that he did not know, but that he wanted to stimulate the disciples...
f. And some say, It was Hillel...
g. R. Joshua says, One who learned but does not work...

2. The versions on the red-heifer exhibit these variations:

Sifré Num.	*Common to both*	*Tos. Parah*
	1. His disciples asked	
2. In what garments is the red-heifer done		2. The red heifer—in what is it done
	3. He said, In golden...	
4. They said to him, Have you not taught us, our rabbi, in white garments		4. You have taught us in white garments
5. —		5. He said to them, Well spoken, and
6a. What my own eyes saw and my own hands served I have forgotten, how much the more so		6a. A deed which my own hands did and my own eyes saw, but I have forgotten, but when my ears hear, how much the more so
6b. that which I have taught		6b. —
7a. —		7a. Not that he did not know
7b. And all this why? In order to stimulate the disciples		7b. but that he wanted to stimulate the disciples
8. And some say it was Hillel		8. And some say it was Hillel the Elder whom they asked.
9. —		9. Not that he did not know but that he wanted to stimulate the disciples
10. —		10. For R. Joshua said...
11. But he could not say, What my own hands served		11. —

The versions are close, but by no means identical. The variations of #2 are minor and insignificant. Those in #4 are of somewhat more interest, for the Tosefta version is briefer and less polite. The real differences begin at #5. Tos. #5 is clearly an embellishment of the story. Tos #6 *a deed which* is added; Sifré #6b is additional; there is no equivalent in the Tos. version, which leaves the *qal veḥomer* to dangle.

A further clear addition is Tos. #7a, *Not that he did not know* which replaces *all this why* with an explication of the problem. 8a is identical in both versions, but Tos. 9 is copied from Tos. 7a, and the intrusion, then exclusion, of Hillel is never actually accounted for. I should regard

Tos. #7a-b as a garbling of Sifré #8 #11, which is a coherent statement. Tos. #9 is absent in the Sifré.

In sum, the Tos. version is not only longer than the Sifré one, but also at several points both augmented and more verbose; Joshua's saying is brought gratuitously. I should therefore regard the Tos. version as a later development of the Sifré. Here again we see that what appears in a later document depends upon, and augments, a version in an earlier compilation. The Sifré story not only appears in the earlier document, but it gives indication of being the earlier *version*. The indications are not so clear-cut, however, as in the *woe* form.

His disciples asked also occurs with analogical exegeses, e.g. Tos. B.Q. 7:1 (see below, XII.iii).

vi. Laws reported by Disciples

1. *The Marriage of an Isah Family*. Mishnah ʿEd. 8:3 (II.i.16) contains R. Gamaliel's saying that he would accept testimony on the eligibility of a class of families for marriage with priests, but Yoḥanan decreed courts may not be called into session for such a purpose, since the priests would not accept their decision. The same passage occurs in b. Ket. 14a (III.ii.15) without alteration. As is common, when a Mishnaic passage is cited in the Babylonian *gemara*, it is cited in exactly, or nearly exactly, the form of its Mishnaic version. We may best account for this fact by supposing that the *gemara* has been made to conform to the Mishnah, either by early copyists or by the first printers. In any event, no variations occur.

2. *Elijah*. Mishnah ʿEd. 8:7 (II.i.17) contains a different teaching on the same theme by Joshua. Elijah will have to repair the violence of the priests in refusing to enter marriages according to Pharisaic teaching. The common theme of the sayings of Gamaliel and Joshua is striking, but we have no evidence that a single saying of Yoḥanan has been recast into two such completely unrelated forms. The Elijah-saying occurs only here.

3. *The Third Loaf*. Joshua's saying that Yoḥanan had predicted a later generation would declare the third loaf incapable of producing uncleanness occurs in Sifra Shemini ed. Weiss p. 54a (I.ii.4), Mishnah Soṭ. 5:2 (II.i.11), and Tos. Soṭ. 5:13 (II.iii.5). The differences are minor:

Sifra	*Mishnah*	*Tosefta*
dust from *between* your eyes	...from your eyes	...from your eyes
Scripture from the Torah	...the Torah *that it is unclean*	[Omits *Scripture...that it is unclean*]
And behold	And does not	And does not
ʿAqiva	ʿAqiva	*Rabbi* ʿAqiva
brought	bring	bring

The Sifra-version differs in minor details, therefore, from the exempla of the Mishnah and Tosefta. These latter are almost identical; ʿAqiva is given the rabbinical title in the Tosefta, and the "Scripture... unclean" clause has been dropped. The differences do not confirm any judgment on which version is earlier. The Tosefta's "Rabbi," and the Mishnah's "from the Torah *that it is unclean*" may be amplifications or improvements. Hence the Sifra version *may* be older. I see no great difference in the omission of *between* or the change from *behold* to *does not* and from *brought* to *brings*.

4. *Receiving Terumah; Preserving its Cleanness*. Ṭarfon's teaching on receiving *terumah* is only in Tos. Ḥag. 3:36 [= Lieberman 3:33, p. 393] (II.iii.4). It is striking that no one else *ever* refers to Yoḥanan's view of the matter.

We do have a story that reflects on eating *terumah* in a state of ritual purity, ARNa ch. 12 (IV.i.4), but the story pertains to whether the man in question actually did follow the purity-laws or not, *not* whether he *ought* to have done so, or when he ought to receive *terumah* from ordinary folk. So we do not have the slightest allusion to Ṭarfon's tradition. There is no parallel to ARN ch. 12.

5. *Poor Man's Tithe in Moab and Ammon*. Eliezer's reference to the tradition Yoḥanan had taught him occurs in Mishnah Yad. 4:3 (II.i.23), Tos. Yad. 2:16 (II.iii.15), b. Ḥag. 3b (III.ii.11), and Midrash on Psalms #25. Of interest is the concluding sentence, "Be not anxious":

Mishnah	*Tos.*	*Bab. Beraita*
who *heard* from his master, and his master from his, until a *law* to Moses from Sinai	who *received* from the pairs, the pairs from the prophets, the prophets from Moses, a *law* to Moses from Sinai	...his master from his, *hilkhata* [instead of *halakhah*

The difference between the Mishnah and the Babylonian *beraita* is slight but important, for *hilkhata* is clearly a Babylonian Amoraic usage inserted in place of the Mishnaic *halakhah*. This shows that where Mishnahs are quoted in the Babylonian Talmud, we cannot take for granted that they have been made to conform to well-known Mishnaic versions, but sometimes, at least, may exhibit minor, local variations.

The Mishnah is simpler, less detailed; no differentiation comes between one kind of master and another. In the Tosefta, the "master" becomes pairs, prophets, Moses, then *Moses* is repeated in a formula. The Tosefta is likely to be later, for the intrusion of *Moses* is immediately followed by a *law to Moses from Sinai*, which suggests that the elaborated formulaic version of *master* has been clumsily inserted into the pre-existing, but unaltered form. (It is also possible that the Toseftan version is simply a separate and different formulation, but this seems to me less likely).

VII. DISPUTES

1. *Ben Bukhri*. Ben Bukhri's dispute with Yoḥanan about the priestly *sheqel* occurs in four places, Mishnah Sheq. 1:4 (II.i.1); b. Men. 21b (III.ii.27) where after *ours* the word *HY'* (it is) is added; b. Men. 46b (III.i.28) where after *ours*, the word *HN* (they are) is added and b. ʿArakh. 4a (III.ii.20), where after *ours*, the word *HM* (they are) is added. Otherwise no variations whatever occur. I find it anomalous that the added pronoun changes in the three Babylonian Talmudic citations of the Mishnah. Obviously it was felt that the diction of the passage required some further syllable, but once something was added, it hardly mattered what pronoun it was. We see once again that a citation of a Mishnah in the Babylonian *gemara* may exhibit some variations, but not many.

2. *Uncleanness of Scriptures*. The Sadducean/Boethusian dispute on the uncleanness of Holy Scriptures occurs in Mishnah Yad. 4:6 (II.i.24) in a form not unique to Yoḥanan-materials, "We cry out against you." In the particular matter of Scriptural uncleanness, Yoḥanan is introduced as a self-described Sadducee. In subsequent matters, the "Pharisees" reply; Yoḥanan is not mentioned. As we have noted, a fragment of the dispute appears in Tos. Yad., ed. Zuckermandel (II.iii.16), "Rabban Yoḥanan ben Zakkai said to them, 'As to Holy Scriptures, as is their preciousness, so is their uncleanness, so that he will not make them into mats for cattle.' " This contrasts with the Mishnaic formulation, "As is their preciousness, so is their uncleanness, but the books of Homer, which are not precious, do not

render hands unclean." The Toseftan attribution is similar to the words of the Sadducees in the Mishnaic version, "As is our love... so that no one will make spoons of the bones of his father and mother." In the Mishnaic version, Yoḥanan does not make use of any simile at all. The Tosefta fragment completes the Mishnaic version.

3. *Sadducean Cleanness Laws and the Red-Heifer Sacrifice.* The story about Yoḥanan's lenient view of the cleanness laws applying to the Red-Heifer sacrifice (Tos. Parah 3:8, II.iii.12) occurs only once. We have no direct allusions to the tale. The students' discussion, "In what garments," seems to be pertinent, though, as I said, it appears in so attenuated a form as to be meaningless for synoptic purposes.

4. *The Date of Pentecost.* The passage is introduced by a citation from the Fasting Scroll (VI.xi.1) then, *for the Boethusians said* (b. Men. 65a, V.ii.18). The Scholion to the Fasting-Scroll repeats the *beraita*, with variations:

b. Men. 55a	*Scholion*
1. Yoḥanan dealt with them and said	1. —
1a. —	1a. One Boethusian said to Yoḥanan
2. Fools, how do you know?	2. —
3. None could answer except an old man who mumbled and said	3. — 3. —
4. Moses loved...	4. Moses loved...
5. Yoḥanan quoted Deut. 1:2	5. Yoḥanan *dealt with him* and quoted Deut. 1:2
6. Old man said, Do you dismiss me with that?	6. Old man said, You are ridiculing us
7. Yoḥanan said, Do not compare our complete Torah to your idle chatter	7. Big fool! Do not let our complete Torah...
8. —	8. Old man: Do you dismiss me with that?
9. Yoḥanan quoted Lev. 23:15, 16	9. Yoḥanan quoted Lev. 23:15, 16
10. How? One Scripture refers to a festival that coincides with the Sabbath, the other with a festival that falls in the middle of the week.	10. How? If the festival coincides with the Sabbath, you count seven weeks. If it falls after the Sabbath, you count fifty days.

The Scholion is thus a rough approximation of the *beraita*. The basic elements are the same; the exegesis of Lev. 23:15,16 is somewhat more complete in the Scholion. The editor of the Scholion clearly had the *beraita* before him, but he did not copy it verbatim. He provided, rather, a version of what must have been a widely known Talmudic *beraita*.

5. *The Daughter's Inheritance.* The Sadducees held that the daughter should inherit alongside the granddaughter, according to a *beraita* in b. B.B. 115b (III.ii.22). Yoḥanan asked how they knew, and none could answer except an old man who mumbled and said that just as the daughter of his son, who inherits on account of him, inherits, his own daughter should even more so inherit. Yoḥanan replied by citing Gen. 36:20 and 36:24. This enigmatic reply is expounded in the Scholion (Lichtenstein, p. 334 = VI.xi.2) at some length. The Scholion's editor most certainly has expanded the account, providing a more elaborate, lucid version of Yoḥanan's answer, which in the *beraita* is elliptical, in fact unintelligible. We may say without any doubt that the version appearing in the later document also constitutes a later development of the simpler account.

A fragment appears in Tos. Yad., ed. Zuckermandel, p. 684, and Yoḥanan is not mentioned at all. The passage begins, "The Boethusians say, 'I cry out against you, O Pharisees. Just as the daughter of my son inherits on account of my son who inherits on my account—behold she inherits me, my own daughter who inherits on my account, is it not logical that she should inherit me?' The Pharisees say, 'No, if you say concerning the daughter of the son...' " This fragment obviously is preferable to the *beraita* in which Yoḥanan does appear. It conforms to the Mishnaic model, "We cry out..." But it does *not* appear in Mishnah Yad., Ch. 4.

6. *The Meal-Offering.* The Sadducees claimed the right to eat the meal offering, according to the Scholion (Lichtenstein, p. 338, Vi.xi.3). The form is the same as earlier:

1. Yoḥanan said, How do you know
2. Only an old man could bring proof
3. Moses loved Aaron
4. Yoḥanan cites a Scripture (Here: Ex. 15:27)
5. The old man asks, What do these have to do with the issue?
6. Old fool! Do not make our complete Torah...
7. Yoḥanan cites Lev. 23:18 and expounds it according to his views.

The dispute has no counterpart in earlier sources. It may be compared to the Ben Bukhri account about whether priests pay the *sheqel*—but only in a general way. In no particular is it similar.

Comment. The Sadducean disputes exhibit a set of relatively fixed forms. In #2, the common form was "We complain against you." The two *beraitot* (#4, 5) are expanded and clarified in the Scholion, an example of the tendency of later texts to amend and augment materials appearing in earlier ones. Since in this instance there can be no reasonable claim that the materials in the Scholion circulated "in some oral form" for a thousand years or more, we may be certain that the Scholion's "versions" in fact are later than, and based upon, those in the Babylonian Talmudic *beraitot*. If so, we here observe the tendency to expand materials in later formulations. In general, what is expanded is often later than the simpler version, though important exceptions do occur, as we have seen.

VIII. The Ordinances of Yavneh

Along with the *ḥomer*-exegeses, the Yavneh ordinances constitute the earliest components of the normative tradition. Conventional forms occur, as we shall see. This indicates that even the earliest strata of Yoḥanan-materials have already been given substantially permanent shape, perhaps after circulating for a time in various unofficial formulations.

1. *The Day of Waving and Lulav*. The Day of Waving saying occurs independently, as well as together with the *Lulav*-decree. The *Lulav*-decree never appears separately. In the earliest documents, the Day of Waving occurs by itself: *When the Temple was destroyed*, Yoḥanan decreed that the Day of Waving should be entirely prohibited [for the eating of new produce], so Sifra ʾEmor Par. 10:10 (I.ii.6). The same document also combines both decrees (Sifra ʾEmor Pereq 16:9, I.ii.7): "*And you will rejoice... And when the Temple was destroyed*, Yoḥanan decreed that the *lulav* should be taken in the provinces seven days... *and* that the Day of Waving should be entirely prohibited." Mishnah R.H. (II.i.5,6,7a,7b,20) reproduces the combined form without much change: *lulav* becomes *the lulav*. Mishnah Suk. 3:12 omits *the*; otherwise it is identical. In neither context is the reference to the Day of Waving essential, even relevant. Therefore the pericope is actually quoted as a conventional and completed unit. The unit must have begun with the Day of Waving; the *Lulav* was added. Once in this form, the pericope was thereafter quoted without change. Mishnah Men. 10:5 and a *beraita*, b. Men. 68b, cite the Day of Waving saying by itself, without change from I.ii.6; similarly in Palestinian Talmud Ḥallah 1:1 (III.i.3) "*And when the Temple was destroyed*, Rabban Yoḥanan ben Zakkai decreed that the day of waving should be entirely pro-

hibited." The addition of *and* in several versions serves the editor's purpose; it is unrelated to the pericope. Tos. Men. 10:26 (II.iii.9) likewise presents the Day of Waving as a single teaching, without change from its earlier appearances. *Beraitot* in b. Suk. 41b (III.ii.9) and b. R.H. 30b also cite the Day of Waving by itself.

The *Lulav*-decree does not occur in *beraitot* in the Babylonian Talmud or in teachings attributed to Tannaim in the Palestinian Talmud. See I.ii.7 for further comment.

2. *Shofar on the Sabbath.* This decree first occurs in the Mishnah; no reference to it is made in the Tannaitic Midrashim. Mishnah R.H. 4:1 (II.i.6) exhibits the *When the Temple was destroyed* form, already seen in the Tannaitic Midrashim. The decree reads, "that they should sound the shofar wherever a court was located." We have already noted R. Eliezer's correction of the saying.

A *beraita* (b. R.H. 29b, III.ii.8) relates to the Mishnaic law, but does not conform to it in any degree. It is a separate story, beginning *One time*, rather than *the story is told about/that. When the Temple was destroyed* is omitted. The *beraita* and Mishnah deal with the same law, but have nothing whatever to do with one another.

3. *Testimony. When the Temple was destroyed* Yoḥanan decreed that evidence concerning the New Moon might be accepted all day long; earlier it was admitted until the afternoon-offering only. R. Joshua b. Qorḥa added that Yoḥanan decreed the witnesses should go only to the place of assembly, so Mishnah R.H. 4:4 (II.i.8), quoted without alteration in b. Beẓ. 5a (III.ii.10).

4. *Priestly Blessing.* A *beraita* (b. R.H. 31a = b. Soṭ. 40a) presents a new form for the Yavnean decrees: "The priests are not permitted to ascend the platform in their sandals, and this is one of the nine decrees which Rabban Yoḥanan ben Zakkai decreed." This is the only decree not introduced by *When the Temple was destroyed.* Another form for ordinances must have existed, in which the decree were listed in some sort of order, "These are the nine decrees which Yoḥanan decreed at Yavneh." Such enumerated lists are found fairly commonly, but never, except here, with reference to Yoḥanan.

This *beraita* is cited, without the usual *beraita*-introduction, in b. Soṭ. 40a. Otherwise it is unchanged.

The enumeration is as follows: "Six in this chapter, one in the preceding chapter, and the following one: A proselyte at the present time... [See below]." The six "in this chapter" are the *shofar*, *Lulav* Day of Waving, Testimony, Witnesses, and Priests. The "one in the preceding chapter" refers to b. R.H. 21b [below]. I assume the enumeration by chapter may derive from Saboraic times, when the Talmud had already received considerable editorial attention.

5. *New Moon Testimony on Sabbath.* The Mishnah states that when the Temple was standing, testimony for the New Moon might be received on the Sabbath in regard to all the months. The following *beraita* (b. R.H. 21b, III.ii.7) is then cited: *Originally* the Sabbath could be profaned for all of them. *When the Temple was destroyed*, Rabban Yoḥanan b. Zakkai said to them, "And is there a sacrifice?" They therefore decreed that one may profane the Sabbath [to bring testimony concerning] Nisan and Tishré only.

The *beraita* is quoted only here. In the Mishnah Judah the Prince ignores Yoḥanan's name while giving Yoḥanan's ruling: "For the sake of two months, the Sabbath may be profaned, namely Nisan and Tishré."

6. *The Proselytes Offering.* A *beraita* (b. R.H. 31b [V.ii.10] = b. Ker. 9a [III.ii.30]) reads: "A proselyte in this time [after the destruction of the Temple] must separate a quarter for his bird-offering. R. Simeon b. Eleazar said, 'Already has Rabban Yoḥanan taken a vote *against it* and annulled it because of [the possibility of] disorder.' " A similar reference is made in the same setting. R. Eliezer had fourth-year vines and wanted to declare them free for the use of the poor. His disciples told him, "Rabbi, your colleagues have already taken a vote on it and declared it permitted." The anonymous editor adds, "Who are his colleagues? Rabban Yoḥanan ben Zakkai." What is of interest is the reference to "taking a vote," which occurs in this context only (and in its parallel, b. Beẓ. 5b).

The proselyte-*beraita* is quoted in y. Sheq. 8:4 (V.i.8), with *bring* in place of *separate* and *of silver* added to *a quarter*. R. Simeon is listed; *b. Eleazar* is omitted. His saying is, "Rabban Yoḥanan ben Zakkai annuled it on account of the possibility of disorder." No reference is made to *took a vote against it*.

The same *beraita* is further quoted in b. Ker. 9a (III.ii.30), in precisely the form that appears in b. R.H. 31b. It occurs in b. Beẓ. 5b, where voted *on it* becomes *against you*. Hence we may note that the Palestinian

Talmud preserves a somewhat different version of the same *beraita*. The most striking difference is the absence of a reference to a vote. Yoḥanan did not have to consult others, according to the Palestinian formulation.

7. *All These Things*. A comment on all the decrees is contained in Tos. R.H. 2:9, R. Joshua b. Qorḥa said, "All these things Rabban Yoḥanan ben Zakkai decreed *when the Temple was destroyed*, and when it will be rebuilt—quickly in our times—these things will return to their former condition." This saying, which echoes the enumeration of the decrees, has no parallel. The context, however, is the reception of witnesses to the New Moon (above #3), and the specific reference may be to that decree only.

R. Joshua's saying here has no relationship to his teaching in the Mishnah R.H. 4:4 about the chief of the court.

Summary: Most of the ordinances of Yavneh seem to have undergone very little development. The Day of Waving never varies from its first formulation, though to it is added the *Lulav*-decree. The *shofar*-decree appears in one version only; the relevant *beraita* has nothing to do with it. The testimony, priestly blessing, new moon testimony on the Sabbath, and proselyte's offering sayings—all likewise exist in one version only. Matters that seem relevant to them in fact relate in subject, never in form. In effect, these are all singletons. Only in #6 did we find a significant parallel. The Mishnah there contains Yoḥanan's decree, but omits his name.

The form, on the other hand, is generally similar: *When the Temple was destroyed* appears as a superscription or in the body of the pericope in #1, 2, 3, 4, 5, and 7. Strikingly, the one place where it lacks is not a direct attribution to, or story about, Yoḥanan. It is rather a *reference* to something Yoḥanan had done. Otherwise, all Yavnean decrees are characterized by the inclusion of that single, unchanging formula.

IX. Conclusion

Yoḥanan's legal sayings and stories contain remarkably few exegeses of Scripture. Occasionally, a secondary formulation will add a Scriptural exegesis where none originally appeared, as in the inclusion of Hos. 14:10 in the *Woe*-sayings. Hos. 4:14 appears in connection with the abrogation of Temple rites, but Yoḥanan says nothing about the verse. The Scripture does not seem to be *cited* for Yoḥanan's particular purposes at all. Even when Yoḥanan-materials appear in collections of legal exegeses of Scripture, they themselves do *not* contain appropriate exegeses.

Yoḥanan's legal sayings certainly were cast into peculiar, fixed forms for the purposes of transmission. This is strikingly clear when we contrast sayings attributed to him with legal opinions cited in the context of stories told by *others* for their own purposes—that is, the *laws reported by disciples*. There we could find nothing characteristic of Yoḥanan-materials at all. Though he is cited as an important authority, he is not the center of interest; the concerns of others have shaped the traditions pertaining to "that day," and Yohanan's laws do not exhibit traditional or conventional forms.[1]

We noted six characteristic forms, phrases, or categories in the legal materials:

1. *Subscriptions*—attached to laws in the Mishnah or Tosefta. Yoḥanan's material is appended, often without close relationship to the substance of the law. We could not conclude that the Yoḥanan-saying or story existed separately in some coherent collection of his disciples. In one instance we know that R. Judah b. Ilai was responsible for the Yoḥanan-story cited as illustration of a legal opinion.

2. *The story is told*—Such stories serve either to illustrate a previously cited law, or to present a theory of law not in abstract, but in casuistic, form.

3. *His Disciples Asked*—These "stories" are closely related in general to the preceding, yet they serve different functions. They do not pertain to the exposition of a law, but rather exemplify Yoḥanan's "mode of teaching." As I suggested earlier, they may well have begun in hostile circles, have been transmitted and then revised by the transforming subscription, *All this why?* Strictly speaking, they do not serve for the transmission of legal materials at all, though their content is law.

4. *Laws Reported by Disciples*—This is merely a category among the several pertinent to Yoḥanan's legal sayings. It is not a *form*.

---

[1] Some of Yoḥanan's legal sayings were therefore carefully edited, while others underwent no editorial processes in his school or among his several disciples. The *on that day* materials are in the latter category, the Yavnean decrees in the former. But we cannot suppose that the former are historically more reliable than the latter; such a supposition would require evidence that the redaction took place under Yoḥanan's own supervision, and we have no such evidence.

5. *Disputes*—This category is divided into three parts. The Ben Bukhri dispute cannot be called a form; it belongs, in fact, with the *laws reported by disciples*, as a further example of a report of legal opinion of Yoḥanan reported later on.

The *We cry out against you* stories do exhibit a roughly coherent form, but we notice immediately that it is not peculiar to Yoḥanan-materials. Rather, Yoḥanan is included within a form generally used for Sadducean dispute stories in the Mishnah and Tosefta.

The two *beraitot* as well as the Scholion equivalents (VIII.vii. 4, 5, 6) obviously adhere to a fixed and conventional form, first a citation of the Fasting-Scroll, then the opinion of the Sadducees-Boethusians, finally, Yoḥanan's encounter, generally turning on the exegesis first of irrelevant, then of relevant Scriptures. This highly developed scheme does not reveal what components shaped earlier have now been revised, and my impression is that the form has not been imposed upon earlier, discrete materials, but in fact the materials and the form in which they are cast were shaped at the same time by a single narrator, editor, or school. The Tosefta fragment (vii.5) shows that the form is not unique to Yoḥanan-materials at all.

6. *When the Temple was Destroyed*—This phrase occurs in almost all Yavnean materials, and I think it likely to be characteristic of reports of Yoḥanan's Yavneh decrees. The decrees have been shaped to conform to a single pattern. The most fundamental, shortest, and least divisible form is simply:

> When the Temple was destroyed, Rabban Yoḥanan ben Zakkai decreed/said...

An alternative form, a list of the "nine decrees," may well have existed, for a fragment was seen in connection with the priestly blessing (VIII.viii.4).

The proselyte's offering is to be compared to the laws reported by disciples, which accounts for the absence of any phrase or formula characteristic of Yoḥanan-materials.

Of the six characteristic forms, phrases, or categories, only one can be called a conventional and characteristic form, as I said, and that is *When the Temple was destroyed.* All the others are commonplace and routine categories, merely useful for our purpose, but in no way suggestive of a traditional form.

A final question must be raised in each segment of our synoptic studies: Does a passage exhibit signs of development in its appearances in later document? Are details dropped or added in the passage of time? We may tentatively suggest that versions of a saying or story appearing in both early and later documents normally do differ from one another. The differences generally are augmentations, inclusion of new details, improvements on diction, or extensions of dialogue, and these are found in versions occuring in *later* documents. It seems to me likely that the versions of legal sayings in later documents are in fact later developments of the versions in earlier ones.

CHAPTER NINE

BIOGRAPHICAL MATERIALS

I. One-hundred-twenty Years

Among the four people, or six pairs who lived the same number of years or died at the age of one-hundred-twenty was Yoḥanan. The pericope occurs in early and late documents:

Sifré Deut. #357 (I.ii.8)	*Mid. Tan. to Deut. 34:7* (I.iv.6)	*b. R.H. 31b=b. Sanh. 41b*		*Ber. R. 100:24* 100:24 (VI.i.5)
1. Deut. 34:7		—	—	[Begins with #7-#13]
2. These are they: Moses, Hillel, Yoḥanan, ʿAqiva		—	—	[Then:]
3. Moses: *was* Egypt, 40 Midian, 40 Sustained	*worked* *served*	—	—	lived in palace of Pharaoh, 40 Midian *served*
4. Hillel: Migrated at 40 Disciple, 40 Sustaine, 40	 *served*	—	—	 *served sages* *served*
5. Yoḥanan *busied* Business, 40 Disciple, 40 Sustained, 40	*worked* *served*	All the years of Yoḥanan were one-hundred-twenty Business, 40 Studied, 40 Taught, 40	*(see b. R.H. 31b)*	*worked* *learned* *served* *worked as a boor*, 40
6. ʿAqiva Studied, 40 Sustained, 40	*studied* *served sages* *served* Israel			*studied* *served*
7. Six pairs lived same number of years		—	—	
8. Rebecca/Kohath		—	—	
9. Levi/Amram		—	—	
10. Joseph/Joshua		—	—	
11. Samuel/Solomon		—	—	
12. Moses/Hillel		—	—	
13. Yoḥanan/ʿAqiva		—	—	

The *one-hundred-twenty-years* pericope thus comes in two versions. In the first, represented by Sifré, Mid. Tan., and Ber. R., Yoḥanan is listed among four, then six pairs who lived one-hundred-twenty years. We may further subdivide these versions into two separate units, the "four," then the "six," or in reverse order in the latest version. Sifré and Mid. Tan. are practically identical; the only variations are in the choice of *worked* for *was*, *served* for *sustained*, in the latter version.

Further, Mid. Tan. corrects the omission in the earlier version of the first forty years of ʿAqiva's life. The tradition on ʿAqiva's early ignorance was well-known and widely attested. It would destroy the symmetry of the passage to make no reference to one-third of ʿAqiva's life, and hence the improvement, which at the same time perfects the saying and cleans up ʿAqiva's early years. See above, I.iv.6, for further comment.

Ber. R., the latest version of all three, not only reverses the order— which is an editorial change— but elaborates the Egyptian period of Moses, changing the general "in Egypt" to the specific "in the Palace of Pharaoh." Likewise ʿAqiva's early years are properly characterized as years of ignorance. But for the rest, the account is close to the early versions.

The two *beraitot*, which are identical, are quite another matter.[1] They ignore all others in the one-hundred-twenty year set and concentrate on Yoḥanan alone. But otherwise the *beraita*-version exhibits striking similarities to the earlier formulations. The forty-year divisions are repeated. Business (*pragmata*) is preserved. The discipleship/sustaining Israel of Sifré Deut. becomes studied/taught, a play on LMD. The *beraita* cannot be divorced from the earlier documents' version. Rather, it revises the tradition to concentrate on Yoḥanan alone; of the four/six, Yoḥanan is singled out. The exegetical framework is dropped as well.

The significant comparison, therefore, is to be made between the version in the earliest document, Sifré Deut., and that in the Babylonian *beraita*. Are the two versions independent but of equal antiquity? Or has the *beraita* formulation been *extracted* from the former

[1] The *beraitot* are as follows:

Has it not been taught, Rabban Yoḥanan ben Zakkai lived for one-hundred-twenty years. Forty years he was in business, forty years he studied, and forty years he taught. b. R. H. 31b

Has it not been taught, Rabban Yoḥanan ben Zakkai lived for one-hundred-twenty years. Forty years he was in business, forty years he studied, and forty years he taught. b. Sanh. 41b

and been slightly rephrased? My guess is that the latter has taken place. What was formerly a complete list is now a story about Yoḥanan alone. The reference to one-hundred-twenty years is the key. Without the exegesis of Deut. 34:7, as well as the list of all those therein included, the reference to Yoḥanan's exception life-span is meaningless; he could be one of hundreds. The tripartite division of his life-span likewise is pointless outside of the earlier convention. The *beraita* standing outside of the exegetical framework and the four/six pattern is enigmatic; within that framework, it makes real sense: These were the four/six who both lived a very long time and whose years were equivalently divided.

Who would have extracted Yoḥanan from the longer list? The most striking relationship in the list is Yoḥanan/ʿAqiva. The others, by the time ʿAqiva had died (second quarter of second century A.D.), were not controversial figures, were not made to serve as protagonists for conflicting principles. But ʿAqiva and Yoḥanan still were highly controversial. ʿAqiva had led a holy war; Yoḥanan had opposed, then abandoned one. Linking the two, perhaps in the school of ʿAqiva, tended to obliterate the important conflict of principle between the two masters. *Separating* Yoḥanan from ʿAqiva would have taught the "true" picture, that those who pair the two do so in error. Yoḥanan stands alone and is not to be compared to ʿAqiva.

We do not know whether the *beraitot* as they appear in the Babylonian Talmud were edited in Tannaitic times or in Amoraic schools. If the former, then some in the circle around Judah the Prince, not hostile to Yoḥanan, would have presented the early master by himself and separate from ʿAqiva, whose leadership had led to the deposition of Judah's grandfather and the disastrous war with Rome. That does not mean the Judahite circle was the only group interested in Yoḥanan. The circle(s) hostile to the patriarch also preserved Yoḥanan-materials. Yoḥanan was, after all, Hillel's disciple— and Simeon and Gamaliel I were *not* Hillel's chosen heirs. Such a story had a very obvious cutting edge: Hillel himself had rejected the principle of hereditary succession in favor of choosing the brightest, even the youngest disciple. It may, therefore, have been this same circle that shaped and transmitted the *beraita* on Yoḥanan's one-hundred-twenty years as well, a *beraita* pointedly ignoring Hillel's sons and heirs. In any event, it is clear that the Aqibans preserved the one-hundred-twenty year sequences in which Yoḥanan and ʿAqiva were paired, and some later masters *then* framed a *beraita* pointedly disconnecting the two men.

II. Eighty Disciples

The tradition on Hillel's eighty disciples occurs in three places:

b. B.B. 134a=b. Suk. 28a (III.ii.24)	*ARN a Ch. 14, ARN b., Ch. 28* (IV.i.5a)	*y. Ned. 5:6* (V.i.12)
Teno Rabbanan	—	—
Hillel had 80 disciples	80 *pairs* of disciples	80 *pairs* of disciples
30 worthy of *Shekhinah* like Moses	30 worthy of *Shekhinah* like Moses *but their generation was unworthy*	—
30 worthy of having sun stand still, like Joshua	[ARN b, Ch. 28: 30 worthy of having sun stand still like Joshua]	—
20 average	20 average	—
Greatest was Jonathan	Greatest was Jonathan	Greatest was Jonathan
Youngest was Yoḥanan	Youngest was Yoḥanan	Youngest was Yoḥanan
They said concerning Yoḥanan...	When Hillel was dying, they all went in, but Yoḥanan did not.	Once Hillel fell sick, disciples came to visit.

The tradition on the eighty disciples appears in the briefest form in y. Ned. There, its basic elements are simply the eighty, greatest, and youngest. The division of the eighty into thirty, thirty, and twenty is elaborated in the b. Suk. *beraita*.

The whole serves to introduce the story of Hillel's last illness/death in ARBb and y. Ned., but comes as a preface of a *they said* saying in b. B.B. and b. Suk. Clearly the common elements are simply:

1. Hillel had eighty disciples
2. Greatest was Jonathan
3. Least was Yoḥanan

These elements then were used by the editor of the Babylonian *beraita*-version for a purpose different from that of the Palestinian Talmud and ARNb. ARNb develops the *eighty-pairs* as does the *beraita*, but attaches it to the same setting as does the Palestinian Talmud. The additional details about the thirty, thirty, and twenty in the *beraita* and ARNa clearly represent a development of the Palestinian Talmudic version, as I said. It seems to me the symmetrical form would precede the unsymmetrical one. As to the death scenes of ARNb and y. Ned:

y. Ned. 5:6	*ARNb*
Once he fell ill	When he lay dying
All entered to visit him	All entered

But Rabban Yoḥanan ben Zakkai stood in the courtyard	but he did not enter
He said to them, Where is the youngest of you, for he is source of wisdom and source of generations (to come) and, needless to say, the greatest of you.	He said to them, Where is Yohanan
They said to him, Behold he is in the courtyard.	They said to him, Behold he is standing by the door.
He said to them, Let him enter.	He said to them, Let him enter, he is worthy
When he had entered, he (Hillel) said to them Prov. 8:21	When he had entered, he said to them, The youngest among you is source of wisdom and source of generations and the oldest how much the more so!
	He said to them, *Concerning all of you* it is said Prov. 8:21.

The ARNb version thus contains all the elements of y. Ned., but in different sequence. The *illness* is now a death scene. Rabban Yoḥanan ben Zakkai becomes merely *he*; the courtyard is omitted. In ARNb, the comment on Yoḥanan is introduced by a question, "Where is Yoḥanan?" The praise of Yoḥanan comes only after he is located. Yoḥanan is told to come in, then "The youngest among you..." Finally, in ARNb comes the praise, while in y. Ned., Yoḥanan is praised, invited to enter, only *then* made the object of the exegesis of Prov. 8:21. In ARNb, Prov. 8:21 applies to *all* the disciples. It is clear that the two versions of the setting for the exegesis of Prov. 8:21 are closely related, and I find it difficult to suggest which version comes first, or how they are connected to one another. ARNa conforms to the Palestinian Talmudic version.

The exegesis of Prov. 8:21 strikingly appears in the *beraita* as well. After much praise of Yoḥanan (below), we find:

> To fulfill what is said in Prov. 8:21
> And since the least of them was so, the greatest—how much the more so.
> They say of Jonathan b. Uzziel that when he studied . . .

We see once again that the *beraita* is a reworking of materials available to ARNb/y. Ned. What all have in common is the exegesis of Prov. 8:21. The exegesis is set into a completely different context. In the Palestinian version, these are the words of Hillel on his death-bed. In the Babylonian one comes a standard exegesis, connected with no particular life-situation whatever. The *beraita* and the Palestinian components compare as follows:

Palestinian	*Babylonian*
1. Eighty disciples	1. Eighty disciples
2. When Hillel fell sick	2. They said concerning Yoḥanan
3. Prov. 8:21 said *by Hillel*	3. Prov. 8:21 stated *anonymously*

The Palestinian version is internally consistent in first making Hillel's death scene the setting and then attributing to Hillel the exegesis of Prov. 8:21 and its application to Yoḥanan in particular. The Babylonian version is more general, less elaborate. The *they said concerning* replaces the whole of the death scene.

If we had a well-established rule that the particular, detailed version precedes the general account, or vice versa, we might be able to ascertain whether the Palestinian version of the exegesis of Prov. 8:21 precedes the Babylonian one, or vice versa. But we do not. The relationships between the two accounts are not obscure; the specific, vivid picture in the Palestinian version becomes the general and more conventional one in the Babylonian *beraita*. But I do not see why we should suppose one *must* precede the other in time of redaction. It is difficult to think they were separately and independently formulated. Still, one may conjecture that several pre-existing elements have been variously shaped. These elements are, as we have seen:

1. Eighty disciples
2. Death scene
3. They said concerning Yoḥanan
4. Exegesis of Prov. 8:21

When #1, 2, and 4 are combined, the exegesis is set into context in the life-situation of Hillel's school. When #1, 3, and 4 are combined, Hillel plays no role whatever. The editor of the *beraita*, presumably a Babylonian—but we do not know of which school or generation—cannot be thought to have held a poor opinion of Hillel. He did not eliminate Hillel-elements, though he did make Yoḥanan the focus of attention. The editor of the Palestinian versions (ARNb, y. Ned.) preserves Yoḥanan as the focus of attention as well, but provides a more literary account of the whole matter. I think the relationships among the several versions are clear. But, as I said, I do not know what they imply about the literary history either of the components or of the final accounts.

III. They Said Concerning Yoḥanan

The form *They said concerning Rabban Yoḥanan ben Zakkai* is imposed on pre-existing materials. This is perfectly evident in the following:

y. A.Z. 3:11 (V.i.18)	*b. Pes. 26a* (V.ii.3)
And Rabban Yoḥanan ben Zakkai (was) sitting and teaching in the shadow of the Temple	*They said concerning Rabban Yoḥanan ben Zakkai* that he would sit in the shadow of the Temple and expound all day long.

The passage in the Palestinian Talmud is not introduced by a particular authority, nor is that in the Babylonian Talmud. The former is simple; it contains a participle, no verb. In the Babylonian *beraita* the verb *to be* is supplied to serve the participle. In the former, the verb ŠNH is used, in the latter DRŠ. *All day long* is added. In the former we have a single clause, in the latter, two clauses. The Palestinian version probably is both more primitive and older; the Babylonian one represents a more artful, later development of earlier components. The *They said concerning* formula is therefore added to the earlier saying. It is never used in the Palestinian Talmudic traditions on Yoḥanan, but is unique to the Babylonian ones.

Other appearances of the *They said concerning* formula are in b. Ber. 17a (V.ii.1), that he always said hello first; and b. B.B. 134a-b. Suk. 28a. The *beraita* in b. Suk. is as follows: *They said concerning Yoḥanan that*

1. he never engaged in profane conversation,
2. he never walked four *'amot* without Torah and *tefillin*,
3. No one ever came to school before him,
4. he never slept in school;
5. he never tarried in alleyways;
6. he never left anyone in school, and he never slept there;
7. he himself always opened the door for his disciples.
8. He never said something he had not heard from his master.
9. He never broke up a study-session.
10. And so did R. Eliezer his disciple behave after him.

Then comes the element considered above, *Hillel had eighty disciples*, then:

They said concerning Yoḥanan that

11. He never left off studying Scripture, Mishnah, gemara, laws, le- ends,... a great matter and a small matter—a great matter, the *Merkavah*—a small matter, the reflections of Abbaye and Rava
12. to fulfill Prov. 8:21
13. They said concerning Jonathan b. Uzziel...

In b. B.B. 134a the order of the elements is reversed:

1. Hillel had eighty disciples
2. *They said concerning Yoḥanan* that he did not leave off studying Scrip- lure.

Thus in b. B.B. 134a, items #1-10 of b. Suk. are omitted. Items #11-13 are identical in both versions.
Item #2 appears in y. Ber. 2:3 (V.i.1) as follows:

> Rabban Yoḥanan ben Zakkai, his *tefillin* did not move from him either in summer or in winter and so did Eliezer his disciple behave after him.

Item #11-12 appears in ARNa Ch. 14 (IV.i.5b) as follows:

> They said concerning Rabban Yoḥanan ben Zakkai that he did not leave off Scripture, Mishnah, Gemara, Laws, Legends, Supplements... And nothing in the Torah did he leave off studying to fulfill that which is said [in] Prov. 8:21.

The *beraita* in b. B.B. 134a clearly is composed of four separate traditions, #1-10 is one corpus; then *Hillel's disciples*; then #11-12; finally #13. The first part has been shaped in Eliezer's school, as I pointed out above. A single element of that tradition existed separately in a Palestinian formulation. The extended list of Yoḥanan's curriculum (#11) is interrupted by the definition of great and small things in terms of the studies of Abbaye and Rava. In ARNa Ch. 14, the list occurs without that interruption.

While the ARNa version of the list seems older than the one in b. B.B. 134a as we now have it, if one excludes the reference to Abbaye and Rava, which is clearly an interjection imposed in a pre-existing formula, then we have no reason to think one version is older than the other.

In their present form the Babylonian *beraitot* must be regarded as the last of the versions. It is clear that the Palestinians omitted the *They said concerning* formula; if so, the ARNa version has now been corrected to conform to the Babylonian formulation of the *beraita*. Since, in its "final form," ARN dates from the ninth century, there is no reason to doubt that the Babylonian *beraita* has been referred to in the ARN's formulation of the Yoḥanan-saying. We cannot, however, claim that *They said concerning* derives from the schools of late fourth-century Babylonia, for the likelihood is that the saying concerning Yoḥanan's studies was older, and was altered to include reference to Abbaye and Rava. So, quite to the contrary, the *They said concerning* formula must date *before* the time of Abbaye and Rava, hence sometime in the third century.

All of the materials on Yoḥanan's early life have one thing in common: They persist in linking Yoḥanan to Hillel and strikingly exclude all reference to Hillel's son, Simeon, his grandson, Gamaliel I, Simeon b. Gamaliel I, Gamaliel II, Simeon b. Gamaliel II, and Judah the Prince. Everyone knew that the Hillelites in fact inherited the authority of Hillel, the scion of their house. No one therefore could have missed the point of a story or exegesis assigning the cloak of the master to Yoḥanan, not to Hillel's own family, indeed stressing that Yoḥanan was the youngest and the least. Any capable master in the Hillelite school would therefore have been worthy of succeeding the dying teacher—anyone but his own son. We can hardly doubt that these sayings were shaped in circles hostile to the Hillelite patriarchate, among men who opposed the principle of hereditary succession and presumably much else about the patriarch. Such men were not revolutionaries in the tradition of the Aqibans before Bar Kokhba. They accepted the policies of the patriarchate and were not looking for trouble with Rome. But its politics was another matter.

The interest of the Pumbeditan-Maḥozan school in traditions linking Hillel to Yoḥanan and suppressing reference to Gamaliel is not difficult to account for. The Pumbeditans were engaged in a struggle to preserve their independence from the exilarch, descended from the Davidic line just as was the patriarch. A story in which the Davidic inheritance mattered far less than knowledge of Torah was particularly useful in this struggle. We shall refer to this matter below (pp. 295 ff.)

IV. Death-Scene

We have four versions of Yoḥanan's death scene, as follows:

y. A.Z. 3:1 (V.i.11)	*y. Sot. 9:16* (V.i.11)	*ARNa Ch. 25* (IV.i.9)	*b. Ber. 28b* (III.ii.1)
R. Jacob b. Idi in the name of R. Joshua b. Levi	*(see y. A.Z. 3:1)*	—	*Teno Rabbanan* When Eliezer was dying, his disciples came to visit...
When Yoḥanan was dying, he said	*commanded and* said	—	And when Yoḥanan fell ill, his disciples came to visit.
—	—	When Yoḥanan was dying, he raised his voice and wept.	When he saw them, he wept.
—	—	Disciples said,	Disciples said Light

		Tall pillar, light of the world, mighty hammer why weep?	of Israel, Right-hand pillar, Mighty hammer Why weep?
—	—	Do I go to judgment before a mortal king, who dies and can be bribed? I go before king of kings and don't know his decision Ps. 22:30	If I were going before mortal king who may be bribed, I'd weep. Now that I go before immortal God, and do not know his decision, should I not weep?
—	—	—	They said, Bless us. He said, May you fear heaven as much as you fear men.
Clear the *house* because of uncleanness	clear the *courtyard*	—	When he died, he said, Clear out the *vessels* and prepare a chair for Hezekiah who comes.
And give a chair for Hezekiah king of Judah	*ordain*	—	
Rabbi Eliezer when dying said	—	—	—
Clear the house because of uncleanness	—	—	—
And set a chair for Rabban Yoḥanan ben Zakkai	—	—	—

The two Palestinian Talmudic versions are simple and unadorned. That in y. A.Z. 3:1 includes the death scene of Eliezer, but in proper chronological order, that is, first Yoḥanan, then Eliezer. The reference to a chair for Yoḥanan is omitted in the corresponding death scene in b. Ber. 28b, which is as different for Eliezer as it is for Yoḥanan. Y. Soṭ. 9:16 omits all reference to Eliezer's death scene. It is otherwise close to the account of Jacob b. Idi in Joshua's name in y. A.Z., and is given the same attribution. The long *beraita* in b. Ber. 28b (III.ii.1) involves an extended account of Eliezer's death, followed by a similarly long version of Yoḥanan's. The "clear out the vessels," which is the point of the Palestinian versions, is rather awkwardly tacked on at the end by the device of having the long sermon introduced by *When he was sick*, and the dying words by *In the hour of his death*. The final blessing is included, parallel to that of Eliezer, but of different content. The ARNa version omits all reference to Eliezer. It begins with Yoḥanan's weeping; the disciples play a less important role; and they do not get a blessing at the end. Light of *Israel* becomes *of the world; right-hand pillar* becomes *tall pillar;* that is, the Babylonian version is more specific, alludes to concrete images. The actual homilies require closer comparison:

ARN	*b. Ber. 28b*
Do I go before a king of flesh and blood — whose anger is of this world — whose punishment is of this world — whose death-penalty is of this world — who can be bribed with words or money?	If I went before a king of flesh and blood, who is here today and in the grave tomorrow — whose anger is not eternal — whose imprisonment is not eternal — whose death-penalty is not eternal And I can bribe him with words or money Even so would I weep
I go before King of Kings — whose anger is eternal — who cannot be bribed with words or money	I go before the eternal God — whose anger is eternal — whose imprisonment is eternal — whose death-penalty is eternal
Before me are two roads, one to Paradise, one to Gehenna And I do not know to which he will sentence me. And of this the verse says—Ps. 22:30.	And before me are two roads, one to Paradise, one to Gehenna And I do not know to which one he will sentence me Should I not weep?
	They said to him, Master, bless us? [As above.]

The homilies are practically identical, certainly close enough to show dependence on one another. It is therefore striking that the concluding blessing is absent in ARNa. Since the Babylonian *beraita*, like the Palestinian one, was shaped in Eliezer's school, or in circles in which Eliezer's relationship to Yoḥanan seemed extremely important, I think the additional clause in the *beraita* was added so that Yoḥanan's death-scene would be symmetrical to Eliezer's. The same factor accounts for the importance of the disciples in the *beraita's* death-scene, by contrast to their role as mere bystanders in ARNa.

It seems to me clear that the primary Palestinian version is y. A.Z. 3:1, for it is unlikely that Jacob b. Idi in Joshua's name would have handed on two separate versions, one long, the other short. Rather the y. Soṭ. 9:16 version has merely been shortened by the omission of reference to Eliezer. It is otherwise so close as to be completely dependent on the longer version. There can be no question of relative age. Both appear in the name of the same master and cannot be thought to come from different schools or periods.

The Babylonian and ARNa versions are another matter. I should imagine, following the former analogy, that b. Ber. 28b is the older, more complete version, shaped along the lines of Eliezer's death scene, as I said. ARNa afterward omits the details involving masters other than Yoḥanan, introduces the exegesis of Ps. 22:30, and concludes with the (probably) famous, "Clear the house..."

What are the primary elements of Yoḥanan's death scene? Clearly they began with "*Clear the house... prepare a chair*," which appears throughout, even to the point of being awkwardly tacked on in b. Ber. 28b and ARNa. In the Palestinian accounts, by contrast, the two-fold message fits together without strain. In the ARNa and b. Ber. versions, we thus find five further, certainly later elements;

1. He wept as he was sick/dying,
2. Disciples [came to visit and] asked why,
3. And heaped on him encomia,
4. He replied saying he was going to eternal judgment and did not know the likely decision,
5. [They asked to be blessed].

I see no reason to suppose all these elements are not late inventions, coming long after the very simple account of Joshua b. Levi. They cannot be called "expansions" of Joshua's account; indeed they bear little or no relationship to it. Rather they make use of some of the same materials as Joshua, particularly the *Clear the house... set a chair...* These may not have been original with Joshua. We do not have to imagine the Babylonian *beraita* was shaped by masters who had ever even heard Joshua's version. Indeed, I doubt they did.

v. A Good Court

Yoḥanan's "good court" is referred to in a brief saying in the Tannaitic Midrashim, and the saying is greatly expanded in a much later *beraita*:

Sifré Deut. 144 (I.ii.8)	*b. Sanh. 32b* (III.i.24)
	Teno Rabbanan.
Righteousness...shall pursue	*Righteousness...shall pursue.*
Go after a good court.	Go after a good court.
After the court of Yoḥanan.	After the court of Eliezer *in Lud*
After the court of Eliezer.	After the court Yoḥanan *in Beror Ḥayil*
	Teno Rabbanan
	Righteousness...shall pursue
	Go after the sages to the academy [*yeshivah*].
	After Eliezer to Lud
	After Yoḥanan to Beror Ḥayil
	After Joshua to Peqi'in
	After Gamaliel to Yavneh
	After 'Aqiva to Bnei Beraq
	After Matthew to Rome
	After Ḥananiah b. Teradion to Sikhnin
	After Yosi to Sepphoris
	After Judah b. Bathyra to Nisibis
	After Ḥananiah nephew of R. Joshua to the Exile
	After Rabbi [Judah] to Bet She'arim
	After the sages to the Hewn Stone Chamber.

The two *beraitot* appear in sequence in the Babylonian Talmud. The first obviously is an expansion of the brief and simple version of Sifré Deut. It adds the details of where their courts were. I think it unlikely that, had those details been at first included, they would later on have been suppressed. It would have deprived the disciples of useful information, and there was no good reason to do so. The third and longest *beraita* cannot date from earlier than the first third of the third century. We see the immense expansion of the one quoted just above. Eliezer and Yoḥanan keep their places. Then follows the first generation of Yavneh, that is, Joshua and Gamaliel; then the generation of 'Aqiva, then the one immediately following the Bar Kokhba war; finally Judah; and at the end, "the sages" to the (presumably eschatological) Hewn Stone chamber. It is again noteworthy that the versions appearing in later documents are elaborated and clearly later than the versions appearing in earlier documents.

A *beraita* in b. R.H. 18a (III.ii.6) is cited without any change whatever in b. Yev. 105a. It concerns Yoḥanan's counsel to the family descended from Eli.

VI. Conclusion

The comparison of several versions of the same saying is here extended. We have seen that the Babylonian *beraitot* in general greatly alter, often augment, pre-existing materials. In the *One-hundred-twenty years* saying, the *beraita*-version (b. R.H. 31b, b. Sanh. 41b) omits all those mentioned in earlier and parallel sayings, and concentrates on Yoḥanan alone. The *beraita* probably comes later than the more complete, standard one. The version appearing in the latest documents of all, that in Ber. R., makes numerous elaborations of the accounts in earlier documents, and this certainly does represent a later formulation. It has no relationship to the *beraita* at all.

The *eighty-disciples* saying proves most complex. In the Babylonian *beraitot* it is only part of a long collection of materials attributed to a Tanna, or to Tannaim, concerning Yoḥanan. In the simplest exemplum, it is the statement that Hillel had eighty disciples, the greatest was Jonathan, the least, Yoḥanan. This is then expanded, with the thirty/thirty/twenty sequence. Finally, the death scenes are attached, in the Palestinian and ARNb forms being closely interrelated, though in different sequence of details. The Babylonian version includes a long *They said concerning Yoḥanan* pericope, which is omitted in a shorter version of the *beraita*. We were able to isolate four basic elements among the several exempla, and I presume that these existed separately before being brought together in various combinations.

It is quite clear that *They said concerning Yoḥanan* is a conventional superscription, imposed on Babylonian materials but absent from similar or identical Palestinian ones in as y. A.Z. and Pes., possibly also in y. Ber. 2:3.

The death-scene went from the simple to the complex, and from the Palestinian Talmud's attribution by R. Jacob b. Idi to R. Joshua, on the one hand, to the fully articulated *beraita*-form *(Teno Rabbanan)* on the other. ARNa again seemed closer to the Babylonian *beraita* than to the simpler Palestinian version.

It seems to me possible that the question of the date of the ARNa will have to be restudied, for it sometimes conforms not to the earlier Palestinian versions, but to the substantially later Babylonian ones. Even though all authorities derive from the third century or earlier, the forms of important sayings which do exhibit Babylonian parallels normally adhere to those Babylonian parallels, hence to later, Babylonian developments of Palestinian materials or to materials invented to begin with in the Babylonian schools.

We once again see clearly that a passage frequently shows development and elaboration when it appears in later documents. Details are added later on. We have every reason to believe, for instance, that the *Righteousness* saying of Sifré Deut. is expanded in the brief *beraita* in b. Sanh. 32b, then greatly augmented in the second, and certainly later one, which *begins* with the *beraita* but then develops it with a long list of later authorities. That the version appearing in the earlier document is in fact the earlier version cannot be seriously doubted; that the versions appearing in the *beraita*-form are expanded and clearly later is equally evident. But the same phenomenon is more or less evident in other materials in this chapter. Even when materials are abbreviated in the version appearing in later documents, as b. R.H. 31b = b. Sanh. 41b in relationship to Sifré Deut. 357, for instance, those materials still exhibit dependence on the versions appearing in the earlier documents.

We cannot, therefore, hold that whatever is expanded is later or that whatever is abbreviated is necessarily earlier. Such a fixed rule would mislead us and ill serve our inquiry. It is, however, ever more obvious that versions appearing in later compilations are generally later than versions appearing in earlier collections. Those who hold that the data are timeless and that what comes late is "not necessarily" later than what comes in earlier documents will have to assume at least a measure of the burden of proof. The contrary seems once and again to be the case. While we cannot regard our observations as definitive proof, they do point in a single direction, and that direction is contrary to the opinion of the traditionalists who hold, for theological reasons, I imagine, that talmudic, like biblical literature is exempt from the normal rules of historical inquiry. *To conclude:* As we follow stories through several recensions, we do find that passages are normally developed, details are added, and these are *prima facie* evidences that later materials are indeed found in the later documents.

CHAPTER TEN

HISTORICAL STORIES

I. The Escape

We have two fundamentally different accounts of Yoḥanan's escape, each in two versions, those in ARNa and ARNb, and in b. Git. 56b and Lam R. It is obvious that all are very late stories. None can possibly date from Tannaitic times; in Tannaitic traditions we find not the slightest reference to an escape. Indeed, we should not know how Yoḥanan reached Yavneh, if we had to rely on the Tannaitic midrashim, Mishnah-Tosefta, and even the *beraitot* in the Babylonian Talmud. Nor does the Palestinian Talmud contain a reference to an escape. If we knew the date of the ARN materials, we should probably have a clear idea about the literary beginnings of the escape legend, though the several components of the ARNa account are probably older and now have been reshaped. We may only imagine that at some point in Amoraic times, it became important to tell escape-stories; no single account was ever widely accepted. I can propose no conjecture on when, where, or why it became important to make up such a story, or to whom it would have been useful. Perhaps opposition to Julian's attempt to rebuild the Temple provoked it, but my guess is that the components of the escape-legends are much older than that.

The Babylonian version is clearly a composite, while ARN is, as usual, more literary, smoother, but also formed from earlier materials. We shall first compare the two ARN versions, then the second pair, and finally contrast one account with the other.

	ARNa (IV.i.2)		*ARNb*. Ch. 6, Schechter, p. 10a
I.	Vespasian asks sign of submission.	I.	*see ARNa (IV.1.2)*
	Yoḥanan counsels Jews to give it, save the Temple, they refuse.		*see ARNa (IV.1.2)*
	Vespasian's men heard of Yoḥanan's loyalty.		*see ARNa (IV.1.2)*
II.	Yoḥanan tells Joshua and Eliezer to help him escape.	II.	*see ARNa (IV.1.2)*

	Make a coffin. Eliezer and Joshua carried coffin. Gatekeepers object, but are told it is a corpse.		*see ARNa (IV.1.2)* *see ARNa (IV.1.2)* Gatekeepers object, want to stab corpse. Disciples reply, You will be said to have stabbled Yoḥanan's corpse.
III.	Coffin carried to Vespasian, Yoḥanan rises from coffin before emperor. Are you Rabban Yoḥanan? What can I give you?	III.	Yoḥanan gets out of coffin, goes and asks after welfare of Vespasian as one asks about a king, saying *Ridumani Imperion.* Are you Ben Zakkai?
	Yavneh, so I may teach, establish prayerhouse, do commandments.		Yoḥanan predicts coming rise to power, citing Is. 10:34.
	Go.		
IV.	Yoḥanan tells Vespasian you are about to be made emperor, on basis of Is. 10:34.	IV.	[*After* his prediction is proved correct, Yoḥanan is permitted to make a request.]
	Two or three days later, news came that Vespasian was emperor.		Give me Yavneh where I may teach Torah and make *ẓiẓit* and do all the other commandments.
			Behold it is given to you as a gift.

Parts I and II are practically identical in both versions. But parts III and IV are not. In the latter, the prediction comes before the emperor gives any favors, as in b. Giṭ. Likewise, gatekeepers are hostile to the disciples. In general, as we shall see, ARNb combines major elements of ARNa and the Babylonian version; it is a composite of the two, standing between them. The Babylonian and Midrashic accounts compare as follows;

	b. Git. 56b (V.ii.14)		*Lam.R. 1.5.31* (VI.ii.2)
I.	Abba Sikra was Yoḥanan's nephew, came to Yoḥanan. How long will you kill the people by starvation? Abba Sikra cannot help. Then, Yoḥanan asks, think of a plan to get me out. Perhaps there may be some slight salvation.	I.	Ben Battiaḥ was Yoḥanan's nephew. When Yoḥanan heard his nephew had burned the city's supplies, he exclaimed "woe". Ben Battiaḥ heard, called Yoḥanan to him, asked why. Yoḥanan said he had praised the burning of the stores because now the people would have to fight. Three days later, he saw people starving, decided to escape. Asked Ben Battiaḥ to help. Ben Battiaḥ

	Pretend to be sick, die, and he did so.		says only dead can leave.
			Yoḥanan determined to escape as corpse.
II.	Eliezer carried one side, Joshua the other.	II.	Eliezer and Joshua carried him, Ben Battiaḥ accompanied cortege. Guards wanted to stab body, Ben Battiaḥ said it will give us a bad name.
	Guards wanted to push, then stab body. Disciples say it will give you a bad name.		
III.	When he reached there, he said, Peace be to you, 0 King.	III.	Disciples returned to city. Yoḥanan wandered among Roman troops, asked where king was. Yoḥanan was brought to Vespasian, *Vive domine Imperator*.[1]
	Vespasian says, You are worthy of death. I am not a king, and if I were, why did you not come earlier.		
	But you are a king, Yoḥanan says, citing Is. 10:34, Jer. 30:21, Deut. 3:25.		Vespasian: You endanger my life, for if king hears, he will put me to death.
	I could not come sooner because revolutionaries would not let me.		But you are a king, Is. 10:34.
IIIb.	Vespasian asks, If you have honey and a reptile is around the cask, would you not break the cask to kill the snake?		—(VI)
	Yoḥanan fell silent.		— (VI)
	R. Joseph/R. ʿAqiva cites Is. 44:25. He should have answered, One takes tongs.		—
IV.	Meanwhile messenger came from Rome, Vespasian is king.	IV.	Yoḥanan put in room without light, but could tell time because of his study.
V.	He had one shoe off, one shoe on, could do nothing.	V.	Vespasian bathes at Gophna, but could not get shoes back on, for word came that Nero died and he was king. Yoḥanan explains, You have heard good news, cites Prov. 15:30 and Prov. 17:22.
	Yoḥanan says, you have heard good news, cites Prov. 15:30. Let someone you dislike pass before you, cites Prov. 17:22.		
VI.	If you were so wise, why did you not come sooner?	VI.	Then they began to speak in parables. If a snake in a cask, what to do? Yoḥanan: Charm the snake.

[1] I do not understand the preference for Latin over Greek.

	I already told you.		Pangar: Break the cask and kill the snake. If a snake in a tower: Yoḥanan, bring a charmer. Pangar: Burn the tower. Yoḥanan to Pangar: You hurt us. Pangar: I seek your welfare. So long as Temple exists, heathen kingdoms will attack you, if it is destroyed, they will not. Yoḥanan: The heart knows what your real intention is.
	So did I.		
VII.	I, Vespasian continued, will soon leave. What can I give you?	VII.	Vespasian: What may I give you?
	Yavneh and its sages, the chain of Gamaliel, and a physician for Ẓadok.		Yoḥanan: Abandon this city and depart. Vespasian: I did not become king to abandon Jerusalem.
	R. Joseph/R. ʿAqiva cites Is. 44-25. He should have asked the Romans to leave them alone.		Yoḥanan: Leave the western gate open for refugees.
	—	VIII.	After the conquest, Vespasian offered to save Yoḥanan's friends.
			Yoḥanan sent Eliezer and Joshua to bring Ẓadoq.
	—	IX.	Vespasian: Why do you stand up before emaciated old man.
			Yoḥanan: If we had one more like him, you would not have conquered Jerusalem. He lives on a fig, teaches many sessions, fasts a lot.
			Vespasian healed Ẓadoq.
	—	X.	Ẓadoq's son: Father, give them reward in this world.
			He gave them calculation by fingers and scales for weighing.
	—	XI.	After conquest, Vespasian assigned destruction of four ramparts to four generals.
			Pangar had western wall, but did not destroy it.
			Pangar explained to Vespasian, I kept it so people would know what you destroyed.

—	Vespasian replied, Well said, but you disobeyed, so commit suicide.
—	He did so, and thus the curse of Rabban Yoḥanan ben Zakkai alighted upon him.

Lam R. has been corrected in important details to conform to the criticism of b. Giṭ.; note the comparison of b. Giṭ. IIIb and VI with Lam. R. VI and VII. Yet in many other, equally important respects, Lam R. stands by itself. The Abba Sikra account is now expanded into two parts. Lam. R. parts IV, VI, VII, VIII, IX, X, and XI have no close counterpart in the earlier version, though the "physician for Rabbi Ẓadoq" of Giṭ. part VI becomes the long encounter of Lam. R. part IX and X.

The central role attributed to Pangar the Arab general has no earlier counterpart. If, as is supposed, Lam. R is a post-Islamic text, then the new interest in the Arabs' role in the destruction of Jerusalem will easily account for the hostile view of the role of Pangar. He claims to be a friend and to mean well, but does the greatest harm of all, though later on "the curse of Yoḥanan" is fulfilled in him. I know no other references to such a curse.

We have no reason to doubt Lam. R. is later than Giṭ. The former is greatly elaborated over the latter. Thus once again we see that the version appearing in the later document is probably later than the one appearing in the earlier document. Indeed, it is expanded both through details common to both stories, and with completely new materials. The following summarizes the points in common as well as the stories found in one account and not in another:

ARN	*b. Giṭ.*	*Lam. R.*
Vespasian asks submission, Yoḥanan agrees.	—	—
Joshua and Eliezer effect the escape of "corpse."	Abba Sikra—"corpse"	Ben Battiaḥ—"corpse."
—	Starvation.	—
—	—	Burning of stores.
Guards went to stab corpse.	*(see ARN)*	*(see ARN)*
Meets Vespasian	*(see ARN)*	*(see ARN)*
What can I give you?	—	—
Yavneh	*(see ARN)*	*(see ARN)*

Prediction, Is. 10:34	*(see ARN)*	*(see ARN)*
News comes.		
—	Honey and reptile.	*(see b. Giṭ.)*
—	Is. 44:25	*(see b. Giṭ.)*
—	Feet bloated, Prov. 15:30, 17:22	*(see b. Giṭ.)*
—	Chain of Gamaliel	—
—	Heal Ẓadoq	*(see b. Giṭ.)*
—	—	Yoḥanan told time miraculously.
—	—	Tower and reptile.
—	—	Pangar.
—	—	Abandon city.
—	—	Accept refugees
—	—	Why honor Ẓadoq?
—	—	Ẓadoq gives calculation.
	—	Pangar fails to destroy Western wall.

All accounts have in common the escape through a ruse, the participation of Joshua and Eliezer, the request for Yavneh, the prediction of Vespasian's coming rise to power on the basis of Is. 10:34, and the arrival of news to verify Yohanan's prediction. Although the order and perspective of ARNa differ from those of the later versions, no important detail in the former is absent in the latter. It seems possible that ARN has served as a source of materials—though as that alone—for the Babylonian and Lam. R. stories. I think it is far more likely, however, that some sort of independent materials circulated widely, and were used by the authors of the several stories independently of one another. Otherwise, I imagine, the relationships between ARN and the other stories would be somewhat more like those between b. Giṭ. and Lam. R. There would be signs of development and augmentation, and we see none. Hence some stories, particularly about the escape and prediction (Is. 10:34) probably antedated the formation of the several accounts. To conclude: ARNa stands by itself, quite apart from b. Giṭ. and its later formulation in Lam. R.; we do not know whether ARNa comes before b. Giṭ. Since the two are not directly related, it hardly matters.

It remains to note that Qoh. R. 7:12:1 (VI.vi.3) contains a fragment of the story of Lam. R. The first part, about Yoḥanan's dealings with Ben Battiaḥ, is cited to illustrated Qoh. 7:12, *The excellency of knowledge is that wisdom preserves the life*... It is virtually certain that Qoh. R. merely quotes Lam. R. and has no independent information whatever.

The tendency to invent stories about Yoḥanan's escape is further illustrated in a Tanḥuma conversation between Yoḥanan and Hadrian, which is obviously a fabrication. Its elements are completely new, unrelated to anything before. The story of Yoḥanan's exegesis of Is. 14:14-15 (III.ii.12) is not cited, though it would have been appropriate. The passage is completely independent. If by some chance the name of Vespasian had been used instead of Hadrian, then those who hold normal considerations of historical study do not apply to Talmudic literature would have doubtless argued we have still another story to be taken seriously and considered possibly, indeed probably, "historical," even though it appears in a late medieval collection. The fact that it comes in such a late collection has no implications whatever for the "historicity" of the story; it merely circulated "in oral form" for thirteen hundred years or more—it thus would have been claimed. But that claim cannot be advanced, for everyone knows Hadrian came half a century after Yoḥanan was dead. We once again have evidence that what appears in a very late document is likely to be a complete fabrication, especially if we are fortunate enough to find a text without any relationships or points in common whatever to stories or sayings appearing in earlier documents. This is important, since we have a number of exegeses (e.g., VI.i.1,2) of just this sort, coming in later midrashic compilations but lacking any sort of antecedent exempla.

II. The Destruction

The exegesis in y. Meg. 3:1 (V.i.9) of II Kings 25:9 by R. Joshua b. Levi includes a reference to Yoḥanan's school, "*And every great house he burned in flames*—"this refers to the school house of Yoḥanan, for there they would rehearse the great deeds of the Holy One blessed be he." The several versions differ slightly:

y. Meg. 3:1 (V.i.9)	*Pesiqta de R. Kahana* (VI.v.3)	*Lam. R.* (VI.iii.14)
II Kings 25:9	II Kings 25:9	II Kings 25:9
This is the schoolhouse of Yoḥanan	And why does he call it a great house?	This is the schoolhouse...
		And why does he call it a great house?
For there they would rehearse the greatness	For there they would rehearse...	For there they would rehearse...

We see that the elements in y. Meg. are briefer: Scripture, application, reason for application. In both the later documents, the exegesis is expanded by some intervening comment, "And why does..." to spell out the point of Joshua's exegesis, that the "*great* house" means Yoḥanan's school, *because* at Yoḥanan's school they would talk about the *great* deeds of God. The latest version simply reverses the sequence of the Pesiqta's elements, but is otherwise no different.

III. Because You Did Not Serve

The sermon on the occasion of seeing a starving child exists in a number of formulations, appearing in the earliest to the latest documents. We shall compare the versions by the sequence of documents.

Mekhilta Baḥodesh (I.i.1)	*Sifré Deut.* (I.i.7)	[*y. Ket. 5:11*]	[*Tos. Ket. 5:9-10*]
They were not satisfied to count.	—	[Marta daughter of Boethus had large dowry...	[The daughter of Naqdimon had a large dowry.
Ezek. 40:1	—		
Hag. 1:15	—	Eleazar b. Ẓadoq said he saw her gathering barley under hooves of horses in Acre, and *I* cited concerning her Deut. 28:56 and Song 1:8]	Eleazar b. Ẓadoq says he saw her gathering barley under the hooves of horses in Acre.
And thus it says, *If you know not* Song 1:8	—		
And it also says, *Because you did not serve* (Deut. 28:47-8)	—		And *I cited* concerning her Song 1:8]
Yoḥanan going to Emmaus saw girl picking barley-corn from horse-dung.	*Story is told* that Yoḥanan was riding an ass and students walking after him, and he saw girl picking barley-corn from the feet of Arab cattle.		
To disciples: What is girl?			
She is Jewish			
The horse belongs to an Arab.	When she saw Yoḥanan, she wrapped herself in her hair and stood before him, asking for food.		
Yoḥanan to disciples: Now I know meaning of *Song 1:8*.			
You are unwilling to be subject to God, are now subject to Arabs.	She: Naqdimon b. Gurion, don't you remember my *ketuvah*?		

You were unwilling to— pay head-tax (Ex. 38:26) now fay fifteen sheqels	He remembers *ketuvah*, also that her family went on carpets to Temple.	—	—
—repair roads for pilgrims now do so for enemy	And all my life I sought meaning of *Song 1:8*	—	—
Thus it says, *Because you did not serve* (Deut. 28:47-8)	Read not…	—	—
	For when Israel do the will of the Omnipresent, no one can rule them, but when they do not, the lowest nation rules them, even the cattle of the lowest nation.	—	—

b. Ket. 66b (III.ii.6)	*ARNa chap. 17* (IV.i.7)
Teno Rabbanan: Story is told that Yoḥanan was riding on ass and *going out of Jerusalem* and his students were walking after him. He saw a girl picking barley-corn from between feet of Arab cattle.	Yoḥanan saw girl in marketplace, picking barley from feet of Arab cattle. Who are you? No answer.
When she saw him, she wrapped self in hair, stood before him, and said, Rabbi, feed me.	Covered self with hair, sat before him, I am daughter of Naqdimon b. Gurion.
He asks, Whose daughter are you?	Yoḥanan: What happened to wealth of father, father in law.
She: Naqdimon b. Gurion.	Girl: Cites proverb.
Yoḥanan: What happened to your father's wealth?	Yoḥanan: Now I understand Song 1:8.
Girl: Cites proverb.	Israel has been surrendered to meanest of peoples, even to cattle-dung.
She: Don't you remember my marriage contract?	Girl: Reminds him about marriage-contract.
Yoḥanan: I remember I signed it.	Yoḥanan: By the Temple service, I signed her marriage-contract and also that her family went on carpets to Temple.
Yoḥanan wept and said, Happy are you O Israel, when you do God's will, no one can rule you, but when you do not, even meanest people rule you, even their cattle.	—

I have cited the Palestinian Talmud and the Tos. Ket. stories merely to indicate how the same Scriptures are used in several different ways. The Toseftan story may be the earlier of the two, for in the Palestinian Talmudic account, we see a proliferation of Scriptures; on the other hand, the daughter in the Tosefta is Naqdimon's, in the Palestinian Talmud, Boethus's. The stories are related, but the latter is not simply an amplified version of the former.

The four accounts in which Yoḥanan appears are certainly interrelated, though the exact relationships are by no means clear. Mekhilta is a play on Deut. 28:47-8 and Song 1:8, while in Sifré Deut., Deut. 28:47-8 does not appear at all. In Mekhilta the girl is unnamed; Yoḥanan has never met her; the pathos of her fall from prosperity is ignored. The meaning of Song 1:8 is elucidated by Deut. 28:47-8. But the girl's plight plays no intrinsic role. And the disciples play an active part. In Sifré Deut., by contrast, the girl is the central figure, asking for food, then identifying herself, reminding Yoḥanan about her *ketuvah;* and he further remembers the luxurious way her family lived. Then comes Song 1:8, now the point of it all. Finally comes the closing homily, "When Israel do..."

Perhaps Sifré Deut. is a development of Mekhilta Baḥodesh, in which the detail about the girl becomes greatly embellished, indeed is made the point of the encounter. Then *You were unwilling* ceases to be an exegesis and becomes an outright homily, independent of a Scripture. But some details of Mekhilta are dropped, first, the conversation with the disciples, second, the location of the trip. When the girl becomes central, the disciples pass out of the picture, serve as a silent audience.

The Babylonian *beraita* clearly depends upon Sifré Deut. Now the location of the trip is once again supplied. The encounter with the girl if further amplified by the question, *What happened to your father's money?* This is inserted before the marriage-contract, so the girl now introduces the topic not in order to identify herself, but as a separate colloquy. Strikingly, all Scriptural exegeses are omitted, but the homily of Sifré Deut. is further expanded by *Happy are you, O Israel.* Otherwise it is identical.

As usual, ARNa is highly literary. The disciples are absent, having no role to play. The marketplace is now the setting. The conversation is dramatic, eloquent. The girl then identifies herself; Yoḥanan asks about her father's money; she replies citing a well-known proverb. Yoḥanan now introduces Song 1:8 and the homily immediately follows, in somewhat abbreviated form. Finally, the details of the marriage-contract and the luxurious way of living of her family are tacked on.

In effect, the version of the Mekhilta stands by itself; Sifré Deut. forms the basis for both the Babylonian *beraita* and ARNa. The components common to all versions are as follows:

1. Starving girl picks barley-corn from dung of Arabian horses/cattle.
2. Yoḥanan sees, asks who she is.
3. He cites Song 1:8 in reference to the girl.

Unique to Mekhilta Baḥodesh is the further exegesis of Deut. 28:47-8; but the homilies appearing in all other accounts in fact are based upon the plainsense of that very Scripture: "If you do well, you will be blessed, but if not, you will be cursed." The additional elements common to Sifré Deut., b. Ket. *beraita*, and ARNa, are as follows:

4. The girl identifies herself as Naqdimon's daughter.
5. Do you not remember you witnessed my marriage-contract?
6. Indeed I do, and what happened to your father's wealth? I remember also how your family went to the Temple on carpets.
7. [Song 1:8 appears in Sifré and ARNa.]
8. When you do God's will, no one can rule you, but when you do not, you are given into the hands of mean people and their cattle.

We may further conjecture that the association of the unnamed girl of Mekhilta with the daughter of Naqdimon in Sifré and afterward derives originally from the fact that an exegesis of Song 1:8 is common to both Yoḥanan and Eleazar b. Ẓadoq, leading to the further assumption that the "you" of "If you do not know" is, in fact, Naqdimon's daughter. Henceforward, the citation of Song 1:8 will remind everyone to whom Yoḥanan was talking, and further details naturally will be supplied from other stories about her. The association of Yoḥanan with her father is drawn quite routinely in the escape stories, but these are very late, certainly much later than the materials before us, and I imagine that the escape-stories have been shaped by *Because you did not serve materials*, rather than vice versa.

IV. Conclusion

No fixed formulae characterize the transmission of materials considered here. The escape stories vary not only in content but also in form. We have seen the persistence of certain primitive components in each of the stories. These generally consist of references to key verses, around which stories are constructed or homilies framed. Such key-scriptures are Is. 10:34 for the escape, with Is. 44:25, Prov. 15:30 and 17:22 as secondary and tertiary scriptural bases in the Babylonian and midrashic versions. Song 1:8 and Deut. 28:47-8 are the chief components of all *Because you did not serve* accounts, though the latter is submerged into a generalized sermon in the later versions.

The escape-stories are all very late, so one might suppose that some kind of primitive components, centered on the designated Scriptures, may have circulated for a very long time before being spelled out in the substantial fabrications before us. On the other hand, Mekhilta and Sifré Deut. are among the earliest documents before us, ca. 250 in final form, it is generally supposed. They make it clear that exegetical traditions quite rapidly were expanded into historical narratives, at least in reference to those exegeses which would easily provoke the imagination of narrators. Few Yoḥanan-exegeses appear outside of a narrative framework, just as in the case of the legal sayings.

We can hardly say that b. Giṭ. and its related versions represent elaborations of ARNa, for on the face of it, they are quite separate and unrelated accounts. Yet the points in common cannot be ignored. In this instance common components have evidently been put together in various ways and set into a narrative framework. The accounts before us probably bear no direct relationship to one another at all. And b. Giṭ.'s honey and reptile and the bloating of Vespasian's feet have certainly produced substantial amendments in Lam. R., another illustration of the tendency of later documents' versions to exhibit development and marks of being later in time than versions appearing in earlier documents.

The b. Ket. 66b and ARNa Ch. 17 versions of the encounter with Naqdimon's daughter probably are developments of Sifré Deut., which is likely to be related to, but separate from, Mekhilta Baḥodesh. Thus stories appearing in documents of approximately the same age do not appear to improve on one another, but do exhibit complex relationships with one another. Stories appearing in later documents as usual seem to be developments of stories appearing in earlier documents. In general, marks signifying a later version normally, though not invariably, include augmentation and other kinds of development. In the historical stories this invariably is the distinguishing trait of the later versions.

CHAPTER ELEVEN

STORIES ABOUT DISCIPLES

Stories about disciples fall into two general categories, those of Avot-ARN built on the form of the five students in the Jerusalem circle, and all others. No relationship exists between Avot-ARN disciple-stories and others; the forms and materials of Avot-ARN rarely occur, directly or by inference, in other compilations.

I. The Five

Avot materials (II.i.18-19) on the five pertain to two matters. Yoḥanan gave nicknames to each; and he listened to their ideas on the good way and on the evil way; and adjudged those of Eleazar b. ʿArakh to be best, because most inclusive. The order is Eliezer, Joshua, Yosi, Simeon, and Eleazar b.ʿArakh; there follows the *three things* each disciple stated, given in the same order. Apart from ARN, no reference is made to these stories elsewhere. ARNa. Ch. 14 serves as a *tosefta* to the Mishnah of Avot (IV.i.5), providing some *gemara* as well, in the story of the death of Yoḥanan's son (IV.i.5h); this follows the Eliezer, Joshua, Yosi, Simeon, Eleazar form. It is otherwise without parallel in any other source.

The form of *the five* appears in a fragmentary way in an exegesis of Prov. 14:34:

b. B.B. 10b (III.ii.20)	*Pesiqta deR. Kahana (VI.iii.1)*
TNY'	—
Yoḥanan said to his disciples, What is the meaning of Prov. 14:34	—
	Prov. 14:34
—	Eliezer, Joshua, and the Rabbis.
R. Eliezer: Righteousness=Israel, II Sam. 7:23; kindness of peoples is only for own aggrandizement, Ezra 7:10.	Liezer: Kindness of peoples is a sin for they take pride in them.
Interjection: But is this not...	—
Joshua: Righteousness=Israel, II Sam.	Joshua: Righteousness=Israel, but

7:23, kindness of peoples is only to prolong their domination, Dan. 4:27.	kindness of peoples is sin, because they take pride when Israel sins and they subjugate them.
Gamaliel: Righteousness=Israel, II Sam. 7:23; kindness of peoples is sin, since they do it only for pride, Prov. 21:24, Zeph. 1:15.	Gamaliel: Righteousness=Israel; kindness of peoples is sin, for so said Daniel to Nebuchadnezzar, Dan. 4:24.
Gamaliel: We still need the Modite.	—
Eleazar the Modite: Righteousness= Israel, II Sam. 7.23; kindness of peoples is sin, since they only do it to reproach us, Jer. 40:3.	—
Neḥuniah b. HaQaneh: Justice and kindness=Israel, but the nations have only sin.	—
Yoḥanan: I prefer Neḥuniah's words to your words.	—
This shows he had an earlier opinion.	—
DTNY': Yoḥanan said to them, just as the sin-offering atones for Israel, so righteousness atones for nations.	—
—	Lazar b. 'Arakh: Righteousness = Israel, but nations of world have only sin.
—	Yoḥanan: I prefer Lazar's words to yours for he gives righteousness and kindness to Israel but sin to the nations.
—	Abin b. Judah: Righteousness = Israel, but Israel receives the kindness of the nations of the world when they sin, for so said Rabshakeh to Hezekiah, II Kings 18:25; Jer. 40.3.
—	Neḥuniah b. HaQaneh: Righteousness = Israel, but righteousness of nations is a sin for Israel, II Kings 3:4.

The *beraita* has mixed up two separate forms, the *five* and the Gamaliel form, *We still need the Modite*, of b. Ber. 40a, b. Ḥul. 92b, etc. The confusion has forced Yoḥanan to praise Neḥuniah's words; this illustrates the persistence of the *I prefer* subscription. The later document has corrected the *beraita* by putting Neḥuniah's words into Eleazar's mouth, so Yoḥanan's normal "praise" follows the usual pattern. But the inclusion of Gamaliel has been preserved. The Scriptural proof-texts of Eliezer and Joshua are omitted, and their teachings are abbreviated and presented in précis. Gamaliel's interpretation in the Pesiqta is in fact a continuation of Joshua's proof-text in the *beraita*. We see, therefore, that the *five* form has guided the Pesiqta's correction and improvement of the Babylonian *beraita's* confused materials, even though in the process of correction, the teaching of Joshua has been divided and shared with Gamaliel. That the Pesiqta version is later than that in the *beraita*, and indeed rests upon the version in the earlier document, is clear. Even though the Pesiqta version is briefer, it stands as a kind of summary. Gamaliel's teaching can only be understood with reference to Joshua's in the *beraita;* the substitution of Eleazar for Neḥuniah and of praise for the former in place of the latter shows the editor's awareness of the *beraita's* departure from the "usual" *five-form*.

II. Eliezer's Origins

The story of Eliezer's origins appears in three versions of Talmudic times, and in others of post-Talmudic origin:

ARNa Ch. 6 (IV.i.3)	*ARNb Ch. 13*	*Gen. R. 41:1* (VI.i.3)
Eliezer was 22, but unlearned. Resolved to study with Yoḥanan. Father: Must plough before eating. Rose early, ploughed, and left for Jerusalem.	*They said concerning* Eliezer that when he sought to study Torah, he was ploughing in difficult ground. He wept. Father gave him easier land, he still wept. He told father he wanted to study Torah. Father: You are 28, too late; have children and send them. He was sad for three weeks. Elijah appeared to him, "Go up to Ben Zakkai in Jerusalem." He went, kept weeping, finally said he wanted to study Torah.	They tell of Eliezer that he was ploughing in difficult ground, his brothers on the plain. His ox broke down. It was for the best. He fled to Yoḥanan.
—	Yoḥanan taught him Prayer, *Shema'*, and Grace. Taught him Mishnah, two a day, reviewed on Sabbath.	—

Some say he ate at father in law's.	Did not eat for eight days, had bad breath, others kept away.	He was eating clods of dirt until his breath stank.
Some say he did not eat from before until after Sabbath.	Eliezer wept.	They told Yoḥanan that his breath stinks.
Put a stone in his mouth, some say, cattle-dung.	Yoḥanan: Whose son are you? Eliezer: Hyrcanus's. Yoḥanan: Eat with me. Eliezer: I already ate at my hostel. Yoḥanan found out he had not eaten for eight days.	He told them, Just as bad breath arose from your mouth for the sake of Torah, so the odor of your learning will go from one corner of the world to the other.
Stayed at hostel.		
Went to Yoḥanan. Breath smelled bad.		
Yoḥanan: Did you eat? No reply.	Joshua, Simeon, Yosi told Yoḥanan that Eliezer had not eaten for eight days.	—
Yoḥanan asked hostellers, Did he eat? They: We thought he ate with you. Yoḥanan: Between us he would have perished.	Yoḥanan tore clothes, saying, Between us he would have perished.	—
Yoḥanan: Just as bad breath arose from your mouth, so will your reputation travel.	Just as bad breath arose from your mouth, so will your reputation travel, Ex. 18:5.	—
Hyrcanus heard he was studying with Yoḥanan, went to disinherit him.	Hyrcanus's sons told him to disinherit Eliezer.	After a time, Hyrcanus came to disinherit him. Found him expounding with the great men of the city before him, Ben Ẓiẓit HaKeset, Naqdimon, and Ben Kalba Shavu'a.
When Hyrcanus came, Yoḥanan made sure he would have to push to the fore.	He went to Jerusalem, found great men of city sitting before Yoḥanan, and these are they, Ben Ẓiẓit *Hakesef*, Naqdimon, and Ben Kalba Shavu'a.	
He reached Ben Ẓiẓit HaKeset, Naqdimon, and Ben Kalba Shavu'a.	Simeon, Joshua, told Yoḥanan that Eliezer's father was coming.	—
Yoḥanan and disciples forced Eliezer to discourse.	He said, Make room for him, and they gave him an honored place.	—
Yoḥanan: Eliezer, you have taught me the truth.	Yoḥanan told Eliezer to say something, and he said I can only say what you have taught me... They forced Eliezer.	—
Hyrcanus: I came only to disinherit him, now he has all, his brothers nothing.		

He expounded things greater than Moses had heard at Sinai, his face shone like the sun, beams of light came out of his face, and no one knew whether it was day or night.

Joshua and Simeon told Yoḥanan, Come and see Eliezer expounding things greater than Moses had heard at Sinai, etc.

Yoḥanan came and kissed him and said, Happy are you Abraham, Isaac, and Jacob, that this one came forth from your loins.

Hyrcanus said, Whom are you referring to?

To your son, Eliezer.

He: Happy am I...

Eliezer sat and expounded, his father stood. Eliezer said his father should sit down. He sat next to Eliezer.

Hyrcanus: I came only to disinherit you, now you get all my property, your brothers nothing.

Eliezer: Silver and gold belong to God, Haggai 2:8. He would give me real estate, Ps. 24:1. I sought only merit in Torah, Ps. 119:128.

His father said, I came to disinherit you, but now my property is given to you as a gift. Eliezer: will only take an equal share with my brothers.

Basically, six components are common to the several narrators:

1. Eliezer was unlearned;
2. He left the plough to come to study;
3. Between us he would have perished;
4. Just as your breath stank from your mouth, so will your Torah go forth and give you a good name;

5. Hyrcanus came to disinherit, but stayed to give Eliezer all his property;
6. But Eliezer refused it.

That these components have been expanded by *all* versions is clear in ARNa Ch. 6, the earliest of the group, for there *some say* recurs, a probable sign that materials from several, unrelated traditions are now moulded into a single account. ARNb is greatly expanded, needless to say.

By contrast, Gen. R. is abbreviated, also not very smooth. Well-known details are alluded to, but then passed by. The framework of Eliezer's origins is there used as the setting for his sermon on Gen. 14:1/Ps. 37:14. In Gen. R. we thus see that the antecedent story is abbreviated and transformed into a context for an exegesis, which is not given, merely alluded to by the citation of the appropriate Scriptures.

ARNb tells the story in great detail, improving on it through invented dialogue, additional information about what the other disciples were saying and doing, elaboration of the glories of Eliezer's public discourse, and improvement on the disinheritance scene.

The medieval compilation, *Pirqé deR. Eliezer*, retells the story, closely following the account of ARNb:

> Hyrcanus had many ploughmen working on flat land, Eliezer ploughed a stony plot.
>
> Eliezer wept, father asked why? He gave Eliezer easier ground, but the son wept again.
>
> He said he wanted to study Torah.
>
> Hyrcanus: You are 28, too old, but get married and send your children.
>
> Elijah came and asked why Eliezer kept weeping, told him to go study with *Rabban Yoḥanan* ben Zakkai.
>
> Eliezer kept weeping, Yoḥanan asked why, Eliezer said he wanted to study Torah, did not tell his name.
>
> Yoḥanan taught *Shema'*, Prayer, Grace, then Mishnah.
>
> Eliezer did not eat, breath stank. Yoḥanan told him to go away. Eliezer

> wept, etc. Finally Yoḥanan said, Who are your hosts? Joshua and Yosi. They said he had not eaten.

Here, PRE omits reference to the rest of the colloquy as well as to Yoḥanan's blessing. Then:

> Sons say, Go and disinherit Eliezer. He went and found the great men of Jerusalem there, Ben Ẓiẓit, etc.
>
> [Here PRE cites the interjections on the strange names of the great men, appearing in ARNb. I have not cited them.]
>
> Yoḥanan told Eliezer to preach, Eliezer said he can only say what Yoḥanan has already taught him.
>
> Yoḥanan agreed to leave if his presence is intimidating. Eliezer expounded, his face shone, no one knew whether it was day or night. They told Yoḥanan what was happening. He: "Happy are you, Abraham...."
>
> Hyrcanus's father asked, Whom is Yoḥanan referring to? To Eliezer your son. Hyrcanus: Happy am I...
>
> Eliezer insisted his father sit down.
>
> Hyrcanus: I came to disinherit, now I give you all. Eliezer: God could give me real estate, Ps. 24:1, and he could give me silver and gold. Hag. 2:8, but I only want merit in Torah, Ps. 119:128.

It is clear that PRE follows the model of ARNb, improving upon it only in matters of detail. No new materials are invented, but existing ones are embellished. The further version in Midrash Tanḥuma is of no interest here; it is a greatly expanded version of the ARNb-PRE account.

Once again we note that accounts in later materials depend upon accounts in earlier ones (ARNa/Gen. R.); and the latest collections of all contain greatly expanded versions of materials appearing in earlier ones.

It is noteworthy that the blessing of Eleazar b. ʿArakh for his *Merkavah* sermon has been borrowed by the later versions of Eliezer's beginnings. I think it likely that the *Merkavah* sermon is very early; hence inclusion of "Happy are you..." for other purposes must be a secondary development.

III. The Merkavah-Sermon and Related Materials

The *Merkavah*-sermon of Eleazar b. ʿArakh is quoted in four versions:

Mekhilta de R. Simeon (I.ii.2)	*Tos. Ḥag. 2:1-2* (II.iii.3)	*y. Ḥag. 2:1* (III.i.4)	*b. Ḥag. 14b* (III.ii.13)
And the story is told that Yoḥanan was riding on an ass and going out of Jerusalem	*(see Mekhilta de R. Simeon)* —	*(see Mekhilta de R. Simeon)* going on the way riding on an ass	*Teno Rabban.* The story is told that Yoḥanan was riding an ass and going on the way, and Eleazar was driving the ass
Eleazar b. Arakh his disciple was going behind him.	*Driving the ass*	going	
Eleazar: Teach me a chapter in the Merkavah	*(see Mekhilta de R. Simeon)*	*(see Mekhilta de R. Simeon)*	*(see Mekhilta de R. Simeon)*
Yoḥanan: Have I not *taught* you. Not of the Merkavah... understand of his own knowledge.	*told*	*(see Mekhilta de R. Simeon)*	*taught*
If not, give me permission to speak before you.	*(see Mekhilta de R. Simeon)*	*(see Mekhilta de R. Simeon)*	before you *something you taught me.*
—	Yoḥanan descended from the ass, covered self with cloak; both sat on a stone under an olive tree.	Yoḥanan descended saying, It is not lawful that I should hear the glory of my creator and be riding on an ass. They went and sat under the tree.	Forthwith Yoḥanan descended from the ass, covered himself, and sat on the *stone* under the olive-tree.
			He said to him, Rabbi, why did you descend.
—	—	—	He said to him, Is it possible that you should expound the Chariot, and the *Shekhinah* be with us, and the ministering angels accompany us, and I should ride an ass?

Eleazar expounded until flames licked around about.	He lectured before him.	Forthwith all the trees broke out in song and said Ps. 96.	Eleazar opened on the Chariot and expounded, and fire went down from heaven and encompassed all the trees round about. What song did the trees sing? Ps. 145.
—	—	—	An angel answered from the fire and said, These, these are the works of the chariot.
When Yoḥanan saw the flames, he got off the ass, kissed him, and said. Eleazar, Happy she that bore you. Happy Abraham our father that such has come forth from his loins.	He stood and kissed him and said, Blessed is the Lord God of Israel who gave a son to Abraham our father who knows how to understand and expound the glory of his father in heaven. Some expound well but do not fulfill well, and vice versa, but Eleazar does both well.	When Eleazar finished the Works of the Chariot, Yoḥanan stood and kissed him on his head and said, Blessed is the Lord, God of Abraham. Jacob who gave to Abraham a son wise and knowing how to expound the glory of our father in heaven. Some preach well... Eleazar does both well.	Yoḥanan stood up and kissed him on his head and said, Blessed is the Lord, God *of Israel*, who gave a son to Abraham our father who knows how to understand and *to investigate*, and to expound the Chariot. Some preach well, etc. Happy are you Abraham our father that Eleazar has come forth from your loins.
—	Happy are you, Abraham our father that Eleazar b. ʻArakh has come forth from your loins, who knows how to understand and expound the glory of his father in heaven.	Happy are you, Abraham our father, that Eleazar has come forth from your loins.	—
He would say, If all sages were on one side of the scale and Eleazar on the other, he would outweigh them all. —	R. Yosi b. Judah: Joshua lectured before Yoḥanan, Aqiva before Joshua, Hananiah b. Ḥakhinai before ʻAqiva. —	When Joseph the priest and Simeon b. Natanel heard, they too opened a discourse on the Chariot. They said, it was, the first day of summer, and the earth trembled, and a rainbow appeared and an echo came and said to them, Behold the pla-	And when these things were told to Joshua, he and Yosi the priest were walking on the way. They said Let us also expound the Chariot. Joshua opened and expounded. That day was the first day of summer, but the heavens clouded over and a kind of a rainbow appeared, and the an-

ce is ready for you and your disciples are slated for the third class.

gels gathered and came to hear like men running to a wedding.

Joshua and Yosi the priest went and told these things to Yoḥanan, who said, Happy are you, and happy are those who bore you. Happy are my eyes who have seen such.

And also you and I in my dream were reclining on Mount Sinai and an echo came forth to us from heaven, "Come up hither, come up hither. Your disciples are slated for the third class.

Is this so? And is it not taught? (TNY'):

Joshua lectured things before Yoḥanan, 'Aqiva before Joshua, Ḥanania b. Ḥakhinai before 'Aqiva.

And Eleazar is not mentioned.

It would be difficult to invent a better example of the development of a tradition from simplicity to complexity, from being relatively unadorned to being full articulated, and from earlier to later versions. In the earliest document the story is shortest, simplest. The Tosefta represents an obvious expansion. The Palestinian Talmudic account is still further enriched with details and entirely new components. And the Babylonian version, last of all in the age of the document in which it appears, clearly is most fully, carefully worked out. The Mekhilta's components are

1. Yoḥanan riding an ass
2. Eleazar with him
3. Teach me—It is illegal.
4. Then let me speak.
5. Eleazar expounded and flames licked round about.
6. Then Yoḥanan blessed him, Your mother and Abraham are happy.
7. Scale

The concluding element (No. 7) is, as I said, a separate and unrelated saying. It plays no integral part whatever in the *Merkavah* tradition. But it is therefore all the more important, for presumably this version, in which no other disciples have any role whatsoever, is how the disciples of Eleazar would have transmitted the story. In fact from the viewpoint of editing, it *is* integral, for after Eleazar's sermon, Yoḥanan's praise for his exceptional student is in order. Hence the fact that it appears in no later version should not be regarded as inconsequential.

The Tosefta's version is close to the foregoing, but it adds that Yoḥanan ceremoniously descended from the ass before the lecture began. Only then did Eleazar say his sermon. The detail about the flames, on the other hand, is absent. But the blessing is greatly expanded. The praise is now extended to Eleazar's ability to achieve a fully realized mystic experience; he does not merely describe the *Merkavah*, but presumably is able to go down in it. Then a second, and separate, blessing is repeated from Mekhilta, *Happy are you...* This clearly indicates dependence, for the first blessing would be sufficient in an independent account. But the second blessing is augmented with reference to the Mekhilta's: Abraham should be happy because you expound well and fulfill well. Thus the narrator tied in the duplicated blessing of the original version. The most important omission is the praise of Eleazar. This is replaced by the story that Joshua did the same before Yoḥanan, ʿAqiva afterward, and so forth. The later version thus emphasized that despite the excellence of Eleazar, which no one denied, the *true* line of transmission extended through Joshua, not through Eleazar. We may assume the first and simplest version derives from Eleazar's school, and the second as been altered, then handed on in the Joshua-ʿAqiva line.

The Palestinian version begins as do the early ones. But it adds a careful explanation of *why* Yoḥanan got off the ass. This explanation is itself rather fulsome. Only afterward do the master and disciple sit down—under a tree, the *olive* is lost. Then fire comes down, but this detail, from the Mekhilta version, is greatly embellished. Angels dance as at a wedding. They even praise Eleazar's sermon, before Yoḥanan has a chance to say anything. He plays no part in the proliferating details. Then the trees sing a Psalm. Only after the expanded element has been completed do we return to the matter of Yoḥanan. He then kisses Eleazar and gives the double blessing. *Blessed is the Lord... Happy are you, Abraham*. Then Joseph/Yosi the priest and Simeon are introduced, with further supernatural events accompanying their never-recorded sermon. The echo invites them to the third level of the heavens.

The Babylonian version is augmented in almost every detail. Eleazar is not merely walking, but driving the ass. He wants to teach something *he has already heard.* Not only does Yoḥanan descend, but Eleazar asks *why* he did so. This is clearly a point at which the Babylonian *beraita* has expanded on a mute detail in the immediately preceding account. Yoḥanan then develops his earlier saying. It is not merely the glory of the creator, but rather both the *Shekhinah* and the Ministering angels are present. Eleazar speaks, and fire (now routinely) pours from heaven. The trees sing a Psalm, this time Ps. 145. An angel repeats the message of the Palestinian version. The order of the trees' psalm and the angels message is therefore reversed. Then comes the kiss—now on his head—and the blessing is expanded to include *to investigate* after to understand and to expound. The *Some preach well* formula comes verbatim, then the second blessing. The further report excludes Simeon b. Natanel, who probably left no disciples, certainly no important school, to insure his position in the traditions. Rather Joshua is now the link. The story is drawn from the earlier version. The rainbow is not enough; now the angels come to a wedding—a detail presumably borrowed from the Palestinian dance of the ministering angels. Then Yosi told Yoḥanan, who expressed approval. The heavenly echo of the Palestinian version becomes the whole dream about the circle of Yoḥanan on Mount Sinai, with a direct invitation to heaven, both elements based upon and developments of *Behold the place is ready for you.*

As I said, I can think of no better demonstration of the fact that versions of a single story appearing in documents of successive age normally proceed from the simpler to the more complex formulation as they pass from an earlier document to a later one. Since they clearly depend on one another, there can be no question as to which comes first, which later, in time of formulation.

We have, further, a tradition on Is. 14:14-15 appearing as follows:

b. Ḥag. 13a (II.ii.12)	*b. Pes. 94a-b*
TNY'	—
Yoḥanan said, What answer did the echo give to that evil man when he said Is. 14:14.	(*see b. Ḥag. 13a*)

The echo said, Evil one son of Nimrod.	*(see b. Ḥag. 13a)*
Man lives seventy years, Ps. 90:	*(see b. Ḥag. 13a)*
Yet from earth to heaven is a journey of five hundred years, etc.	[*Yet* omitted.]
Yet you said Is. 14:14?	Above them the holy ḥayyot, etc.
No, but Is. 14:15 applies.	*(see b. Ḥag. 13a)*

The *beraita* is far longer than the version in b. Pes. The whole passage of measurements from the reference to the *ḥayyot* to the king on *his throne* is omitted. From the thicknesses of the firmaments, the b. Pes. version proceeds to the citation of Is. 14:15. I imagine that the *beraita* was shaped as a complete set of measurements, and merely abbreviated for purposes of citation in b. Pes., where the *beraita*-introduction is omitted.

IV. CONCLUSION

We have seen that the Avot-ARN materials stand entirely apart from other disciple-stories. The *five*-form is attempted in a *beraita* as well, but is garbled and incomplete. Only two of the Jerusalem circle actually appear. Eliezer's origins show the usual development from the version appearing in the earliest source to the ones appearing later on. Basic components recur, but generally in much augmented form. In the medieval pseudepigraphic materials, we see the recurrence of ARNb. The most striking example of change from earlier to later documents, demonstrating beyond doubt that earlier documents do contain earlier versions, appeared in the *Merkavah*-materials, which showed in striking sequence how the simple becomes complicated, the unadorned embellished. The interstices of an earlier account are filled in later on. Earlier components are repeated, but new elements are added as well.

The *beraita* and the allusion thereto in b. Ḥag. 13a and b. Pes. 94a-b are sufficiently close to one another as to be regarded as a single item, undeveloped from one place to the other, but simply cited in the latter in abbreviated form.

CHAPTER TWELVE

SCRIPTURAL EXEGESIS

i. Disputes with Gentiles

The stories about Yoḥanan's disputes with gentiles form a single *type* of material, but exhibit no common form. Only one appears in an early document, Agrippas the hegemon asked Yoḥanan how many Torahs were given to you from heaven, Midrash Tannaim 33:10, ed. Hoffmann, p. 215 (I.iv.5), but in Sifré Deut. #351 it is *agenitos* and Gamaliel.

The enumeration of the Levites (Num. 4:46) is the common theme in the following:

b. Bekh. 5a (V.ii.20)	*y. Sanh. 1:4* (V.i.15)	*Num. R. 4:9* (VI.vii.1)
Quntroqis asked Yoḥanan	Antoninus Hegemon asked Yoḥanan	Agentus the Hegemon asked Yoḥanan
When Levites are enumerated in detail, you find 22,300. But when counted as a group, 22,000. Where did the 300 go?	In general they lack, in particular they are too many.	Moses your teacher was either a thief or poor at arithmetic. Why?
Three hundred were first-born and a first-born cannot redeem a first-born (Num. 3:44).	The three hundred extras were the first born of the priesthood, and holy can not redeem holy.	Because there were 22,273, and God commanded: Levites redeem the first-born. Now there were still 300 Levites left over when counted in detail, for we find 273 gave five *sheqels* each.
—	—	Further, when he sums up the number, he deducts the 300 of the original number. So he left them out so that those 273 first-born might each give 5 *sheqels* to his brother Aaron.
—	—	or bad at arithmetic

—	—	Yoḥanan: He was no thief and was good at arithmetic. But you read but cannot expound Scripture.
—	—	Moses thought, The 22,000 Levites will redeem the 22,000 first-born, and the 300 Levites will remain, and of the first-born another 273. First-born cannot redeem a first born, so when he summed up the number he omitted them because they were first-born.

Num. R. has obviously provided a careful spelling out of the reasons for the dispute, in the form of supplied dialogue. The Palestinian version is too brief to have been comprehended without additional explanation. Whether this depended on the Babylonian story or not I cannot say. Perhaps some sort of brief reference was meant to call to mind a well-known, more complete account. But in its current form, without Scriptural references, even without an antecedent for *they lack* and *they are too many*, the Palestinian version is garbled. The assertion that Moses was either poor at arithmetic or a thief, of Num. R. 4:9 is borrowed from y. Sanh. 1:4 (V.i.16), which concerned *not* the enumeration of the Levites, but the collection of the *sheqel* for use in the sanctuary and the final accounting for the use of the money. The passage continues, after some intervening material, in both b. Bekh. 5a and y. Sanh. 1:4, as follows:

b. Bekh. 5a	*y. Sanh. 1:4*
And again he was asked	Antoninus the Hegemon asked Yoḥanan
With reference to collection, you count 201 *kikkar* and 11 *maneh*.	Moses was either a thief or not good at arithmetic, Ex. 38:27. If a centaurius...he stole one sixth/one half.
But when Moses gave the money, you find only 100 *kikkar*. Was Moses a thief or bad at arithmetic? He gave half, took half, and did not return a complete half.	—
Yoḥanan: Moses was reliable and good at arithmetic. The sacred *maneh* was double the common one.	Yoḥanan: Moses was a faithful treasurer and good at arithmetic [See V.i.16 for details, none of which recurs in b. Bekh. 5a]

The *again he was asked* becomes a separate story in y. Sanh., and while the point of both stories is roughly the same, namely that Temple measurements were different from ordinary ones, there is no close relationship between the two accounts. Clearly some sort of common tradition underlies both versions; it had to do with the gentile's ignorance of Scripture and of the Temple's measurements, on the one hand, and of the redemption rules, on the other. But beyond that, I see little in common in the literary accounts produced in the schools of the two countries.

A story appearing only in late collections is told about "a gentile" or a star-worshipper, who asked Yoḥanan:

Num. R. 19:8 (VI. ii. 12)	*Pes. deR. Kahana p. 74* (VI. ii. 13)	*Pesiqta Rabbati # 14*
These rites appear to be witchcraft. You burn heifer... you are unclean.	*(see Num. R. 19:8)*	*(see Num. R. 19:8)*
Yoḥanan: Demon of madness.	*(see Num. R. 19:8)*	*(see Num. R. 19:8)*
This is spirit of uncleanness, Zech. 13:2.	*(see Num. R. 19:8)*	*(see Num. R. 19:8)*
Disciples: What do you tell *us?*	*(see Num. R. 19:8)*	*(see Num. R. 19:8)*
Yoḥanan: Dead does not defile, but I have issued a decree, etc., Num. 19:1.	*(see Num. R. 19:8)*	*(see Num. R. 19:8)*
		[No reference to Num. 19:1]

I have found no substantial differences among the several versions appearing in late documents. I doubt that any considerable developments took place. I cannot suggest which version is earliest, but clearly as soon as a version had made its way, it repeatedly was copied quite faithfully, with no more than minor alterations.

The brief reference in Midrash Tannaim 33:10 certainly must be regarded as dubious, since Sifré Deut. #351 has the same material in Gamaliel's name. If the reference to Yoḥanan in I.iv.5 is not accurate, then the earliest clear dispute with a gentile occurs in Amoraic materials and is much augmented afterward. The name of the gentile prince or *hegemon* is given in various forms, some quite unrelated to the others, or merely as "a gentile/star-worshipper", as follows:

Agrippas Hegemon	*Qunṭroqis the Prince*	*Agenṭos the Hegemon*
Midrash Tannaim 33:10 (I.iv.5) [= Sifré Deut. #351, Gamaliel, Agenṭos]	b. Bekh. 5a	(Sifré Deut. #351) Num. R. 4:9

Antoninus the Hegemon	*A Gentile*
y. Sanh. 1:2 y. Sanh. 1:4	Deut. R. 7:7 Num. R. 19:8 Pesiqta deR. Kahana, ed. Mandelbaum, p. 74 Pesiqta Rabbati #14 Tanḥuma Huqat #26 (star-worshipper)

Obviously, no single, clear-cut, and well-shaped tradition on the name of the *hegemon* actually existed. This would suggest that the later accounts rested on no well-known earlier ones, but were separately invented without reference to one another. Alternatively, the story existed, but the name was supplied—or garbled—later on. This would account for coincidences of theme. I suppose that the dispute-with-gentiles stories do not begin to take shape much before the later Amoraic period and did not circulate widely even then.

II. Exegesis in "Standard" Form

"Standard" form refers simply to an exegesis attached to a Scripture without the adornment of a historical setting or conversation, or to an exegesis not described as being of a particular type (e.g. *kemin ḥomer*). Yoḥanan's sayings on Gen. 1:15 in Pesiqta deR. Kahana, ed. Mandelbaum p. 126 and Pesiqta Rabbati #17 exhibit no variation whatever. Gen. R. 17:19 and 19:7 contain comments of Yoḥanan on Gen. 2:19 and 3:7; these have no parallels in earlier or later documents. R. Judan's sayings in Yoḥanan's name appear in Gen. R. 19:7 and 44:18, the latter on Gen. 15:18, also without parallel elsewhere.

A striking exegesis appears in Midrash Tannaim to Deut. 12:1 (I.iv.1) Hoffman, p. 58, *These are the statutes...which you will be careful to do in the land which the Lord...has given you to possess all the days that you live upon the earth:* From here, Yoḥanan would say, "If you have made your Torah great." The exegesis is dropped in the famous saying in Avot. 2:1 and in ARNa ch. 14, "*He* would say, 'If you have made your Torah much, do not take pride, for to this end were you created, for mortals were created only on condition that they busy themselves in Torah.' " In ARNb ch. 31, Deut. 30:20 is then cited, *For it is your life* etc. Neither version refers to Deut. 12:1.

Midrash Tannaim to Deut. 12:2, *You shall surely destroy all the places where the nations whom you shall dispossess served their gods* (I.iv.2) is accompanied by a similar form, *From here*, Yoḥanan would say, Do not make haste to destroy the altars of gentiles that you will not rebuild them with your own hands, not of mortar so you do not have to make them of stone, of stone, wood..." This likewise recurs in ARNb Ch. 31, ed. Schechter p. 33b. The latter passage is somewhat briefer: "Do not destroy their altars that you do not have to rebuild them with your own hands. Do not destroy of mortar, that they not say to you, Come and make them of stone." The omissions of *do not make haste* and *stone/wood* are not important. What is important is that the exegetical connection is once again omitted. The reasons for these differences must be sought in interrelationships and literary history of ARN and Midrash Tannaim; I do not think they tell much, if anything, about the history of Yoḥanan-traditions.

Yoḥanan's saying on Malachi 3:5, in b. Hag. 5a (V.ii.11) recurs in expanded form in Tanḥuma Shofeṭim #7.

Yoḥanan's parable, pertinent to Qoh. 9:8, cited in b. Shab. 153a, makes no reference to his exegesis of the same Scripture in Qoh. R. 9:8:1. A somewhat similar parable is quoted in the latter document in the name of Judah the Prince. On the relationships of these materials, see my *Life*, second ed., p. 239.

III. Analogical Exegeses (Kemin Ḥomer)

The *ḥomer* exegeses occur both with that designation and without. The list in Tos. B.Q. 7:2-5 counts five in all, but as we shall note, there are additional exegeses in the *ḥomer*-style, both so designated and otherwise. We shall first compare the versions of the five in Tos. B.Q. 7:3-7:

Tos. B.Q. 7:3: Why was Israel exiled to Babylonia?
— no parallels.
Tos. B.Q. 7:4: First tablets, second tablets
— no parallels

Tos. B.Q. 7:5 (II.iii.8)	*Sifra VaYiqra* (I.ii.3)	*y. Hor. 3:2* (III.i.6)	*b. Hor. 10b* (III.ii.26)
—	—	—	*Teno Rabbanan*

Lev. 4:22	*(see Tos. B.Q. 7:5)*	*(see Tos. B.Q. 7:5)*	*(see Tos. B.Q. 7:5)*
Happy is the generation whose prince brings a sin-offering for his unwitting sin.	*(see Tos. B.Q. 7:5)*	*(see Tos. B.Q. 7:5)*	*(see Tos. B.Q. 7:5)*
—	—	—	If the prince brings, do you have to ask about an ordinary person?
—	—	—	If for an unwitting sin, do you have to ask an intentional sin?

What is striking, first of all, is that no version of the saying on Lev. 4:22 ever designates the exegesis as analogical, except for the superscription of Tos. B.Q. The Babylonian *beraita* expounds Yoḥanan's meaning, extending his message. It obviously is a later elaboration, and once again illustrates the tendency of the Babylonian *beraitot* to augment and improve upon earlier materials.

Tos. B.Q. 7:5-6 (II.iii.8)	*Mekhilta Neziqin* (I.i.3)	*y. Qid. 1:2* (III.i.5)	*b. Qid. 22b* (III.ii.18)
And it says Ex. 21:6	Yoḥanan interprets it *kemin ḥomer*.	His disciples asked Yoḥanan	Yoḥanan *would* interpret this Scripture *kemin ḥomer*.
Why ear pierced more than all other limbs?		Why is this slave to be pierced in his ear more than all limbs?	Why is the ear differentiated from all the limbs of the body?
Since it heard from Mt. Sinai Lev. 25:55 Yet it broke from itself the yoke of heaven and accepted the rule of mortals	The ear heard Ex. 20:13. Yet went and stole.	He said to them, The ear heard Ex. 20:2 Yet broke the yoke of the kingdom of heaven and accepted the yoke of mortals	The Holy One, blessed be he said, The ear which heard my voice on Mt. Sinai when I said Lev. 25:55 and not slaves to slaves.
—	—	The ear heard Lev. 25:55 yet went and acquired for itself another master.	Yet it went and acquired for itself a master.

Therefore Scripture says, Let the ear come and be pierced, for it did not keep what it heard.	Therefore it alone of all limbs will be pierced.	Therefore let the ear come and be pierced.	Let it be pierced.
	—	Because it did not keep what it heard.	—
Another matter: It did not wish to be subjugated to its creator, let it come and be subjugated to his daughters.	—	—	—

The version of Pesiqta Rabbati #21 is closest to y. Qid. We see that the simplest version is the Mekhilta, in which Ex. 20:13 is cited. The assumption is that by stealing and being unable to pay recompense, the man was forced to sell himself into slavery. This version stands apart. Even though it is briefer than Tos. B.Q., we cannot suppose that the latter was built upon it, for the whole exegetical framework in Tos. B.Q. is different.

The comparisons are to be made, rather, between Tos. B.Q. and the two Talmudic versions. We note that the Palestinian version inserts Ex. 20:2 before Lev. 25:55, and omits the "other matter," which seems adequately spelled out in reference to Lev. 25:55 and to require no further repetition. The version in b. Qid. is closer to Tos. B.Q. and I assume it is copied from it, with the inclusion of the *kemin ḥomer* designation. Lev. 25:55 is further expounded, an improvement on *therefore Scripture says*. In place of *Scripture*, the verse is introduced by reference to *God*, a *voice*, *Mt. Sinai*, and so forth; that is, it is made more vivid. The interrelationship between Tos. B.Q. and b. Qid. thus is close, but the differences all point toward the latter's being a later development of the former. The account in y. Qid. does not depend upon the Babylonian one, and is a secondary development of the Tos. B.Q. one, also considerably improved.

Tos. B.Q. 7:6 (II.iii.8)	*Mekhilta deR. Ishmael* (I.i.2)
And it says Deut. 27:5 Why was iron prohibited more than all metals? Because the sword may be made from it.	This is what Yoḥanan says: *(see Tos. B.Q. 7:6)*
The sword is a sign of punishment and the altar of atonement.	*(see Tos. B.Q. 7:6)*

Remove something which is a sign of punishment from something which is a sign of atonement.	*(see Tos. B.Q. 7:6)*	
And it is a *qal veḥomer*:	*(see Tos. B.Q. 7:6)*	
Stones which do not see, hear, speak—	*(see Tos. B.Q. 7:6)*	
Because they bring atonement between Israel and their father in heaven.	*(see Tos. B.Q. 7:6)*	
Scripture says Deut. 27:5.	*(see Tos. B.Q. 7:6)*	
Sons of Torah who are atonement for the world	*(see Tos. B.Q. 7:6)*	
How much the more so that any of all the demons should not touch them	*(see Tos. B.Q. 7:6)*	

Tos. B.Q. 7:7 (II.iii.8)	*Mekhilta Baḥodesh* (I.i.2)	*Sifra Qedoshim* (I.ii.5)
Behold it says Deut. 27:6	Yoḥanan says, Behold It says Deut. 27:6	*(see Mekhilta Baḥodesh)*
Stones which bring peace between Israel and their father in heaven, the Omnipresent says, should be perfect before me	Stones which bring peace.	*(see Mekhilta Baḥodesh)*
	It is a *qal veḥomer:*	*(see Mekhilta Baḥodesh)*
Sons of Torah, who perfect the world	Stones do not see, hear, speak.	*(see Mekhilta Baḥodesh)*
How much the more so should they be perfect before the Omnipresent.	Because they bring peace between Israel and their father in heaven, the Holy One said Deut. 27:5.	*(see Mekhilta Baḥodesh) Scripture*
—	How much the more so the *one who brings peace* between man and man, husband and wife, nation and nation, family and family, government and government	*(see Mekhilta Baḥodesh)* [Man/man *omitted*] *family*/family, city/city, state/state, nation/nation.
—	be protected so no harm should come to him.	How much the more so should punishment not overtake him.

We see that the *stones which bring peace* and the prohibition of iron appear both together and also separately in Tos. B.Q. 7:6-7. The first version contains the prohibition of iron, and adds to it the *stones*, the second treats *stones* alone. The *qal-veḥomer* appears only in connection with *stones*. The Aqiban version seems copied directly from the Tosefta's, or vice versa. The Ishmaelean version is clearly longer and more elaborate than the Tosefta's. Differences between it and the Sifra's account are striking, and it is not difficult to assign priority. I have already pointed out (I.i.2) that the Aqiban revisions of the Ishmaelean exegesis were intended to change condemnation of war and swords and praise of peacemakers into praise of study of Torah and disciples of Torah. These revisions clearly reflect the *tendenz* of the Aqiban school.

Tos. B.Q. 7:1 (II.iii.8)	*Mekhilta Neziqin* (I.i.5)	*b. B.Q. 79b* (III.ii.19)
His disciples asked Yoḥanan:	—	His disciples asked...
What did the Torah see to be more stringent with the thief than the robber?	(*see Tos. B.Q. 7:1*)	(*see Tos. B.Q. 7:1*)
He said, The robber equated the honor of the slave to that of his owner.	(*see Tos. B.Q. 7:1*)	(*see Tos. B.Q. 7:1*)
The thief paid greater respect to the slave than to the master.	(*see Tos. B.Q. 7:1*)	(*see Tos. B.Q. 7:1*)
As if the thief made the eye above not to see, the ear not to hear.	(*see Tos. B.Q. 7:1*)	(*see Tos. B.Q. 7:1*)
Is. 29:15	(*see Tos. B.Q. 7:1*)	(*see Tos. B.Q. 7:1*)
Ps. 94:7.	(*see Tos. B.Q. 7:1*)	(*see Tos. B.Q. 7:1*)
Ezek. 9:9.	(*see Tos. B.Q. 7:1*)	(*see Tos. B.Q. 7:1*)

There are in fact no variations whatever among the several versions of this exegesis. A related, though different, exegesis is found in Mekhilta Neziqin (I.ii.4).

Similar to the analogical exegeses, but not so designated, are Yoḥanan's explanation of the requirement to pay the half-*sheqel*, y. Sheq. 2:3 (V.i.7), cited with minor variations in Pesiqta de R. Kahana, ed. Mandelbaum, p. 32. Yoḥanan's explanation of the draft exemptions appears in Sifré Deut. 192 (I.ii.9) and Midrash Tannaim to Deut. 20:8 (I.iv.3). The former is far more vivid and detailed than the latter.

IV. CONCLUSION

Only a few forms (apart from *teno rabbanan*) recur in separate categories of materials. These are the editorial connector-forms, specifically, *the story is told that*, *they said concerning*, and also *his disciples asked* as well as the plain *Yoḥanan says/said*. The recurrences of the former are in the legal and exegetical categories. Apart from these, no identifiable form used for one genre or type of materials appears in connection with any other. No usages of fixed formulae whatever can be found with reference to biographical and historical materials. The disciple-stories exhibit none either, except for the curious *five*-form of Avot-ARN, and, in other connections, *his disciples asked*, which we find in both legal and exegetical settings, as I just said.

In the exegetical materials we noticed that the themes of some of the dispute-stories recur, but the developments in the several versions are not much related to one another. *Again he was asked* serves as an editorial device to connect one story to another; but the component stories appear separately and unrelated as well. The "conventional" or standard form was simply, (1) the statement of a Scripture; followed by (2) *Rabbi X says/would say*. Alternatively, we find: (1) statement of Scripture; (2) Rabbi X, Rabbi Y; (3) One says... The other says... These occur in V.ii.11, in Midrash Tannaim and in Gen. R., and the latter have no antecedent versions at all. We thus may say that the bulk of Yoḥanan's exegeses rarely appeared in the most commonplace form.

The *ḥomer*-materials were not invariably so designated, as I said.

We have repeatedly observed that when a story appears in both an earlier and a later document, the account appearing in the earlier one is normally the earlier version. This result is important for the historical evaluation of Yoḥanan-materials.

PART III

CONCLUSION

CHAPTER THIRTEEN

FORMATION OF A LEGEND

I. The Cumulative Tradition

The synoptic studies repeatedly show that stories and sayings in later collections are very likely later in origin than materials appearing in earlier collections. When we are able to compare versions of a single story or saying, we find time and again that the earlier document contains what seems to be the earlier version; the later document's version is normally a more elaborate, much augmented later story, clearly dependent on the account in the earlier document. Further, later versions repeatedly exhibit signs of considerable imaginative improvement, including the attribution to Yoḥanan of sentences of direct discourse, exegeses, and other materials which never earlier made an appearance. I think it reasonable to suppose that the new material was not known earlier, but was in fact fabricated by the later tradents for the purposes of their improved accounts. This is not the place to speculate on the pseudepigraphic mentality, but it is a fact that much that is put into Yoḥanan's mouth is likely to be pseudepigraphic—perhaps nearly the whole of the tradition, for all we know. In this respect, we are in a position similar to that of New Testament scholars who have reached what seems to be the earliest stratum of the traditions. Bultmann (quoted by Edgar V. McKnight, *What Is Form Criticism?* [Philadelphia, 1969], p. 67) confessed that " 'Jesus' means the message of the oldest layer of the Synoptic tradition which may not be the message of the earthly Jesus—although Bultmann believed that it was." Here too we find ourselves unable to build a usable bridge between the earliest strata of the Yoḥanan-traditions and the actual life of, and events pertaining to, Yoḥanan ben Zakkai.

Through the tables that follow, we shall see what materials in the whole tradition appear in which collections. Having compared one tradition to another, and one collection to another, we now review the whole corpus. Two possible principles of ordering the materials presented themselves. I could have organized the corpus by the categories of the synoptic studies, or, to the contrary, by the order of the documents of part one. I preferred the latter. It made possible a clearer understanding of what came first and what came afterward, and that, after all, is our primary interest, rather than speculative, form-critical arrangements by categories which have yet to establish their analytical suggestiveness. The categories—legal, historical, exegetical, and so forth—turned out to be mere conveniences, but contributed little new knowledge; and the forms uncovered within the several categories produced no new insight, so far as I can tell. Hence, as I said, I chose to lay out each unit of the whole tradition in the order of the document in which it first makes its appearance. This allows us further to exploit the thesis proposed above concerning the relative age of the components of the tradition.

	Tannaitic Midrashim	Mishnah	Tosefta	Tannaitic Materials in Palest. *Gemara*	Babylonian *Beraitot*	ARNa	Palestinian *Gemara*	Babylonian *Gemara*	Later *Midrashim*
1) "If you do not know" "You were unwilling"	I.i.1 I.i.7				III.ii.16	IV.i.7			
2) "Whole stones"	I.i.2, I.ii.5		II.iii.8e						
Iron/altar	I.ii.1		II.iii.8f						
3) Slave's ear	I.i.3		II.iii.8d	III.i.5	III.ii.18				VI.iv.11
4) Ox/lamb	I.i.4				III.ii.19b				
5) Thief pays double	I.i.5		II.iii.7		III.ii.19a				
6) Garments for heifer-ceremony	I.i.6		II.iii.13						
7) 120 years	I.i.8 I.iv.6								VI.i.5
8) *Merkavah*	I.ii.2		II.ii.3	III.i.4	III.ii.13				
9) Prince sins	I.ii.3		II.iii.8c	III.i.6	III.ii.26				
10) Uncleanness of third loaf	I.ii.4	II.i.11	II.iii.5			(see #56)		V.ii.12	
11) Day of Waving	I.ii.6	II.i.20	II.iii.9	III.i.3	III.ii.9			V.ii.17 V.ii.19	
12) *Lulav*-Day of Waving	I.ii.7	II.i.5 II.i.7					V.i.3 V.i.5	V.ii.9	
13) After good court	I.ii.8				III.ii.24				

	Tannaitic Midrashim	Mishnah	Tosefta	Tannaitic Materials in Palest. *Gemara*	Babylonian *Beraitot*	ARNa	Palestinian *Gemara*	Babylonian *Gemara*	Later *Midrashim*
14) Frail-hearted	I.ii.9 I.iv.3								
15) Created to study Torah	I.iv.1	II.i.18a							
16) Destroy altars	I.iv.2					IV.i.6a			
17) Letters *re* fourth-year produce	I.iv.4								
18) How many Torahs-dispute	I.iv.5								
19) I doubt he is not liable to sin offering		II.i.1 II.i.2							
20) Ben Bukhri *re* priest's *sheqel*		II.i.3			III.ii.27 III.ii.28 III.ii.29		V.i.6		
21) Brought food to Sukkah		II.i.4			III.ii.4			V.ii.5	
22) Shofar on Sabbath		II.i.6			III.ii.8		V.i.4		
23) New Moon evidence all day long		II.i.8a	II.iii.2		III.ii.10				
24) New Moon evidence to court, not chief		II.i.8b							
25) Ḥanan said well		II.i.9 II.i.10			III.ii.17				
26) Job served in love		II.i.12							
27) Abrogation of breaking heifer's neck, bitter waters	III.i.13	II.iii.6							

28) When died		II.i.14							
29) Ben Zakkai tested evidence		II.i.15			III.ii.25				
30) Marriage of Isah-family		II.i.16			III.ii.15				
31) Elijah		II.i.17							
32) Five Disciples		II.i.18b				IV.i.5d-g			
33) Capacity of fragments		II.i.21							
34) Woe if I say it		II.i.22	II.iii.10		III.ii.21				VI.vi.2
35) Ammon, Moab pay poor-man's tithe in seventh year		II.i.23	II.iii.15		III.ii.11				VI.x.1
36) Sadducee-dispute: Uncleanness of Scriptures		II.i.24	II.iii.16						
37) Do guests tithe dates?			II.iii.1	III.i.1		IV.i.2			
38) Ṭarfon on heave-offering			II.iii.4						
39) Israel exiled to Babylonia			II.iii.8a						
40) First/second tablets			II.iii.8b						
41) One who searches (see #6)			II.iii.11						
42) Heifer-priest made unfit			II.iii.12						
43) Shema'yah, go sprinkle waters			II.iii.14						
44) Death-scene					III.ii.1	IV.i.9	V.i.11 V.i.17		
45) Son saved by Ḥanina's prayer					III.ii.2				
46) Zech. 11:1-predicted destruction					III.ii.3				

	Tannaitic Midrashim	Mishnah	Tosefta	Tannaitic Materials in Palest. *Gemara*	Babylonian *Beraitot*	ARNa	Palestinian *Gemara*	Babylonian *Gemara*	Later *Midrashim*
47) Hillel's disciples (compare #60)					III.ii.5, 23	IV.i.5a-b	V.i.12	V.ii.16 (in part)	
48) Family of Eli					III.ii.6 III.ii.13				
49) New Moon testimony on Sabbath (see #23,24)					III.ii.7				
50) Is. 14:14					III.ii.12			V.ii.4	VI.iii.1
51) Prov. 14:34					III.ii.20				(VI.v.5-Hadrian)
52) Sadducee dispute: daughter's inheritance					III.ii2.2				VI.xi.2
53) Hosea 6:6						IV.i.1			
54) Escape in coffin						IV.i.2		V.ii.14	VI.ii.2 VI.vi.3
55) Beginnings of Eliezer						IV.i.3			VI.i.3 VI.v.1
56) Priest eats heave-offering						IV.i.4 (Comp. #10)			
57) Son's death						IV.i.5h			
58) Sprout-pride-sins						IV.i. 6b-d			
59) Wise/fear sin						IV.i.8			

60) Always wore *tefillin*, etc:							V.i.1	V.ii.6 V.ii.7	
61) 'Ulla-18 yrs. in 'Arav							V.i.2		
62) Ten *gerahs*							V.i.7		V.iii.2
63) Proselyte in this time					(III.ii.30)		V.i.8	V.ii.21	
64) II Kings 25:9							V.i.9		VI.ii.1 VI.iii.4 VI.v.3
65) Yoḥanan as rainmaker							V.i.10		
66) Ordination							V.i.13		
67) Why is ox stoned Ex. 21:29							V.i.14		
68) Census							V.i.15	V.ii.20	VI.vii.1
69) Moses as accountant							V.i.16		
70) Teaching in Temple's shadow							V.i.18	V.ii.3	
71) Greeted gentiles								V.ii.1	
72) Cut grapes uncleanness								V.ii.2	
73) Valley of Ben Hinnom								V.ii.8	
74) Fourth-year fruit								V.ii.10	
75) Mal. 3:5								V.ii.11	VI.v.4
76) Priests bless barefooted								V.ii.13	
77) Nephews lost money								V.ii.15	
78) Date of Pentecost								V.ii.18	VI.xi.1
79) Gen. 2:9									VI.i.1

	Tannaitic Midrashim	Mishnah	Tosefta	Tannaitic Materials in Palest. *Gemara*	Babylonian *Beraitot*	ARNa	Palestinian *Gemara*	Babylonian *Gemara*	Later *Midrashim*
80) Gen. 3:7									VI.i.2
81) Gen. 15:18									VI.i.4
82) Hocus-pocus									VI.iii.3 VI.v.2 VI.iv.1 VI.vii.2
83) Gen. 1:5									VI.iii.5 VI.vi.2
84) Simeon the trench-digger									VI.vi.1
85) Qoh. 9:8									VI.vi.4
86) Celebrate in common									VI.viii.1
87) Song 7:14									VI.ix.1
88) Priests eat meal-offering									VI.xi.3

II. YOḤANAN AND THE TANNAIM

We shall here consider the configuration of the Yoḥanan-tradition as it was shaped by various Tannaitic masters and circles. The Yoḥanan-tradition at the end of the formation of the major Tannaitic collections basically consisted of three major components: exegeses of Scripture, including the mystical tradition, legal traditions, particularly related to Yavneh, and some dispute-stories, involving both gentiles and Sadducees. Of the forty-three components, fifteen are exegeses of Scriptures. Among these, numbers 1, 2, 39 and 40 relate to Yoḥanan's theological interpretation of Israel's fate in general and of the Temple in particular. Numbers 3, 4, 5, 9, 14, 20, pertain to Scriptural bases of laws. It is clear that a large segment of the earliest Yoḥanan-tradition was composed of exegetical materials; in addition to those just noted, many other sorts of traditions either contain, or directly pertain to, Scriptural interpretation and application. Numbers 7, 13, 21 relate to Yoḥanan's biography, not telling stories about him, but merely referring to him. The disciples form the center of interest in numbers 8, 32, 37, and 43; they further constitute the setting in numbers 6 and 41. The Yavneh decrees consisted of numbers 11-12, the *lulav* and Day of Waving rulings, to which were later added numbers 22, 23, and 24. Dispute-stories involving gentiles may begin as early as Midrash Tannaim, number 18, but more likely first occur in the latest stratum of Tannaitic materials, number 36. Dispute-stories involving Sadducees and priests are much earlier, as in numbers 20, 30, 31, 36.

Tannaitic traditions in the Palestinian Talmud duplicated numbers 3, 8, 9, and 11, that is, the slave's ear, the *Merkavah*, the prince-sin-offering, and the Day of Waving decree, and in addition referred to the Tosefta story about Joshua's instructions on whether guests have to tithe or not. No Tannaitic attribution in the Palestinian Talmud contained essentially new materials. All simply repeated earlier and well-known materials. This is striking, for the Babylonian Tannaitic materials, introduced by *Teno Rabbanan*, by contrast included important new elements, specifically, numbers 44, 45, 46, 47, 48, 49, 50, 51, and 52. These materials have in common the tendency to tell stories about Yoḥanan; they in fact constitute the first truly narrative biographical data. If we had a history of Talmudic literature we might be able to suggest whether the new style of story-telling about Yoḥanan reflects a more widespread literary innovation, turning brief sayings or traditions into rich and artistic narratives, for example, in the manner of

Rav's stories about the Messianic house. At any rate, it is clear that the *beraita*-corpus added the dramatic death-scene. (This occurs in simpler form, to be sure, in the Palestinian Talmud, in V.i.11, 17, but there it is not attributed to Tannaim.) In addition we find the ʿArav story about Ḥanina ben Dosa's prayer in behalf of Yoḥanan's son; the prediction of the destruction; the first appearance of the *Hillel's eighty disciples* material; the way Yoḥanan's exegesis saved the life of the descendents of Eli; New Moon testimony on the Sabbath only for Tishri and Nisan; the exegeses of Is. 14:14 and Prov. 34:14; and another Sadducean dispute, this time about the daughter's inheritance. Of all the *beraitot* which contain new material, therefore, only numbers 49 and 52 are of legal interest; all the others pertain to biography. *Beraitot* which certainly repeat earlier Tannaitic materials appear in numbers 1, 3, 4, 5, 8, 9, 11, 13, 20, 21-23, 25, 29-30, 34-5. All other *beraita*-material is new. This is important, for we should not have predicted that a great many *beraitot* would exhibit *no* close relationship to antecedent collections. On the contrary, we should have expected *beraita*-materials to contain a very high proportion of references to what had already been redacted in Tannaitic collections, just as the Palestinian Talmud's *TNY* and related forms do indeed introduce citations of, or at least clear allusions to, earlier collections. In fact, of twenty-nine *beraitot* in our collections, eleven contain new materials, eighteen repeat earlier traditions.

ARN may or may not be Tannaitic origin. We earlier followed Goldin's judgment. If it is Tannaitic, however, it must be the latest of all Tannaitic collections, and since it is generally agreed that the compilation was edited (whatever that may mean) in the ninth century, we certainly cannot with certainty attribute its stories to the Tannaitic stage in the development of the Yoḥanan-tradition. In any event, as we noticed, ARN introduces the colloquy with Joshua on the Temple mount (number 53), the first great account of the escape from Jerusalem (number 54), the first account of Eliezer's beginnings (number 55), and the long story about the disciples' comfort when Yoḥanan's son died (number 57), as well as relatively minor matters: the priest who ate heave-offering in a state of purity, the messianic saying, and the saying about the wise man who fears sin. This certainly constitutes a new and important stage in the formation of the Yoḥanan-legend, one in which literary considerations clearly play an important part. From a literary viewpoint ARN is far closer in spirit and in style to the Babylonian *beraita*-literature than to Palestinian materials. Even the modest stories in the Tannaitic midrashim cannot be compared to the smooth and powerful narratives of ARN.

Amoraic additions to the Yoḥanan-legend include new details added to earlier *beraitot*, as in number 60 (= 47). Palestinian Amoraic contributions include 'Ulla's saying about eighteen years in 'Arav, provoked by the reference to the Sabbath cases cited by Judah b. Ilai; the saying on ten *gerahs*; Joshua b. Levi's inclusion of Yoḥanan's school in his exegesis of II Kings 25:9; two further references to Yoḥanan in Jerusalem, numbers 65 and 70; a new Yavnean decree, number 63, this one about the proselyte "in this time" (though this may be as early as Simeon b. Yoḥai); colloquys with gentiles about Moses as an accountant, in two forms, first as to the census, second as to the Temple treasury, numbers 68 and 69; and the saying on ordination, which falls into the Yavnean group. In addition to the new account of the escape in b. Giṭ. 56a-b, the Babylonian Amoraim added stories about Yoḥanan's early life, number 72, about his nephews, number 77, and about his personality, number 73; a new exegesis of Mal. 3:5, number 75; two more Yavnean ordinances on the priestly benediction, number 76, and on fourth-year fruit, number 74; and a saying about use of the valley of Ben Hinnom's produce for the *lulav*, number 73.

New materials in the later midrashic compilations included exegeses of Gen. 1:5, 2:19, 3:7, 15:18, Qohelet 9:8, Song of Songs 7:14 (in which Yoḥanan is merely mentioned); and several dispute stories, two with gentiles (numbers 82, 86) and two with Temple authorities and Sadducees, numbers 84 and 88.

In all, we have counted 88 components of the Yoḥanan tradition. Of these, we find the following proportions of new items contributed by each group of documents:

Tannaitic Midrashim	18	20.0%	ARN	7	7.9%
Mishnah-Tosefta	25	28.3%	Amoraic materials	19	21.5%
Babylonian *beraitot*	9	10.2%	Later collections	10	11.3%

If we suspend judgment both on whether Babylonian *beraitot* are actually of Tannaitic origin and on the date of ARN materials, we find that almost half of all components of the tradition were shaped by the end of Tannaitic times, 48.3% to be exact, and a fifth of the whole tradition was shaped by the Bar Kokhba War or shortly thereafter. If, further, we suppose the *beraitot* and ARN in fact *are* Tannaitic, then we find that 66.4% of the materials are of Tannaitic origin. Approximately a third of the tradition is of Amoraic or later origin by any standard, and perhaps more than half if we suppose the ARN and *beraita* materials are later.

Early Tannaitic interest in Yoḥanan is not difficult to trace, for while some components of the Tannaitic segment of the tradition first occur without prior attestation in the Mishnah and Tosefta, (in particular numbers 21, 22, 27, 28, 29, 33, 34, 36, 39, 40, 42, 43), some of these same items do refer to, and probably derive from, Tannaitic masters earlier than the circles around Judah the Prince. These have been signified in the charts[1] by parentheses around their entry prior to the Mishnah-Tosefta. Some materials, on the other hand, refer to Jerusalem years, but we have no grounds to permit assigning their original formulation to that period. But to Yavneh, Beror Ḥayil, Emmaus, not to mention the schools of Ishmael and ʿAqiva, Usha, and Bet Sheʿarim (in the time of Judah the Prince), we can safely attribute many stories.

Eleazar b. ʿArakh (Emmaus): This circle is certainly responsible for the *Merkavah*, number 8, in its primary form, though, as we saw, Joshua, Yosi, and others augmented it; and the *five*-form, number 32, including the colloquy about the good and evil way in its *present* formulation. But the form is not the creation of Emmaus. Eleazar's circle may additionally have contributed the story of how Yoḥanan was comforted when his son died (number 57), though it is difficult to say so for certain. It is also possible that a much later narrator has taken up the Eleazar-version of the *five*-form and made use of it to shape materials actually composed long after Eleazar's death. The story of Eleazar's departure following Yoḥanan's death (IV.i.5i) lays much greater claim to origins in Eleazar's circle, for, as I said, it puts a good face on the matter. It certainly would have left a negative impression, had it been alleged that Eleazar departed while Yoḥanan was still alive, even when he was in Yavneh. Hence that story is likely to be attributed to Eleazar's Emmaus circle, at least in some primitive version; but the account as we have it has been completely reshaped to offer criticism of *anyone* who departs from a center of Torah-study merely for considerations of climate or other material benefit. I think it not unlikely that Eleazar's circle originally claimed he left Yoḥanan after death, and then others, later on, added that Emmaus was not a center of Torah—despite Eleazar's presence! Indeed, Eleazar himself

[1] pp. 278-287.

forgot what he knew. The circles around ʿAqiva who preserved Eleazar's *Merkavah*-stories cannot have been responsible for such a teaching, for, so far as they were concerned, Eleazar was most certainly remembered his Torah, which was authoritative as precedent, therefore worth quoting and preserving. Since Eliezer's circle was aloof from the *Merkavah*-tradition, perhaps that group reshaped the story in its current form; but this is merely conjecture, and since we do not know enough about the date of ARN, I can offer no better.

Eleazar's circle thus concentrated on the mystical and moral side of Yoḥanan's teachings. The *Merkavah* vision (without the substance of the mystery, to be sure), the good way-evil way sayings, and words of comfort when Yoḥanan's son died—these are the substance of Eleazar's contribution. Exegeses, legal sayings, Yavnean decrees, stories of Yoḥanan's life and work—none of these occurs. The Yoḥanan ben Zakkai of Emmaus was a mystic and a homilist, a moralist and a visionary. He was neither a lawyer nor a teacher nor a judge. He played no part in great historical events. Eleazar himself likewise seems to have conformed to this view of the master. While his students do not preserve stories of "how the master did so and so, just like *his* master Yoḥanan," in the manner of Eliezer's school, nonetheless we discern a striking resemblance between Yoḥanan ben Zakkai and Eleazar, the moral master, the mystic visionary, who came to Emmaus rather than struggling in Yavneh.

Eliezer b. Hyrcanus (Yavneh, Lud): Eliezer's circle preserved a version of the *what garments for the heifer-ceremony* story, number 6; the advice to go to a good court, including Yoḥanan's number 13; the Yavneh-decree about sounding the shofar on the New Year that coincides with the Sabbath, number 22; the law pertaining to tithing in Moab and Ammon in the seventh year, number 35, the instructions about uncleanness laws given to Shemaʿyah, number 43; and the death scene, number 44.

We may also attribute to the circle of Eliezer and Joshua the first great escape story (number 54). Certainly the beginnings of Eliezer (number 55) were given shape by followers of Eliezer—if ARN is as early as is claimed. But if, as is also possible, ARN is much later, then we cannot attribute to Eliezer's group even the narrative of his origins and early studies, and in that case, we must suppose the group responsible for pseudepigraphic use of Eliezer's name for later narratives (e.g. Pirqé de R. Eliezer) is also responsible for this account. My guess is that the material actually is early, for the ARN version contains

	Jerusalem	Eleazer	Yavneh Eliezer	Yavneh Joshua	Yavneh Other
1) "If you do not know" "You were unwilling"					
2) "Whole stones"–Iron altar					I.ii.5
3) Slave's ear					
4) Ox/lamb					
5) Thief pays double					
6) Garments for heifer-ceremony			(I.i.6)	II.iii.13	
7) 120 years					
8) *Merkavah*		(I.ii.2a)		II.iii.3 III.ii.13	III.i.4 Yosi & Simeon
9) Prince sins					
10) Uncleanness of third loaf				(I.ii.4) II.i.11 II.iii.5	
11) Day of Waving				(I.ii.6)	
12) *Lulav*—Day of Waving				(I.ii.7)	
13) After good court			(I.ii.8)		
14) Frail-hearted					
15) Created to study Torah					
16) Destroy altars					
17) Letters *re* fourth-year produce					
18) How many Torahs-dispute					
19) "I doubt he is not liable to sin offering"					
20) Ben Bukhri *re* priests' *sheqel*			(II.i.3)		

Second Century — to 140		140-180 Usha	180-220 Judah the Prince et. al.	Third-Century Pales-tine	Third-Century Baby-lonia	Fourth-Century Pales-tine	Fourth-Fifth-Century Baby-lonia	Later
Ishmael	ʿAqiva							
I.i.1 I.i.7				IV.i.7			III.ii.16	
I.i.2	I.ii.1 I.ii.5		II.iii.8e II.iii.8h					
I.i.3			II.iii8d.	III.i.5	(III.ii. 18?)	IV.ii.19a		VI.iv.iii
I.i.4					(III.ii. 19?)	IV.ii.19b		
I.i.5			II.iii.7					
I.i.6			(II.iii.13)					
I.i.8 I.iv.6	(I.i.8)							VI.i.5
	I.ii.2 II.iii.3c		II.iii.3	III.i.4	(III.ii. 13?)			
	I.ii.3		II.iii.8c	III.i.6			III.ii.26	
	I.ii.4		II.i.11 II.iii.5				V.ii.12	
	I.ii.6	II.i.20	(II.i.20) II.iii.9	III.i.3			III.ii.9 V.ii.17 V.ii.19	
	I.ii.7 (II.i.5)		IIi.5 II.i.7			V.i.3 V.i.5	V.ii.9	
	I.ii.8				III.ii.24			
I.iv.3	I.ii.9							
I.iv.1			II.i.10a	IV.i.5c				
I.iv.2				IV.i.6a				
I.iv.4								
I.iv.5								
		II.i.1 II.i.2						
		II.i.3				V.i.6	III.ii.27 III.ii.28 III.ii.29	

	Jeru-salem	Eleazer	Yavneh		
			Eliezer	Joshua	Other
21) Brought food to Sukkah	(II.i.4)				
22) Shofar on Sabbath			(II.i.6)		
23) New Moon evidence all day long					
24) New Moon evidence to court, not chief					
25) "Ḥanan said well"	(II.i.9) (II.i.10)			(II.i.9) (II.i.10)	
26) Job served in love					II.i.12-Joshua b. Hy-canus
27) Abrogation of breaking heifer's neck, bitter waters	(II.i.13) (II.iii.6)				
28) When-died					
29) Ben Zakkai tested evidence	(II.i.15)				
30) Marriage of Isah-family				(II.i.16) III.ii.15	
31) Elijah				II.i. 17	
32) Five Disciples		(II.i.18b)			
33) Capacity of fragments					
34) Woe if I say it					
35) Ammon, Moab pay poor-man's tithe in seventh year			(II.iii.15) (II.i.23)		
36) Sadducee-dispute; Uncleanness of Scripture				(II.i.24)	
37) Do guests tithe dates				Beror Ḥayil-II.iii.1 III.i.1,2	
38) Ṭarfon on heave-offering					(II.iii.4)
39) Israel exiled to Babylonia					
40) First/second tablets					
41) One who searches (see #6)				(II.iii.11)	

Second Century — to 140 Ishmael 'Aqiva	140-180 Usha	180-220 Judah the Prince et. al.	Third-Century Pales-tine	Third-Century Baby-lonia	Fourth-Century Pales-tine	Fourth-Fifth-Century Baby-lonia	Later
		II.i.4		III.ii.4(?)		V.ii.5	
		II.i.6			V.i.4	III.ii.8	
	II.iii.2	II.i.8a				III.ii.10	
	II.i.8b						
		II.i.9,10				III.ii.17	
		II.i.12					
		II.i.13 II.iii.6					
		II.i.14					
		II.i.15				III.ii.25	
		II.i.16				III.ii.15	
		II.i.17					
		II.i.18b	IV.i.5d-g				
		II.i.21					
		II.i.22 II.iii.10	III.ii.21	(IV.ii. 21?)			VI.vi.2
		II.i.23 II.iii.15		(III.ii. 11?)			VI.x.1
		II.i.24 II.iii.16					
		II.iii.1	III.i.1 III.i.2				
		II.iii.4					
		II.iii.8a					
		II.iii.8b					
		II.iii.11					

	Jeru-salem	Eleazar	Yavneh		
			Eliezer	Joshua	Other
42) Heifer-priest made unfit					
43) Shema'yah, Go sprinkle waters			(II.iii.14)		
44) Death-scene			(III.ii.1) (IV.i.9)		
45) Son saved by Ḥanina's prayers					(III.ii.2 Ḥanina)
46) Zech. 11:1 Predicted Destruction					
47) Hillel's 80 disciples (compare #60)		(III.ii.5)			
48) Family of Eli					
49) New Moon testimony on Sabbath (See #23, 24)					
50) Is. 14:14					
51) Prov. 14:34					(Gamaliel III.ii.20)
52) Sadducee dispute: daughter's inheritance					
53) Hosea 6:6			(IV.i.1)		
54) Escape in coffin			(IV.i.2)		
55) Beginnings of Eliezer			(IV.i.3)		
56) Priest eats heave-offering				(IV.i.4)	
57) Son's death		(IV.i.5h)			
58) Sprout-pride-sins					
59) Wise/fear sin				(IV.i.8 Ḥanina?)	
60) Always wore *tefillin*				(V.i.1) (V.ii.6)	

Second Century — to 140 Ishmael 'Aqiva	140-180 Usha	180-220 Judah the Prince et. al.	Third-Century Pales-tine	Third-Century Baby-lonia	Fourth-Century Pales-tine	Fourth-Fifth-Century Baby-lonia	Later
		II.iii.12					
		V.iii.14					
			III.ii.1 IV.i.9 Vii.i. V.i.17				
			III.ii.2				
				II.ii. 3(?)			
			IV.i. 5a-c V.i.12			III.ii.5 III.ii.23 V.ii.16	
						III.ii.6 III.ii.13	
				III.ii.7			
				(III. ii.12?)	V.ii.4	V.ii.4	(VI.v.5- Hadrian)
						III.ii.20	VI.iii.1
						III.ii.22	VI.xi.2
			IV.i.1				
			IV.i.2		V.ii.4	V.ii.4	VI.ii.2 VI.vi.3
			IV.i.3				VI.i.3 VI.v.1
			IV.i.4				
			IV.i.5h				
			IV.i. 6b-d				
			IV.i.8				
			(V.i.1)	V.ii.6 V.ii.7	V.i.1		

	Jeru-Salem	Eleazer	Yavneh		
			Eliezer	Joshua	Other
61) Ulla—18 years in Arav					
62) Ten *gerahs*					
63) Proselyte in this time					
64) II Kings 25:9					
65) Yoḥanan as rainmaker					
66) Ordination					
67) Why is ox stoned Ex. 21:29					
68) Census					
69) Moses as accountant					
70) Teaching in Temple's shadow					
71) Greeted gentiles					
72) Cut grapes in cleanness					
73) Valley of Ben Hinnom					
74) Fourth-year fruit		(V.ii.10)			
75) Mal. 3:5					
76) Priests to bless barefooted					
77) Nephews lose money					
78) Date of Pentecost					
79) Gen. 2:9					
80) Gen. 3:7					
81) Gen. 15:18					

Second Century — to 140		140-180 Usha	180-220 Judah the Prince et. al.	Third-Century Palestine	Third-Century Babylonia	Fourth-Century Palestine	Fourth-Fifth-Century Babylonia	Later
Ishmael	'Aqiva							
				V.i.2				
						V.i.7 (Joshua b.R. Nehemiah)		VI.iii.2
		III.ii.30 V.i.8 Simeon b. Yoḥai			V.ii.21			
				V.i.9 Joshua b. Levi				VI.ii.1 VI.iii.4 VI.iv.3
						V.i.10		
						V.ii.13 R. Ba		
						V.i.14		
						V.i.15	V.ii.20	VI.vii.1
						V.i.16		
						V.i.18	V.ii.3	
							V.i.1	
					V.ii.2 (Huna)			
							V.ii.8	
							V.ii.9	
				V.ii.11				VI.v.4
							V.ii.13	
				V.ii.15				
							V.ii.18	VI.xi.1
								VI.i.1
				(VI.i.2)				VI.i.2
								VI.i.4

	Jeru-salem	Eleazer	Yavneh		
			Eliezer	Joshua	Other
82) Hocus-pocus					
83) Gen. 1:5					
84) Simeon the trench digger					
85) Qoh. 9:8					
86) Celebrate in common?					
87) Song 7:14					
88) Priests eat meal-offering?					

Second Century — to 140 Ishmael	Second Century — to 140 'Aqiva	140-180 Usha	180-120 Judah the Prince et. al.	Third-Century Palestine	Third-Century Babylonia	Fourth-Century Palestine	Fourth-Fifth-Century Babylonia	Later
								VI.iii.3
								VI.iv.1
								VI.v.2
								VI.vii.2
								VI.iii.5
								VI.iv.2
								VI.vi.1
								VI.vi.4
								VI.vii.1
								VI.ix.1
								VI.xi.3

numerous hints that existing, well-known stories are hammered together into a single account. The obvious components—ploughing, *hunger/bad breath* apophthegm, great sermon and blessing, disinheritance—all these may have circulated in primitive form. If so, Eliezer's circle must be credited with the stories, at least in the first instance.

For Eliezer's circle, the master and the master's master, Yoḥanan, were much the same. Both were devoted students of Torah. Both conducted good courts. Both played an important role in the legislative activities of the day. The work of Yavneh was advanced by Yoḥanan, just as did Eliezer his disciple after him; the legislation of Yoḥanan himself as well as his legal traditions were carefully preserved. But the Yoḥanan who saw the *Merkavah* and heard voices calling him to heaven—of that Yoḥanan ben Zakkai we hear not a single word. Eliezer was no mystic. He was a lawyer, judge, staunch defender of the traditions he received. And the Yoḥanan of Eliezer ben Hyrcanus's circle set the precedent. The law of tithing came from Moses; the priests required careful instruction on the law; a few important exegeses of legal and theological interest were likewise handed on. Yoḥanan, and Eliezer after him, never said anything his master had not said first; he never neglected his *tefillin;* and he never saw the *Merkavah;* he probably never played a great role in historical events; but faithfully, against all odds, preserved the true traditions of the law.

Joshua b. Ḥananiah (Yavneh): Joshua and his disciples are responsible for a version of the *garments for the heifer ceremony* story, number 6; the *Merkavah*, number 8; the *uncleanness of the third-loaf* colloquy with 'Aqiva, number 10; Yavneh decrees about the Day of Waving and the *lulav* (in *both* forms) numbers 11 and 12; the rule about the marriage of an Isah-family into the priesthood, number 30; the mission of Elijah in dealing with the priesthood, number 31; whether guests tithe their food, number 37; and a version of the story about how Yoḥanan pretended to forget only to stimulate the students, number 41 (compared to number 6). Joshua's disciples may well be responsible for number 53, a story in which Joshua alone plays the central role as Yoḥanan's important disciple; and I suspect the story of the foolish priest who did not know purity rules, number 56, is attributable to them also.

Joshua's traditions stand between the mystical and moral Yoḥanan of Eleazar on the one side, and the traditional, legal conservative Yoḥanan of Eliezer on the other. Joshua's Yoḥanan saw the *Merkavah*, but also taught important laws, exegeses, and moral rules which only later on were recognized as valid. He was responsible for the Yavnean ordinances about the *lulav* and Day of Waving and struggled with the priesthood. In all, like Joshua himself, Joshua's Yoḥanan never withdrew from, but took a vigorous part in, political life, gladly facing up to the opposition and overcoming it. Like Joshua, Yoḥanan lived a deep and mystical inner life. He served as lawyer and judge; and above all, he attended to the needs of the day through the Yavnean legislation.

The Yoḥanan of the several disciples' schools or circles thus conformed to the lives the several disciples actually lived later on. This rather general judgment requires refinement in closer study of the lives of Joshua and Eliezer, in particular; since Yoḥanan appears in almost all Eleazar-materials, we are on firmer ground in comparing the disciple's view of the master to the later disciple's traditions about the disciple, Eleazar himself.

Hostile priests and/or Hillelites: We earlier speculated that a number of stories may have been given their primary form by priests hostile to Yoḥanan, by Gamaliel and his friends, or by both. Among these stories were numbers 6 = 41, about the garments in which the heifer is sacrificed; number 29, about how "Ben Zakkai" conducted a murder trial. Perhaps the omission of Yoḥanan's authoritative action about a Temple rite in II.iii.6 (number 27) in favor of a mere report represents a deliberate revision, to demonstrate he did not have the authority some people attributed to him. The hostile-priestly tradition, later revised by both of Yoḥanan's chief disciples in several ways so as to reflect credit on him, thus was concerned with the heifer-ceremony. I imagine that in the years immediately preceding the war of 66, some ceremony took place in the Temple, and a Pharisee presumably criticized the conduct of a ceremony, saying the priests did not do it according to "the whole Torah." The priests would then have paid slight attention. But after the war, the incident must have been remembered and dramatized by priestly circles to demonstrate the incapacity of even Yoḥanan ben Zakkai himself to claim to have directed the cult, or to direct once again what would be done in the Temple. If the story was told, it was quickly taken up by Yoḥanan's circle, as I said, and then given a far more satisfactory form.

III.ii.8, a version of the *shofar* on New Year-Sabbath decree, may derive from a hostile-priestly circle.

It is striking that Hillelites (Gamaliel II, for instance) never seem to have shaped stories about Yoḥanan as did the disciples Eliezer, Eleazar, and Joshua. We indeed do not have a single statement handed on by Yoḥanan in Hillel's name. Since, at least according to Eliezer, Yoḥanan never said anything he had not first heard from his master, and since his master was supposedly Hillel, that fact is striking. It would suggest that no one was interested in attributing to Yoḥanan any sayings in Hillel's name. The Hillelite house would have been the obvious candidate for the preservation, fabrication or invention of such attributions. Those friendly to Jonathan b. Uzziel and hostile to the Hillelites said Yoḥanan was Hillel's youngest, or least, disciple and passed silently by the actual heirs of Hillel: Simeon b. Gamaliel, Gamaliel, and Simeon b. Gamaliel. The Hillelites, in the persons of Gamaliel II, Simeon b. Gamaliel II of Usha, and Judah, as well as the circles of masters close to the patriarchate—these important authorities said nothing whatever.

But it is equally important that none of Yoḥanan's disciples claimed Yoḥanan ever quoted Hillel. This must mean that in the context of Yavneh, they did not choose to link their master's authoritative statements to those of *any* former master whatever, including Hillel. It was one thing to assert Yoḥanan received the Torah, that is, normative *authority*, from Hillel. It was quite another to admit that anything Yoḥanan ever said required anterior precedents, and this the disciples never confessed. On the contrary, Eliezer advised the consistery of "that day" not to doubt its rightness, for Yoḥanan taught him—in the name of Moses, but *not* of Hillel!—just what they had concluded.

I think the circles that might have cited Hillel-Yoḥanan sayings failed to do so for opposite reasons. Both the disciples of Yoḥanan and the heirs of Hillel either suppressed what they had or failed to fabricate what they did not have. The former must have preferred to ignore their master's alleged dependence on Hillel, thus avoiding the inference that they now should subordinate themselves to Hillel's heir. The latter must have wanted to avoid any unnecessary reference to the "fact" that Hillel had neglected their own forebears in favor of their present (or, immediately past) competition for authority in Yavneh. Further study of the formation of the Hillel sayings may make clearer the original context in which Hillel's sayings actually were handed on.

Ishmaelean and Aqiban stories: These are summarized above, pp. 32-35. Original to the Ishmaelean school were numbers 1, 3, 4, 15, 16, 17, 18. These are *ḥomer*-exegeses (numbers 1, 3, 4) and other sorts of Scriptural interpretations. The Aqibans may have contributed number 9, the exegesis of Lev. 4:22.

The generation of Usha (ca. 140-180) is represented by Judah b. Ilai (numbers 11 [II.i.20], 19, 20) and Joshua b. Qorḥa (numbers 23, 24). Both men concentrated on the Yavneh ordinances. We may safely say that interest in the Yavnean laws was greater now than earlier. Since Usha was responsible for issuing a number of new *taqqanot* in the manner of Yoḥanan, the sages probably devoted more attention to the study—possibly including fabrication—of what Yoḥanan had done in the earlier disaster. But I see no direct connection between the content of the decrees now attributed to Yoḥanan and the circumstances of Usha. It is probably the more general need to issue *taqqanot*, rather than any search for specific precedents for what the Ushans actually needed to do, that accounts for their increased interest in the Yavnean decrees.

Perhaps, additionally, Judah's interest in Yoḥanan's Galilee experience, reflected in the ʿArav materials, was provoked by the establishment in Galilee of rabbinical centers. A search for early precedents for the new situation may have elicited concern for the Yoḥanan of ʿArav.

Judah the Prince and his circle: The latest Tannaitic contributors added the story of Gamaliel I and Yoḥanan, number 20, the approval of Ḥanan, number 25, the authority of Yoḥanan over the Temple cult, numbers 27 and 42, Yoḥanan's court-precedures in a murder trial, number 29, uncleanness rulings, numbers 33, 34, 36 (Scriptures, in a dispute with Sadducees), the explanation for the exile to Babylonia, number 39, and of the first and second tablets (a related exegesis), number 40.

The most striking additions are in numbers 25, 27, 42, 29, and 36, for all make the same point: Yoḥanan had great authority in the Temple. He furthermore was friendly with Judah's ancestor, Gamaliel (whether the first or second was intended hardly matters), certainly a new fact. Thus Yoḥanan's role in Jerusalem before 70 was of special interest to Judah. Judah's and his circle's interest in that particular question probably was provoked by the possibility that the Temple might in fact be restored. We do not know whether Judah was really friendly with "Antoninus," but we do know that he achieved excellent relations with the Romans. It is not out of the question that Judah hoped to use his influence with the imperial government to secure permission to restore the Temple, now that the after-effects of

Bar Kokhba's war had been forgotten. He may well have maintained that while the Romans could not entrust the project to revolutionaries, they could well trust Judah, their proven friend, and the sages around him. And this would certainly have solidified his rule over the Jews, for what war had failed to accomplish, the Hillelite heir would have won. Indeed, since Judah claimed to descend from David—and was worried about the equivalent claim of the Babylonian exilarch—his expected success in rebuilding the Temple would have been widely interpreted, with his encouragement, to mean that he was the Messiah. We do not know whether he openly sought permission to restore Jerusalem, but it is beyond doubt that he would have profited from doing so and would have been unwise to fail to consider the consequences for Jewish government.

It therefore was useful to point to the role of Yoḥanan in the earlier war. Even then, had the Romans placed into power a wise sage such as Yoḥanan, he could have prevented the great upheavals. With this in mind, Judah may have further stressed that if and when the Temple is rebuilt, he and the subordinated rabbis, not the ancient priesthood, would in fact run it, just as Yoḥanan ben Zakkai had done one hundred fifty years earlier. That may be why the bulk of the new material in the Mishnah and Tosefta pertains to this issue.

Babylonians played so great a role in Judah's court that a *ḥomer*-explanation, attributed to Yoḥanan, of how Babylonian Jews came to Babylonia in the first place, must have easily been provoked. It was not a very friendly exegesis: Jews are there only because their ancestors played the whore, so were sent back where they came from—where they belonged. The exegesis appears nowhere else and may be pseudepigraphic in origin.

It is difficult to know whether Judah's circle or some later students bear responsibility for any of the ARN materials. The collection of sayings about the need to plant a sprout before receiving the messiah, avoiding pride, and the sins of the householders, number 68, is all quite new, and if the sayings have no roots in earlier materials, and if ARN also dates from this period, then it would not be farfetched to suppose Judah's circle is in some degree responsible for the sayings. It would be easy enough to trace the anti-Messianic saying to Judah's court, for it is quite congruent to Judah's interests and policies. But it is equally useful in earlier and later settings, and for much the same reasons. The other sayings could be related to Judah's interests. The escape-story obviously conforms to the patriarch's Roman policy. I think it would be wise, however, to avoid further speculation on ARN materials, because of the difficulty in definitively attributing them to Judah the Prince's group.

III. YOḤANAN AND THE AMORAIM

Our interest is in two separate questions. First, what new materials appear for the first time in Amoraic collections, and how can we account for them? Second, what Amoraim discuss Tannaitic materials well-attested in earlier sources?

Materials first occuring in Amoraic literature: Amoraic additions include, as we have noted, a number of new ordinances at Yavneh (numbers 63, 66, 74, 76) and important dispute stories (numbers 67, 68, 69). No entirely new type or genre of material is now invented. Once the escape story is introduced, the biography is in effect complete, though to be sure new details are added to every kind of tradition.

Palestinians: We have seen that Yoḥanan was cited by the following Palestinian masters:

Palestinian masters:

Jonah—III.i.1

Simeon b. Laqish—II.i.2, 6, V.i.1,
Yoḥanan b. Nappaḥa—V.i.12,
V.ii.11

Yosi b. R. Bun—II.i.3, V.i.12, 14
R. Jeremiah

Isaac b. Ṭavlai—III.ii.3
Zuṭra b. Ṭuvyah

Ḥama b. Ḥanina—III.ii.8

Hoshaia—III.ii.17

Samuel b. Isaac—III.ii.21

'Ulla—V.i.2

Berekiah—V.i.6

Joshua b. Neḥemiah—V.i.7

Joshua b. Levi—V.i.9, 11 (=17)
V.ii.8

Ba—V.i.13

Judah b. Shalom—V.ii.15

Babylonians: Sayings of Yoḥanan were cited or discussed by the following:

Pumbedita

Rav Judah b. Ezekiel—III.ii.4

Rabbah, R. Joseph—III.ii.10, 25, 26, 28, 29
V.ii.14e

Abbaye, Rava—III.ii.5, 6, 14, 15, 17, 22, 23
V.ii.1, 3, 4, 5, 7, 8, 16, 20

Maḥoza-Pumbedita (after 355)

Naḥman b. Isaac—III.ii.9, V.ii.9, 17, 19

5th C. Sura: Ashi
III.ii.16, 24, 27
V.ii.13

The school of Pumbedita and its continuator at Maḥoza under Naḥman b. Isaac thus are responsible for the bulk of references to, and citations of, Yoḥanan in the Babylonian Talmud, twenty-six clearcut citations. R. Ashi, afterward, is certainly responsible for an additional four references. In the third century, a single saying may be attributed to Huna, another (V.ii.21) to Adda b. Aḥva. Thus of the approximately thirty-one exempla which may without doubt be assigned to Babylonia, twenty-six, or more than 83%, pertain to a single school. This fact becomes still more astonishing when we compare the scattering of Palestinian references. Of twenty-two clearcut attributions, we may locate the following divisions by schools:

Sepphoris: None
Caesarea: Hoshaia—1
Lydda: Joshua b. Levi—4
Tiberias: Yoḥanan/Simeon b. Laqish 5; Jeremiah—3

The others are scattered. Thus of all the sayings, approximately eight derive from Tiberias. Slightly more than 36% are attributed to heads of the Tiberian school; approximately 18% are attributed to a head of the Lyddan one. It certainly is a striking contrast to note that the heads of a single Babylonian school produced the great bulk of Yoḥanan-discussions and citations.

Actually, these figures are not probative, but merely suggestive, for until we have a thorough calculation of the number of sayings attributed to all Amoraic masters, and until these are divided among the schools, we shall not know whether the proportions before us are sufficiently disproportionate to be genuinely significant. Moreover, it would be important to know just what proportion of the whole of the literature was framed originally at the several named schools, and, in addition, to what extent sayings are framed in the schools given in the name of the head of the school of the age in which the sayings are declared normative. Without such knowledge, it is difficult to draw sound conclusions. For example, it may have been the practice in Pumbedita to attribute sayings to the head of the school; but that may not have been the case in Tiberias. Hence the comparison of sayings according to attributions to the heads of the schools would not be decisive. And, as I said, we have no idea whether a larger proportion of the Palestinian Talmudic materials indeed derive from one or another school, and if so, just what that proportion actually is. Still, I think it unlikely that, whatever future statistical studies may reveal, we shall be found in error if we suppose Pumbedita from start to finish took a remarkably keen interest in Yoḥanan ben Zakkai.

Yoḥanan at Pumbedita: Yoḥanan-traditions cited at Pumbedita-Maḥoza pertained to bringing food to the Sukkah, with Gamaliel; the eighty disciples of Hillel; the family of Eli saved by Yoḥanan's advice; the struggle with the Bené Bathyra; the decrees on the Day of Waving and *Lulav;* Gamaliel's acceptance of Yoḥanan's rule that one does not call into session courts to deal with priestly marriage practices; Yoḥanan's approval of Ḥanan's ruling; praise of Yoḥanan's court (this may not be Pumbeditan, but the pertinent Mishnah certainly was discussed there); Yoḥanan's procedure in examining witnesses at a murder trial; the prince's sin-offering; the Ben Bukhri dispute about the priests' paying a *sheqel;* Yoḥanan's practice of greeting everyone in a friendly way; Yoḥanan's teaching in the Temple mount's shadow; the *Shi'ur Qomah* saying; the escape story (b. Giṭ. 56a-b); and the dispute about the census. We may thus describe the Yoḥanan ben Zakkai of Pumbedita-Maḥoza: He was closely associated with Hillel, as the leading disciple, and with Gamaliel (I). Gamaliel II accepted his authority. His decrees at Yavneh and his disputes with the priests about their offerings to the Temple show that he was the leading authority over priests and patriarch alike. He was obeyed and respected not only by the Hillelites, but also by the assembled sages of Yavneh. In Temple times, he could give the stamp of his approval to the decrees of the 'sons of the high priests'. His court was worthy of special praise, and his court-procedures elicited close interest. His mysticism may have attracted some attention because of Rava's interest in similar doctrines. The escape story was subjected to Joseph's criticism, but Yoḥanan's escape was nonetheless regarded as the means by which some small salvation was achieved in the debacle of 70. He held princes should confess even unwitting sins.

The Yoḥanan of Pumbedita was, therefore, primarily a political figure, a judge and administrator, rather than a mystic, moralist, or legislator. What interested the Pumbeditans was, specifically, Yoḥanan's relationships with the Hillelite house and the priesthood, his discipleship at Hillel's school, his subsequent position of equality with Gamaliel I and dominance over Gamaliel II. If we did not know that the Pumbeditans were involved in a bitter struggle with the Davidic scion of Babylonia, the exilarch, we might have supposed some such difficulty lay at the root of the Pumbeditans' interest in Yoḥanan. But, in fact, what is known about Pumbedita is precisely this: its half-century effort to raise its own funds and to preserve its independence from the exilarchate. The stories and references to Yoḥanan conform to that effort and serve its cause. Simply translating Gamaliel, Hillel, and the like to *the Davidic exilarch*, we find that the rabbi, or collegium of rabbis, is here alleged in times past to have been superior to the exilarch; to have even been selected disciple of the Davidide to the exclusion of the exilarch; to have proved equal to the high priests of old; to have judged at the best court of the day; to be worthy precedent in murder trials (and the only known murder trial of Babylonian Jewish history came toward the end of this period). The prince-exilarch is to be praised if he confesses his unwitting sin and brings a sin-offering, and happy the generation whose prince does so (—would that ours did!). Torah and good deeds avert the curse of the house of Eli—that and not the blessing of the priest or king-messiah.[1] The rabbi, not the exilarch, decrees what is to be done about

[1] References to the sons of Eli and their sin may be accounted for in two ways. First, Rava and Abbaye were supposedly related to that family. Second, the contemporary Christian church-father Aphrahat repeatedly refers to the hopeless sin of Eli's sons; nothing could redeem them. The assertion that study of Torah could save them represents a rabbinical response. References to Eli and his sons will be found in R. Graffin, ed., *Patrologia Syriaca*, I, vol. i-ii, Ioannes Parisot, ed., *Aphraatis Sapientis Persae, Demonstrationes* (Paris, 1894), Vol. i, p. 177, l. 24-6; 592, l. 25; 616, l. 18-22; 617, l. 8-10; 620, l. 26; 624, l. 18; 629, l. 11; 641, l. 22-4; 657, l. 4; 689, l. 6; 752, l. 6; 832, l. 17; 949, l. 19; Vol. ii, p. 88, l. 14-16. Still, we have no evidence whatever that Abbaye and Rava ever heard of Aphrahat, or vice versa. The point of their exegesis is directed not against those who say the cult is of no value, as did Aphrahat with reference to this Scripture, but rather against priests who do not appreciate the equivalent salvific value of study of Torah and doing commandments. The rabbis asserted that these constituted more effective means of atonement than sacrifice—an assertion important in an anti-priestly polemic. Hence the supposed derivation of the sages in the family of Eli may have drawn their attention to the Scripture, along with their eagerness to assert their own immunity to the ancient curse.

troublesome priests. In other words, Yoḥanan-sayings and stories served the Pumbeditans as important precedents in their struggle with the exilarch, for it is clear that his relationships to Hillel and the Hillelites provided a vital example of what ought even now to be the case in Babylonia.

It seems to me that the disproportionate interest in Yoḥanan at Pumbedita had no equivalent provocation in Palestine, or, if it did, the issues were argued in a different way. In any event, it is a fact that Pumbedita bears by far the largest—practically sole—responsibility for the Yoḥanan-references in the Babylonian Talmud, and Pumbeditans may even have formed some of the *beraitot* as we now have them. So far as I can tell, no similar interest in Yoḥanan was localized at any other Babylonian or Palestinian academy.

IV. Conclusion

The earliest and most primitive elements constituted the Yoḥanan-*tradition;* the later and more polished, literary ones became the Yoḥanan-*legend.* The former related to things the master had said and done, the latter to the interests of the later schools in those same things. Materials appearing in early documents *are* earlier and historically pertinent to the tradition of the life of the master. Those in later collections are later and historically pertinent only to the place of the master in the mind and imagination of later generations.

No element in the tradition is without historical consequence, but the significance is for different issues. If one asks, Who was Yoḥanan ben Zakkai? What did he do? How did he respond to the events and issues of his time?—then he must turn primarily to the early second-century data. That does not mean he will find unequivocal and unambiguous answers, for we have no writings of Yoḥanan, no sayings demonstrably redacted under his authority and transmitted at his instructions, no eye-witness accounts of historians, biographers, or other relatively reliable informants. But it does mean that, standing among the chief disciples, not long after the master's death, while the issues of his actual life and times still lived, one may listen to the recollections of men who knew what they were talking about and whose motives in saying what they did in a measure may be discerned. The first collections of materials, therefore, present responses both to the man and to the times of those who made the collections. The later ones respond to their own setting but contain little, if anything, derived from Yoḥanan's life and context. They contain exact and entirely valuable information on the mind of the later schools and how later masters found it pertinent and meaningful to tell about Yoḥanan. A critical biography of Yoḥanan ben Zakkai would have to rely mainly on the former; an intellectual history of talmudic Judaism on the latter as well.

Relying on the former, however, the biographer will still not gain much. The earliest materials, in Mekhilta, Sifra, Sifré, Mishnah, and Tosefta, are generally not very primitive, but already show the marks of considerable development. I was able to suggest some of the earliest components of the tradition, but rarely do these components appear to stand pretty much in their original state. We noticed, for instance, that the whole stones/iron homilies occur in both Aqiban and Ishmaelean forms; the Aqibans clearly altered the tradition to suit their view of war and Torah. Yoḥanan's essential idea was that peace-makers perform the function of the altar; the Temple and its instruments can be replaced by human virtues. This, I assume, is Yoḥanan's original message. But it occurs only in the document of a school fifty years after the event (or more). Early exegeses of Scripture normally were taken up and given dramatic settings, a sign of later development. "Events" in Yoḥanan's life, such as his forgetting Temple laws, turn out to have been stories told about him by hostile parties, then revised by friendly ones. Many such stories reveal more about partisan politics at later Yavneh, Usha, and Bet She'arim than about Yoḥanan in Jerusalem or in early Yavnean times. Yoḥanan's homilies show independent development of an original anecdote; sometimes we can isolate the original element. We are never able to demonstrate that the element was *how things actually happened.* On the contrary, not infrequently even the original element reveals signs of development. Some materials, to be sure, seem to have come from pre-70 Jerusalem, but they survive in so generalized a form that the original setting and polemic have been removed or lost.

Two themes seem to me historically well founded on the actual life of Yoḥanan ben Zakkai, first, the opposition to the war of 66-73, second, the promulgation of decrees afterward. The former so permeates the traditions that it attains the status of an axiom, as I said in the preface. If Yoḥanan really did not oppose the war of 66-73, then he contributed his name, if nothing else, to the formation of traditions about a man who did. The second is better founded on form-critical analysis, for the traditions about the Yavnean decrees include some decrees, innocuous in content to be sure, in most primitive and undeveloped form; these appear in the earliest documents in that form, recurring unchanged later on, and were discussed, even emulated, from the end of the first-century onward.

Two further themes seem to me probably related to Yoḥanan's own life and thought, the *Merkavah* vision and the *ḥomer*-exegeses. That Yoḥanan was a mystic is attested by the apparent competition with him felt by the disciples of Jonathan ben Uzziel, a competition shown by their revision of Hillel-stories to denigrate Yoḥanan's role and highlight Jonathan's.[1] This fact and the preservation of the *Merkavah* stories in Aqiban circles and afterward constitute two different and unrelated sorts of evidence pointing toward the same conclusion. The *ḥomer*-materials, while highly formalized, lay a strong claim to historical relationship to Yoḥanan. Both the content and the peculiarities of form suggest so.

The relationship of Yoḥanan to ʿAqiva dominated the formation of traditions in the first century after Yoḥanan's death. ʿAqiva recurs in numerous items in the early tradition, shaped not around what Yoḥanan said, but rather around what ʿAqiva said about what Yoḥanan said. As noted, important early stories are revised in ʿAqiva's school to conform to the policies of the later master.

The second-century materials, while on the whole not interrelated, thus evolved not at random or episodically, but in relationship to living traditions about the master and to genuine concern for what he had said and done. Later on, the Yoḥanan-tradition developed into the Yoḥanan-legend: stories were invented out of whole cloth, exhibiting little or no relationship with what had gone before. The most striking invention is the story of Yoḥanan's escape from Jerusalem, which first occurs in Amoraic times, possibly very late. The sole "fact" we should have known had we access only to Tannaitic collections was that Yoḥanan opposed the war. Within a century or so, this had become the elaborate account, replete with conversations and dramatic episodes, of b. Giṭ. and elsewhere. The *beraitot* are another achievement of this stage. Also characteristic of the second stage in the formation of the Yoḥanan-story was discussion of materials in the first stage; talmudic masters studied some of the materials, e.g. from the Mishnah-Tosefta, in their final form. So the second stage was marked by two quite different sorts of activity, first telling accounts

[1] But this judgment will be modified in the light of the history of the Jonathan b. ʿUzziel tradition, in my *The Rabbinic Traditions on the Pharisees before 70.*

fabricated out of, but independent from, older materials, second, discussing quite old, entirely completed ones.

The third and final stage is constituted by the materials in Chapter Six. By then, Yoḥanan was merely a name, to be used for the purposes of pseudepigraphy. The escape story related to the fact of Yoḥanan's opposition to the war and was probably necessitated by the question, How did Yoḥanan survive the destruction? The stories of Yoḥanan's evaluation of the red-heifer sacrifice and his encounter with Temple authorities, by contrast, exhibit no similar relationship to what had gone before. The later midrashic collectors either took over without much alteration what existed in earlier collections or made up, without any attention to "facts", whatever they liked. The old was copied without discussion: the new was fabricated without manifest concern for the existing corpus of materials.

What are the implications of these findings for the study of the Babylonian Talmud and related literature for historical purposes? The first, obvious conclusion is that talmudic literature simply cannot be converted into historical narrative until the varied processes of historical analysis and criticism have been undertaken. No passage can be treated as an eye-witness account. None can be supposed to tell "just how things were." Each must be closely and carefully examined. Some materials are more credible than others. These must be specified. But credibility only occasionally produces facts, as we have seen. For historians the form-critical inquiry has not been wholly sterile. On the contrary, we have been able to isolate a number of items which are as firm evidence of historical facts as one is ever apt to have about rabbis in late antiquity.

The second is that the historical question is not the only one of interest. On the contrary, we have seen that three sorts of "lives" of Yoḥanan ben Zakkai are possible, and all are interesting. The first is the account of the actual man: What can we say with some certainty about his life and opinions? The answer is meager but not unavailable. The second is the story of the life of the man after his death: What importance did he have in the mind of the immediate disciples and those who followed in later schools and communities? The answer consists of a considerable corpus of facts, for the sources accurately testify to the mind of the schools of the second, third, and fourth centuries that produced them. The third is a composite portrait of the first two, done for the purposes of characterizing the phenomenon that produced the whole: Who was a hero to the rabbis of late antiquity? How did they preserve their views? What religious values are revealed? What reality did their imagination perceive, then shape? The third kind of biography in a measure depends upon the results of the first two, but really constitutes a quite different historical statement. It is a statement given in the context of the history of religions, for the study of which the question, Did these things "really" happen? is not important. What is important is the question, What view of reality shaped the minds of men who told these stories, lived by these laws, believed these myths? Each of the three "lives," to be sure, is critical, but the criticism in each instance is different. All of them together may contribute in the end to the interpretation of both the data and the men who created them.

INDEX OF BIBLICAL AND TALMUDIC REFERENCES*

I. Bible

Genesis 1.5 170
1.24 159
2.19 159, 183
3.7 159, 256
4.25 124
14 161
14.1 247
14.15 160
15.18 161
36.20 105, 181, 207
36.24 181, 207
50.22 161
Exodus 15.27 181, 207
18.5 245
20.2 171, 173, 358-85
20.3 59
20.13 18, 72, 86, 100, 258-59
20.25 16, 24
21.3 100-01
21.6 18, 71, 258
21.29 138, 157
22.1 18
22.7 18, 70
24.7 130
31.25-26 140
32.16 71
38.26 15, 154, 236
38.27 254
38.28 141
38.29 140
Leviticus 4.22 71, 86, 108, 258, 291
6.16 108-09
6.23 42
10.3 124
11.33 26, 48-49, 121-22, 131
11.35 121
23.11 43
23.14 56
23.15 153, 180, 206
23.16 153, 180-81
23.18 206
23.40 29
25.55 71-72, 86, 100-01, 171, 259-61
Numbers 3.39 139, 153
3.44 253
4.46 253
19.1 19, 168, 173, 255
19.2 178
Deuteronomy 1.2 153, 180, 204
3.25 149, 230
12.1 36, 257
12.2 36
16.20 107
20.3 31
20.8 36
20.19 159
27.5 24,27-28,71,259-60
27.5-6 33
27.6 16-17, 28, 71
27.26 128
28.5 148
28.47-48 15, 235-39
28.56 235
28.57 150
30.20 128, 257
34.7 23, 217
Judges 9.25 101
I Samuel 3.14 98
3.31 92, 98
4.13 116
II Samuel 7.23 102, 240
12.24 125
23.21 101
II Kings 3.4 241
18.25 241
25.9 117, 136, 162, 169, 173, 234, 275
27.9 136, 155
Ezra 6.10 102
7.10 240
Song of Songs 1.8 15, 21-22, 32, 129, 235-39
7.14 179
Isaiah 10.34 115, 119, 151, 163, 166, 230, 233 ,239
14.14 95, 112, 142-43, 157, 182-83, 251-52, 270, 273-

* Indices were prepared by Mr. Arthur Woodman, Canaan, New Hampshire, under a grant from Brown University.

Isaiah 74, 282
14.14-15 174, 234, 251
14.15 143, 252
29.15 19, 70, 101, 261
44.25 4, 149, 230, 233, 239
Jeremiah 30.21 230
40.3 241
Ezekiel 7.19 148
9.9 19, 70, 101, 261
25.14 147
40.1 15, 235
45.12 141
Daniel 4.24 241
4.27 102, 241
24.4 167
Hosea 4.14 50-51, 70, 193, 209
6.6 131, 270, 282, 288
14.10 175, 194, 209
Amos 2.96 173
Zephaniah 1.15 102, 241
Job 1.1 49
1.21 124
13.15 49
27.5 49
Psalms 22.30 131, 224
24.1 244, 246
25.14 58
37.14 160, 245
37.14-15 161
37.15 160
37.21 55, 123
Psalms 65.14 178
66.1 178
89.3 113
90. 252
90.10 95, 143
91.7 70
94.7 19, 101, 261
96 248
96.12 84
111.10 129
119.128 244, 246
145 248, 251
147.7 9, 14, 96
Proverbs 5.16 123, 126
8.15 137, 152
8.21 122, 217-21
14.34 102-04, 112, 167-68, 183, 240, 270, 273-75, 282
15.30 149, 164, 230, 233, 239
17.22 150, 164, 230, 233, 239
21.24 102, 241
28.14 146
34.14 274
Haggai 1.15 15, 235
2.8 244, 246
Zechariah 11.1 89, 269, 273, 282
13.2 168, 170, 172, 178, 255
Malachi 3.5 145, 173, 183, 257, 271, 275, 284

II. Sifra

Sifra 'Emor 10.10 29, 206
16.9 206
Sifra Qedoshim 10.4 28
Sifra Shemini 201
7.12 26
Sifra Vayiqra 5.5 26

III. Sifré

Sifré Num.
Ḥuqat # 123 19, 199
Sifré Deut. 80 8
144 30, 225
Sifré Deut. 192 31, 38, 261
305 21
351 37, 253, 255-56
357 23, 213, 227

IV. Mishnah

Avot 2.8-9 55
Ed. 8.3,7 53, 201
Kel. 2.2 57, 192
17.16 58, 193
Ket. 13.1,2 48, 195
Men. 10.5 55, 209
R.H. 4.1 44, 207
4.2,3 44
4.4 44, 207, 209
Sanh. 1.1 64
5.2 52, 198
Shab. 16.7 41, 196
22.3 41
Sheq. 1.4 42, 203
Soṭ. 5.2 5, 49
9.9 50, 192

Soṭ 9.15 50, 64
Suk. 2.5 43, 197
3.12 43, 206
Yad. Ch. 4 205
4.3 69, 202
4.6 60, 203

V. Tosefta

'Ahilot 16.8 74, 199
B.Q. 3-7 257
7.1 70, 201, 261
7.2-5 257
7.3-7 72
7.5 258
7.5-6 258
7.6 259-60
7.6-7 260
7.7 260
Ḥag. 2.1 67
2.1-2 247
3.33 69
3.36 202
Kel. B.M. 7.9 73
Ma'aserot 2.1 65, 198
Men. 10.26 73
20.26 207
Parah 3.7 199
3.8 75, 204
4.7 77
10.2 77
R.H. 2.3 65
2.9 65, 209
Soṭ. 5.13 69, 201
14.1 69, 192
Yad. 1.19/2.9 78
2.16 78, 202

VI. Palestinian Talmud

Avot 2.1 259
2.9 81
A.Z. 3.1 141, 221-22, 224
3.11 141, 219
Ber. 2.3 133, 220, 226
Demai 3.1 83, 198
Ḥag. 2.1 85, 247
Ḥallah 1.1 84, 207
Hor. 3 257
3.2 82
Ket. 5.11 235
Lam. 1.5 162
Ma'aserot 2.2 83, 198
Meg. 3.1 136, 234
Ned. 5.6 137, 216
Qid. 1.2 86, 258
R.H. 4.2 134
4.3 134
Sanh. 1.2 138, 256
1.4 139, 141, 253-54, 258
5.2 7
Shab. 16.7 8
16.8 133
22.3 7
Sheq. 1.3 134
2.3 135, 261
8.4 135, 208
Soṭ. 9.16 137, 222, 224
Suk. 3.11 134
Ta'anit 3.11 136

VII. Babylonian Talmud

'Arakh 4a, 109, 203
B.B. 10a 151
10b 103, 240
60b 114
89b 104, 194
115a 182
115b 205
115b-116a 105
134a 106, 153, 216, 219
134a-b 219
Bekh. 5a 141, 154, 253-54, 256
Ber. 17a 142, 219
28a-b 47
28b 87, 221-24
Ber. 34b 88
50a 241
Beẓ. 5a 94, 207
5b 208-09
B.Q. 79b 261
Giṭ. 55b-56b 150
56a 166, 188
56b 4, 229-30
56a-b 275
Ḥag. 3b 95, 202
5a 145, 257
13a 95, 144, 251
13b 252
14b 97, 247

Hor. 10a 257
10b 108
Ḥul. 92b 241
Ker. 9a 109, 155, 208
Ket. 14a 99, 201
66b 99, 236, 239
Men. 21b 108, 205
46b 109, 203
55a 204
65a 183, 204
65a-b 154
68a 154
68b 153
Ned. 33b 100, 195
Pes. 3b 143
26a 143, 219
94a-b 144, 254
Qid. 22b 100, 258
79b 101
R.H. 18a 92
18a 92, 225
21b 92, 208
29b 207
R.H. 30b 94, 207
31a 207
31b 207-08, 213, 226-27
29b 93
Sanh. 32b 107, 225-27
41a 107, 198
41b 213, 226-27
Shab. 121b-122a 197
146a-b 197
152a 257
Soṭ. 29b 146
40a 146, 207
Suk. 26b 144
28a 90, 216, 219
28b 144-45
31b 145
32b 145
41a 145
41b 207
Yev. 105a 98, 225
Yoma 39b 89
79a 89, 197

VIII. Avot de Rabbi Natan

ed. Goldin
Chap. 4, p 34 113
Chap. 6, pp 43-44 120
Chap. 12, p 71 121
Chap. 14, pp 74-78 125
Chap. 17, pp 88-89 129
Chap. 22, p 99 130
Chap. 25, pp 105-107 131
ARNa
Chap. 4 113
Chap. 6 244, 247
Chap. 12 202
ARNb
Chap. 6 228
Chap. 13 242
Chap. 14 216, 220, 240, 256
Chap. 17 236, 239
Chap. 25 221
Chap. 27 121
Chap. 28 214
Chap. 31 128, 257

IX. Midrashim

Der. R. 100.24 213
Deut. R. 178
7.7 170, 256
Genesis R. 158-62
15.18 256
17.4 159
17.19 256
19.6 159
19.7 256
41.1 242
42.1 160
44.18 256
44.21 161
100.10 161
Lamentations, R. 162-69
1 5.31 4, 165, 229
Lamentations R. Proem # 12 162
Numbers, R. 176-78
3.14 139, 156
4.9 177, 253-54, 256
19.8 78, 178, 255-56
Pesiqta R. 169-71
14 170, 255-56
17 170, 256
21 171, 259
Qohelet R. 174-76
4.17 174
6.1 174-75, 194

Qohelet R., 7.2 163, 175, 235
9.7 176
9.8 175
Song of Songs R 178-79
7.14 179
Pesiqta de Rav Kahana 167-69, 255-56, 261

Tanḥuma 171-74
Additions to Deut # 7 173
Ḥuqat # 26 256
Ḥuqat # 28 173
Lekh Lekha # 10 172
Shofetim # 7 173, 257

GENERAL INDEX

A

Aaron, 124, 177, 181, 205
Abaye, 98-99, 109, 111, 126, 220, 294;
    Babylonian Talmud, 142-45, 152-54;
    daughter's inheritance, 105-06; *Merkavah*, 90-92
Abba Saul, 54-55, 82, 123, 126
Abbahu, R., 103, 138
Abba Sikra, 149, 151, 229, 232
Abin, R., 142
Abin b. R. Judah, 168, 241
Abraham and covenant, 161, 177-78, 183, 272, 284
Abraham, I., 95, 97
Adda b. Aḥva, R., 136, 154, 294
'Admon, 47
Ageniṭos, 37, 156, 177, 253, 256
Agrippas the Hegemon, 37, 39
Aḥa b. Jacob, R., 96
Aḥi, R., 154
Akko, 100
Albeck, Ḥ., 49n, 159-61
Allon, G., 7, 8n
Altar: destroying gentile's, 36, 40, 79, 128, 132, 257, 268, 278, 290; stones and iron, 16-17, 24, 27-28, 32, 40, 71, 79, 259-61, 267, 278
Ammi, R., 103
Amoraic traditions, 133-59, 293-97
Amram, 23, 38, 161, 213-15
Amraphel, 160
'Anah, 105, 181
Antoninus, 139-41, 156, 253, 291
Apollonius of Tyana, 187
'Aqiva, R., 67-69, 121, 276, 290, 299; age, 23, 38, 161, 213-15; Amoraic traditions, 135, 138, 149; Babylonian Talmud, 150; escape story, 230-31; Ishmaelean School compared, 32-35; *Merkavah* sermon, 249-50; Midrashim, 24-32, 36-38, 159-61, 166, 179; Mishnah texts, 48-50, 57, 59, 63; Palestinian Talmud, 135, 138; Tannaitic traditions, 97-98, 103, 107; Tosefta texts, 67-69; tradition, 3-4, 17, 23
'Arav, 'Ulla in, 133, 155-56, 158, 196, 271, 275, 284, 293
Ascend to heights, 95, 112, 143-44, 157, 182-83
Ashi, R., 100, 107-08, 111, 146, 294
Avot de Rabbi Natan, 4, 36, 39, 113-132, 188

B

Ba, R., 155, 293
Babylonia, Israel's exile, 71-73, 257, 269, 276, 280, 291
Balaam, 166
Barefooted, blessing by priests, 145, 157, 271, 275, 284, 293
Bar Kappara, 176

Bar Kokhba War, 2, 27, 32, 34, 58, 103-04, 114, 118, 221, 225, 275, 289, 292, 298
Bar Qamẓa, 146, 151
Ben 'Azzai, 50
Ben Baṭṭiaḥ, 162-63, 166-67, 175, 229, 232-33
Ben Bukhri, priest's *sheqel*, 42-43, 63, 80, 108-10, 112, 134-35, 156, 158, 203, 206, 268, 273-74, 278, 291, 295
Ben Ḥinnom, Valley of, 144, 157, 271, 275, 284
Ben Kalba Shavu'a, 120, 147, 160, 162, 175, 243
Ben Ẓiẓit Hakkeset, 120, 147, 160, 162, 175, 243, 245
Ben Zoma, 50, 85
Berekiah, R., 134-35, 159, 185, 293
Beror Ḥayil, 45-46, 65, 69, 83, 107, 198, 276
Bethar, 146
Bet Ramah, 121
Bet She'arim, 276
Bitter water, 50, 193-94, 267, 276, 280, 289, 291
Bné Bathyra, 93
Boethius, 148, 151, 237
Braude, W. F., 169-71, 179-80
Bultmann, R., 188u, 190

C

Caesarea, 162
Cashdan, Eli, 108-09, 153
Celebrate in common, 178, 182, 183, 272, 275, 286
Census, 139-40, 153, 157, 176-77, 184, 253-54, 271, 284, 292-93
Chariot, Works of, 24, 66-67, 84-85, 96-98
Cohen, A., 162, 165, 174-76
Conventional sayings, 192-93
Court, after good court, 30-31, 40, 79, 1%7, 110, 112, 224-25, 267, 273, 273-74
Covenant with Abraham, 161, 177-78, 183, 272, 284
Create/gather, 159, 183, 271, 284

D

Danby H., 41-44, 48, 50, 52-53, 55-60
Daniel, 167
Dates: guests and tithes, 65, 79, 111, 197-99
Daughter's inheritance, 105-06, 110, 112, 181, 184, 205, 270, 273-74, 282
David, King, 124-25
Day/night, both called day, 169-70, 183-84, 272, 286
Day of Waving, 29-30, 40, 46, 56, 63, 73, 78-79, 84, 94, 110-12, 134, 151-53, 206-07, 209, 267, 273-74, 278, 288, 295
Death-scene, 87-88, 111, 130-32, 137, 141-42, 155, 157-58, 221-24, 226, 269, 273, 277, 282; son, 124-25, 132, 270, 276, 282
Destruction predicted, 89, 269, 273, 282
Dibelius, M., 188n
Disciples: five, 54-56, 63, 80, 122-27, 132, 240-42; Hillel's, 90-91, 106, 110-12, 122,28, 132, 154, 157-58, 216-18, 220, 226, 270, 273, 282, 295
Dosa b. Harkinas, R., 48, 100, 195
Dosethai b. R. Yannai, R., 103

E

Editorial tendencies, 6-8, 32-35
Eleazar, R., 55, 64, 81, 124, 126, 165
Eleazar b. 'Arakh, R., 166, 190, 276-77; Avot de Rabbi Natan, 117, 123, 125, 127; disciples' stories, 240-42, 246; *Gemarot*, 84-85, 96-97; *Merkavah* sermon,

247-52; Mishnah texts, 40, 54-55; Tannaitic midrashim, 24-25, 34; Tosefta texts, 66-67, 82
Eleazar b. ʿAzariah, 46, 50
Eleazar b. Dinai, 50
Eleazar b. R. Ẓadoq, 100, 235, 238
Eli family, 91-92, 98, 110, 112, 117, 270, 273-74, 282, 295
Eliezer, R., 62, 223-27; Amoraic traditions, 133, 136-37, 144-45, 149, 156; Avot de Rabbi Natan, 113, 115, 117, 124-27, 131; Babylonian Talmudic tradition, 87, 90-91, 94-95, 102, 104, 107; disciples' stories, 240, 242-43; escape story, 228-34; good court, 30-31; Midrashim, 163, 165, 167, 176, 179-81; Mishnah texts, 42, 44-45, 51, 56, 58-60; Tannaitic Midrashim, 19-21, 27; Tosefta texts, 75, 77, 81-82; Yavneh ordinances, 206-07; as
Eliezer b. Hyrcanus, 30, 41, 43, 47, 54-55, 82, 122-23, 277-88; beginnings, 119-21, 132, 160-61, 171-72, 182-83, 242-47, 270, 274, 277
Eliezer b. Jacob, 86
Eliezer b. R. Simeon b. Yoḥai, 118
Eliezer b. R. Yosi, 103
Elijah, 53-54, 118, 201, 242, 269, 273, 280, 288
Emmaus, 15, 22, 68, 125-26, 235, 276-77
Epstein, Y. N., 15n, 24-25, 31, 38-39, 42n, 43n, 48n, 51n, 52n, 58n, 69n, 74
Escape in coffin, 34-35, 114-19, 132, 146-52, 156-57, 162-67, 175, 182-84, 190, 228-34, 239, 270, 277, 282, 295
Evidence tested, 52, 80, 107, 112, 199, 269, 274, 276, 280, 289, 291
Exile, Israel to Babylonia, 71-73, 269, 276, 280, 282, 291
Eyes opened, 159, 182, 272, 284
Ezekiel vision, 98

F

Faint-hearted, 31-32, 36, 38, 40, 64, 79, 268, 273, 278
Fear sin, 129, 270, 282
Finkelstein, Louis, 22n, 25n
Five disciples, 54-56, 63, 80, 122-27, 132, 240-42, 269, 276, 280
Food, in Sukkah, 43, 80, 89-90, 110-11, 144, 157, 268, 276, 280, 295
Fourth-year fruit, 145, 158, 208-09, 268, 271, 275, 284, 293
Fourth-year produce, letters *re*, 37, 40, 79
Fragments, capacity, 56-58, 80, 269, 276, 280, 291
Freedman, H., 143
Fruit; fourth-year, 145, 158, 208-09, 268, 271, 275, 284, 293, 295; orchard fruit, 179, 184, 272, 286

G

Gamaliel I, 3, 5, 43, 50-51, 59, 82, 88-89, 107, 110, 150, 168, 179, 215, 221, 225, 233, 242, 255, 291, 295-96
Gamaliel II, 7, 43-47, 52-53, 55, 59, 93, 104, 221, 290, 295-96
Gamaliel, R., 99, 102, 107, 167, 201, 256, 290, 295
Garments always white, 175-76, 182, 184, 272, 286; heifer-ceremony, 19-21, 40, 64, 74-76, 78-79, 200-01, 267, 277-78, 289-90
Gather/create, 159, 183, 271, 284
Gemarot, 83-112
Gentiles: celebrate in common, 178, 182, 183, 272, 275, 286, destroying altars 36, 40, 79, 128, 132, 257, 268, 278, 290; disputes, 253-57, greeted, 142, 158, 272, 295
Gerahs, ten, 135, 155, 157, 159, 182-83, 271, 284

Gerhardson, Birger, 2n
Goldberg, Abraham, 9n
Goldenberg, Robert, 50n
Goldin, J., 113, 116, 118, 120-21, 125, 129-31, 274
Gophna, 164
Grapes, uncleanness, 142-43, 157, 271, 275, 284
Guests, tithes and dates, 65, 79, 198-201, 269, 280, 288

H

Hadrian, 173, 234, 270, 282
Ḥama b. R. Ḥanina, R., 94, 293
Hamnuna, R., 86, 134-35
Ḥanan said well, 47-48, 80, 100, 112, 190, 195-97, 268, 274, 280, 291
Ḥananiah, R., 8
Ḥananiah b. Ḥakhinai, 67, 249
Ḥananiah b. Teradion, R., 107
Ḥanina b. Dosa, R., 42, 50-51, 81, 129-30, 133; prayer saves son, 88-89, 110, 269, 273-74, 282
Heave-offering, priest eating, 121-22, 132, 202, 270, 282, 288; Ṭarfon, 68-69, 78-79, 202, 268, 280
Heifer: breaking neck, 50, 69-70, 78, 193, 268, 276, 280, 289, 291; priest unfit, 75-76, 78-79, 204, 269, 276, 282, 291
Heifer-ceremony, garments for, 19-21, 40, 64, 74-76, 78-79, 200-01, 267, 278 288-89
Ḥezekiah, 87, 131, 137, 141, 241
Hillel, 3, 54, 179, 221, 290, 296, 299; age, 23, 38, 161, 213-15; Amoraic traditions 142-43; disciples, 90-91, 106, 110, 112, 122-27, 128, 131-32, 137-38, 155, 158-59, 215-18, 220, 226, 270, 273, 282, 295; legal sayings, 199-201;
Tannaitic Midrashim, 19-21, 23; Tosefta texts, 74-75, 77
Hillelites, 289-90
Hillel b. Berekiah, R., 162, 165, 185
Ḥinena, R., 86
Ḥisda, R., 5, 86, 142, 147, 154
Ḥiyya, R., 84-85
Ḥiyya b. Abba, R., 89
Hocus-pocus, 167-69, 182-84 255, 272, 275, 286 ,288
Hoffmann, David, 36-38
Homeros, 60
Hoshaia, R., 100, 136, 293-94
House of Kings, 117, 136, 157-58, 162, 169, 173, 182, 234, 271, 275, 284
Huna, R., 105, 142, 294
Hyman, A., 48
Hyrcanus, 119-20, 243-45

I

Idi, R., 108
Idi b. Gershom, 154
Ifra Hormiz, 103
Inheritance, Sadducee and daughter, 105-06, 110, 112, 181, 184, 205, 270, 273-74, 282
Iron and altar, 16-17, 24, 27-28, 32, 40, 71, 79
Iron Mountain, 145
Isaac b. Kappara, 176

Isaac b. Ṭavlai, R., 89, 293
'Isah family, marriage, 53, 63, 80, 99, 201, 269, 273-74, 282, 288
Ishmael, R., 57, 276, 290; Aqiban school compared, 32:35; Mekhilta, 16-19; Midrash Tannaim, 37-39; School and Tannaitic Midrashim, 15-23, 28, 30; tradition, 3
Ishmael b. Phiabi, R., 50-51
Ishmael b. R. Yosi b. Ḥalafta, 118
Israel, Babylonian exile, 71-73, 258, 269, 276, 280, 291

J

Jacob b. Idi, 137, 141, 221-22, 227
Jeremiah, R., 84, 162, 293
Jerusalem, 2, 6, 52, 113-14, 126-27, 162, 165, 172; destruction, 34, 114-19; Temple, 42-43, 45, 47, 51, 65; *see also* escape in coffin
Jesus, 1-2, 6, 187, 190, 265
Job, 124; served in love, 49-50, 80, 268, 280
Jonah, R., 83, 293
Jonathan, R., 8
Jonathan b. 'Uzziel, 90-91, 106, 122, 126, 137, 152, 219, 226, 290, 299
Joseph, R., 3-4, 8, 294; Amoraic traditions, 144, 149-50; escape story, 230-31; *Gemarot*, 107, 109, 111; *Merkavah* sermon, 248; Midrashim, 161, 166; years, 213-15; Tannaitic Midrashim, 23, 38
Joseph the Priest, R., 85
Josephus, 20, 89
Joshua, R., 8, 223, 225, 226, 273, 274, 288; Amoraic traditions, 136, 138, 149; Avot de Rabbi Nathan, 113-15, 117, 122-27, 131; disciples, 240, 242-44, 248-50; escape story, 229-33; *Gemarot*, 83, 85, 97, 99, 102, 107; legal sayings, 198-99, 201; Midrashim, 160-61, 163, 165, 167, 179; Mishnah texts, 50-51, 53-54, 61; 120 years, 213-15; Tannaitic Midrashim, 20, 23, 25, 27, 37-39; third loaf, 48, 69; Tosefta texts, 65, 67, 74-75, 77, 81-82; Joshua b. Ḥananiah, 47, 49, 53-54, 62, 68, 82, 122, 288-89
Joshua b. Hyrcanus, 49
Joshua b. Levi, R., 136-37, 141, 144, 155, 224, 293-94
Joshua b. R. Neḥemiah, 135, 168-69, 183, 293
Joshua b. Qorḥa, R., 44, 46-47, 65-66, 82, 207, 209
Joshua son of Nun, 90, 106
Judah, R., 41, 108-09, 134-35, 145, 152-53, 161, 185, 225, 290
Judah b. Bathyra, R., 8, 53, 61, 107
Judah b. Ilai, 41-42, 46, 56, 58, 61-62, 66, 82, 103, 196, 210, 275, 291
Judah b. R. Shalom, 103, 151, 293
Judah the Prince, 8-9, 126, 176, 221, 257, 291-92; Amoraic traditions, 142-43; *Gemarot*, 85, 90, 107; legal sayings, 193, 208; Mishnah texts, 42-43, 48, 51-52, 62; Tannaitic traditions, 34, 36, 38-39; Tosefta texts, 66, 68, 70, 81
Judan, R., 159-61, 185
Judea, 15
Jung, Leo, 109

K

Knowing, unwillingness, 15-16, 21-22, 34, 40, 79, 99-100, 112, 128-29, 132, 235-38, 267, 278, 290
Kohath, 23, 38, 139, 161, 213-15

L

Lamb/ox, 18, 40, 112, 267, 273-74, 278, 293

Lauterbach, J. Z., 16-19, 171
Levi, R., 23, 38, 96, 135, 160-61, 213-15
Levi b. Laḥma, R., 94
Levine, Baruch A., 141
Lieberman, S., 65-67, 69, 202
Liezer, R., 137-38, 141, 160-167. See Eliezer b. Hyrcanus.
Lot, 160
Love; Job served in, 49-50, 80, 268, 280; loving kindness, 113-14, 131, 270, 282, 288
Lulav-day of waving, 29-30, 40, 43-46, 79-80, 84-85, 94, 157-59, 206-07, 209, 267, 273, 278, 288, 295
Lydda, 58, 164

M

Mandelbaum, B., 167-69
Marriage, Isah family, 63, 63, 80, 99, 201, 269, 273-74, 280, 288
Marsh, John, 188n
Mattiah b. Ḥeresh, R., 8, 107
McKnight, Edgar V., 265
Meal-offering, priest eats, 181-82, 184, 272, 275, 286
Meir, R., 9, 18, 50-51, 63, 138, 147, 179
Mekhilta of R. Ishmael, 16-19
Mekhilta of R. Simeon b. Yoḥai, 24-25
Melamed, E. Z., 24-25
Merari, 139
Merion, R., 144
Merkavah, 24-26, 32, 35, 40, 68, 78-79, 81, 85, 91, 96, 98, 110-12, 127, 152, 247-52, 267, 273-74, 276-78, 288, 299
Midian, 38, 161
Midrashim, 159-85; Deuteronomy Rabbah, 178-79; Genesis Rabbah, 159-61; Lamentations Rabbati, 162-67; Numbers Rabbah, 176-78; Pesiqta de Rav Kahana, 167-69; Pesiqta Rabbati, 169-71; Psalms, 179-80; Qohelet Rabbah, 174-75; Scholion to Megillat Ta'anit, 180-82; school of 'Aqiva, 24-32; School of R. Ishmael, 15-32, 28, 30; Song of Songs Rabbah, 178-79; Tanḥuma, 171-74; Tannaitic, 15-40
Mishnah texts, 41-61
Mordecai, R., 108
Moses: accountant, 140-41, 154-55, 158-59, 254-55, 271, 275, 284, 293; 120 years old, 23, 37-38, 40, 79, 161, 213-15

N

Naḥman b. Isaac, R., 94, 111, 145, 153, 294
Naqdimon ben Gurion, 21, 99-100, 120, 129, 147, 151, 160, 162, 174, 235-39
Nathan, R., 4
Nebuchadnezzar, 143, 156, 162, 167
Nebuzaradan, 162
Neḥemiah, R., 134-35
Neḥunya b. HaQaneh, R., 88, 103-04, 168, 241-42
Nephew lost money, 151, 157, 271, 275, 284
Nero, 147, 164
New Moon, evidence, 44, 46, 65-66, 78-80, 92-94, 110, 112, 207-09, 268, 273-74, 280

New Year: *see Shofar*
Night: *see* Day/night
Nimrod, 95, 143, 252
Nisan, 92

O

One hundred and twenty years, 23, 37-38, 40, 79, 161, 183, 213-15, 226, 267, 278
Orchard fruit, 179, 186
Ordinances of Yavneh, 207-10
Ordination, 138, 155, 157, 271, 284, 293
'Otenai, 77
'Oved Bet Hillel, fourth year letter, 37
Ox/lamb, 18, 40, 112, 267, 273-74, 278, 293
Oxen, when stoned, 138-39, 157, 272, 284, 293

P

Palestinian Talmud, Amoraic traditions, 133-42
Pangar, 162, 164-67, 231-33
Papa, R., 103, 105, 107, 111
Pentecost, date, 153-54, 157, 180-81, 184, 204-05, 271, 284
Pinḥas, R., 135-36
Pirqé de R. Eliezer, 277
Prayer: Ḥanina's son saved, 88-89, 110, 269, 273-74, 282
Priest: blessed barefooted, 145, 157, 271, 275, 284, 293; heave-offering, 121-22, 132, 202, 270, 282, 288; heifer-priest unfit, 75-76, 78-79, 203, 269, 276, 282, 291; meal-offering, 181-82, 183, 272, 275, 286; *sheqel*, 42-43, 63, 80, 108-10, 112, 134-35, 156, 158, 203, 206, 267, 273-74, 278, 291, 295
Prince sins, 26, 32, 40, 71, 79, 86, 108, 111-12, 267, 273-74, 278, 290
Produce, fourth-year letters *re*, 37, 40, 79
Proselyte, 135-36, 155-58, 208-09, 271, 275, 284, 293
Psalms, Midrash, 179-80
Pumbedita, 294-98

Q

Qamẓa, 146, 151
Quntroqes, 154-55, 253

R

Rabbah, 98, 108-10
Rabbah b. Meri, 144
Rabbinowitz, J., 178
Rabbinowitz, R., 44n
Rabina, 108
Rabshakeh, 241
Rainmaking, 155, 157, 271, 275, 284
Rami b. Ḥama, 107
Rav, 5, 100, 105, 117, 142-43, 274
Rava, 105, 126, 219-20, 294; Amoraic traditions, 141-44, 152; *Gemarot*, 90-92, 94' 99-100, 103, 105-06, 111

Rav Judah, 100, 111, 117, 293
Rebecca, 23, 38, 161, 213-15
Rehoboam b. Solomon, 128
Righteousness, 102-04, 112, 167-68, 184, 241, 271, 275-76, 284

S

Sabbath: *Shofar*, 43-45, 80, 93-94, 110, 112, 134, 156, 158, 207, 209, 268, 273-74, 276-77, 280, 289
Sadducee: daughter's inheritance disputed, 105-06, 110, 112, 181, 184, 205; uncleanliness of Scriptures, 60-61, 63, 78-80, 203-04, 270, 273, 276, 280, 291
Samuel, 5, 23, 38, 105, 160, 213-15
Samuel b. Ammi, R., 98, 174-75, 185
Samuel b. R. Isaac, R., 104, 194, 293
Schechter, Solomon, 36, 38, 113, 116, 121, 125, 128
Schools: 'Aqiva and Ishmael compared, 32-35; 'Aqiva and Tannaitic Midrashim, 24-32; Ishmael and Tannaitic Midrashim, 15-23, 28, 30
Scriptures, Sadducee uncleanliness, 60-61, 63, 78-80, 203-04, 269, 273, 276, 280, 291
Shammai, 54, 122, 128, 180
Shapur, 105
Sheqel, Ben Bukhri, 42-43, 63, 80, 108-110, 112, 134-35, 156, 158, 203, 206, 268, 273-74, 278, 291, 295
Shila, R., 180
Shisha, R., 108
Shofar, Sabbath, 43-45, 80, 93-94, 110, 112, 134, 156, 158, 207, 209, 268, 273-74, 276-77, 280, 289
Simeon, R., 109, 124-27, 138, 154, 215, 240, 243-44
Simeon b. Gamaliel I, 3, 17, 39, 46, 50, 53, 61, 221, 290
Simeon b. Gamaliel II, 221
Simeon b. HaSegan, 65
Simeon b. Laqish, R., 84, 86, 96, 107, 135, 146, 293-94
Simeon b. Nathaniel, 54, 85, 123, 248, 251
Simeon b. R. Judah, 136
Simeon b. R. Yoḥai, 135-36, 277; Mekhilta, 24-25
Simeon the trench digger, 174, 182, 184, 272, 275, 286
Simeon b. Eleazar, R., 16-17
Simon, M., 87-88, 103, 150, 152, 179
Sins: light/heavy, 145-46, 173, 183, 257, 271, 275, 284; offering, 41, 64, 78-80, 267, 278, Prince, 26, 32, 40, 71, 86, 108, 111-12, 267, 273-74, 278, 291; sprout-pride, 128, 132, 270, 282; wise/fear, 129-30, 132
Slave's ear, 18, 32, 40, 71, 79, 85, 100-01, 111-12, 170-71, 183, 258-59, 267, 273-74, 278, 290
Slotki, I. W., 90, 99, 104-06, 140, 152
Slotki, J. J., 177-78
Smith, Morton, 1-2, 17n, 22n, 25n, 27n, 45n, 48n, 52n, 54n, 55n, 60n, 72n, 76n, 103n
Solomon, 23, 38, 161, 213-15
Son's death, 124-25, 132, 270, 276, 282
Sprinkling waters, Shema'yah, 77-79, 269, 276-77, 282
Sprout-pride sins, 128, 132, 270, 282
Stones for altar, 16-17, 24, 27-28, 32, 40, 71, 79, 260-62, 267, 278
Strack, H., 160, 163, 168, 170, 175
Sukkah, food, 43, 80, 89-90, 110-11, 144, 157, 198-99, 268, 276, 280, 295

T

Tablets, first and second, 71, 257, 269, 276, 280, 291
Talmud: Amoraic traditions, 133-55; Babylonian traditions and Tannaim, 86-109; Historiography, 8-9; Palestinian traditions and Tannaim, 83-86
Tannaim, 273-93
Tannaitic materials, 83-112; Midrashim, 15-40; School of R. 'Aqiva, 24-32; School of R. Ishmael, 15-23, 28, 30
Ṭarfon, R., 55, 82; heave-offering, 68-69, 78-79, 202, 269, 280
Ṭavi, R., 134-35
Teaching, shadow of Temple, 141-42, 156-57, 221, 271, 275, 284, 295
Tefillin, always wearing, 133, 151-52, 220-21, 271, 275, 282
Teḥinah b. Parishah, 50
Ten *gerahs*, 135, 155, 157-58, 168, 182, 261-62, 271, 284
Thief, double penalty, 18, 32, 70, 79, 101-02, 112, 261-62, 273-74, 278
Third loaf, uncleanliness, 26-27, 40, 48-49, 63, 65, 69, 78-80, 145, 201-02, 267, 278, 288
Tiberias, 294-95
Tishré, 92
Tithes, 58-60, 63, 77-80, 94-95, 112, 179, 184, 202-03, 269, 274, 277, 280; guests and dates, 65, 79, 111, 197-200, 269, 280, 288
Titus, 151, 162, 166
Torah: created to study, 36, 40, 79, 167-68, 267, 278, 290; disputes, 38, 40, 253, 268, 278, 290
Tosefta texts, 65-78
Tur Malka, 146

U

'Ulla in 'Arav, 133, 156-57, 159, 196, 271, 275, 284, 293
Uncleanness: grapes, 142-43, 157, 271, 275, 284; Scriptures, 60-61, 63, 78-80, 202-03, 269, 273, 276, 280, 291; third loaf, 26-27, 40, 48-49, 63, 65, 69, 78-80, 146, 201-02, 267, 278, 288
Unwillingness, 15-16, 21-22, 34, 79, 99-100, 112, 128-29, 132, 235-38, 267, 278, 290
Usha, 42, 57, 276, 291

V

Valley of Ben Ḥinnom, 144, 157, 271, 275, 284
Vespasian, 4-5, 82, 114-19, 147, 149, 150, 162-66, 228-32, 239

W

Waving, Day of, 29-30, 40, 46, 56, 63, 73, 78-79, 84, 94, 110-12, 134, 151-52, 206-07, 209, 267, 273-74, 278, 288, 295; *Lulav*-Day of Waving, 29-30, 40, 43-46, 84-85, 134, 157-59, 206-07, 209, 273, 278, 288, 295, 297
Waxman, M., 159, 167, 176, 178
Weiss, Abraham, 151-52
Weiss, I. H., 26
When died, 50, 269, 276, 280
White garments, 175-76, 182, 184, 272, 286
Wise/fear sin, 129, 270, 282

Woe if I say it, 58, 73-74, 79-80, 110, 112, 174-75, 194-95, 198, 269, 274, 208, 291,
Works of the Chariot, 24, 66-67, 84-85, 96-98

Y

Yannai, R., 133, 155
Yavneh, 4, 6-7, 9, 25, 32-35, 106-07, 113, 125-27, 156, 276, 290-91, 295; ʻArav cases, 41-82; ordinances, 207-10; privileges, 46-47
Yoḥanan ben Nappaḥa, 143, 146, 151, 155, 293
Yoḥanan ben Zakkai; age, 23, 38; ʻArav cases, 41-82; Vespasian, 4-5, 82, 114-19, 147, 149, 150, 162-66, 228-32, 239; when died, 50, 269, 276, 280
Yosi, R., 97, 278; Avot de Rabbi Natan, 124-27, disciples, 240-42, 246, 250-52; Midrashim, 180-81; Mishnah texts, 41, 54, 58
Yosi b. R. Bun, R., 84-85, 137-38, 293
Yosi b. Ḥalafta, 58, 107
Yosi b. R. Judah, R., 67, 82, 97
Yosi the Priest, 123

Z

Ẓadoq, R., 4, 43, 148, 150, 165-66, 232-33
Zechariah b. ʻIddo, 89
Zedekiah, 136
Zekhariah b. Abqulas, R., 146
Zibeon, 105
Zunz, L., 162, 167, 169, 176, 178
Zuṭra b. Ṭuvyah, R., 89, 293